AF790473

The Exercise of the Right to a Fair Trial in the Era of the COVID-19 Pandemic

Ius, Lex et Res Publica
Studies in Law, Philosophy and Political Cultures

Edited by Barbara Janusz-Pohl and Anna Jaron

Volume 36

Maciej Świder

The Exercise of the Right to a Fair Trial in the Era of the COVID-19 Pandemic

PETER LANG

Berlin - Bruxelles - Chennai - Lausanne - New York - Oxford

Bibliographic Information published by the Deutsche Nationalbibliothek
The Deutsche Nationalbibliothek lists this publication in the Deutsche Nationalbibliografie; detailed bibliographic data is available in the internet at http://dnb.d-nb.de.

Library of Congress Cataloging-in-Publication Data
A CIP catalog record for this book has been applied for at the Library of Congress.

The cover image courtesy of Benjamin Ben Chaim.

ISSN 2191-3250
ISBN 978-3-631-92027-5 (Print)
E-ISBN 978-3-631-92801-1 (E-Book)
E-ISBN 978-3-631-92802-8 (E-PUB)
DOI 10.3726/b22434

© 2024 Peter Lang Group AG, Lausanne Published by Peter Lang GmbH, Berlin, Deutschland

info@peterlang.com - www.peterlang.com

All rights reserved.
All parts of this publication are protected by copyright.
Any utilization outside the strict limits of the copyright law, without the permission of the publisher, is forbidden and liable to prosecution.
This applies in particular to reproductions, translations, microfilming, and storage and processing in electronic retrieval systems.

This publication has been peer reviewed.
www.peterlang.com

Table of contents

Introduction

In the early months of 2020, the world was faced with a challenge of unprecedented scope and magnitude in the 21st century: the rapid development of the SARS-CoV-2 virus epidemic. The first case of COVID-19 disease caused by this pathogen was reported in Poland on 4 March 2020. In turn, the COVID-19 epidemic was declared a pandemic by the World Health Organisation on 11 March 2020. The epidemiological situation forced a number of significant social changes. Face-to-face human contact had to be minimised, including the closure of many public institutions and a shift to remote working wherever possible. A number of far-reaching changes had to be made to the existing legal system, including the adaptation of the rules governing the operation of the judicial system, which had also been significantly affected by the pandemic.

The judiciary has been subject to significant restrictions. The regulations most relevant to the civil procedure model were adopted in the so-called COVID-19 Special Act, i.e. the Act of 2 March 2020 on Special Solutions Related to the Prevention and Control of COVID-19, Other Infectious Diseases and Crisis Situations Caused by Them[1]. In the early stages of the pandemic, all procedural time limits were suspended, effectively freezing the functioning of the judiciary. Court buildings were partially closed to the public and emphasis was placed on the computerisation of civil proceedings to allow remote participation in court hearings and the introduction of solutions for electronic communication with parties to proceedings. Undoubtedly, the new instruments introduced by the legislature to combat the spread of the coronavirus also had a significant impact on the work of the courts.

In the public discourse, representatives of the academic and legal communities raised a number of objections to the solutions introduced. They were also raised by the courts and the Polish Ombudsman. The most important of these concerns related to the possible impact of the new rules on the right to a fair trial. This right, also referred to as the right to court, which is regulated primarily in Article 45(1) of the Constitution of the Republic of Poland and in a number of other international legal instruments, is the basic means of protecting an individual against the arbitrary actions of public authorities and is one of the most important principles of a democratic rule of law. Due to the importance of the matter to which the doubts expressed in the public debate relate, they require in-depth consideration.

The research problem to be addressed below is the impact of selected provisions of the COVID-19 Special Act on the civil procedure model, on the one hand, and on the individual's right to a fair trial, on the other. The lively public debate and

1 Journal of Laws – Republic of Poland, 2024, item 340 (consolidated text).

academic discourse, as well as the importance of the legal issues raised, which require further analysis, make the problem raised here worthy of discussion in a separate work. So far, the issue has been the subject of individual academic papers and studies in the form of commentaries or guides to the amended provisions. In the last three years, several academic articles have been published, but they can only contribute to the further discussion of the amended model of civil procedure in the era of the COVID-19 pandemic. At the same time, there is no monography that deals with the changes in a comprehensive and systemic way. None of the studies to date has examined the changes introduced by the COVID-19 Special Act in relation to the issue of the right to a fair trial. Despite the fact that more than three years have passed since the entry into force of the COVID-19 Special Act, the jurisprudence on the institutions discussed in this work is not extensive. It must be stressed that, despite the end of the COVID-19 pandemic, the problems presented are still relevant, as some of the cases initiated during this period are still pending.

The issues presented in the following chapters also have a practical dimension, since they attempt to discuss the different approaches taken by the courts in applying the instruments provided for by the COVID-19 Special Act and to draw attention to the need to develop a uniform procedural model in order to guarantee an adequate level of protection of the parties' procedural rights. The paper also puts forward a number of *de lege ferenda* postulates, the implementation of which would make it possible to introduce some of the institutions discussed into the civil procedure model on a permanent basis and to regulate them in a comprehensive manner. A more complex discussion of the issues addressed in this work seems necessary in order to determine the status of a party in civil proceedings in the era of the COVID-19 pandemic, to compare it with the status of a party before the introduction of a number of new procedural institutions into the legal order, and to present a prognosis of the position of an individual after the end of the COVID-19 pandemic.

The primary objective of the analysis is to present the most significant changes in the model of civil proceedings introduced by the COVID-19 Special Act and to examine whether the adopted provisions fully implement the standard of the right to a fair trial. This can be achieved by defining and comparing the standards of the right to a fair trial resulting from the Constitution of the Republic of Poland, the European Convention on Human Rights and the Charter of Fundamental Rights of the European Union. The study also aims to show the differences between the models of protection of the right to a fair trial defined in the constitutional, European and EU order. The analysis also seeks to resolve fundamental problems that arise in practice in the application of the provisions discussed by the courts. In addition, the study aims to assess whether any of the discussed institutions should be permanently introduced into the Code of Civil Procedure and, if so, under what conditions.

The provisions introduced into the civil procedure model in the course of the efforts to counteract COVID-19 will be examined with regard to the following issues:

1) remote hearings (Article 15zzs^{1}(1) points 1 and 2 of the COVID-19 Special Act),
2) hearing of the case in closed session (Article 15zzs^{1}(1) point 3 and Article 15zzs^{2} of the COVID-19 Special Act),
3) composition of the court (Article 15zzs^{1}(1) point 4 of the COVID-19 Special Act),
4) electronic service of court documents (Article 15zzs^{9} of the COVID-19 Special Act),
5) suspension of procedural time limits (Article 15zzs of the COVID-19 Special Act)
6) suspension of public auctions in the course of real estate enforcement (Article 952^{1} § 5 of the CCP) and the execution of eviction orders (Article 15zzu of the COVID-19 Special Act).

The above provisions contained in the COVID-19 Special Act (and in one case directly in the CCP) had the greatest impact on the conduct of civil proceedings during the pandemic and on the realisation of the individual's right to a fair trial. Some of them were permanently incorporated into the rules of civil procedure after the end of the pandemic. The issues discussed are therefore still relevant.

The main thesis of the research is that the normative solutions adopted by the legislator and listed above do not fully achieve the declared purpose justifying their introduction and do not comply with the minimum standard of the right to a fair trial guaranteed to the individual, and thus remain in contradiction with Article 45 of the Constitution, Article 6(1) of the ECHR and Article 47 of the CFR.

The research problem outlined above also allows for the identification of a research hypothesis that, after the end of the COVID-19 pandemic, remote court hearings and the possibility of deciding cases in closed sessions, as well as electronic service of court documents, may constitute a permanent element of the civil procedure model and significantly contribute to increasing its efficiency, provided that normative changes are adopted that allow for the adjustment of these institutions to the minimum standard of the right to a fair trial.

The following questions must be answered before the thesis can be examined:

1) How is the right to a fair trial defined in the Constitution, the ECHR and the CFR, and are the standards derived from these instruments identical, and what is their scope of application?
2) What is the real purpose of the changes to the civil procedure model introduced by the COVID-19 Special Act, and is this purpose consistent with the legislator's stated aim of protecting health?

The entire study is divided into eleven chapters. Chapters I and II analyse the model of protection of the right to a fair trial in the European Convention on Human Rights and the Charter of Fundamental Rights of the European Union.

There is no doubt that the solution of the research problem presented at the beginning requires first of all a detailed explanation of the concept of the right to a fair trial. To this end, Chapter I attempts to define the scope of the right to a fair trial in civil matters under the European Convention on Human Rights by analysing the various components of this right, i.e. the right of access to court, the right to impartial, independent court and to court established by law, the right to a fair procedure before a court and the principle of openness and expediency of proceedings. Chapter II discusses the standard of the right to a fair trial under the EU Charter of Fundamental Rights. Given the nature of this legal instrument, the discussion is preceded by an outline of the historical background to its adoption and an explanation of the scope of the Charter. The purpose of this is to identify the cases in which an individual may invoke the right to a fair trial under the Charter of Fundamental Rights.

Chapters III and IV deal with the right to a fair trial in the domestic legal order. The considerations in Chapter III focus primarily on the right to a fair trial in the constitutional order. The analysis carried out serves to define the concept of the right to court under Article 45(1) of the Constitution of the Republic of Poland and therefore, as in Chapter I, the considerations in Chapter III concern the right of access to court, the concept of a competent, independent and impartial court, the right to a fair procedure before a court and the principle of openness and expediency of proceedings. This discussion will allow for a comparison of the Convention and EU standards with the constitutional standard. This, in turn, will allow for the development of a single standard of the right to a fair trial, which seems necessary for the later detailed considerations in the following chapters of the work. Chapter IV is devoted to questions of the implementation of the right to a fair trial on the basis of the Code of Civil Procedure[2]. This part presents the concept of procedural principles and discusses the principles of equality, expediency and openness of proceedings, also indicating the basic manifestations of their implementation in the CCP. These principles are fundamental to the realisation of the right to a fair trial in civil proceedings. Moreover, the introduction of the provisions of the COVID-19 Special Act discussed in this work has left its mark on the implementation of the procedural principles just mentioned, which is why it is necessary to discuss them in detail.

Chapter V, entitled 'The COVID-19 pandemic as a premise for the limitation of civil rights and freedoms', provides an introduction to the issue of normative changes relevant to the model of civil procedure in the era of the pandemic. The chapter first discusses the question of the validity of the restrictions resulting from the COVID-19 Special Act over time. For this purpose, it was necessary to establish a time calendar of legislative changes introduced in Poland during the COVID-19 pandemic, including a description of the type of instruments introduced into

2 Code of Civil Procedure (CCP) – Law of 17 November 1964 Code of Civil Procedure, Journal of Laws 2023, item 1550 (consolidated text).

the legal system. The chapter analyses the question of the validity of individual provisions of the COVID-19 Special Act over time in the context of their compliance with the principle of proportionality of the restriction of civil rights and freedoms. The reason for placing these considerations in a separate chapter is that the way in which the issues discussed are regulated is common to most of the institutions of the COVID-19 Special Act examined. The assessment of whether the legislative technique applied can be considered correct in the light of the principle of proportionality has allowed relevant conclusions to be drawn regarding the compatibility of the regulation with the right to a fair trial. The chapter also presents the solutions adopted in other EU countries to combat the pandemic. These considerations contribute to the further analysis of the instruments introduced into the legal order by the Polish legislator. At the same time, the observations made in this part of the chapter are not intended to be a comprehensive discussion of foreign legislation, but only to outline the background, which will make it possible to identify similarities and differences between the solutions adopted in the Polish legal system and the regulations of other EU Member States. The considerations presented in Chapter V provide the necessary context for a more detailed analysis of the legislative solutions that are the subject of research in this study.

The issues addressed in the following chapters concern the various institutions of the COVID-19 Special Act (and the CCP) adopted to combat the spread of the coronavirus. These considerations, through a detailed discussion of the instruments under consideration, aim to compare them with the previously presented standard of protection expressed in the ECHR, the CFR and the Constitution. Chapter VI is devoted first of all to remote hearings in the era of the COVID-19 pandemic. The considerations begin with a detailed presentation of the institution in question, including the historical background of its introduction, as well as the resolution of interpretive doubts arising in the practice of its application. On the basis of these findings, the compliance of the regulation with the standard of the right to a fair trial was then assessed and own legislative postulates of a *de lege ferenda* nature were presented. A similar approach was taken with regard to the provisions of COVID-19 concerning in camera hearings (Chapter VII) and the composition of the court (Chapter VIII).

The next Chapter IX deals with electronic service through the Information Portal. The considerations begin with an approximation of the material and personal scope of application of Article 15zzs9 (2)-(5) of the COVID-19 Special Act, as well as the premises for waiving electronic service under the provision in question. Only the development of a unified model for the application of the institution of electronic service and the clarification of emerging interpretative doubts made it possible to assess the compatibility of the provision in question with the right to a fair trial. The next part of the Chapter also sets out *de lege ferenda* postulates for electronic service in civil proceedings.

The last two chapters are devoted to the impact of the COVID-19 pandemic legislation on the course of civil proceedings. First, the solutions related to the suspension of procedural time limits under Article 15zzs of the COVID-19 Special

Act are presented and the compatibility of this institution with the right to a fair trial standard set out in Chapters I and II is assessed (Chapter X). Subsequently, the provisions relating to enforcement proceedings, i.e. the suspension of judicial auctions of real estate serving the debtor's housing needs and the suspension of enforcement of eviction orders, were analysed in accordance with the above scheme (Chapter XI). As these provisions have been repealed, the considerations are of a historical nature and therefore do not include *de lege ferenda* postulates. Despite the fact that the above-mentioned provisions are revoked from the legal order, their detailed analysis was necessary due to their significant impact on civil proceedings and the realisation of the individual's right to a fair trial.

The study concludes with a verification of the initial thesis and research hypothesis and a concise synthesis of the considerations presented in the previous chapters.

1. European Convention on Human Rights

1.1. Introductory remarks

Article 6(1) of the Convention for the Protection of Human Rights and Fundamental Freedoms[3] establishes the right to a fair trial, i.e. fair and public proceedings before a court. According to the first paragraph of article 6 (first sentence): 'In the determination of his civil rights and obligations or of any criminal charge against him, everyone is entitled to a fair and public hearing within a reasonable time by an independent and impartial tribunal established by law'. The quoted article provides for the right to a fair trial, guaranteeing the right to a fair and public hearing within a reasonable time.

The provision introduces a broad set of fair trial guarantees, formulating a general principle setting out the basic elements of civil and criminal justice[4] . The second sentence of the first paragraph of Article 6 guarantees the openness of the proceedings before the court, while introducing permitted exceptions to this principle. Paragraphs 2 and 3 of Article 6 of the Convention indicate a number of specific conditions to be met by criminal proceedings and are beyond the scope of this publication. Article 6(1) of the Convention not only establishes a number of individual rights, but also introduces the procedural guarantees necessary for the realisation of the other rights and freedoms provided for in the Convention. In this sense, the right to a fair trial is an expression of the principle of subsidiarity, whereby it is the task of national courts to protect individual rights and freedoms under the ECHR[5].

In *Golder v UK*, the European Court of Human Rights noted that Article 6 of the Convention reflects the fundamental principle of the rule of law underlying the Convention[6]. It further pointed out that in civil matters, the rule of law is inconceivable without access to courts[7]. The rule of law is not viable if there is no justice system capable of remedying violations of universally accepted norms[8].

---

3 Convention for the Protection of Human Rights and Fundamental Freedoms drawn up in Rome on 4 November 1950, subsequently amended by Protocols Nos. 3, 5 and 8 and supplemented by Protocol No. 2, hereinafter: European Convention on Human Rights, Convention or ECHR.

4 P. Hofmański, A. Wróbel, [in:] *Konwencja o Ochronie Praw Człowieka i Podstawowych Wolności. Komentarz do artykułów 1–18*, L. Garlicki (editor), Warsaw 2010, p. 246.

5 P. Hofmański, A. Wróbel, [in:] *Konwencja o Ochronie...*, p. 247.

6 M. A. Nowicki, *Wokół Konwencji Europejskiej. Komentarz do Europejskiej Konwencji Praw Człowieka*, Warsaw 2013, p. 510.

7 Judgment of the European Court of Human Rights of 21 February 1975, Application No. 4451/70.

8 M. A. Nowicki, *Prawo do rzetelnego procesu sądowego: część „cywilna“*, Palestra 1996/7–8, p. 141.

As the right to a fair trial is a purely procedural guarantee, the Court, when hearing individual complaints, does not examine the correctness of the application of substantive and procedural law. The Strasbourg Court is not a court of 'fourth instance' and its role is limited to assessing whether there has been a violation of the right to a fair trial guaranteed by the Convention before a national authority[9].

The guarantees under the provision of Article 6(1) of the ECHR are procedural in nature, with the Convention imposing an obligation on the Member States to achieve a certain result in terms of a fair, public trial, rather than to adopt specific solutions. Member States are left with procedural autonomy, while at the same time the ECHR imposes an obligation to organise the administration of justice in such a way that it meets the standards set by Article 6. The right set out in Article 6(1) ECHR consists of: (1) organisational guarantees of an independent and impartial court established by law; (2) the right of access to a court; (3) fair trial guarantees in the strict sense, i.e. procedural fairness[10].

The right to a fair trial set out in Article 6(1) of the ECHR does not include a right of appeal[11] (with regard to criminal cases, such a requirement is introduced by Article 2 of Protocol No. 7). However, if national law provides for a right of appeal, also the proceedings before the appellate instance must meet the Convention requirements of a fair trial[12]. Indication by the Strasbourg Court of a violation of Article 6(1) does not give rise to an obligation to reopen the proceedings before the national court or to annulment of a final judgment[13].

1.2. Scope of application of Article 6(1) of the ECHR

Article 6(1) of the Convention relates to 'the determination of civil rights and obligations'. This is an autonomous Convention term and should be interpreted separately from the meaning given to it by the domestic law of the Member State[14]. The guarantees set out in this provision will only apply if the following conditions are cumulatively met: (1) the proceedings concern rights or obligations derived from national law; (2) there is a real and serious dispute, the outcome of which affects those rights or obligations; (3) the right or obligation is of a civil nature[15] .

The right or obligation must derive from domestic substantive law, and the Court cannot in its jurisprudence create new rights not provided for in the Member State's legal order. However, the question arises as to whether the Court has the power to grant such a right to an individual where domestic law omits one of the

9 P. Hofmański, A. Wróbel, [in:] *Konwencja o Ochronie ...*, p. 328.
10 P. Hofmański, A. Wróbel, [in:] *Konwencja o Ochronie ...*, pp. 248–249.
11 M.A. Nowicki, *Wokół Konwencji ...*, p. 512.
12 P. Hofmański, A. Wróbel, [in:] *Konwencja o Ochronie...*, p. 253.
13 P. Hofmański, A. Wróbel, [in:] *Konwencja o Ochronie...*, p. 248.
14 M. A. Nowicki, *Wokół Konwencji ...*, p. 513.
15 P. Hofmański, A. Wróbel, [in:] *Konwencja o Ochronie...*, p. 254.

fundamental rights of the individual which is generally granted by other domestic systems[16]. The judgment in *Zavoloka v Latvia*[17] answered this question in the negative, stating that, in view of the great diversity of the legal systems of the Member States, the Court could not infer an absolute and general right to compensation for immaterial damage following the death of a close relative if the national legal order did not provide for such a right. The Court's assessment must be agreed with. The right to a fair trial is intended to guarantee, on the procedural side, the realisation of other existing rights provided for in the domestic legal order of the State, and not to establish, through the jurisprudence of the Court, new substantive rights not articulated elsewhere. On the other hand, it is emphasised that the Court is not bound by the interpretation of the national court as to the existence of a particular right, and that the legal classification made by the national court is not binding for the Strasbourg Court, since this would lead to the protection of the Convention being subject solely to the decision of the Member State, which would be contrary to the purpose of the Convention. The Court is therefore free to conclude that an individual may derive a right from a substantive national provision, even if the national court has held that such a right does not exist. However, this cannot in any event lead to the recognition of rights which have no substantive legal basis in the domestic legal order of the State[18].

For the purposes of recognising the existence of a 'civil right or obligation', it is irrelevant whether it belongs to a specific branch of law (civil law, administrative law, public law) or to the type of body empowered to adjudicate (general court, administrative court, administrative body). Nor does it matter whether the public authority exercises its jurisdiction in the sphere of government authority, power (i*mperium*) or non-power (*dominium*). It cannot be ruled out that a right or a claim is of a civil nature, even if it derives from regulations that are considered public under national law. In order to determine the civil nature of a right or a duty, reference must be made to its substantive content and to the consequences it entails for the individual[19]. The rights or obligations must be the subject matter or one of the subjects of the dispute, and the outcome of the proceedings must directly determine such rights or obligations, without any remote connection[20]. If the proceedings concern rights or obligations of a monetary, personal or private nature, the case is in principle civil[21]. However, on the other hand, matters falling

---

16 P. Hofmański, A. Wróbel, [in:] *Konwencja o Ochronie...*, pp. 254–255.

17 Judgment of the European Court of Human Rights of 7 July 2009, Application No. 58447/00.

18 P. Hofmański, A. Wróbel, [in:] *Konwencja o Ochronie...*, p. 255.

19 Guidelines on the application of Article 6 issued by the European Court of Human Rights, available at www.echr.coe.int, p. 8.

20 Judgment of the European Court of Human Rights of 19 October 2006, Application No. 1855/02.

21 P. Hofmański, A. Wróbel, [in:] *Konwencja o Ochronie...*, pp. 263–264.

exclusively within the sphere of public law will be excluded from the operation of Article 6(1), e.g. fines or obligations arising from tax laws or other civil obligations, even though they are of a monetary nature[22].

The Court recognises that where a Member State grants a right to an individual and a legal remedy to enforce that right, that right must, in principle, be regarded as a civil[23]. The Court considered the following cases to be cases concerning the settlement of civil obligations: protection of reputation, family, change of name, social security and social assistance, patent cases[24]. On the other hand, according to the Court, the following cases are not of this nature: the right to asylum[25], electoral rights[26], prohibition of association in organisations[27].

A dispute concerning a civil right or obligation must be real and serious. It may concern the very existence of the right or obligation or the extent and manner of its exercise. The outcome of the proceedings must be directly decisive for the right in question[28]. A dispute is presumed to be real and serious unless there are clear indications to the contrary. A dispute is 'serious' if it is fundamental to the existence or exercise of a right. By contrast, the 'real' nature of a dispute means that it must exist objectively. The dispute must be capable of being resolved directly by the courts[29]. Since the dispute must be real, hypothetical cases would therefore have to be excluded from the scope of Article 6(1) of the ECHR. The seriousness of the dispute means that Article 6(1) of the ECHR does not apply to situations where the violation of rights is minimal[30].

Article 6(1) of the ECHR applies to civil proceedings, not only at the actual judicial phase, but also at the pre-litigation stage[31] and in enforcement proceedings, which are a natural extension of the trial[32]. Otherwise, the right to a fair trial would be illusory[33] if it did not cover the enforcement stage. The State must therefore

---

22 M. A. Nowicki, *Wokół Konwencji...*, pp. 515–516.
23 Judgment of the European Court of Human Rights of 19 October 2006, Application No. 1855/02.
24 M. A. Nowicki, *Wokół Konwencji...*, pp. 517–518.
25 Judgment of the European Court of Human Rights (Grand Chamber) of 5 October 2000, Application No. 39652/98.
26 Decision of the European Court of Human Rights of 25 January 2000, Application No. 51501/99.
27 Decision of the European Court of Human Rights of 12 June 2012, Application No. 31098/08.
28 Judgment of the European Court of Human Rights (Grand Chamber) of 5 October 2000, Application No. 33804/96.
29 M. A. Nowicki, *Wokół Konwencji ...*, p. 515.
30 P. Hofmański, A. Wróbel, [in:] *Konwencja o Ochronie...*, p. 256.
31 P. Hofmański, A. Wróbel, [in:] *Konwencja o Ochronie...*, p. 252.
32 M. A. Nowicki, *Europejski Trybunał Praw Człowieka. Orzecznictwo. Tom 1 Prawo do rzetelnego procesu sądowego,* Kraków 2001, p. 27.
33 P. Hofmański, A. Wróbel, [in:] *Konwencja o Ochronie...*, p. 254.

guarantee the effective enforcement of the judgment, otherwise there can be no judicial protection of individual rights.

As the right to a fair trial occupies a non-negligible place in a democratic society, it is of particular importance for the proper functioning of democratic mechanisms and cannot therefore be interpreted restrictively. It is accepted that in cases of doubt as to whether Article 6 of the ECHR applies, the answer should be in the affirmative[34]. As the Court has pointed out, a narrow interpretation of Article 6 § 1 of the Convention - as regards respect for the fundamental principle of the impartiality of the courts - would be incompatible with the object and purpose of that provision. In interpreting that provision, account must be taken of the important place which the right to a fair trial occupies in a democratic society within the meaning of the Convention[35].

1.3. The right of access to court

The right of access to justice implies the possibility of bringing a civil claim before a court for consideration. It is an integral part of the right to a fair trial enshrined in Article 6(1) of the ECHR and is an expression of one of the fundamental principles of international law which prohibits the 'denial of justice'[36].

Access to justice must be real. The Convention does not guarantee individual rights that are illusory and hypothetical, but rights that are practical and effective[37]. It does not satisfy the requirements of Article 6(1) of the Convention to formally grant an individual access to court, while at the same time imposing restrictions that make this right theoretical. The right of access to court must be seen in legal and factual terms. For example, if an individual is given the opportunity to formally initiate proceedings but is denied the assistance of counsel, the actual access to court is restricted[38]. Access to justice is therefore not achieved simply by providing a judicial channel. It is also necessary to ensure that access to justice is effective, i.e. that the individual is able to present his or her case effectively before the court. Effective access to justice requires the existence of a coherent legal system governing access to legal remedies, with sufficiently clear and certain grounds for admissibility.

The right of access to justice does not require that an individual be granted the right to appeal a decision. Such a right cannot be derived from Article 6 (1) of

34 M.A. Nowicki, *Europejski Trybunał ...*, p. 23.
35 Judgment of the European Court of Human Rights of 26 October 1984, Application No. 9186/80.
36 P. Hofmański, A. Wróbel, [in:] *Konwencja o Ochronie...*, p. 288.
37 Judgment of the European Court of Human Rights of 15 February 2000, Application No. 38695/97.
38 P. Hofmański, A. Wróbel, [in:] *Konwencja o Ochronie...*, p. 289.

the ECHR. However, where national law provides for an appeal, access to such a remedy cannot be restricted and all fair trial guarantees apply[39].

The need to ensure effective access to court requires that free legal aid be granted to an individual in certain situations. An infringement of the right of access to court by refusing to grant legal aid may, in principle, occur in two cases: firstly, because of the complexity of the case and, secondly, because of the compulsory legal representation by a professional[40]. Given that legal aid is publicly funded, the State may limit or even exclude this right in certain categories of cases. The right to legal aid does not have to be granted in every case, but only when there are sufficient grounds. In order to determine whether free legal aid is necessary to ensure effective access to justice, it is necessary to examine the circumstances of the case, i.e. its importance, complexity, but also the prospects of success of the proceedings and the ability of the party to represent himself. It is not the duty of the State to ensure absolute 'equality of arms', but only to ensure that an individual is able to present his case adequately and in a way that does not put him at a serious disadvantage vis-à-vis the other party[41]. However, where the assistance of a professional is necessary to ensure effective access to justice (either because of compulsory legal representation or because of the complex nature of the proceedings), the State has an obligation to ensure that a lawyer participates in the proceedings free of charge. The introduction of compulsory legal representation in cases requiring specific expertise does not conflict with Article 6(1) of the ECHR, but then requires the establishment of an effective mechanism for free legal aid[42].

The Court has repeatedly emphasised that the right of access to a court is not absolute and may be subject to certain limitations. Since it is for the Member state to determine how the right of access to court is to be regulated, it must enjoy a certain margin of discretion in this respect. However, the restrictions in place must not be such as to affect the essence of the right[43]. They must also be proportionate and pursue a legitimate aim[44]. When restricting the right of access to court, such an objective will normally be the justified by the interests of the administration of justice, its proper functioning, avoiding an excessive burden on the courts or ensuring legal certainty[45] .

---

39 P. Hofmański, A. Wróbel, [in:] *Konwencja o Ochronie...*, pp. 289–290.
40 M. A. Nowicki, *Wokół Konwencji...*, pp. 536–537.
41 Judgment of the European Court of Human Rights of 15 February 2005, Application No. 68416/01.
42 P. Hofmański, A. Wróbel, [in:] *Konwencja o Ochronie...*, pp. 293–294.
43 Judgment of the European Court of Human Rights of 12 November 2002, Application No. 46129/99.
44 Judgment of the European Court of Human Rights of 19 May 2009, Application No. 18353/03.
45 P. Hofmański, A. Wróbel, [in:] *Konwencja o Ochronie...*, p. 295.

The most frequently cited forms of restriction of access to courts, which the ECHR nevertheless considers acceptable in principle, are limitation periods, court fees, compulsory legal representations and the immunities of defendants.

The need for the stability of the law and the interest of a well-functioning judiciary may require the introduction of time limits for the commencement of proceedings. However, such limitations must be proportionate[46]. A fair balance must therefore be struck between the protection of legal certainty in the public interest and the individual's right to have his case heard by a court. For this reason, excessively short limitation periods must be regarded as contrary to the right of access to justice. The application of limitation periods, like any restriction on access to justice, must be proportionate and achieve the purpose for which it was introduced[47].

The level of court fees and an individual's ability to bear them are crucial in assessing whether a person enjoys or is deprived of the right of access to court. National courts have a duty to strike a fair balance between the financial interests of the state and those of individuals seeking judicial protection. The imposition of excessive court fees on an applicant may be a disproportionate infringement of the right of access to justice[48]. Courts therefore have a duty to ensure that access to court is not economically impossible. Court fees must not be excessive, and the assessment of proportionality must be made in relation to the circumstances of the particular case[49].

The right of access to justice may also be restricted by excessive formalism and by obstacles of a procedural nature. Imposing certain obligations may result in the court refusing to hear the case and denying access to justice. This does not preclude the imposition of formal limitations, provided that such limitation is not excessive and is proportionate to the objective pursued by the procedural regulation[50].

Access to justice is not only the ability to bring a case before a court, but also the right to have the decision enforced by means of state power. The right of access to a court is not only a theoretical right to obtain recognition of an individual's right by reaching a final verdict, but also involves a legitimate expectation that a binding court decision will be enforced. According to the ECHR, enforcement proceedings are an integral part of the judicial process and the right to court also protects the right of access to execution proceedings[51]. Otherwise, the right to a fair trial would

---

46 M. A. Nowicki, *Wokół Konwencji ...*, p. 538.
47 P. Hofmański, A. Wróbel, [in:] *Konwencja o Ochronie...*, pp. 300–301.
48 Judgment of the European Court of Human Rights of 20 January 2009, Application No. 32971/03.
49 P. Hofmański, A. Wróbel, [in:] *Wokół Konwencji...*, pp. 298–299.
50 O. Piaskowska, *Prawo do sądu a oddalenie oczywiście bezzasadnego powództwa w świetle projektu zmian z 27.11.2017 r. do Kodeksu postępowania cywilnego*, Studia Prawnicze 2018/1, p. 34.
51 Judgment of the European Court of Human Rights of 28 November 2006, Application No. 40765/02.

be incomplete if the individual is not provided with mechanisms to enforce the judgment[52]. Therefore, access to justice in civil matters must also be guaranteed in enforcement proceedings.

1.4. Access to an impartial and independent court established by law

An individual's access to court is only guaranteed if it is an independent and impartial court. A 'court' for the purposes of the Article 6(1) of the Convention is a body which exercises a judicial function and decides disputes within the limits of the powers conferred upon it, in accordance with the procedure laid down by the law[53]. The decision of this body must be legally binding and cannot be overturned by any authority other than a court of law. This body must also be established by law, which excludes the recognition of *ad hoc* bodies as courts[54].

The expression 'court established by law' means 'established in accordance with the law', which does not merely refer to the existence of a legal basis for the establishment of the 'court', but to the establishment of the court in accordance with specific provisions regulating its functioning and the composition of the court in a given case. This, however, does not imply imposing uniformity on the practice of appointing judges in the Member States, but an obligation to ensure that national law prevents arbitrary interference by the executive in appointing judges[55].

The European Court of Human Rights, in the case of *Ástráðsson v. Iceland*, recalled that a judicial body which does not meet the requirements of independence (in particular in relation to the executive branch) is not a court within the meaning of Article 6(1) of the ECHR. Judicial independence implies the personal and institutional autonomy necessary for an impartial decision-making process and is thus a precondition for impartiality. Judicial independence consists of an internal component, manifested in the 'state of mind' of the judge, which shows resistance to external pressure, and an external component, i.e. a set of institutional and operational features designed to protect the court from undue influence[56]. In assessing whether a judicial body is independent, the following should be

---

52 T. Koncewicz, *Prawo do egzekucji wyroku jako element prawa do rzetelnej procedury w prawie europejskim*, Palestra 2014/7–8, p. 218.

53 Judgment of the European Court of Human Rights (Grand Chamber) of 1 December 2020, Application No. 26374/18.

54 J. Kociubiński, *Dostęp do niezawisłego i bezstronnego sądu jako element prawa do rzetelnego procesu karnego w orzecznictwie Europejskiego Trybunału Praw Człowieka*, Nowa Kodyfikacja Prawa Karnego. Tom XXVII, Wrocław 2011, p. 133.

55 Judgment of the European Court of Human Rights (Grand Chamber) of 1 December 2020, Application No. 26374/18.

56 Judgment of the European Court of Human Rights (Grand Chamber) of 1 December 2020, Application No. 26374/18.

considered: the way in which the members of the body are appointed, the length of their term of office, the existence of guarantees against external pressure, the perception of the body as independent[57].

An 'impartial' court is one that is free from prejudice or bias. It is not influenced by information from outside the courtroom, such as pressure from public opinion, but bases its decisions on objective reasons that emerge during the course of the trial[58]. The ECHR has emphasised that a judge's impartiality has two aspects: the subjective, in relation to the judge's personal convictions in a particular case, and the objective, in relation to the existence of guarantees which exclude reasonable doubts as to the judge's impartiality[59]. The objective test will be whether the organisation of the tribunal may cast doubt on the impartial character of any member of the tribunal or of the tribunal itself. Under the objective approach, it is not the party's belief that is determinative, but whether its concern is objectively justified. It is the 'appearance' and the question of the confidence that the tribunal should inspire in the public that matters[60]. The impartiality of the judge is to be presumed as long as there is no evidence to the contrary[61]. It is not necessary to prove the actual lack of impartiality of the judge, but the existence of reasonable doubts as to impartiality is sufficient.

Each of the guarantees described above concerning the court's 'establishment by law', its independence and its impartiality, are separate guarantees of a fair trial, but they share the common objective of preserving the fundamental guarantees of the rule of law and the separation of powers. The ECHR emphasises that the need to maintain the confidence of the public in the judiciary and the need to safeguard the independence of the judiciary are at the root of these principles[62].

1.5. Fair trial

The right to a fair trial in civil matters guaranteed by Article 6(1) of the Convention consists, in addition to the right of access to an independent and impartial tribunal established by law, of the right to a fair hearing in terms of procedural fairness – the right to a fair (just) trial. As indicated above, the right to a fair trial comprises a number of individual procedural guarantees and rights[63]. Since the right to a fair

57 P. Hofmański, A. Wróbel, [in:] *Konwencja o Ochronie...*, p. 314.
58 P. Hofmański, A. Wróbel, [in:] *Konwencja o Ochronie...*, pp. 318–319.
59 Judgment of the European Court of Human Rights of 1 October 1982, Application No. 8692/79.
60 P. Hofmański, A. Wróbel, [in:] *Konwencja o Ochronie...*, p. 321.
61 Judgment of the European Court of Human Rights of 1 October 1982, Application No. 8692/79.
62 Judgment of the European Court of Human Rights (Grand Chamber) of 1 December 2020, Application No. 26374/18.
63 T. Koncewicz, *Prawo do egzekucji...*, p. 209.

trial is, in fact, a bundle of individual rights which, taken together, condition a fair trial, the question that needs to be answered at this point is what are the main rights that make up this standard?

In broad terms, the right to a fair trial consists of the principle of equality of arms and the right to an adversarial procedure. In addition, it follows from the very wording of the provision of Article 6(1) of the ECHR that the right to a fair trial includes an open (oral) hearing and a guarantee of a speedy (within a reasonable time) conclusion. The catalogue of specific guarantees includes, inter alia, the right of access to the case file, the right to be heard, the right to a statement of reasons, the right to be present at the trial, the right to an adversarial procedure and the principle of *res judicata*. The above list is open-ended and covers the main elements of the right to a fair trial. This list may be subject to further development by the ECHR[64].

The right to an adversarial process means that each party must have an equal opportunity to know the position of the other party and to respond to it[65]. A trial can be said to be adversarial when a party has knowledge of, and the opportunity to comment on, all evidence presented in the case or submissions made (not only by the opposing party but also by the court) with a view to influencing the court's decision[66]. Whether the adversarial nature of a trial is an absolute value or can be subject to certain limitations has been a matter of debate[67]. Initially, it was assumed that the opposing party was entitled to see all materials relating to the case, regardless of their relevance, as it is up to the opposing party to decide whether it wants to respond to the opponent's position[68]. However, this concept has been modified and the Court now emphasises that the right to an adversarial procedure is not absolute, and its scope may vary depending on the individual nature of a particular case[69]. The adversarial nature of the proceedings in the ECHR's jurisprudence is not understood in the same way as the adversarial nature of the trial on the grounds of civil procedure in the Polish legal system, where it means that the burden of proof is on the parties[70].

The principle of 'equality of arms' implies the requirement of a 'fair balance', i.e. to ensure that each party has a reasonable opportunity to present its case under conditions which do not put it at a substantial disadvantage vis-à-vis the other

64 P. Hofmański, A. Wróbel, [in:] *Konwencja o Ochronie...*, p. 329.
65 M. A. Nowicki, *Europejski Trybunał ...*, p. 40.
66 Guidelines on the application of Article 6..., p. 50.
67 P. Hofmański, A. Wróbel, [in:] *Konwencja o Ochronie...*, p. 333.
68 Judgment of the European Court of Human Rights of 22 February 1996, Application No. 17358/90.
69 Judgment of the European Court of Human Rights of 27 April 2010, Application no. 23083/05.
70 A. Jakubecki, *Naczelne zasady postępowania cywilnego w świetle nowelizacji kodeksu postępowania cywilnego,* [in:] *Czterdziestolecie Kodeksu postępowania cywilnego. Meeting of Chairs of Civil Procedure in Zakopane (7–9.10.2005),* Krakow 2006, p. 358.

party[71]. Equality of arms may be seen as an element of adversarial procedure, but the case ECHR emphasises the distinction between the two concepts[72]. The adversarial process focuses on the ability of one party to challenge the evidence and arguments presented by the other party, whereas equality of arms refers to the position and procedural situation of the parties, which should not differ to the extent that one of the parties is prevented or impeded from presenting its case. The difference between the two guarantees is also reflected in the fact that the principle of equality of arms means that both parties must be treated in the same way, whereas the right to an adversarial procedure means that one party must be guaranteed access to all the material in the case, whether or not the other party is granted such access[73].

The adversarial procedure requires that a party must have the opportunity to comment on any document in the case, including those received at the initiative of the court[74]. The consequence of the above must be the right to access the case file. The principle of equality of arms implies that access to the file and other case documents must be equal for both parties[75]. The party must be informed of the contents of the file and of any new documents or evidence placed on the file, even if represented by a legal representative who cannot be expected to enquire regularly and on his own initiative whether new documents have been placed on the file[76].

A further guarantee of a fair trial is the right to participate in the proceedings in person. This right derives firstly from the adversarial principle and secondly from the principle of the openness of the proceedings, which also implies their oral nature. In civil cases, the right to attend in person is not absolute, as the standard in this respect is lower than in criminal cases[77]. However, it will be different in cases where the personal participation of one of the parties is of crucial, decisive importance, e.g. in guardianship cases. As a general rule, the personal presence of a party is not as important in appeal proceedings as in hearings before the court of first instance. To determine whether personal attendance is required, the ECHR will take into account the particular nature of the case, the subject-matter of the proceedings, their importance to the applicant and the manner of exercising and safeguarding the rights of the parties[78].

---

71 Guidelines on the application of Article 6..., p. 52.
72 P. Hofmański, A. Wróbel, [in:] *Konwencja o Ochronie...*, p. 343.
73 P. Hofmański, A. Wróbel, [in:] *Konwencja o Ochronie...*, p. 346.
74 Judgment of the European Court of Human Rights of 18 February 1997, Application No. 18990/91.
75 P. Hofmański, A. Wróbel, [in:] *Konwencja o Ochronie...*, p. 347.
76 Judgment of the European Court of Human Rights (Grand Chamber) of 11 July 2002, Application No. 36590/97.
77 P. Hofmański, A. Wróbel, [in:] *Konwencja o Ochronie...*, p. 348.
78 A. Pagiela, *Zasada „fair trial" w orzecznictwie Europejskiego Trybunału Praw Człowieka*, Ruch Prawniczy, Ekonomiczny i Socjologiczny 2003/2, p. 138.

In criminal matters, the Convention standard allows participation in the trial by videoconference as a substitute measure[79]. It therefore appears that, in the context of civil proceedings, the participation of a party in a court hearing by videoconference does not, in principle, constitute a violation of the right to a fair trial. This was also stated by the ECHR ruling *Jallow v Norway*[80]. The Court indicated that it is permissible for a party to be present at a court hearing by means of an Internet connection allowing direct transmission of video and audio, provided that this means serves a legitimate purpose in the particular case and that the technical solutions do not conflict with the right to a fair trial. The Court noted, however, that in some cases a party who is physically present in court may be in a better position than a person who participates online (for example, it may be difficult to consult a lawyer in confidence during the examination of witnesses). It should be noted that the right to a fair hearing guaranteed by Article 6(1) of the ECHR means effective (adequate) participation[81]. It is therefore not just a question of attending the hearing *per se*, but also of the right to follow the hearing (for example, in *Stanford v UK*, the ECHR held that the right to a fair trial had been violated because a party had difficulty hearing due to poor acoustics)[82].

The right to a fair trial does not end with the delivery of the judgment but extends to the actions of the court after that moment. It follows that an element of the right to a fair trial is also the right to a statement of reasons for the judgment. A statement of reasons for the court's decision not only enables a party to lodge an appeal, which would be impossible or at least much more difficult without knowledge of the court's reasoning, but also helps to convince the public that the court proceedings were fair and the judgment correct. The reasoning of the judgment also reinforces the right to be heard, as it makes it possible to ascertain whether the arguments put forward by a party during the proceedings have been considered[83]. The right to a statement of reasons applies not only to the final judgment. It also applies to other decisions of more incidental nature[84].

It should be noted that the right to justice guarantees not only the right to any statement of reasons, but also to a statement of reasons of an appropriate nature and quality, given its important role in enabling social control of the administration of justice and ensuring that the parties themselves are aware of the reasons

---

79 P. Hofmański, A. Wróbel, [in:] *Konwencja o Ochronie...*, p. 347.

80 Judgment of the European Court of Human Rights of 2 December 2021, Application no. 36516/19.

81 P. Hofmański, A. Wróbel, [in:] *Konwencja o Ochronie...*, p. 348.

82 Judgment of the European Court of Human Rights of 23 February 1994, Application No. 16757/90.

83 A. Lach, *Werdykt ławy przysięgłych w świetle prawa do rzetelnego procesu*, Palestra 2011/1–2, p. 45.

84 I. Rzucidło-Grochowska, *Brak obowiązku uzasadnienia i uzasadnienie skrócone a prawo do sądu*, Studia Prawnicze 2014/4, p. 62.

for the court's decision. While there is no obligation on the part of the court or tribunal to give a detailed response to each and every argument raised, the court or tribunal should not omit those points which are of fundamental importance to the outcome of the case. Depending on the type of judgment and the nature of the proceedings, the content and scope of the statement of reasons will vary. One standard should be applied to judgments of courts of first instance and another to judgments of courts of appeal, where it is normally permissible to confine to confirming the reasoning of the court of first instance. Exceptions to the principle of stating reasons for all judgments made during proceedings are permitted, particularly in simplified proceedings. Restricting the right to a statement of reasons may indeed contribute to the effectiveness of these proceedings, which is also an element of the right to a fair trial. However, in accordance with the principle of proportionality, a balance must be struck between the objectives of the statement of reasons and the organisational capabilities of the judiciary[85].

1.6. The principle of openness of justice

The judiciary plays an important role in society as the guardian of justice – a fundamental value in a constitutional state. It is therefore essential that the judiciary enjoys public confidence, otherwise it will not be able to fulfil its role[86]. One of the means of maintaining confidence in the judiciary is the public nature of the proceedings, which, by being subject to public scrutiny, contributes to the objective of Article 6(1) of the ECHR, i.e. a fair trial[87].

The function of the right to a public hearing is primarily to protect a party from the arbitrariness of the court. But this is not the sole reason for introducing the guarantee. The principle of publicity also serves to strengthen the independence and impartiality of the judge and is a means of ensuring a party's right to a fair hearing[88] .

The Convention does not define the 'openness' of the procedure, nor does it specify what it should consist of. This is a deliberate feature of the Convention. It is intended to provide flexibility to enable Member States to comply with its obligations. The Court avoids setting rigid limits and decides on the basis of the specific circumstances of the case. Nevertheless, the case law of the European Court of Human Rights has developed a certain minimum standard from which follows that the right to public proceedings includes at least three specific rights: the right

---

85 I. Rzucidło-Grochowska, *Brak obowiązku...*, pp. 63–64.

86 M.A. Nowicki, *Europejski Trybunał Praw Człowieka – Przegląd orzecznictwa (styczeń-marzec 2021 r.),* Palestra 2021/4, p. 101.

87 M.A. Nowicki, *Wokół Konwencji...*, pp. 599–600.

88 M.A. Nowicki, *Wokół Konwencji...*, pp. 351–352.

to be present at a trial, the right to have access to the case file and the right to be informed of the court's decision[89].

The right to participate in a court hearing is not limited to access to the courtroom, but also includes effective notice of the date and place of the hearing, in sufficient time to enable one to prepare to attend, and the opportunity to make an oral statement (the right to be heard)[90]. According to the European Court of Human Rights, the principle of publicity includes the right to an oral hearing, which of course does not exclude the written form at certain stages[91].

The right to a public hearing is not absolute and circumstances may exist where an oral hearing is not necessary. This is particularly the case in proceedings where there is no dispute as to the facts or where the issue of the credibility of the evidence has not arisen and the case can be decided on the basis of the parties' statements or written documents[92] . In *Ramos Nunes de Carvalho e Sá v Portugal*[93], the Court has summarised the permissible exceptions to the principle of a public hearing. In addition to the point made above concerning the absence of any dispute as to the facts or the credibility of the evidence, the ECHR has indicated that there is no need for an oral hearing when a case involves only legal arguments or purely technical issues. In certain cases, procedural economy may justify dispensing with a public hearing, in particular where the nature of the case justifies giving priority to the principle of promptness. In the cited judgment, the Court stated that a public hearing is required: (1) where it is necessary to assess the correctness of the findings made by the public authorities; (2) where it is necessary for the judge to form a personal impression of a party, thereby giving that party the right to explain his or her situation in person; and (3) where the court needs to obtain clarification of certain issues by means of a hearing. The circumstances justifying a departure from the principle of openness depend on the nature of the issues to be decided in the case. Refusing to hear a case does not only apply in rare cases, since the reason for not hearing a case in open court does not lie in the frequency with which the situations mentioned occur, but in the nature of the case concerned. However, the overriding principle of justice (fairness) must always be the determining factor[94].

A party may waive the right to a public hearing. The waiver may be express or implied, for example by not making or sustaining a request for a hearing. A party's

---

89 J. Roszkiewicz, *Jawność postępowania sądowego w świetle Europejskiej Konwencji Praw Człowieka,* Radca Prawny. Zeszyty Naukowe 2021/2, pp. 13–14.
90 J. Roszkiewicz, *Jawność postępowania...,* pp. 14–15.
91 P. Hofmański, A. Wróbel, [in:] *Konwencja o Ochronie...,* p. 356.
92 P. Hofmański, A. Wróbel, [in:] *Konwencja o Ochronie...,* p. 357.
93 Judgment of the European Court of Human Rights (Grand Chamber) of 6 November 2018, Application Nos. 55391/13, 57728/13, 74041/13.
94 Judgment of the European Court of Human Rights of 9 April 2019, Application no. 11236/09.

intention must be clear. However, the waiver of a public hearing must not be contrary to the public interest[95].

The right to participate in the hearing can also be guaranteed by means of videoconferencing, which in itself does not violate the principle of a fair trial[96]. The technical requirements must be appropriate in terms of the quality and security of the link, the ability of the participant to follow the proceedings, the opportunity to speak and the confidentiality of communication with legal representation[97].

Court proceedings must also be open to the public. The standard set out in Article 6(1) of the ECHR is met if the public can be informed of the date and place of the hearing, provided that it is a place easily accessible to them[98]. If the hearing is held by videoconference, the public should also be able to participate in the hearing, either through an Internet connection or by allowing access to the courtroom[99].

The principle of open justice also includes the right to public pronouncement of judgment. This right is not explicitly mentioned in the Polish translation of the Convention, but it follows directly from other language versions, which indicate that the judgment must be publicly announced. Unlike the right to a public hearing, the right to public proclamation of judgment cannot be restricted for the reasons set out in Article 6(1) of the Convention. Publication of the judgment alone is not sufficient to meet the objective of Article 6(1) of the ECHR and must also include the reasons for the judgment[100]. Contrary to the literal wording of the provision (in the English version: *judgment shall be pronounced publicly*), The ECHR accepts that the requirement to publish the judgment must be treated with some flexibility. Other means of making the judgment public may also be compatible with Article 6 of the Convention[101]. In particular, the judgment may be published in an official publication, or a copy of the judgment may be made available to the interested party[102]. The requirement to publish a judgment is also satisfied by making its content available to the parties in an on the court's website, after appropriate anonymisation of personal data.

The second sentence of Article 6(1) of the Convention lists the situations in which it is permissible to exclude the public: in the interests of morals, public order or national security in a democratic society; where the interests of juveniles or the

---

95 Judgment of the European Court of Human Rights of 26 July 2011, Application No. 58222/09.
96 Judgment of the European Court of Human Rights of 2 October 2018, Application no. 66580/12.
97 J. Roszkiewicz, *Jawność postępowania...*, pp. 16–17.
98 P. Hofmański, A. Wróbel, [in:] *Konwencja o Ochronie...*, p. 350.
99 J. Roszkiewicz, *Jawność postępowania...*, p. 17.
100 P. Hofmański, A. Wróbel, [in:] *Konwencja o Ochronie...*, p. 359–361.
101 Judgment of the European Court of Human Rights of 21 September 2006, Application No. 12643/02.
102 P. Hofmański, A. Wróbel, [in:] *Konwencja o Ochronie...*, p. 360.

protection of the private life of the parties so require; or to the extent strictly necessary in the opinion of the court in special circumstances where publicity would prejudice the interests of justice.

Only the public and representatives of the media are excluded (the provision refers explicitly to the 'press', but there is no reason not to extend the application of this provision to other representatives of the media[103]). It is therefore not permissible to limit the openness of the proceedings with regard to the parties concerned.

1.7. The principle of promptness

Article 6(1) of the Convention provides for the right to be tried 'within a reasonable time'. The question arises as to why this requirement is so important that it has to be expressed explicitly in the text of the Convention. As Vincent De Gaetano, judge at the European Court of Human Rights from 2010 to 2019, points out, lengthy court proceedings threaten the effectiveness (efficiency) of any legal system. The lack of efficiency in turn leads to a lack of credibility of the courts. Such a lack of confidence, in turn, undermines the very idea of the rule of law[104]. According to the English maxim, 'justice delayed is justice denied'.

The ECHR has not developed a uniform definition of protracted proceedings, using the broad phrase 'processing the case within a reasonable time'. A court case will be considered to be protracted if a reasonable period of time has been unreasonably exceeded[105].

Although the Court has not attempted to give a definition of a protracted case, it emphasises that certain categories of cases should, by their very nature, be treated as urgent. These include social security cases, cases concerning civil status, the protection of personal rights or compensation for road traffic accidents[106].

In principle, the period from the filing of the complaint to the final decision of the appellate court should be taken into account when assessing whether proceedings have been completed 'within a reasonable time'. Sometimes, in cases where an administrative decision has to be obtained first, the duration of the administrative procedure preceding the court case should also be taken into account. In some cases, the duration of the proceedings before the Constitutional Court should

103 P. Hofmański, A. Wróbel, [in:] *Konwencja o Ochronie...*, p. 363.

104 V. De Gaetano, *Reasonable time and hasty decisions - the article 6 and dilemma for domestic courts,* [in:] *Przewlekłość* postępowania sądowego, O. Piaskowska, P. Piesiewicz (red.), Warsaw 2018, p. 26.

105 P. Piesiewicz, *Korzystanie z uprawnień procesowych przez stronę a przewlekłość postępowania sądowego,* [w:] *Przewlekłość postępowania sądowego*, O. Piaskowska, P. Piesiewicz (red.), Warsaw 2018, p. 46.

106 O. Piaskowska, P. Piesiewicz, *Instytucja przewlekłości postępowania. Wprowadzenie do problematyki,* [w:] *Przewlekłość* postępowania sądowego, O. Piaskowska, P. Piesiewicz (red.), Warsaw 2018, pp. 15–16.

also be added to the duration of the proceedings, provided that the outcome of the proceedings can affect the final outcome of the case, i.e. is conclusive for civil rights and obligations[107]. This position was confirmed by the ECHR in its judgment of 21 July 2022 in the case of *Bielinski v Poland,* where the Court concluded that the suspension of the proceedings pending the judgment of the Constitutional Tribunal contributed to the excessive length of proceedings[108]. The assessment also includes the enforcement procedure, which is an integral part of the judicial process. It is only then that a final decision on a civil right is taken and becomes effective for the claimant[109].

The assessment of whether a reasonable time limit has been observed should be made on the basis of the specific circumstances of the individual case, taking into account criteria such as the complexity of the case, the conduct of the parties and the authority responsible for the proceedings, and the importance of the subject-matter of the dispute for the applicant[110]. The ECHR has developed guidelines for assessing the reasonable length of proceedings. However, it does not explicitly state when (after how many months or years) the procedure can be considered to be protracted[111]. In assessing the length of proceedings, the Court is bound to consider the proceedings as a whole and not their individual stages. The individual stages of the duration of the proceedings, considered separately, may not indicate a problem of excessive length but, taken together, may indicate that a reasonable duration of the proceedings has been exceeded. Nevertheless, even individual, longer periods of unjustified inactivity may in themselves justify the assessment that the right to be tried within a reasonable time has been violated, if they lead to the clear conclusion that the proceedings are not being conducted without delay[112].

The complexity of a case may justify the length of the proceedings if it involves an extensive evidentiary process, e.g. a large amount of material evidence or a large number of witnesses to be heard[113]. As a rule, the 'complexity' of a case should not relate to questions of law, as the national court is required to be fully aware of the law, even if it is complex[114]. However, the factual complexity of a case does not

107 M. A. Nowicki, *„Rzetelny proces w rozsądnym terminie" w orzecznictwie europejskim,* Studia Europejskie 1997/2, pp. 2–4.

108 Judgment of the European Court of Human Rights of 21 July 2022, Application no. 48762/19.

109 M. A. Nowicki, *„Rzetelny proces w rozsądnym terminie"...,* pp. 5–6.

110 O. Piaskowska, P. Piesiewicz, *Instytucja przewlekłości postępowania. Wprowadzenie do problematyki,* [w:] *Przewlekłość* postępowania sądowego, O. Piaskowska, P. Piesiewicz (red.), Warsaw 2018, pp. 15–16.

111 V. De Gaetano, *Reasonable time...,* p. 31.

112 V. De Gaetano, *Reasonable time...,* p. 33.

113 A. Pagiela, *Zasada „fair trial"...,* p. 136.

114 V. De Gaetano, *Reasonable time...,* p. 33.

always justify the length of the process, in particular when the nature of the case requires a prompt decision[115].

The length of the proceedings can be influenced by the conduct of the party itself, even if only by repeatedly requesting an adjournment or failing to produce requested documents or evidence[116]. In fact, the State can only be held liable for delays caused by its own fault[117].

However, the State is not only responsible for the actions of the judicial authorities. The court is obliged to ensure the efficiency of the proceedings and not to allow them to be prolonged by the opposing party, e.g. by granting an unjustified adjournment of the hearing or by accepting requests for evidence which are not essential to the resolution of the case and which lead to an excessive prolongation of the proceedings. This principle also applies in systems where the procedural initiative belongs exclusively to the parties[118]. The court is also responsible for other persons who do not have the status of a party and who, at the request of the court, perform ancillary tasks during the proceedings. This includes court experts who perform their duties under the control of the court[119]. The court is responsible for the manner and timing of the forensic reports and has a duty to ensure that there are no periods of inactivity in the delivery of the report by court experts.

It is the responsibility of the State to organise an efficient judicial system. The State may be held responsible not only for the delay in the adjudication of a particular case, but also for failing to increase the measures taken in the event of a backlog of cases in the courts or for structural deficiencies in the judicial system that cause delays. Addressing the systemic problem of lengthy proceedings may require the State to take remedial action in legislative, organisational, budgetary, and other respects[120]. While an excessive workload excuses a judge who, even with proper scheduling, is unable to complete proceedings within a reasonable time, this does not absolve the State party of its responsibility[121].

In civil cases, a party has a duty to refrain from filing motions and appeals intended to prolong the proceedings. It is also their duty to take all necessary steps to ensure the efficient conduct of the proceedings[122]. However, this does not mean that a party should waive its procedural rights, as the overriding objective is to reduce the length of the proceedings as much as possible. Generally, a party cannot be faulted for exercising its rights, but must nevertheless be aware that

---

115 O. Piaskowska, P. Piesiewicz, *Instytucja przewlekłości postępowania...*, pp. 16–17.
116 A. Pagiela, *Zasada „fair trial"...*, p. 136.
117 M. A. Nowicki, *„Rzetelny proces w rozsądnym terminie"...*, pp. 7–8.
118 P. Piesiewicz, *Korzystanie z uprawnień...*, p. 50.
119 M.A. Nowicki, *„Rzetelny proces w rozsądnym terminie"...*, p. 9.
120 Judgment of the European Court of Human Rights of 7 July 2015, Application nos. 72287/10, 13927/11, 46187/11.
121 P. Piesiewicz, *Korzystanie z uprawnień...*, p. 48.
122 M. A. Nowicki, *„Rzetelny proces w rozsądnym terminie"...*, p. 8.

their conduct may increase the length of the proceedings[123]. A party can only be held liable for delay if it abuses its procedural rights. The use of tactics by a party to prolong the proceedings does not relieve the court of its duty to avoid delay[124].

While the requirement for a reasonable length of proceedings is central to the credibility of any justice system, the quality of the judgments delivered by the courts is also important. A judgment based on incorrectly established facts or on the incorrect application of law is equally likely to undermine confidence in the administration of justice. Moreover, it may ultimately lead to a prolongation of the whole process, in cases where it results in the annulment of the first instance judgment and the need for a retrial[125].

In the case of *Nideröst-Huber v. Switzerland*[126], The European Court of Human Rights pointed out that, although the objective of saving time and speeding up proceedings is a value to which the Court attaches great importance, it does not justify disregarding the fundamental principle of the adversarial nature of proceedings. Indeed, the primary purpose of Article 6(1) of the Convention is to safeguard the interests of the parties and the proper administration of justice.

123 Judgment of the European Court of Human Rights of 10 October 2006, Application No. 69129/01.
124 P. Piesiewicz, *Korzystanie z uprawnień...*, pp. 50–51.
125 V. De Gaetano, *Reasonable time...*, p. 27.
126 Judgment of the European Court of Human Rights of 18 February 1997, Application No. 18990/91.

2. The right to a fair trial under the law of the European Union

2.1. Introductory remarks

The Charter of Fundamental Rights of the European Union[127] was proclaimed at the Nice European Council on 7 December 2000. In 2003–2004, efforts were made to incorporate the Charter of Fundamental Rights into the 'Constitution for Europe' (the Treaty establishing the Constitution for Europe, signed in Rome on 29 October 2004). The Charter of Fundamental Rights was to form Part II of the Constitution for Europe, but it has not been ratified by all the Member States of the European Union[128]. Nevertheless, the European Court of Justice in Luxembourg (now the Court of Justice of the European Union[129]) has repeatedly referred to the Charter of Fundamental Rights, for the first time in its judgment of 27 June 2006 in case C-540/03[130]. In assessing the European Parliament's action against the Council of the European Union for annulment of Directive 2003/86/EC of 22 September 2003 on the right to family reunification, the Court referred to Article 7 of the CFR, which governs the right to respect for private and family life. It also pointed out that, although the CFR is not a binding legal instrument, its importance should be stressed. The Court noted that the EU legislature has recognised the importance of the CFR by confirming in the Directive that it respects the principles recognised not only by Article 8 of the European Convention on Human Rights but also by the Charter[131].

The CJEU's position has been confirmed in subsequent judgments, including C-303/05 (reference for a preliminary ruling from the Belgian Court of Arbitration), in which it was pointed out that the Court must examine the validity of the Framework Decision on the European Arrest Warrant in the light of the principles set out in Articles 49, 20 and 21 of the CFR. In this respect, the opinion of the Advocate General of the ECJ, Damas Ruiz-Jarab Colomer, delivered on 12 September 2006, is particularly noteworthy, in which it is pointed out that, although the proclamation of the Charter is a mere political declaration without binding legal value, the

---

127 The Official Journal of the European Union (OJ EU) C 202, 7.6.2016, hereinafter: Charter of Fundamental Rights, EU Charter or CFR.

128 Z. Brodecki, T. Koncewicz, *Karta Praw Podstawowych i zasady ogólne prawa wspólnotowego,* [in:] *Karta Praw Podstawowych w europejskim i krajowym porządku prawnym*, Wróbel A. (ed.), Warsaw 2009, p. 16.

129 Hereinafter: CJEU.

130 R. Mazur, *Karta Praw Podstawowych,* [in:] *Ochrona Praw Podstawowych w Unii Europejskiej. Wybrane zagadnienia*, A. Florczak (ed.), Warsaw 2009, p. 43.

131 Judgment of the CJEU of 27 June 2006, C-540/03, ECLI:EU:C:2006:429.

event can hardly be ignored. The Charter of Fundamental Rights did not emerge from nowhere, but confirms rights derived from the common legal heritage of the Member States, both at national and international level. According to the Advocate General, the Charter should be the main instrument for interpreting the guarantees to which citizens are entitled[132].

The situation regarding the binding nature of the Charter changed on 1 December 2009 with the entry into force of the Lisbon Treaty[133], which amended the current wording of Article 6 of the Treaty on European Union[134]. Paragraph 1 of this provision states that 'the Union recognises the rights, freedoms and principles set out in the Charter of Fundamental Rights of the European Union of 7 December 2000, as adapted at Strasbourg on 12 December 2007, which shall have the same legal value as the Treaties'. The Treaty of Lisbon has thus not only made the Charter of Fundamental Rights binding but has also placed it on an equal footing with the Treaties, giving it the status of primary law. This is all the more important because the secondary legislation of the European Union (i.e. legal acts adopted by the institutions of the EU) must be consistent with primary law. If an act of secondary legislation is found to be contrary to primary law, and thus to the Charter, it must be declared void, which the Court of Justice may do either by an action for annulment (Article 263 TFEU[135]) or by a reference for a preliminary ruling (Article 267 TFEU)[136].

The legal nature of the Charter of Fundamental Rights means that the legal order of a Member State must also comply with the provisions of the Charter, but only to the extent that the Charter is applicable. The actions of Member States must comply with the requirements of the CFR when they are subject to the EU law, but not outside it[137]. Antonio Tizzano, former Judge at the Court of Justice of the European Union, and its Vice-President from 2015 to 2018, underlined the exceptional nature of the Charter in a speech delivered on 10 April 2014 on the occasion of the visit of a delegation from the Court of Justice to Warsaw. He pointed out that the Charter of Fundamental Rights could in a certain sense even take

132 Opinion of Advocate General Ruiz-Jarabo Colomer delivered on 12 September 2006, Advocaten voor de Wereld VZW v Leden van de Ministerraad, EUR-LEX 62005CC0303.

133 Treaty of Lisbon amending the Treaty on European Union and the Treaty establishing the European Community, done at Lisbon on 13 December 2007, Journal of Laws 2009, No. 203, item 1569.

134 Treaty on the European Union, Journal of Laws 2004, No. 90, item 864/30, as amended, hereinafter referred to as the TEU.

135 Treaty on the Functioning of the European Union, Journal of Laws 2004, No. 90, item 864/2, hereinafter TFEU.

136 P. Marcisz, [in:] *Podręcznik prawa Unii Europejskiej*, A. Zawidzka-Łojek, A. Łazowski (eds.), Warsaw 2018, pp. 100–101.

137 Judgment of the CJEU of 26 February 2013, C-617/10 *Fransson*, OJ EU C 114, 20.4.2013.

precedence over the Treaties themselves, since it expresses the fundamental principles of the Union[138]. For his part, the President of the Court of Justice, Koen Lenaerts, in a speech delivered on 12 November 2019 to mark the tenth anniversary of the Charter of Fundamental Rights as a source of primary law, considered that the entry into force of the Charter under the Treaty of Lisbon was, in retrospect, one of the greatest achievements in the history of European integration, as it demonstrated that the European Union was 'a union of democracy, a union of justice, and a union of rights and values based on constitutional traditions common to the rights of the Member States'[139].

The Charter of Fundamental Rights of the European Union consists of a preamble and seven chapters (titles). The first six contain a grouping of the fundamental rights reaffirmed in the Charter: I - Dignity, II - Freedoms, III - Equality, IV - Solidarity, V - Citizens' rights, VI - Justice. Finally, Title VII sets out the principles for applying the Charter and addresses questions of interpretation. These are the so-called horizontal provisions[140].

The fundamental rights in the Charter do not introduce new categories of human rights protected by the UE law and not enshrined elsewhere but confirm existing rights deriving from the constitutional traditions of the Member States, international obligations contained in the European Convention on Human Rights, general principles of Union law and the case law of the Court of Justice[141]. The above follows directly from the preamble to the Charter. The provisions of the Charter of Fundamental Rights in no way extend the competences of the Union as defined in the Treaties, in accordance with Article 6(1) of the TEU. The role of the Charter is therefore to specify and reaffirm fundamental rights and to make them more visible[142].

An extremely important document related to the CFR is the Explanations relating to the Charter of Fundamental Rights[143] prepared by the Praesidium of the European Convention. The Convention is the body set up at the meeting of the European Council of 14 and 15 December 2001 on the basis of the Laeken Declaration on the Future of the European Union[144]. The Convention's tasks

---

138 A. Tizzano, *Stosowanie Karty Praw Podstawowych UE w państwach członkowskich (art. 51 ust. 1 Karty)*, Europejski Przegląd Sądowy 2014/9, p. 29.

139 K. Lenaers, *Aby Karta Praw Podstawowych Unii Europejskiej była rzeczywistością dla wszystkich: 10 lat, odkąd Karta jest prawnie wiążąca*, Europejski Przegląd Sądowy 2020/2, p. 8.

140 A. Wyrozumska, *Znaczenie prawne zmiany statusu Karty Praw Podstawowych Unii Europejskiej w traktacie Lizbońskim oraz Protokołu polsko-brytyjskiego*, Przegląd Sejmowy 2008/2, p. 26.

141 Z. Warso, [in:] *Podręcznik prawa Unii Europejskiej*, A. Zawidzka-Łojek, A. Łazowski (eds.), Warsaw 2018, p. 62.

142 A. Wyrozumska, *Znaczenie pawne...*, p. 25.

143 Explanations on the Charter of Fundamental Rights, OJ EU C 303, 14.12.2007.

144 F. Jasiński, *Karta Praw Podstawowych Unii Europejskiej*, Warsaw 2003, p. 175.

included drawing up the text of the Charter of Fundamental Rights. As the document itself states, the Explanations do not have the force of law, but are 'a valuable interpretative tool intended to clarify the provisions of the Charter'. Although the Explanations do not constitute a source of law, their nature is not self-evident, since consideration of the content of this document is expressly required by the Treaty on European Union, which provides in Article 6(1) that the rights, freedoms and principles set out in the Charter shall be interpreted in accordance with the general provisions of Title VII of the Charter governing its interpretation and application and with due regard to the Explanations referred to in the Charter, which set out the sources of those provisions. The Explanations are also expressly referred to in Article 57(7) of the CFR, which provides that the courts of the Union and of the Member States shall take due account of the Explanations drawn up for the purpose of interpreting the Charter. Reference to the Explanations is also made in the preamble to the Charter itself. It is recalled that the Explanations are closest to a doctrinal interpretation in that they are not legally binding and that the courts of the Member States are not relieved of the obligation to interpret the provisions of the Charter themselves, even if they do so contrary to the Explanations[145]. However, it should be borne in mind that both the TEU and the CFR require 'due account' to be taken of the content of the Explanations when interpreting the Charter, so that their role cannot be reduced to merely non-binding doctrinal interpretation. The Explanations therefore appear to be closer to EU soft law than to a mere instrument of interpretation. Although the Explanations have no binding force, they certainly have a certain legal value.

2.2. Scope of application of the Charter of Fundamental Rights of the European Union

The scope of the Charter of Fundamental Rights is defined in Article 51(1), which states that the provisions of the Charter are addressed to the institutions and bodies of the Union, with due regard for the principle of subsidiarity, and to the Member States 'only when they are implementing Union law'. The extent to which the Union institutions are bound by the Charter of Fundamental Rights is not the subject of this analysis.

From the outset, the term 'implement' used in this provision has given rise to controversy and problems of interpretation, exacerbated by the inconsistent terminology used in the various language versions of the Charter[146]. Some of them refer to the 'execution' of EU law, others more precisely to the 'application' of EU

---

145 A. Wróbel, *O niektórych problemach sądowego stosowania Karty Praw Podstawowych*, [w:] *Karta Praw Podstawowych w europejskim i krajowym porządku prawnym*, A. Wróbel (ed.), Warsaw 2009, p. 104.

146 N. Półtorak, *Zakres związania państw członkowskich Kartą Praw Podstawowych Unii Europejskiej*, Europejski Przegląd Sądowy 2014/9, p. 19.

law[147], and still others 'implementation'. The term 'application' (stosować) used in the Polish version of the CFR has an autonomous (independent) meaning and cannot be interpreted in the same way as in Polish legal language. It should be understood in a much broader sense, as the 'implementation' of EU law, referring not only to legislative implementation, but also to the implementation of the law by the courts[148]. The 'application of Union law' covers all situations in which a Member State is required to fulfil an obligation imposed by the Treaties or by secondary Union law, and this does not mean only the obligation to transpose Union directives. It covers all situations in which national law constitutes an obstacle to the exercise of the freedoms laid down in the Treaties and the Member State justifies the restriction on the basis of overriding reasons relating to the public interest. The application of European Union law within the meaning of Article 51(1) also implies its interpretation, which leads to the conclusion that national law must be interpreted by national courts in accordance with the Charter[149]. The national court must therefore take account of the fundamental rights enshrined in the Charter when interpreting national law, provided that the application of national law in a given case falls within the scope of UE law.

In *Yoshikazu Iidia v Stadt Ulm,* the CJEU stated that, in order to determine whether a national authority is applying Union law, it must first be ascertained whether the national rule 'is intended to implement a provision of Union law, what the nature of that rule is and whether it pursues objectives other than those pursued by Union law, even if it may indirectly affect the latter, and whether there are provisions of Union law which specifically govern the field in question or which may be relevant to it'[150].

The issue of the interpretation of Article 51(1) of the CFR was addressed by the ECJ in, inter alia, the *Fransson* judgment[151]. This judgment arose in response to a preliminary question from the Haparanda tingsrätt (a Swedish district court) seeking an interpretation of the above provision of the CFR. The question concerned the interpretation of the *ne bis idem* principle in EU law. Hans Åkerberg Fransson was charged with serious tax offences in relation to tax obligations for the years 2004 and 2005. However, the Swedish tax authorities had previously issued a decision against him, determining his tax liabilities and imposing an obligation to pay interest. The Swedish court raised doubts as to whether it was permissible to conduct criminal proceedings against the defendant in a situation where he had previously been subject to an administrative sanction and whether this was not contrary to, inter alia, Article 50 of the Penal Code, which prohibits re-punishment for the same act.

147 A. Tizzano, *Stosowanie Karty...*, p. 30.
148 A. Wróbel, *O niektórych problemach ...*, p. 88.
149 K. Lenaers, *Aby Karta Praw...*, pp. 4–5.
150 Judgment of the CJEU of 8 November 2012, C-40/11, OJ EU C 9, 12.1.2013.
151 Judgment of the CJEU of 26 February 2013, C-617/10 *Fransson*, OJ EU C 114, 20.4.2013.

The European Commission and the governments of five Member States challenged the admissibility of the Swedish court's request for a preliminary ruling, arguing that neither the legislation giving rise to the additional tax liability nor the legislation on which the criminal proceedings were based constituted an application of EU law. However, the Court of Justice held that the legislation giving rise to Fransson's additional tax liability and the criminal proceedings constituted the implementation of Articles 2, 250(1) and 273 of Directive 2006/112/EC of 28 November 2006 on the common system of value added tax. Furthermore, under Article 325 of the TFEU[152], Member States are obliged to combat fraud affecting the financial interests of the Union with the same measures as they apply to combat crime affecting their own interests. Therefore, measures such as those imposed on the defendant in the main proceedings on account of false statements he made in relation to VAT, constitute an act of application of EU law within the meaning of Article 51(1) of the CFR.

The CJEU held, firstly, that respect for the fundamental rights protected by the Charter is required when national rules fall within the scope of EU law. There can therefore be no situation governed by UE law in which fundamental rights are not applicable. In other words, the application of EU law always requires the application of the Charter of Fundamental Rights. On the other hand, if a legal situation does not fall within the scope of UE law, the CJEU has no competence to assess its compatibility with the CFR. The CJEU recalled that, in accordance with Article 51(2) of the CFR, the Charter does not extend the field of application of UE law beyond its competences, nor does it establish new competences and tasks for the Union, nor does it modify the competences and tasks conferred on it by the Treaties. the Court of Justice interprets Article 51 of the CFR strictly and with some caution, upholding the principle of conferred powers, which is enshrined in a number of relevant instruments. According to this principle, the European Union can only act in areas in which it has been empowered to do so by the Member States. It follows that the Court of Justice may also interpret Union law in relation to fundamental rights only within the limits of the powers conferred on the European Union[153]. The Charter of Fundamental Rights therefore applies wherever Union law applies. It is argued that although the Fransson judgment has set a certain standard for the application of the Charter, drawing a clear line between the scope of application of purely national law and that of Union law remains an extremely difficult and often controversial task[154].

The above considerations also remain relevant in the context of the right to a fair trial. Article 47 of the CFR guarantees the right to an effective remedy and to

152 The Treaty on the Functioning of the European Union, OJ EU C 202, 7.6.2016, hereinafter: TFEU.

153 Judgment of the CJEU of 15 November 2011, C-256/11, ECLI:EU:C:2011:734.

154 J. Skrzydło, *Karta Praw Podstawowych UE w praktyce brytyjskiej*, Europejski Przegląd Sądowy 2015/10, pp. 27–28.

an impartial tribunal. A party can only claim a violation of this right if the case has an EU dimension. It is therefore necessary for the national court to consider, at each stage of the proceedings, whether the case is 'UE in nature', i.e. whether the facts on which the parties base their claim fall within the scope of European Union law or solely within the scope of national law[155]. If the answer is in the affirmative, the court is obliged to ensure the protection of the fundamental rights guaranteed by the Charter, including the right to an effective remedy and to an impartial tribunal. If the case does not have an EU dimension, a party does not have the right of access to court under Article 47 of the CFR. Indeed, the Charter of Fundamental Rights does not guarantee the right to court as such, but only when it is intended to protect claims based on the EU law[156]. This, moreover, follows directly from the wording of Article 47 of the CFR ('Everyone whose rights and freedoms guaranteed by the law of the Union are violated...'). The above does not, of course, mean that in such a situation the right to a fair trial is not protected by other legal systems (primarily national and Strasbourg systems).

2.3. Protocol No 30 on the application of the Charter of Fundamental Rights

Additional doubts as to the scope of application of the Charter of Fundamental Rights by Polish courts may be raised by the provisions of Protocol No. 30 on the application of the Charter of Fundamental Rights to Poland and the United Kingdom[157], also referred to as the Polish-British Protocol. According to Article 1(1) of the Protocol, the Charter does not extend the ability of the Court of Justice of the European Union, or any court or tribunal of Poland or of the United Kingdom, to find that the laws, regulations or administrative provisions, practices or action of Poland or of the United Kingdom are inconsistent with the fundamental rights, freedoms and principles that it reaffirms. In particular, and for the avoidance of doubt, nothing in Title IV of the Charter creates justiciable rights applicable to Poland or the United Kingdom except in so far as Poland or the United Kingdom has provided for such rights in its national law (section 2). In turn, Article 2 of the Protocol states: 'To the extent that a provision of the Charter refers to national laws and practices, it shall only apply to Poland or the United Kingdom to the extent that the rights or principles that it contains are recognised in the law or practices of Poland or of the United Kingdom'.

Protocol 30 was drafted by the United Kingdom as part of the Lisbon Treaty negotiations. It was designed to limit the application of the Charter, in particular to prevent British citizens from claiming social rights before the courts where the

155 M. Kożuch, *Karta Praw Podstawowych – samoistne źródło prawa czy zbiór zasad interpretacyjnych*, Europejski Przegląd Sądowy, pp. 31–32.
156 *Ibid*, p. 33.
157 OJ EU C 115, 9.5.2008, pp. 313–314.

national legal order did not allow them to do so. The Protocol therefore had legal significance for the United Kingdom. In addition, the British government wanted to convince public opinion that the Lisbon Treaty and the Charter of Fundamental Rights would not lead to a change in the constitutional legal order. Poland, on the other hand, expressed its willingness to join the Protocol in the second half of 2007, but for different reasons than those for which the United Kingdom had prepared the document. This circumstance is considered to be the reason for the discrepancy between the wording of the Protocol and the Polish conditions[158]. The plans to make the Charter legally binding have led to a debate in Poland about the dangers of the Charter. Criticism came mainly from right-wing circles and the Catholic Church, and was linked to the fear that the Charter and the Court would violate a certain standard that was incompatible with public morality. The main objection was to Article 21 of the CFR, which prohibits discrimination on grounds of, inter alia, sex and sexual orientation. It was feared that making the Charter a binding source of law would be a first step towards legalising same-sex marriage and the adoption of children by such couples[159]. Opponents of the Charter feared that it would provide a basis for imposing a change in the national order on Poland and introducing the right to euthanasia and abortion. Another argument against the Charter was the notion that it would provide a basis for claims by German citizens to property left in the Polish Regained Lands[160].

Poland's accession to the Protocol 30 was therefore 'a manifesto of restraint towards the European Union' and was politically rather than legally motivated. The government justified this move by threatening to block the ratification process of the Lisbon Treaty by the President of Poland[161]. Due to strong criticism of Poland's decision to accede to the British protocol, especially from trade unions, Poland added a unilateral declaration – Declaration (No. 62) of the Republic of Poland concerning the Protocol on the application of the Charter of Fundamental Rights of the European Union in relation to Poland and the United Kingdom, which states that 'in view of the tradition of the Solidarność social movement and its significant contribution to the struggle for social and labour rights, [the Republic of Poland] fully respects the social and labour rights established by European Union law, in particular those reaffirmed in Title IV of the Charter of Fundamental Rights of the European Union'.

---

158 S. Biernat, *Czy Karta Praw Podstawowych Unii Europejskiej obowiązuje* w Polsce, [w:] *Państwo prawa i prawo karne. Księga jubileuszowa profesora Andrzeja Zolla, t. I*, P. Kardas, T. Sroka, W. Wróbel (eds.), Warsaw 2012, pp. 62–63.

159 R. Mazur, *Karta* ..., pp. 51–52.

160 M. Wyrzykowski, [in:] *Ochrona praw podstawowych w Unii Europejskiej*, J. Barcz (ed.), Warsaw 2008, pp. 29–30.

161 J. Barcz, *Odniesienia do Karty Praw Podstawowych w toku procedury ratyfikacyjnej Traktatu z Lizbony w Polsce*, [in:] *60 lat Rady Europy. Tworzenie i stosowanie standardów prawnych*, H. Machińska (ed.), Warsaw 2009, p. 70.

The intention of some political elites was that the Polish-British protocol would provide a mechanism for derogation of the Charter's provisions (*opt-out* clause)[162]. Meanwhile, the majority of the doctrine accepts that its purpose is by no means to exclude the application of the Charter of Fundamental Rights in relation to Poland[163], which is fully bound by its provisions. Rather, the Protocol should be understood as a guarantee that the fundamental rights set out in the Charter can be invoked by an individual once they have been confirmed in Polish law[164]. Thus, a theoretical obstacle to invoking the provisions of the Charter can only arise if the same rights do not derive from another legal systems, i.e. the Polish constitutional order or the ECHR. Since all three systems of protection offer a similar standard, in practice these situations will be rare[165].

As the text of the Protocol makes clear, the Charter does not extend the jurisdiction of the Court of Justice of the European Union or create rights which may be enforced by the courts. The Protocol 30 therefore does not exclude the application of the Charter to Poland. This is also clear from the preamble to the Protocol, which states, first, that the purpose of the Protocol is to clarify certain aspects of the application of the Charter and, second, that it is without prejudice to the application of the Charter.

The meaning of the Polish-British Protocol was clarified by the Court of Justice in its judgment of 21 December 2011[166], in which it stated that Article 1(1) of the Protocol does not call into question the application of the Charter to the United Kingdom or to Poland, which is confirmed in the recitals of the Protocol. The Charter is applied and interpreted by the Polish and UK courts in strict compliance with the Explanations, and Article 1(1) of the Protocol 'confirms the content of Article 51 of the Charter concerning its scope of application and is not intended to exempt the Republic of Poland and the United Kingdom from complying with the Charter or to prevent the courts and tribunals in those Member States from ensuring compliance with those provisions'.

2.4. Rights and principles in the Charter of Fundamental Rights of the European Union

The preamble to the Charter of Fundamental Rights concludes by stating that 'the Union recognises the rights, freedoms and principles set out below'. The categorisation of the fundamental rights set out in the Charter into the above groups plays

162 J. Skrzydło, *Karta Praw Podstawowych...*, p. 25. Similarly: A. Wyrozumska, [in:] *Ochrona praw podstawowych w Unii Europejskiej*, J. Barcz (ed.), Warsaw 2008, p. 89.
163 Anna Wyrozumska, [in:] *Ochrona Praw Podstawowych...*, p. 89.
164 Anna Wyrozumska, [in:] *Ochrona Praw Podstawowych...*, p. 91.
165 A. Bodnar, [in:] *Ochrona praw podstawowych w Unii Europejskiej*, J. Barcz (ed.), Warsaw 2008, p. 147.
166 Judgment of the CJEU of 21 December 2011, C-411/10 *N.S.*, ECLI:EU:C:2011:865.

an important role in the judicial application of the law. 'Rights' as defined in the Charter can be invoked directly by individuals. 'Principles', on the other hand, will require prior transposition into EU or national law. 'Freedoms' will be closer to the framework rules and sometimes the aspirations of the Union[167]. The individual fundamental rights guaranteed by the Charter thus imply different levels of protection.

The terms 'right', 'freedom' and 'principle' have an autonomous meaning in Union law, which means that they cannot be interpreted according to the meaning attributed to them in national law[168]. The CFR does not provide a clear answer as to which provisions contain rights and which contain principles. Nor do the Explanations provide a precise and exhaustive indication, although in some cases they recognise a particular fundamental right as a right or a principle (e.g. the Explanations to Articles 25, 26, 37 of the CFR explicitly state that it is a principle, while Articles 23, 33 and 34 of the CFR contain both a right and a principle)[169].

A provision of the Charter will contain rights if it is intended to confer protection on the individual or if the object of the protection is the benefit of the individual[170]. Rights are therefore an individual claim (subjective right), as confirmed by Article 54 of the CFR, which introduces the prohibition of abuse of rights[171]. Principles protect the individual in a different way from rights, as they have to be transposed into national law in accordance with the constitutional requirements of the Member States. The level of implementation of these rights may therefore vary. According to Article 52(5) of the CFR, the principles of the Charter may be invoked before a court to interpret and review the legality of acts of Member States only when they are implementing Union law in the exercise of their respective powers. It is recognised that the nature of the principles are mainly social rights under Chapter IV of the Charter, which do not require the same level of protection as political rights[172]. The national court, which is under an obligation to give a pro-union interpretation, must nevertheless ensure the full effectiveness of the Charter's social rights[173].

Adam Bodnar proposes to distinguish between two categories, 'rights and freedoms' and 'principles'. The first category comprises the provisions of the Charter, which are similar to the typical rights and freedoms found in national constitutions and which can be invoked directly before the courts, since they can be used to

167 A. Wyrozumska, *Znaczenie prawne...*, p. 30.
168 A. Wróbel, *O niektórych problemach...*, pp. 90–91.
169 A. Wyrozumska, *Znaczenie prawne...*, pp. 30–31.
170 A. Wróbel, *O niektórych problemach ...*, p. 92.
171 Cezary Mik, [in:] *Ochrona praw podstawowych w Unii Europejskiej*, J. Barcz (ed.), Warsaw 2008, pp. 66–67.
172 A. Wróbel, *O niektórych problemach ...*, p. 93.
173 A. Wróbel, *O niektórych problemach ...*, p. 94.

create an effective legal norm. The principles, on the other hand, set out the general values to which the Union is committed[174]. Andrzej Wróbel treats 'freedoms' as a separate category, while pointing out that this distinction has no consequences in terms of application other than those related to 'rights'[175]. Cezary Mik also places rights and freedoms in a single category, arguing that the difference between them is normatively irrelevant[176].

The distinction between rights and principles is important because the former can be invoked directly before the UE institutions as well as before national courts, which means that there is no need to refer to additional grounds for the direct application of a legal norm. A typical example of a right contained in the Charter is the right to a fair trial[177].

2.5. Admissibility of limitations to fundamental rights

Another important consequence of the Charter's distinction between rights and principles is found in Article 52 of the CFR. According to paragraph 1, 'Any limitation on the exercise of the rights and freedoms recognised by this Charter must be provided for by law and respect the essence of those rights and freedoms. Subject to the principle of proportionality, limitations may be made only if they are necessary and genuinely meet objectives of general interest recognised by the Union or the need to protect the rights and freedoms of others'. In turn, paragraph 3 provides that: 'In so far as this Charter contains rights which correspond to rights guaranteed by the Convention for the Protection of Human Rights and Fundamental Freedoms, the meaning and scope of those rights shall be the same as those laid down by the said Convention. This provision shall not prevent Union law providing more extensive protection'. The purpose of these provisions is to define the scope for introducing possible limitations to the rights contained in the Charter. Since the term 'right' is specific to EU law, it must be assumed that Article 52(1) and (3) of the CFR does not refer to the principles set out in the Charter.

Article 52(1) provides a general clause for the admissibility of limitations to fundamental rights, which is possible only if the following conditions are cumulatively met 1) they concern rights and freedoms recognised by the Charter; 2) they are provided for by law; 3) they respect the essence of the right being restricted; 4) they are necessary; 5) they genuinely meet objectives of general interest recognised by the EU or the need to protect the rights and freedoms of others; 6) they are proportionate.[178] .

174 A. Bodnar, [in:] *Ochrona Praw Podstawowych...*, p. 147.
175 A. Wróbel, *O niektórych problemach...*, pp. 92–93.
176 Cezary Mik, [in:] *Ochrona Praw Podstaowych...*, pp. 66–67.
177 A. Bodnar, [in:] *Ochrona Praw Podstawowych...*, p. 148.
178 A. Wróbel, [in:] *Karta Praw Podstawowych Unii Europejskiej. Komentar*, A. Wróbel (ed.) Warsaw 2020, p. 1291.

The term 'law' also has an autonomous EU meaning and refers to general and abstract acts of national law, but also to EU law, both primary and secondary. Limitations must be expressly provided for in these acts and it must be assumed that all blanket authorisations are prohibited. It should be noted, however, that the provision of paragraph 1 will in principle be relevant only to limitations provided for in derived EU law, since Article 52(2) of the CFR introduces a *lex specialis* to paragraph 1. According to this provision, the rights recognised in the Charter which are subject to the provisions of the Treaties shall be exercised under the conditions and within the limits laid down therein. While the requirement in the Charter that any limitation of rights and freedoms be made by law is identical to the provision of Article 31(3) of the Polish Constitution, in other constitutional systems (e.g. Germany and the Netherlands) it is permissible to make such limitations by sub-statutory law[179].

Restrictions can only apply to rights and freedoms 'as recognised in this Charter' and therefore do not apply to fundamental rights which are general principles of European Union law. Absolute rights such as the right to life or dignity may also not be subject to limitations[180].

The need to respect the 'essence' of a right means that, from the point of view of the function of the right in question, restrictions must not constitute an unacceptable interference which would threaten the very *raison d'être* of that right. According to Andrzej Wróbel, the Charter advocates an absolute conception of the essence of a right, according to which there is a rigid and abstract limit that can never and under no circumstances be exceeded[181]. Meanwhile, in its earlier jurisprudence[182], the CJEU noted that fundamental rights are not absolute, but must be considered in relation to their social function. The exercise of these rights may be subject to limitations, provided that the interference is not disproportionate and infringes the very essence of the right. The restrictions must be 'necessary' and meet objectives of general interest (as expressed primarily in the Treaties) and must also comply with the principle of proportionality, which is a general principle of EU law. According to the CJEU, 'the principle of proportionality requires that the acts of the institutions of the Union must be suitable for achieving the legitimate objectives pursued by the legislation in question and must not go beyond what is necessary to attain those objectives'[183].

179 A. Wróbel, [in:] *Karta Praw Podstawowych...*, pp. 1294–1295.
180 A. Wróbel, [in:] *Karta Praw Podstawowych...*, pp. 1291–1292.
181 A. Wróbel, [in:] *Karta Praw Podstawowych...*, pp. 1295–1296.
182 Judgment of the CJEU of 13 July 1989, C-5/88 *Wachauf*, ECLI:EU:C:1989:321.
183 Judgment of the CJEU of 16 June 2015, C-62/14, OJ EU C 279, 24.8.2015.

The Explanations to Article 52 of the CFR indicate that the purpose of above-mentioned paragraph 3 is to ensure consistency between the Charter of Fundamental Rights and the European Convention on Human Rights. The *ratio legis* of this provision is undoubtedly to guarantee a minimum standard of protection which cannot be lower than that resulting from the Convention[184]. To the extent that the fundamental rights guaranteed by the Charter correspond to the rights set out in the Convention, the permissible limitations on fundamental rights are the same as those provided for in the Convention. When defining limitations of rights, the EU institutions (as well as the authorities of a Member State when applying Union law) must respect the standards on limitations contained in the Convention and its protocols. This also applies to the obligation to respect the interpretation of the Convention in the judgments of the European Court of Human Rights. The authors of the Explanations emphasise that the provision of Article 52(3) of the CFR in no way affects the autonomy of the Court of Justice to give a binding interpretation of UE law. Articles of the Charter whose scope overlaps with the provisions of the European Convention on Human Rights are listed in the Explanations to Article 52.

In accordance with Article 53 of the CFR, 'nothing in this Charter shall be interpreted as restricting or adversely affecting human rights and fundamental freedoms as recognised, in their respective fields of application, by Union law and international law and by international agreements to which the Union, the Community or all the Member States are party, including the European Convention for the Protection of Human Rights and Fundamental Freedoms, and by the Member States' constitutions'. This provision introduces a minimum standard of protection for the fundamental rights reaffirmed in the Charter. In 2005, the European Court of Human Rights delivered its judgment in the *Bosphorus* case, stating that the EU meets human rights standard comparable to that of the Convention and that the ECHR therefore accepts the presumption that a Member State acts in accordance with the Convention when implementing acts of EU law[185]. EU law is presumed to guarantee the Convention standard and is in principle not subject to review. However, this presumption can be rebutted[186]. In the *Fransson* judgment, the CJEU pointed out that EU law does not regulate the relationship between the European Convention on Human Rights and the legal systems of the Member States, nor does it determine the consequences that a national court should draw from a conflict between a rule of national law and the rights protected by the Convention.

184 A. Wróbel, [in:] *Karta Praw Podstawowych...*, p. 1305.

185 Judgment of the European Court of Human Rights (Grand Chamber) of 30 June 2005, Application No. 45036/98, LEX No. 154344.

186 N. Półtorak, *Przystąpienie Unii Europejskiej do Konwencji o Ochronie Praw Człowieka – projekt umowy akcesyjnej a prawo UE*, Europejski Przegląd Sądowy 2012/9, p. 12.

The provision of Article 53 of the CFR provides for a minimum standard of protection, but in certain cases the minimum standard will be at the same time a maximum standard and the application of other (national) systems of protection of fundamental rights will not be possible[187]. In the *Melloni* judgment[188], the CJEU held that in certain cases it would be contrary to the principle of uniformity and effectiveness of EU law to grant a wider scope of protection in a national constitutional system. The minimum standard of protection is therefore set by the Charter of Fundamental Rights and the maximum standard by the principle of the primacy, uniformity and effectiveness of Union law. In certain situations, the higher standard of protection must be reduced in order for the UE law to remain fully effective[189].

The right of access to court, which is the subject of this study, and which is guaranteed by Article 6 of the ECHR, is not an absolute right and may be subject to certain limitations, as long as the essence of the right to a court is not violated[190]. Thus, the right guaranteed by Article 47 of the CFR may be subject to limitations, under the conditions set out in Article 52 of the CFR, if they serve to guarantee other fundamental rights[191].

2.6. Right to an effective remedy and access to a fair trial

Article 47 of the Charter of Fundamental Rights, found in Title VI - Justice, provides for 'the right to an effective remedy and to a fair trial'. According to paragraph 1, 'everyone whose rights and freedoms guaranteed by the law of the Union are violated has the right to an effective remedy before a tribunal in compliance with the conditions laid down in this Article'. Paragraph 2, in turn, states that 'Everyone is entitled to a fair and public hearing within a reasonable time by an independent and impartial tribunal previously established by law. Everyone shall have the possibility of being advised, defended and represented'. According to paragraph 3, 'legal aid shall be made available to those who lack sufficient resources in so far as such aid is necessary to ensure effective access to justice'.

According to the Explanations, Article 47(1) of the CFR corresponds to Article 13 of the European Convention on Human Rights, which provides for the right to an effective remedy, while Article 47(2) corresponds to Article 6(1) of the

---

187 M. Taborowski, *Poziom ochrony praw podstawowych wynikający z Karty Praw Podstawowych UE jako przeszkoda dla przystąpienia Unii Europejskiej do Europejskiej Konwencji Praw Człowieka,* Europejski Przegląd Sądowy 2015/12, p. 29.

188 Judgment of the CJEU of 26 February 2013, C-399/11 *Melloni,* OJ EU C 114, 20.4.2013.

189 M. Taborowski, *Poziom Ochrony...*, p. 29–30.

190 P. Hofmański, A. Wróbel, [in:] *Konwencja o Ochronie...*, p. 295.

191 N. Półtorak, [in:] *Karta Praw Podstawowych Unii Europejskiej. Komentarz,* A. Wróbel (ed.), Warsaw 2020, pp. 1169–1170.

Convention, which provides for the right to a fair trial, although the Charter protection is broader because Article 6(1) of the Convention provides for the right to a court only in civil and criminal matters, whereas the Charter does not contain this limitation[192]. Article 47 contains three distinct subjective rights: the right to an effective remedy before a court, the right of access to an impartial tribunal and the right to legal aid. All three paragraphs of Article 47 together form the principle of effective judicial protection[193], which is at the same time recognised as a general principle of Union law stemming from the common constitutional tradition of the Member States and protected under Articles 6 and 13 of the European Convention on Human Rights[194] .

Article 47 of the CFR confers on individuals a right (in line with the distinction between rights and principles set out above) which they may invoke directly before national courts, without the need to lay down specific rules in EU or national law[195], but only to the extent that court applies EU law. The right to effective judicial protection is one of the so-called 'meta-rights', since the realisation of other fundamental rights guaranteed by UE law depends on the exercise of this right[196]. Ensuring effective judicial protection of individuals' rights under EU law is 'at the heart of the rule of law within the meaning of Article 2 TEU, which defines the values on which the European Union is founded'[197]. Respect for the fundamental right to a fair trial is also the cornerstone of mutual trust and the recognition of judgments between Member States[198].

On the question of terminology, it should be noted that the CJEU uses an inconsistent nomenclature in which the rights contained in Article 47 CFR are primarily referred to collectively as the right to 'effective judicial protection' or 'effective legal protection'. Sometimes the CJEU refers to the right to a 'fair trial' in its jurisprudence[199]. These terms are used inconsistently by the CJEU as equivalent. The principle of effective judicial protection includes procedural and institutional guarantees such as the right of access to a court, the right to a fair trial and the right to a court decision[200]. There is no obstacle to equating the concept of effective judicial

---

192 R. Wieruszewski, [in:] *Ochrona praw podstawowych w Unii Europejskiej*, J. Barcz (ed.), Warsaw 2008, p. 140.

193 A. Wróbel, [in:] *Karta praw Podstawowych...*, p. 1128.

194 Judgment of the CJEU of 22 December 2010, C-279/09 *DEB*, ECLI:EU:C:2010:811.

195 Judgment of the CJEU of 17 April 2018, C-414/16 *Egenberger*, ECLI:EU:C:2018:257.

196 M. Safjan, *Prawo do skutecznego środka prawnego i bezstronnego sądu – art. 47 Karty Praw Podstawowych w relacjach horyzontalnych – kilka uwag w związku z wyrokiem TSUE w sprawach połączonych C-585/18; C-624/18, C-625/18*, Palestra 2020/5, p. 7.

197 A. Wróbel, [in:] *Karta Praw Podstawowych...*, p. 1110.

198 P. Filipek, *Rozproszona europejska kontrola przestrzegania prawa do rzetelnego procesu sądowego w świetle zasady wzajemnego zaufania i wyroku C-216/18 PPU, LM*, Europejski Przegląd Sądowy 2019/2, pp. 15–16.

199 Judgment of the CJEU of 6 November 2012, C-199/11, OJ C 9, 12.1.2013.

200 A. Wróbel, [in:] *Karta Praw Podstawowych...*, p. 1111.

protection with the right to a fair trial. Both terms refer to the same set of principles aimed at giving effect to the protection of individual rights guaranteed by EU law. The Court of Justice has emphasised that the principle of effective judicial protection enshrined in Article 47 of the Charter consists of various elements, in particular the right of defence, the right of access to a court and the right to legal advice, assistance and representation[201].

The right to effective judicial protection will include the following specific rights: the right to a fair trial, the right to a public hearing, the right to be tried within a reasonable time, the right to be tried by an independent tribunal, the right to be tried by an impartial tribunal, the right to be tried by a tribunal established by law, the right to legal aid and the right to free legal aid[202].

As regards the scope of Article 47 of the CFR, it should be noted that the provision uses the term 'everyone'. It follows from the established case law of the Court of Justice that the right to an effective remedy is available to any natural person and that this concept cannot be limited to citizens of the EU. The right to effective judicial protection also applies to nationals of third countries when they are the subject of rights and freedoms guaranteed by the Union[203]. However, the protection may also be invoked by a legal person in order to challenge before a court an act which adversely affects that legal person[204]. Nevertheless, organisations that are part of the public authority structure, as well as legal persons that are not part of that structure but perform tasks of public authority, should be excluded from the scope of the term 'everyone'[205].

The term 'effective remedy' referred to in paragraph 1 is an EU concept and must therefore, in accordance with the principle of the uniform application of EU law, be given an autonomous meaning independent of the interpretation given to it by the courts or doctrine of the Member States. It must be interpreted in accordance with the meaning given to the term 'effective remedy' in Article 13 ECHR and in the light of the case law of the European Court of Human Rights. Indeed, Article 47(1) of the CFR is modelled precisely on this provision. The term 'remedy' refers to any legal means by which a case may be adjudicated (including the possibility of an action, interlocutory proceedings, appeal, compensation or restitution). The existence of an effective remedy means that, on the one hand, that the national authorities must ensure that the substance of the allegation based on the

---

201 Judgment of the CJEU, C-199/11.

202 K. Szczepankowska-Kozłowska, *Prawo do skutecznego środka prawnego i bezstronnego sądu – art. 47 Karty Praw Podstawowych w relacjach horyzontalnych – kilka uwag w związku z wyrokiem TSUE w sprawach połączonych C-585/18, C-624/18, C-625/18,* Palestra 2020/5, p. 105.

203 A. Wróbel, [in:] *Karta Praw Podstawowych...*, p. 1140.

204 Judgment of the CJEU of 6 October 2020, C-245/19 and C-246/19, OJ EU C 414, 30.11.2020.

205 A. Wróbel, [in:] *Karta Praw Podstawowych...*, pp. 1139–1140.

Convention can be presented to them, and, on the other hand, the need to ensure that such a violation can be rectified[206].

The right to court under Article 47 of the Charter consists not only of the right to petition, but above all of the right of access to court established by law. Unlike Article 13 of the Convention, Article 47 of the CFR explicitly states that 'everyone has the right to an effective remedy before a tribunal'. The principle of uniform interpretation of EU law requires that 'tribunal' be considered as a concept of EU law. Accordingly, a tribunal can only be an institution established as a judicial authority in accordance with the rules of the legal system concerned[207]. The control of the violation of Article 47 of the CFR will therefore consist of examining whether access is guaranteed to a body with the corresponding constitutional characteristics, which fulfils the conditions for being entrusted with the administration of justice[208]. The question of the concept of a court and how to distinguish it from an administrative body has been examined by the CJEU on several occasions. In the *Wilson* judgment[209], the CJEU set out the minimum requirements a national court must meet under EU law. These are: 'appointment by law, permanence, exclusive jurisdiction to hear a particular type of dispute, adversarial procedure and application of the law, as well as independence and impartiality'. On the basis of the case cited, the Court considers that the Luxembourg Bar Association, as a body hearing cases concerning the right to practise the profession of lawyer, is not a court, since it is composed exclusively of practitioners of that profession. It could be in the interests of those practitioners to prevent newcomers from practising on the market, which supports the view that that body is not sufficiently impartial. The independence of the tribunal means first and foremost that the body is a 'third party' in the sense that there is no organisational and functional link between the tribunal and a party (e.g. the body whose decision is being challenged before the tribunal)[210].

The concept of judicial independence has two elements: an external one, which presupposes the protection of the institution from interference and outside pressure, and an internal one, which concerns impartiality and equal distance from the litigants and their interests[211]. The guarantees of independence require the existence of rules, in particular on the composition of the body, the procedure for its appointment, the duration of its term of office, the grounds for exclusion and the removal of members of the body, which make it possible to exclude any doubt as to the independence of the body from external factors and its neutrality with

206 A. Wróbel, [in:] *Charter of Fundamental Rights...* pp. 1135–1136.
207 M. Safjan, The *right to an effective remedy...*, p. 20.
208 R. Grzeszczak, M. Krajewski, *„Sąd" w świetle przepisów art. 47 KPP oraz art. 267 TFUE*, Europejski Przegląd Sądowy 2014/6, p. 10.
209 Judgment of the CJEU of 19 September 2006, C-506/04 *Wilson*, ECLI:EU:C:2006:587.
210 Judgment of the CJEU of 30 May 2002, C-516/99, ECLI:EU:C:2002:313.
211 Judgment of the CJEU C-506/04 *Wilson*.

regard to the parties[212]. Institutional guarantees of independence are, according to the CJEU, inter alia the irremovability of judges, the appropriate level of their remuneration[213] or the existence of a disciplinary system for judges which excludes the risk of such a system being used to politically control the content of judicial decisions[214]. In interpreting the concept of court (tribunal) in Article 47 of the CFR, the case law of the European Court of Human Rights may be helpful[215].

According to the principle of procedural autonomy, a Member State is competent to determine the jurisdiction of the courts and the judicial procedures for hearing claims based on EU law. This does not mean, however, that systemic and procedural issues relating to the claims based on EU law are entirely excluded from the competence of the EU[216]. The establishment of procedural rules on remedies to ensure the protection of rights derived from EU law by the Member States is only possible in an area where there is no EU regulation[217]. The principle of procedural autonomy gives way to the principle of the primacy of Union law. Moreover, in accordance with the principle of equivalence set out in the *Rewe/Comet* formula[218], a national remedy to resolve an EU case may not be less favourable than a remedy established for a similar national claim[219].

The procedural autonomy of the Member States in the area of civil procedure is significantly limited in cross-border cases. Under Article 81 of the TFEU, the European Union has legislative competence in the area of judicial cooperation in civil matters. In addition, provisions of secondary law sometimes impose procedural standards on a Member State that limit national autonomy and require the adoption of certain procedural solutions in order to ensure the effectiveness of EU law (for example, Article 10 of the Equality Framework Directive[220], which requires Member States to adopt certain solutions regarding the burden of proof in equal treatment cases). The principle of procedural autonomy also gives way to the principle of effectiveness, according to which a Member State's procedural rules must not make it impossible in practice to pursue claims based on EU law[221].

---

212 Decision of the CJEU of 14 May 2008, C-109/07, ECLI:EU:C:2008:274.

213 Judgment of the CJEU of 27 February 2018, C-64/16 *Associação Sindical dos Juízes Portugueses v Tribunal de Contas, Portuguese judges' case,* ECLI:EU:C:2018:117.

214 Judgment of the CJEU of 25 July 2018, C-216/18, ECLI:EU:C:2018:586.

215 R. Grzeszczak, M. Krajewski, *"Sąd" w świetle przepisów...*, p. 11.

216 A. Wróbel, *Autonomia proceduralna państw członkowskich. Zasada efektywności i zasada efektywnej ochrony sądowej w prawie Unii Europejskiej,* Ruch Prawniczy, Ekonomiczny i Socjologiczny 2005/1, pp. 35–36.

217 Judgment of the CJEU of 16 December 1976, 33/76 *Rewe,* ECLI:EU:C:1976:188.

218 Judgment of the CJEU 33/76 *Rewe* and judgment of the CJEU of 16 December 1976, 45/76 *Comet,* ECLI:EU:C:1976:191.

219 R. Grzeszczak, M. Krajewski, *"Sąd" w rozumieniu prawa ...*, p. 4.

220 Council of the European Union Directive 2000/78/EC of 27 November 2000, OJ L 303, 2.12.2000.

221 A. Wróbel, [in:] *Karta Praw Podstawowych...*, p. 1122.

The principle of procedural autonomy is closely linked to the principle of effective judicial protection, as Member States are responsible for ensuring the effective protection of the rights conferred by EU law[222]. Thus, the principle of procedural autonomy cannot limit the principle of effective judicial protection, as this would be contrary to the principle of effectiveness. This, in turn, is the guiding principle of the system of EU law, according to which the provisions of EU law must be given practical effect[223].

Paragraph 2 of Article 47 concretises the right to an effective remedy guaranteed in paragraph 1. The right to a fair trial within the meaning of Article 47(2) of the CFR ('Everyone is entitled to a fair and public hearing...') must be interpreted by reference to the standard set by the European Convention on Human Rights, as is clear from Article 52(3) of the CFR, which indicates that the scope and meaning of the rights guaranteed by the Charter are the same as those granted by the Convention. In order to determine the standard set by the Charter, it will therefore be necessary to refer to the case law of the European Court of Human Rights on Article 6(1) of the ECHR. The guarantees provided by the two systems are in principle to be understood in a similar way (with the Court having the power to establish a higher level of protection in EU law).

An essential element of the principle of effective judicial protection is the right of access to justice. According to the CJEU[224], the European Union is a union governed by the rule of law, in which individuals have the right to challenge before the courts the legality of any decision or other national act concerning the application of an act of the Union. Guaranteeing access to an impartial tribunal in order to protect rights under EU law is an obligation for Member States[225]. This means that any decision taken by a public authority on the basis of EU law must be subject to review. Even if national law does not provide for a judicial remedy in a given situation, national courts must interpret the procedural rules in such a way as to provide for a judicial remedy for the enforcement of EU law claims in any event, and even apply solutions not expressly provided for by national law[226]. However, this does not mean that every single decision taken by a public authority must be subject to judicial review, but rather the final decision closing the proceedings on a claim conferred by EU law[227].

The conditions for the realisation of the right to a fair trial are not specified in detail in Article 47, nor does the CJEU define this right exhaustively[228]. However,

222 Judgment of the CJEU of 15 April 2008, C-268/06, ECLI:EU:C:2008:223.
223 A. Wróbel, [in:] *Karta Praw Podstawowych...*, p. 1124.
224 Judgment of the CJEU, C-64/16 The *Portuguese judges' case.*
225 Judgment of the CJEU of 19 June 1990, C-213/89 *Factortame*, ECLI:EU:C:1990:257.
226 N. Półtorak, [in:] *Karta Praw Podstawowych...*, p. 1156.
227 Judgment of the CJEU of 28 July 2011, C-69/10, ECLI:EU:C:2011:524.
228 N. Półtorak, [in:] *Karta Praw Podstawowych...*, p. 1191.

it is recognised that it includes the principle of adversarial procedure and equality of arms, the right to be heard and to participate in the proceedings, the right to access the case file, the right to a reasoned decision by the court, the principle of *res judicata* and the right to an effective defence[229].

As the CJEU pointed out in its judgments in cases C-514/07 and C-199/11[230], the principle of equality of arms, which is a corollary of the very notion of a fair trial, entails the obligation to give each party a reasonable opportunity to present its case, including its evidence, under conditions which do not place it in a clearly less favourable position than the opposing party. The principle of equality of arms is therefore intended to maintain a balance between the parties and to ensure that each party is able to evaluate and challenge any document submitted to the court. The adversarial principle means that a party must have a real opportunity to participate in the proceedings, i.e. to know and understand the subject matter and course of the proceedings and to be able to refer to them. A party should have the right to know and refer to all documents and submissions made by an opponent to influence the court's decision[231].

The right to a defence, which according to the CJEU is not limited to the accused in criminal cases, but applies to all proceedings which may adversely affect an individual, means first and foremost the right to be heard (to present a position on circumstances relevant to the decision)[232]. According to the Court of Justice of the EU[233], the right of defence includes the possibility of submitting one's views to the competent authority before a decision is taken which could adversely affect the interests of the individual. It is also a corollary of the right of defence that the authority is under an obligation to respond to the observations submitted by the person concerned, to examine them carefully and impartially and to give detailed reasons for its decision so that the reasons for any refusal to take account of the observations submitted can be understood. Respect for the rights of the defence, as an element of the right to effective judicial protection, applies even where such a procedure is not formally provided for by national law. The principle of effective judicial protection requires compliance with the obligation to communicate the reasons on which a decision is based, in order to enable individuals to defend their rights under the best possible conditions and to decide whether it is appropriate to assert them before the Union courts[234].

229 M. Górski, *Prawo do skutecznego środka prawnego w art. 47 Karty Praw Podstawowych UE – znaczenie i deficyty*, Europejski Przegląd Sądowy 2016/8, p. 40.
230 Judgment of the CJEU of 21 September 2010, C-514/07, ECLI:EU:C:2010:541, judgment of the CJEU of 6 November 2012, C-199/11.
231 M. Górski, *Prawo do skutecznego...*, p. 40.
232 N. Półtorak, [in:] *Karta Praw Podstawowych...*, p. 1192.
233 Judgment of the CJEU of 11 December 2014, C-249/13, OJ EU C 46, 9.2.2015.
234 Judgment of the CJEU of 3 September 2008, C-402/05 *Kadi*, ECLI:EU:C:2008:461.

However, the CJEU does not regard the rights of the defence as an absolute value and accepts that ensuring the fairness and efficiency of the administration of justice may justify restricting them[235]. Such limitations must in fact correspond to the objectives of general interest pursued by the measure in question and must not constitute, in the light of the objective pursued, a manifest and disproportionate restriction of the rights thus guaranteed. Such an objective may, according to the Court, be to counteract delaying tactics 'which ultimately lead to an offence against the administration of justice'. In civil proceedings, which are essentially adversarial in nature, it is therefore permissible to deliver a judgment by default in the absence of the defendant[236]. In order to avoid a situation in which the plaintiff is deprived of access to justice, it is permissible to introduce national procedural rules under which proceedings against a person whose domicile is unknown are conducted in his absence, but only if the court hearing the case has satisfied itself that all searches required by the principle of diligence and good faith have been made to locate the defendant[237]. According to the CJEU, a party may expressly or even tacitly withdraw from a trial and there is no breach of the right to a fair trial if the party has been informed of the time and place set for the trial or if is represented by a lawyer to whom the party has given a mandate[238].

The Court of Justice allows a restriction of the rights of the defence in order to protect public health, indicating that it is permissible for the public authorities to take the necessary measures (to protect health) without the person concerned having been heard. Such a restriction can only constitute a disproportionate and unacceptable interference with the very essence of the rights of the defence if the persons concerned are deprived of the possibility of challenging the measure in question in subsequent proceedings and of putting forward their views effectively in those proceedings[239].

Article 47(2) of the CFR guarantees the right to a 'public' trial. This right is an essential feature of a fair trial, and its purpose is to subject judicial proceedings to public scrutiny in order to reinforce the other guarantees of the right to a fair trial[240]. It should be noted that, unlike Article 6(1) of the ECHR, Article 47 of the CFR does not expressly provide for limitations on the right to a public hearing. On the contrary, the Convention allows for such exceptions ('the press and public may be excluded from all or part of a trial in the interests of morals, public order or national security in a democratic society, where the interests of juveniles or the protection of the private life of the parties so require, or to the extent strictly necessary in the opinion of the court in special circumstances where publicity

235 N. Półtorak, [in:] *Karta Praw Podstawowych...*, p. 1195.
236 Judgment of the CJEU of 2 April 2009, C-394/07, ECLI:EU:C:2009:219.
237 Judgment of the CJEU of 17 November 2011, C-327/10, ECLI:EU:C:2011:745.
238 Judgment of the CJEU, C-399/11 *Melloni*.
239 Judgment of the CJEU of 15 June 2006, C-28/05, ECLI:EU:C:2006:408.
240 M. Górski, *Prawo do skutecznego...*, p. 41.

would prejudice the interests of justice'). The question to be answered, therefore, is whether the Charter really does not provide for any restrictions on the openness of proceedings, or whether restrictions on the right to a public hearing along the lines of those provided for in the Convention are permissible.

It would appear that, although the Charter does not expressly define exceptions to the principle of openness, the right to a public trial cannot be regarded as an absolute value and that exceptions to it should be allowed[241]. Since the right to effective judicial protection corresponds in essence to the right to a fair trial set out in Article 6(1) of the ECHR, the scope of this right should be understood in the same way (Article 52(3) of the CFR is intended to ensure the necessary consistency between the two standards, while respecting the autonomy of EU law[242]). While the provisions of the Charter may provide greater protection than those of the Convention, it would not be reasonable to assume that the principle of openness is absolute. The Convention allows for restrictions on the openness of judicial proceedings in order to protect other overriding values such as public safety or the protection of privacy. The inadmissibility of restrictions on the openness of judicial proceedings could in some cases conflict with other rights and principles guaranteed by the Charter, such as the right to respect for private and family life (Article 7 of the CFR) or the principle that public authorities must have regard to the best interests of the child (Article 24(2) of the CFR). It should be recalled that any limitations to the principle of publicity – in accordance with Article 52(1) of the CFR – must be introduced by law and respect the essence of the right to a fair trial, and must also be proportionate and necessary and genuinely meet objectives of general interest recognised by the EU or the need to protect the rights and freedoms of others. There is no doubt that the exceptions to the principle of publicity provided for in Article 6(1) of the ECHR are in the general interest of the EU, which includes, inter alia, the protection of security or the rights of the child (Article 2 TEU, Article 3(5) of the TEU). Ultimately, therefore, it must be assumed that the provisions of Article 47 of the CFR do not preclude the introduction of certain restrictions on the openness of proceedings, but no more extensive than those provided for in Article 6(1) of the ECHR.

It should be noted that in its jurisprudence, the CJEU has generally not undertaken to define exceptions to the principle of openness, but has merely referred to the case law of the ECHR and stated that the content and scope of the right to effective judicial protection (including the right to a public trial) should be interpreted in the same way (if not more broadly) as in the Convention[243]. In its judgment of

241 A. Skowron, *Rzetelny proces karny w ujęciu Karty Praw Podstawowych Unii Europejskiej oraz Europejskiej Konwencji o Ochronie Praw Człowieka i Podstawowych Wolności*, Prokuratura i Prawo 2017/11, p. 18.
242 Judgment of the CJEU of 29 March 2022, C-132/20, ECLI:EU:C:2022:235.
243 Judgment of the CJEU of 30 June 2016, C-205/15, ECLI:EU:C:2016:499.

26 July 2017[244], the Court, referring to the ECHR judgment in *Jusilla v Finland*, indicated that Article 47 of the CFR does not impose an absolute obligation to hold a public trial and does not necessarily require a trial in all proceedings. However, the infringement of the right to effective judicial protection must be assessed in the light of the specific circumstances of the case, in particular the nature of the act in question, the circumstances in which it was adopted and the law governing the field in question. The judgment[245], cited by the CJEU, pointed out that although an oral and public hearing is a fundamental principle protected by Article 6(1) of the Convention (particularly in criminal cases), there may be proceedings in which it is not necessary: for example, where there is no question of credibility or challenge to the facts justifying a hearing and the courts can decide the case fairly and reasonably on the basis of the parties' submissions and other written material. At the same time, the ECHR emphasised that the fact that an open and public hearing is of great personal importance to the applicant is not determinative of the need for a hearing.

The right to effective judicial protection in Article 47 of the CFR also includes the right to have a case heard within a reasonable time[246]. In the context of proceedings before the General Court of the EU, the Court of Justice has indicated that the assessment of whether proceedings before the Court are unduly lengthy should be based primarily on criteria such as the overall length of the proceedings; the importance of the case for the parties; the number of appeals lodged and the languages in which the proceedings are conducted; the volume of the file and the complexity of the factual and legal issues involved; any conduct of the appellants and the competent authorities which may have influenced the length of the proceedings; the period between the end of the written procedure and the opening the oral procedure; any interim measures of organisation of procedure and measures of inquiry; the period between the end of the proceedings and the judgment[247].

In its judgment of 19 December 2012[248] following a reference for a preliminary ruling from the Polish court, the Court of Justice interpreted Article 1(1) of Regulation (EC) No. 1393/2007 on the service of documents[249] and held that that provision must be interpreted as precluding legislation of a Member State which provides that court documents intended for a party whose domicile or habitual residence is in another Member State are to be placed on the file of the proceedings

244 Judgment of the CJEU of 26 July 2017, C-348/16, OJ C 309, 18.9.2017.
245 Judgment of the European Court of Human Rights of 23 November 2006, Application No. 73053/01, LEX No. 199099.
246 N. Półtorak, [in:] *Karta Praw Podstawowych...*, p. 1201.
247 Judgment of the CJEU of 25 January 2007, C-403/04 P, ECLI:EU:C:2007:52.
248 Judgment of the CJEU of 19 December 2012, C-325/11, OJ EU C 46, 16.2.2013.
249 Regulation No 1393/2007 of the European Parliament and of the Council of 13 November 2007 on the service in the Member States of judicial and extrajudicial documents in civil or commercial matters, and repealing Council Regulation (EC) No. 1348/200, OJ EU L 324, 10.12.2007.

with effect for service, where that party has not appointed an agent for service of process residing in the first Member State in which the court proceedings are taking place. The Court held that the mechanism of fictitious service provided for in Article 1135[5] of the Code of Civil Procedure was incompatible with the attainment of the objectives of the protection of the rights of the defence set out in Regulation No. 1393/2007. The Court emphasised that the objective of ensuring the efficiency of judicial proceedings cannot be achieved at the expense of any weakening of the rights of defence to which the addressees are entitled and which derive from the right to a fair trial. According to the CJEU, the objective must be to reconcile the efficiency and speed of the procedure with the need to ensure that the rights of the defence of the addressees are adequately protected, in particular by guaranteeing the actual and effective receipt of court documents.

The right to court, guaranteed by Article 47 of the CFR, includes the right to legal aid to the extent necessary to ensure effective access to justice[250] ('Legal aid shall be made available to those who lack sufficient resources in so far as such aid is necessary to ensure effective access to justice').

As mentioned above, the right to court is not absolute and may be subject to restrictions. One of the limitations of the right to court may be the obligation to pay court fees. The Court of Justice recognises that the charging of court fees is in principle a desirable measure, since it contributes to the good functioning of justice by providing a source of funding for the judicial activities of the Member States and discourages applications which are manifestly unfounded or whose sole purpose is to delay proceedings[251]. In accordance with the principle of equivalence, court fees for actions seeking to ensure the protection of rights which individuals derive from EU law may not be less favourable than those for internal proceedings. Nor may they render impossible or excessively difficult in practice the exercise of rights conferred by the UE legal order[252]. This means that a Member State, which in principle has the autonomy to lay down procedural rules on the obligation to pay court fees, is obliged, on the one hand, to ensure that court fees are not excessive and, on the other hand, to take account of the possibility of applying for an exemption from court fees.

Another guarantee for the implementation of the principle of effective judicial protection is the possibility to invoke the right to legal assistance. The Court of Justice has held that this right is not limited to natural persons and that Article 47 of the CFR must be interpreted as meaning that legal persons are not excluded from exercising this right[253]. The European Court of Human Rights, on the other hand, does not require that the applicant be granted the right to assistance in every case, but only where assistance is genuinely necessary. Moreover, there must be

250 N. Półtorak, [in:] *Karta Praw Podstawowych...*, pp. 1202–1203.
251 Judgment of the CJEU of 6 October 2015, C-61/14, ECLI:EU:C:2015:655.
252 Judgment of the CJEU, C-205/15.
253 Judgment of the CJEU, C-279/09 *DEB*.

specific criteria for granting it, and the right must be concrete and not merely theoretical[254]. This standard will also apply to the right to assistance confirmed in Article 47(3) of the CFR. Among the criteria to be examined by the national court in order to determine whether the conditions for granting the right to legal aid constitute a restriction of the right of access to court, the CJEU has identified the following: the subject-matter of the dispute, the reasonable prospects of winning the case, the importance of the case to the party, the complexity of the rules applicable to the case, the ability of the applicant to manage the case effectively. With regard to legal persons, the national court should also examine their situation, i.e. the form and nature of their activity (profit-making or non-profit-making), the financial capacity of their shareholders and the possibility of obtaining the sums necessary to bring an action[255].

An expression of the EU legislator's pursuit of the right to a court in the area of the right to legal aid is Council Directive 2003/8/EC of 27 January 2003, which was transposed into Polish law by the Act of 17 December 2004 on the right to assistance in civil proceedings conducted in the Member States of the European Union and on the right to assistance for the purpose of settling a dispute amicably before the institution of such proceedings[256]. The Act sets out the conditions and procedure for granting the right to assistance, including exemption from court costs, the appointment of a legal representation and the payment by the Treasury of the necessary travel expenses of the applicant in connection with their personal appearance ordered by the court.

2.7. Relation between Article 47 of the CFR and Article 19(1) of the TEU

The scope of the Charter of Fundamental Rights, including Article 47 of the CFR, has already been clarified in previous subsections. According to Article 51(1) of the CFR, it applies to the Member States in so far as they apply the law of the European Union. In order to be able to invoke the principle of effective judicial protection, it will therefore be necessary for the national court to recognise that the legal situation on which the decision on the facts established is based falls within the scope of EU law[257], i.e. that the case has a Union dimension.

The right to effective judicial protection is part of the EU rule of law as expressed in Article 2 of the TEU[258]. Effective judicial protection is also referred to in Article 19 of the TEU, which is also a concretisation of the rule of law set out in Article

254 N. Półtorak, [in:] *Karta Praw Podstawowych...*, p. 1204.
255 Judgment of the CJEU, C-279/09 *DEB*.
256 Journal of Laws 2022, item 284 (consolidated text).
257 K. Szczepankowska-Kozłowska, *Prawo do skutecznego...*, p. 108.
258 A. Wróbel, [in:] *Karta Praw Podstawowych...*, p. 1130.

2 of the TEU[259]. According to Article 19 of the TEU, 'Member States shall provide remedies sufficient to ensure effective legal protection in the fields covered by Union law'.

The relationship between Article 47 of the CFR and the second subparagraph of Article 19(1) of the TEU deserves consideration. As the Court of Justice has pointed out, the second subparagraph of Article 19(1) of the TEU is a general principle of the Union, now confirmed by Article 47 of the Charter of Fundamental Rights. This means that Article 47 of the CFR must be taken into account when interpreting the second subparagraph of Article 19(1) of the TEU[260]. The provision refers to 'the fields covered by Union law'[261]. Although both provisions express the principle of effective judicial protection, the second subparagraph of Article 19(1) of the TEU is of a jurisdictional nature[262], and imposes an obligation on the Member State to provide for a system of remedies which meets the requirements of effective judicial protection in areas covered by EU law[263]. In turn, Article 47 of the CFR contains a subjective right to an effective remedy before a court[264].

In the case of the Portuguese judges[265,266], the CJEU pointed out that, since the Court of Justice has jurisdiction to rule on questions concerning the application and interpretation of EU law, the Member State is obliged to ensure that it complies with the integral requirements of effective judicial protection under the second subparagraph of Article 19(1) of the TEU. This provision entrusts not only the Court of Justice but also the national courts with the task of ensuring judicial review in the EU legal order[267]. The Court clarified that the second subparagraph

259 Judgment of the CJEU of 16 November 2021, C-748/19 to C-754/19, ECLI:EU:C:2021:931.
260 Judgment of the CJEU, C-132/20.
261 Judgment of the CJEU, C-132/20.
262 A. Wróbel, [in:] *Karta Praw Podstawowych...*, p. 1130.
263 Judgment of the CJEU, C-64/16.
264 A. Wróbel, [in:] *Karta Praw Podstawowych...*, p. 1130.
265 Judgment of the CJEU, C-64/16.
266 The facts of the case concerned the temporary reduction in the salaries of persons employed in the public sector, including judges of the Court of Auditors, under Portuguese Law No. 75/2014. The Portuguese Judges' Association (Associação Sindical dos Juízes Portugueses) challenged this legislation, claiming that it violated not only the Portuguese Constitution but also the principle of judicial independence enshrined in Union law. The Portuguese Supreme Administrative Court requested a preliminary ruling on the interpretation of the second subparagraph of Article 19(1) of the TEU and Article 47 of the CFR. The European Commission argued that the national court had failed to demonstrate the relationship between the national provisions in question and EU law. The CJEU rejected the plea that the question referred was inadmissible.
267 A. Sikora, *Glosa do wyroku TSUE z 27.02.2018 r., C-64/16, Associação Sindical dos Juízes Portugueses (art. 19 TUE jako autonomiczny i samodzielny wzorzec kontroli legalności)*, Państwo i Prawo 2018/11, p. 138.

of Article 19(1) of the TEU concerns 'areas covered by Union law, whatever the situation in which the Member States apply that law, within the meaning of Article 51(1) of the Charter'. The Court thus extended the scope of the principle of effective judicial protection in the second subparagraph of Article 19(1) of the TEU beyond its scope under Article 47 in conjunction with Article 51(1) of the CFR[268], since a national court which is a court of the EU must satisfy the requirements of effective judicial protection not only in a matter of Union law, but as a court potentially applying Union law[269]. The Court of Justice has held that the second subparagraph of Article 19(1) of the TEU constitutes an autonomous basis for assessing allegations of breach of the principle of effective judicial protection, even where they do not concern the application of EU law but 'in fields covered by Union law'[270]. This 'EU link', according to the CJEU, is the principle of the rule of law as an overarching value of the EU (Article 2 of the TEU) and the principle of loyal cooperation between the EU and the Member States. The Court of Justice has opened up the possibility of examining whether a Member State fulfils its obligation to provide effective judicial protection, and the criterion for assessing whether a case has an EU dimension is whether the court is an EU court, i.e. whether it has the potential to apply and interpret EU law[271]. However, it does not seem appropriate to extend this interpretation by the CJEU to the provision of Article 47 of the CFR, which, as mentioned above, is of a different nature and, unlike the second subparagraph of Article 19(1) of the TEU, is directly applicable in horizontal relations (disputes between individuals).

2.8. The principle of effective judicial protection as a general principle of EU law

EU law distinguishes between primary and secondary law. Primary law consists of acts of international law adopted by the Member States, while secondary law is adopted by the institutions of the EU. Primary law includes the founding Treaties, the general principles of EU law and the Charter of Fundamental Rights.

The general principles of EU law have been developed by the Court of Justice on the basis of the Treaties, international agreements to which the Member States are party (in particular the European Convention on Human Rights) and the constitutional traditions common to the Member States[272]. The identification of general

---

268 *Ibid*, p. 138.

269 K. Szczepankowska-Kozłowska, *Prawo do skutecznego...*, p. 110.

270 J. Barcik, *Niezawisłość sędziowska jako wartość konstytucyjna Unii Europejskiej – glosa do wyroku Trybunału Sprawiedliwości z 27.02.2018 r., C-64/16, Associação Sindical dos Juízes Portugueses*, Europejski Przegląd Sądowy 2018/5, p. 25.

271 J. Barcik, *Niezawisłość sędziowska...*, pp. 28–29.

272 A. Wróbel, *Stosowanie prawa Unii Europejskiej przez sądy*, A. Wróbel (ed.), Warsaw 2005, p. 37.

principles as sources of law was intended to fill gaps in EU law and to complement the legal systems of the Member States. General principles provide interpretative guidance for the interpretation of secondary EU law[273]. The general principles contain the most fundamental rules for the functioning of the European Union, such as the principle of the primacy of EU law, the principle of direct effect, the principle of proportionality, the principle of effectiveness, the principle of non-discrimination, the principle of the protection of fundamental rights and, finally, the principle of effective judicial protection.

As early as the 1980s, the Court of Justice of the European Union emphasised that the principle of effective judicial protection is a general principle of Union law, 'deriving from the common constitutional tradition of the Member States and protected by Articles 6 and 13 of the European Convention on Human Rights'[274]. Following the proclamation of the Charter of Fundamental Rights in 2000, the Court has often supplemented the above formula by stating that this principle is now also 'reaffirmed in Article 47 of the Charter of Fundamental Rights of the European Union'[275]. Even after the Charter became legally binding, the Court of Justice referred in its judgments to the principle of effective judicial protection as 'a general principle of Union law reaffirmed in the Charter'[276]. Thus, the Court first refers to a general principle of Union law and only later points out that this right is 'reaffirmed' in Article 47 of the CFR, treating the Charter as a secondary source[277].

Under Article 6(3) of the TEU, fundamental rights, as guaranteed by the European Convention on Human Rights and as they result from the constitutional traditions common to the Member States, form part of EU law as general principles of law. Given the characterisation of the Charter of Fundamental Rights as a source of primary law (and thus equivalent to general principles), the question arises as to the point of distinguishing and protecting fundamental rights (including the principle of effective judicial protection) as general principles of EU law in Article 6(3) of the TEU, when a reference to the Charter seems sufficient. This leads to the existence of two different sources of law within a single system – and of a different nature (written and unwritten)[278].

Given that the binding nature of the Charter of Fundamental Rights was intended to 'make fundamental rights more visible', as the preamble itself states, it would be preferable to take the view that the general principles should be

---

273 A. Wróbel, *Stosowanie prawa...*, p. 39–40.

274 Judgment of the CJEU of 15 May 1986, 222/84, LEX No. 130212.

275 Judgment of the CJEU of 13 March 2007, C-432/05, ECLI:EU:C:2007:163.

276 See for example: judgment of the CJEU of 23 January 2020, C-578/18, ECLI:EU:C:2020:35, judgment of the CJEU of 18 April 2013, C-463/11, ECLI:EU:C:2013:247.

277 T. Jurczyk, *Zasady ogólne prawa Unii Europejskiej a Karta Praw Podstawowych*, [w:] *Rządy prawa i europejska kultura prawna*, A. Bator, J. Helios, W. Jedlecka (eds.), Wrocław 2014, p. 201.

278 T. Jurczyk, *Zasady ogólne prawa...*, p. 201.

subsidiary and possibly form the basis of the Court's decisions in the absence of a corresponding provision in the Charter[279]. By referring to general principles, the Court leaves itself an 'open door' with regard to the catalogue of rights that can be defined. As the general principles are not codified, the scope for interpretation is certainly wider than if it were limited to the Charter[280].

It should be recalled that it is the provisions of the Charter which reaffirm the fundamental rights derived, inter alia, from the case law of the Court of Justice, and not the other way round. Further developments in society and the evolution of fundamental rights could theoretically lead to the Court identifying new fundamental rights which are not enshrined in the Charter. It may then be useful to distinguish fundamental rights as general principles of EU law. However, with regard to the fundamental rights reaffirmed in the Charter, their additional identification as general principles leads to a lack of a clear hierarchy of sources of law and thus reduces the transparency of the system of protection of fundamental rights and weakens the position of the Charter of Fundamental Rights[281], the very premise of which was the opposite.

Whatever the intentions of the EU legislator, it must be assumed that the Court accepts a pluralist system of fundamental rights protection and does not seek to establish an internal hierarchy[282].

2.9. Accession of the European Union to the European Convention on Human Rights

Attempts to have the European Communities accede to the Convention were first made in 1979 and 1990, and the proposal was renewed and made explicit in 1993. In 1996, the European Court of Justice ruled that the European Community did not have the competence to accede to the ECHR, which would require an amendment to the Treaties[283].

The Lisbon Treaty provides for such an amendment. Article 6(2) of the TEU (as amended by the Lisbon Treaty) provides that the Union shall accede to the European Convention for on Human Rights. Accession to the Convention is without prejudice to the Union's competences under the Treaties. Protocol No 8 on Article 6(2) of the TEU on the accession of the Union to the European Convention on Human Rights was signed together with the Treaty of Lisbon. This document contains three articles setting out the conditions to be met by an accession agreement. The purpose of the Protocol was to ensure that the European Union's accession to the

279 T. Jurczyk, *Zasady ogólne prawa...*, pp. 201–202.
280 T. Jurczyk, *Zasady ogólne prawa...*, p. 200.
281 T. Jurczyk, *Zasady ogólne prawa...*, p. 202.
282 T. Jurczyk, *Zasady ogólne prawa...*, p. 203.
283 N. Półtorak, *Przystąpienie...*, p 5.

ECHR would not affect the competences of the EU, in particular those of the Court of Justice.

The basic purpose of the European Union's accession to the Convention was to enhance its credibility as an organisation whose core value is fundamental rights. This step was intended to underline the importance of and respect for fundamental rights and to expose the EU to external scrutiny by the European Court of Human Rights. The rationale for the EU's accession to the Convention was also to create a single system for the protection of fundamental rights by bringing together two co-existing systems in which the jurisdiction of the two Courts overlapped[284].

The European Union's accession to the ECHR also required amendments to the Convention itself, which were made by Protocol 14, which entered into force on 1 June 2010. Currently, Article 59(2) of the ECHR states that 'The European Union may accede to this Convention'. On the EU side, the procedure for accession to the Convention is laid down in Article 218 of the TFEU, which provides for a procedure for the negotiation and accession of the Union to international agreements or organisations.

Following the entry into force of the provision of Article 6(2) of the TEU, negotiations for an accession agreement started. In July 2011, a draft international agreement enabling the European Union to accede to the Convention was presented[285].

In its opinion of 18 December 2014[286], the CJEU considered that the negotiated agreement on the accession of the European Union to the Convention was in breach of Article 6(2) of the TEU and Protocol No. 8. In the Court's view, the European Union's accession to the Convention could jeopardise the limitations identified in the *Melloni* judgment[287] with regard to Article 53 of the CFR. It should be recalled that in this judgment, the CJEU recognised that a national standard cannot be lower than that laid down in the CFR, but neither can it diminish the primacy, uniformity and effectiveness of EU law[288]. The fundamental problem, however, is that the interpretation of the standard of protection of fundamental rights made by the CJEU in the *Melloni* judgment is not binding on the ECHR. The risks identified by the CJEU are therefore in fact threats to the effectiveness of the CJEU's own case-law, which is binding on the Member States and the EU institutions but not on the ECHR. This creates an asymmetry between the binding effect of ECHR judgments

284 N. Półtorak, *Przystąpienie...*, p. 6

285 N. Półtorak, *Przystąpienie..., p.* 4.

286 Opinion of the CJEU No 2/13 of 18 December 2014 on the accession of the European Union to the Convention for the Protection of Human Rights and Fundamental Freedoms, EU:C:2014:2454

287 Judgment of the CJEU, C-399/11.

288 A. Wróbel, *Dekalog akcesyjny, czyli dziesięć argumentów Trybunału Sprawiedliwości przeciwko przystąpieniu Unii Europejskiej do Europejskiej Konwencji Praw Człowieka,* Europejski Przegląd Sądowy 2015/12, p. 5.

on the CJEU and the lack of binding effect of CJEU judgments on the ECHR. The CJEU has noted the need to 'ensure coordination' between Article 53 of the CFR and Article 53 of the ECHR[289] (according to which: 'Nothing in this Convention shall be construed as limiting or derogating from any of the human rights and fundamental freedoms which may be ensured under the laws of any High Contracting Party or under any other agreement to which it is a party'). The Court of Justice has insisted that Article 53 of the ECHR takes account of the limitations on the standard of protection of fundamental rights under Article 53 of the CFR (in the sense of the *Melloni* judgment). The Court's concern is that a Member State, while taking into account the minimum standard set by Article 53 of the ECHR, would not take into account the maximum standard set by Article 53 of the CFR, which would jeopardise the primacy, uniformity and effectiveness of EU law. It should be stressed, however, that EU law contains mechanisms for the enforcement of the Charter of Fundamental Rights by the CJEU, and accession to the Convention will not change this fact. The concerns of the CJEU are therefore unfounded. Moreover, the problem outlined by the CJEU is only potential in nature and it is difficult to imagine that it will be of great practical significance. The implementation of the CJEU's demand would require amendments to the European Convention on Human Rights, which would guarantee the binding force of the CJEU's decisions on the European Court of Human Rights. Such a change in the position of the ECHR seems difficult, if not impossible, to implement[290].

It should be noted, however, that Article 6(2) of the TEU is categorical in its wording and orders the European Union to accede to the European Convention on Human Rights. The problem of competing standards for the protection of fundamental rights should therefore be resolved as soon as possible in order to fully implement the European Union's treaty obligations under Article 6 of the TEU.

289 M. Taborowski, *Poziom Ochrony..*, pp. 32–33.
290 M. Taborowski, *Poziom Ochrony...*, pp. 33–34.

3. Constitution of the Republic of Poland

3.1. Introductory remarks

The right to a fair trial has its source not only in international law but also in the Constitution of the Republic of Poland[291]. Article 45(1) of the Constitution provides that everyone has the right to a fair and public hearing without undue delay by a competent, independent, impartial and autonomous court.

One of the basic functions of the above-mentioned regulation is to protect the individual against the arbitrariness of the authorities[292]. The second role of the right to court is to resolve a claim in a situation where at least one of the parties to the legal relationship is an individual[293]. However, the function of the right to court is not to provide a subject seeking legal protection with a favourable outcome, but only with the opportunity to petition a court to hear their case and render a legally binding decision after a fair hearing of evidence[294].

On the one hand, the right to court is instrumental in nature – it enables the individual to exercise other rights and freedoms confirmed by the Constitution. On the other hand, this right is autonomous in nature and must be protected regardless of the violation of other guaranteed rights[295]. The right to court is one of the fundamental rights of the individual and a guarantee of the rule of law. Article 45(1) of the Constitution imposes an obligation on the State to create an adequate system of justice, which enables an individual's case to be heard in proceedings that meet constitutional standards[296].

Article 45(1) of the Polish Constitution refers to the right of everyone to a fair and public 'consideration of the case'. The subject-matter boundaries of the right to court are therefore determined by the concepts of 'consideration' and 'case'. The individual's right provided for in Article 45(1) of the Constitution will be valid only if it is a 'case' within the meaning of that provision[297]. The first of these terms, consideration, means 'a sovereign intervention by the court, an examination by the court and a determination of whether the conduct of other parties infringes

291 Journal of Laws 1997, no. 78, item 483.

292 E. Tkaczyk, *Konstytucyjne prawo do sądu jako jedna z najważniejszych gwarancji praw człowieka w państwie demokratycznym. Aspekt teoretyczny*, Studia Prawnicze i Administracyjne 2017/2, p. 40.

293 M. Kutwin, *Prawo do sądu w orzecznictwie Trybunału Konstytucyjnego oraz Europejskiego Trybunału Praw Człowieka*, Studia Iuridica, vol. LXXVI, p. 272.

294 E. Tkaczyk, *Konstytucyjne prawo do sądu...*, p. 44.

295 E. Tkaczyk, *Konstytucyjne prawo do sądu...*, pp. 40–41.

296 E. Tkaczyk, *Konstytucyjne prawo do sądu...*, p. 45.

297 P. Grzegorczyk, K. Weitz, [in:] *Konstytucja RP. Komentarz. Tom I*, M. Safjan, L. Bosek (eds.), Warsaw 2016, p. 1105.

the legally protected interests'[298]. The consideration of a case is the legal qualification of a given state of facts, contained in a concrete and individual norm, from which certain legal consequences, i.e. rights or obligations, arise[299]. According to the Polish Constitutional Tribunal[300] a 'case' is a specific task of a court consisting in the legal qualification of a concrete factual situation with the aim of issuing an individual norm regulating the rights or obligations of a specific subject (addressee)'. The term 'case' includes disputes arising from civil law relations, administrative law relations, resolution of the validity of criminal charges, but not only[301]. Thus, it concerns any decision on the rights of a subject, regardless of the field of legal relations from which they arise. This is an expression of the intention to include the widest possible range of cases in the application of Article 45(1) of the Constitution[302].

The right to court specified in Article 45(1) of the Constitution of the Republic of Poland is developed in Article 77(2), according to which statutes shall not bar the recourse by any person to the courts in pursuit of claims alleging infringement of freedoms or rights. Article 45(1) formulates the right to court from the positive side, while Article 77(2) completes the right to a court from the 'negative' side, prohibiting the closure of the judicial path. The provision of Article 77(2) of the Constitution is thus intended to guarantee the right to court[303]. At the same time, the question arises as to the scope of this prohibition, i.e. whether it refers only to rights and freedoms guaranteed by the Constitution or also to those derived from subordinate sources of law[304]. On the one hand, it is argued that the provision of Article 77 has been placed among the provisions concerning measures for the protection of constitutional rights and freedoms and cannot be understood as a simple repetition of Article 45(1) of the Constitution. The second position assumes that Article 77(2) is not limited exclusively to the rights and freedoms guaranteed by the Constitution of the Republic of Poland. However, it would be very difficult to draw a straight line between constitutional and non-constitutional rights and freedoms and could lead to arbitrary decisions. Therefore, the second view should be accepted. There is a symmetry between the positive aspect of the right to court (Article 45(1) of the Constitution) and the prohibition of closing the judicial path (Article 77(2) of the Constitution). Thus, wherever there is a 'case' within

298 Z. Czeszejko-Sochacki, *Prawo do sądu w świetle Konstytucji Rzeczypospolitej Polskiej (Ogólna charakterystyka)*, Państwo i Prawo 1997/11–12, p. 93.
299 Judgment of the Constitutional Tribunal of 27 May 2008, SK 57/06, LEX No. 380075.
300 SK 57/06.
301 G. Zalizowski, *Prawo do sądu na tle Konstytucji Rzeczypospolitej Polskiej w kontekście europejskiej Konwencji o ochronie praw człowieka i podstawowych wolności*, [w:] *Duch praw w krajach Europy Środkowo-Wschodniej*, Wrocław 2016, p. 23.
302 P. Grzegorczyk, K. Weitz,[in:] *Konstytucja RP...*, p. 1106.
303 P. Grzegorczyk, K. Weitz,[in:] *Konstytucja RP...*, p. 1093.
304 P. Grzegorczyk, K. Weitz,[in:] *Konstytucja RP...*, p. 1777.

the meaning of Article 45(1), the Constitution provides for the prohibition of closing the judicial path[305]. It should therefore be assumed that Article 77(2) of the Constitution cannot refer only to constitutionally guaranteed rights and freedoms.

In accordance with the established judicature of the Constitutional Tribunal, the right to court, guaranteed by Article 45(1) of the Constitution, includes in particular: 1) the right to initiate court proceedings, 2) the right to an appropriate judicial procedure in accordance with the principles of justice and openness, 3) the right to obtain a binding decision[306]. A. Łazarska also identifies, as a separate, fourth element of the right to court, the right to proper formation of the system and position of the bodies adjudicating the case[307]. It is also argued that another component of the right to a court is the right to enforce a court decision[308]. Indeed, if the legislator fails to create the conditions for the effective enforcement of a judgment, the right to court would become illusory[309].

It is a matter of debate whether the right to court includes the right to challenge a decision. According to one view, expressed, inter alia, by the Constitutional Tribunal in its judgment of 12 September 2006, the principle of a two-instance procedure is one of the essential elements determining the content of the right to court[310]. The opposite view is that the right to appeal against a decision of the first instance (Article 78 of the Constitution) and the principle of a two instance procedure (Article 176(1) of the Constitution) are not components of the right to court, although they are closely related to this right. The possibility of subjecting a decision to review by a second instance clearly increases the likelihood that the procedure will fulfil the guarantees of the right to court. Article 78 of the Constitution, which contains the subjective right to challenge a decision, has the function of strengthening and supplementing the right to court. The right to court, which derives from Article 45(1) of the Constitution, is not the source of the right to challenge a decision in any of its three elements (the right to initiate proceedings, the right to a fair trial and the right to a binding decision). In this sense, Article 78 of the Polish Constitution is the source of a separate individual right. Article 176(1) of the, on the other hand, does not have the character of a subjective right and contains only a constitutional provision addressed to the legislator[311]. Article 176(1) does not establish the right of a party to have a case heard in two instances. Since this provision is not a source of a subjective right, and since Article 78 of the

305 P. Grzegorczyk, K. Weitz,[in:] *Konstytucja RP...*, p. 1778.

306 Judgment of the Constitutional Tribunal of 24 October 2007, SK 7/06, LEX No. 322157.

307 A. Łazarska, *Rzetelny proces cywilny*, Warsaw 2012, p. 259.

308 G. Zalizowski, *Prawo do sądu...*, p. 20.

309 Judgment of the Constitutional Tribunal of 24 February 2003, K 28/02, LEX No. 76811.

310 Judgment of the Constitutional Tribunal of 12 September 2006, SK 21/05, LEX No. 208363.

311 P. Grzegorczyk, K. Weitz, [in:] *Konstytucja RP...*, pp. 1093–1094.

Constitution has such a character, it should be recognised that although an individual has the right to appeal against any court decision, this does not mean that it must necessarily be exercised in the course of two instances. Access to court, as guaranteed by Article 45(1) of the Constitution, is therefore not the same as access to a court of second instance. This is due to the fact that the problem of appealing against the decision of the court of the first instance only arises when the access to court has already been realised and only the party is not satisfied with the result. As mentioned above, the right to court does not imply that an individual is entitled to a decision of a certain content, but only that they may demand that their case be heard by a court. The source of the right to challenge a decision is not the right to a fair trial, since it cannot be argued that a single-instance procedure automatically fails to meet the requirement of fairness. Consequently, the right to a fair and public hearing without undue delay by a competent, independent, impartial and autonomous court must be clearly distinguished from the right to appeal a decision. Therefore, in a situation where the legislator has not provided for the possibility of appeal against the decision of the court of first instance, the benchmark for constitutional review should be Article 78 and not Article 45(1) of the Constitution. The above argument is further strengthened by the fact that the right to a fair trial within the meaning of Article 6(1) of the ECHR does not include the right to appeal against the decision of the court of first instance[312].

The right to court provided for by the Constitution, as in the case of the European Convention on Human Rights and the Charter of Fundamental Rights, is not absolute. It has the character of a formal guarantee and is therefore an instrument for the protection of other rights and freedoms. To accept that the right to court may not be subject to limitations resulting from the application of Article 31(3) of the Constitution would lead to an internal contradiction of constitutional rules. Since other rights and freedoms may be subject to certain restrictions under the conditions specified in the above provision of Article 31(3), the right to court, which is of an instrumental nature in relation to the other rights and freedoms, may be subject to such restrictions all the more[313]. The Constitutional Tribunal notes that in no legal system is there an absolute and unconditional right to court, which is not subject to any limitations, and which would provide an unlimited possibility to protect the rights of an individual by means of a court. The very organisation of the judicial procedure constitutes a significant and actual limitation of the right to court, which is manifested, inter alia, in the rules governing the initiation of proceedings before the court, the time limits for proceedings, the obligation to pay court fees, the mandatory representation of the parties or the rigours of the evidence procedure[314].

---

312 P. Grzegorczyk, K. Weitz, [in:] *Konstytucja RP...*, pp. 1094–1096.

313 J. Juchniewicz, *O granicach swobody ustawodawcy w kształtowaniu standardów prawa do sądu*, Przegląd Prawa Konstytucyjnego 2016/3, pp. 33–34.

314 Judgment of the Constitutional Tribunal of 10 May 2000, K 21/99, LEX No. 40330.

Restriction of the right to court is possible only to the extent specified in Article 31(3) of the Constitution, in accordance with the principle of proportionality. This principle consists of three specific rules, which together form the so-called proportionality test. The first of these, the principle of suitability means that a restriction on the right to court may be imposed only by means which make it possible to achieve the objective justifying the restriction. The second, the principle of necessity (the principle of the most lenient measure), means that where there are several possible ways of restricting a right in order to achieve the objective pursued, the least restrictive means must be chosen. The third element is the principle of proportionality *sensu stricto*, which requires an assessment of which of two or more conflicting principles takes precedence[315]. The Constitutional Tribunal has stated that the assessment of compliance with the principle of proportionality requires the answer to three questions: 1) whether the introduced legal regulation is capable of producing the intended effects, 2) whether the regulation is necessary for the protection of the public interest to which it is linked, 3) whether the effects of the introduced regulation remain in proportion to the burdens imposed on the citizen[316]. The principle of proportionality is addressed not only to the legislator at the level of law-making, but also at the level of application of the law, i.e. to the courts[317], which are obliged to ensure that any limitation of the right to a court is implemented in accordance with the principle of proportionality.

Restriction of access to court is not permitted during a time of martial law or a state of emergency, as it is included in the catalogue of higher protected rights (Article 233(1) of the Constitution) and may not be restricted during a state of emergency, as it is not included in the catalogue of lower protected rights (Article 233(2) of the Constitution)[318].

3.2. The constitutional and the European standards of the right to a fair trial

In the context of the provisions of Article 45(1) of the Constitution, the term 'right to court' has become established, which primarily emphasises the element of access to a court. However, the established understanding of this term also includes other procedural guarantees, in particular concerning the organisation and composition of the court and the course of the proceedings. It is therefore reasonable to assume that the concept of the 'right to a fair (just) trial' used in the European

315 P. Tuleja, [in:] *Konstytucja Rzeczypospolitej Polskiej. Komentarz*, P. Tuleja (ed.), Warsaw 2019, pp. 116–117.

316 Judgment of the Constitutional Court of 26 April 1995, K 11/94, LEX No. 25538.

317 P. Tuleja, [in:] *Konstytucja...*, p. 118.

318 M. Florczak-Wątor, *Prawo do sądu jako prawo jednostki i jako gwarancja horyzontalnego działania praw i wolności*, Przegląd Prawa Konstytucyjnego, 2016/3, pp. 50–51.

Convention on Human Rights or the Charter of Fundamental Rights of the EU is the counterpart of the 'right to court' regulated by the Constitution of the Republic of Poland[319].

According to the Constitutional Tribunal, the constitutional right to court provides the same guarantees as the right to a fair trial under Article 6(1) of the ECHR. Due to the convergence of the content of the two provisions, the Convention standards should be used to construct the constitutional standard. Both the constitutional and the Convention standards cover the organisational and institutional aspects, the guarantee of access to court, the fairness of the proceedings, in particular the reasonable time for obtaining a decision and their efficiency. The right to a fair trial under both the Convention and the Polish Constitution includes openness of proceedings, equality of arms, the right to be heard and the adversarial nature of the proceedings, as well as the right to obtain reasons for the court decision and the principle of *res judicata*. Consequently, all these guarantees based on the Polish legal system acquire a double basis of validity (constitutional and Convention)[320]. In EU cases, the basis for the right to a fair trial will even be threefold, as it will also follow from Article 47 of the EU Charter of Fundamental Rights. It is therefore a question of the superposition of autonomous legal orders, in other words the phenomenon of legal multicentrism.

However, the provisions of Article 45(1) of the Constitution and Article 6(1) of the European Convention on Human Rights are not identical, and their scope differs in concrete terms, in particular as regards their scope of application. The right to court provided for by the Constitution does not contain the limitation provided for by the Convention, according to which Article 6(1) of the ECHR applies only when deciding on rights and obligations of a civil nature. In this respect, Article 45(1) of the Polish Constitution is more similar to Article 47(2) of the CFR, which also contains no such limitation. Article 45(1) of the Constitution, unlike Article 6(1) of the ECHR, also does not impose the condition that the case falling within the scope of this provision must be real and sufficiently serious[321].

At this point it is necessary to signal the problem of the relationship between the Constitution of the Republic of Poland and the Convention and EU law in the context of the hierarchy of sources of law. Poland's membership of the European Union and, in particular, the characteristics of EU law, which include, first and foremost, the principle of primacy and direct effect, compel a discussion of the traditionally understood principle of the supremacy of the Constitution of the Republic of Poland over other sources of law. As R. Grzeszczak points out, Poland's membership in the European Union shakes the dominant paradigm that the Constitution occupies the highest place in the hierarchy of sources of law. EU law proposes a new point of reference (in relation to EU matters), namely the EU Treaties

---

319 P. Grzegorczyk, K. Weitz,[in:] *Konstytucja RP...*, p. 1088.
320 P. Grzegorczyk, K. Weitz,[in:] *Konstytucja RP...*, pp. 1089–1090.
321 P. Grzegorczyk, K. Weitz,[in:] *Konstytucja RP...*, p. 1090.

(TEU and TFEU)[322]. As previously mentioned, one of the fundamental principles of the European Union is the supremacy of EU law over the law of the Member States. However, according to the Polish legal system, it is the Constitution of the Republic of Poland that prevails and takes precedence over all legal acts in force in the Polish constitutional system, including EU law. This position of the Polish Constitution follows from its Article 8(1)[323] .

In examining the compatibility of the Accession Treaty with the Polish Constitution, the Constitutional Tribunal reserved the status of the Polish Constitution as the supreme law of the Republic of Poland. The Constitutional Tribunal noted, however, that this provision is accompanied by an obligation, stemming from Article 9, to respect and favour the norms of international law duly established and in force on the territory of the Republic of Poland. At the same time, the Tribunal emphasised that EU law is not created arbitrarily by the European institutions, but is the result of joint action by the Member States. EU law is based on an axiology common to all Member States. In this context, however, it cannot be ruled out that a situation may arise in which there is an irreconcilable contradiction between the provisions of the Polish Constitution and those of EU law, which cannot be resolved by means of an interpretation that respects the relative autonomy of EU law and the national order. The Constitutional Tribunal pointed out that such a contradiction may arise only in exceptional cases, due to the aforementioned shared foundations and values of the system. However, the interpretation favourable to EU law has its limits and may in no case consist in exceeding the minimum threshold established by the provisions of the Constitution of the Republic of Poland in the field of individual rights and freedoms. At the same time, the Constitutional Tribunal indicated how the procedure should be followed in the event of such an irreconcilable contradiction. The Polish legislator should then either decide to amend the Constitution in order to align it with EU law, or take steps to amend EU law accordingly, or – as a last resort, decide to withdraw from the European Union[324].

When examining the compatibility of the Treaty of Lisbon with the Constitution of the Republic of Poland, the Constitutional Tribunal also stated that the values expressed in the Constitution and the Treaty of Lisbon determine the axiological identity of Poland and the European Union. The economic, social and political system resulting from the Treaty, which is based on respect for the dignity and freedom of the individual and respect for the national identity of the Member

322 R. Grzeszczak, *„Mapa" judykatury Trybunału Konstytucyjnego dotyczącej członkostwa Polski w Unii Europejskiej,* [in:] *Wokół kryzysu praworządności, demokracji i praw człowieka. Księga jubileuszowa Profesora Mirosława Wyrzykowskiego k,* A. Bodnar, A Ploszka (eds), Warsaw 2020, pp. 786–787.

323 Judgment of the Constitutional Tribunal of 16 November 2011, SK 45/09, LEX No. 1027531.

324 Judgment of the Constitutional Tribunal of 11 May 2005, K 18/04, LEX No. 155502.

States, is fully consistent with the fundamental values of the Constitution. At the same time, the Constitutional Tribunal emphasised that the basis for this is the identity of axiological inspiration derived from the European Convention on Human Rights. However, the Constitutional Tribunal noted that membership in the European Union entails for each Member State the emergence of a constitutional problem concerning the relationship between national and EU law. According to the Tribunal, the territory of Poland is covered by a number of sub-systems of legislation, originating from various centres of legislation, that must coexist on the basis of the principle of friendly interpretation and joint application of the law. Notwithstanding the foregoing, the Tribunal emphasised that the views expressed in its judgment of 11 May 2005 (K 18/04) on the supremacy of the Constitution remain fully valid. However, the emphasis placed on the role of the Constitution must not jeopardise the uniform validity and application of EU law and the harmonious fulfilment of Poland's obligations as a Member State[325].

In its judgment of 16 November 2011[326], the Constitutional Tribunal recognised its competence to review EU secondary law, contrary to the principle of supremacy of EU law, while acknowledging that this competence is subsidiary to the Treaty competences of the CJEU. At the same time, the Constitutional Tribunal stated that, according to the wording of Article 8 of the Polish Constitution, it must retain its position as the 'court of last word' with regard to the Polish Constitution. The presumption of compatibility of EU law with the Constitution must be exercised with restraint, and the Constitutional Tribunal and the Court of Justice of the European Union cannot be positioned as competing courts[327]. The Tribunal, taking into account the specificity of acts of EU law, indicated that the party filing a constitutional complaint should be required to demonstrate plausibly that the challenged act of EU secondary law significantly reduces the level of protection of rights and freedoms as compared to the Constitution. If this requirement is not met, the Tribunal will in future consider that the constitutional and legal requirements for a constitutional complaint have not been met, which will lead to a refusal to proceed with the complaint[328].

However, in an earlier ruling of 17 December 2009, the Constitutional Tribunal held that it was not competent to examine the compatibility of EU secondary law with the Polish Constitution, as the law adopted by international organisations was not included in the catalogue set out in Article 188 of the Constitution. On the basis of the decision in the case SK 45/09, the Constitutional Tribunal, without

325 Judgment of the Constitutional Tribunal of 24 November 2010, K 32/09, LEX No. 621758.

326 Judgment of the Constitutional Tribunal of 16 November 2011, SK 45/09, LEX No. 1027531.

327 R. Grzeszczak, *"Mapa" judykatury...*, pp. 794–795.

328 Judgment of the Constitutional Tribunal of 16 November 2011, SK 45/09, LEX No. 1027531.

departing from this approach, stated that, when examining a constitutional complaint, it is not bound by the catalogue specified in this provision and that it is competent to examine the secondary law of the EU[329].

Not only the Polish Constitutional Tribunal allows the examination of EU acts for compatibility with the national constitution. Already in its judgment of 29 May 1974, known as *Solange I*, the German Federal Constitutional Court indicated that the primacy of EU (then European Communities) law could be questioned by the German Court and that the examination of the constitutionality of secondary law was permissible and necessary as long as the process of integration of the European Communities had not progressed to such an extent that its own guarantees for the protection of fundamental rights had been established[330]. This view was later revised by the Federal Constitutional Court which, in its *Solange II* judgment of 22 October 1986[331], stated that Community law provided an adequate level of protection of fundamental rights (in particular, it guaranteed the right to a fair trial) equivalent to that guaranteed by the German Constitution. As long as the level of protection of fundamental rights in the European Community is maintained, the Federal Constitutional Court will not examine this law for compliance with the German Constitution. In contrast, in its ruling of 15 December 2015 (also referred to as *Solange III*), the Federal Constitutional Court held that the monitoring of compliance with the protection of fundamental rights must be carried out without restriction, irrespective of the protection afforded by EU law. Contrary to the CJEU ruling in the *Melloni* case, the Court thus recognised its competence to review the constitutionality of provisions of EU law, pointing out that it is the German Constitution that determines the minimum level of protection of fundamental rights.

Other constitutional courts of the Member States have also confirmed their competence to review the constitutionality of EU secondary law. One example is the judgment of the Czech Constitutional Court of 13 January 2012 in the *Landtova* case, in which the Court refused to apply an EU regulation as interpreted by the CJEU, thereby indicating that it had exceeded its competence. In a judgment of 19 April 2016, the Danish Constitutional Court refused to apply the general principle of EU law expressed by the CJEU in the *Mangold* case, finding that at the time of Denmark's accession to the European Union, EU law did not contain such a principle[332].

---

329 Order of the Constitutional Tribunal of 17 December 2009, U 6/08, LEX No. 562830.

330 Judgment of the Federal Constitutional Court of 29 May 1974, available at: https://www.servat.unibe.ch/dfr/bv037271.html (in German, own translation).

331 Judgment of the Federal Constitutional Court of 22 October 1986, available at: https://www.servat.unibe.ch/dfr/bv073339.html (in German, own translation).

332 M. Krajewski, [in:] *Podręcznik prawa Unii Europejskiej*, A. Zawidzka-Łojek, A. Łazowski (eds.), Warsaw 2018, pp. 21–22.

Meanwhile, Article 267 of the TFEU gives the Court of Justice of the European Union exclusive jurisdiction to review the validity of acts of EU law, which was further confirmed by the CJEU in the *Foto-Frost*[333] case, recognising that this is a necessary condition for the unity of EU law. The roots of the principle of the primacy of EU law can be traced back to the 1960s and the judgment in *COSTA v ENEL*[334], in which the CJEU held that Treaty rights cannot be overridden by national law, even if enacted subsequently (the principle of *lex posteriori derogat legi priori*), and that the effectiveness of EU law requires that it be applied uniformly in all Member States, which would be jeopardised if its effects could be unilaterally revoked by Member State legislation. In its judgment in the *Internationale Handelsgesellschaft*[335] case, the CJEU stated that Treaty law takes precedence over national law, irrespective of its rank. In contrast, in its judgment of 8 June 2000 in the *Giovanni Carra and Others*[336] case, the CJEU stated that the principle of primacy applies to all acts of EU law, including those adopted before a Member State's accession to the EU.

The above analysis leads to the conclusion that the issue of the principle of supremacy of EU law in relation to the Constitution of the Republic of Poland remains unresolved. So far, the Constitutional Tribunal has taken a conservative position on the application of EU law, which highlights the importance of the Polish Constitution as the supreme law[337]. However, the Constitutional Tribunal stated that the order based on EU law should not be set in opposition to the provisions of the Polish Constitution; on the contrary, given the axiological identity of the two orders, solutions should be sought which allow for an interpretation friendly to EU law[338]. So far, this dispute has been mainly ideological and political in nature, and its practical dimension has been limited. As E. Łętowska points out, it concerned the question of sovereignty, where the admissibility of 'abandoning the field' itself was questioned[339].

In its judgment of 7 October 2021[340], the Constitutional Tribunal, rejecting further dialogue with the CJEU within the framework of friendly interpretation, ruled that Article 1(1) and (2) in conjunction with Article 4(3) of the TEU were unconstitutional, inter alia, to the extent that the Polish Constitution is not the supreme law of the Republic of Poland with priority of validity and application, as well

---

333 Judgment of the CJEU of 22 October 1987, C-314/85 *Foto-Frost*, ECLI:EU:C:1987:452.

334 Judgment of the CJEU of 15 July 1964, C-6/64 *COSTA v ENEL*, ECLI:EU:C:1964:66.

335 Judgment of the CJEU of 17 December 1970, C-11/70 *Internationale Handelgesellschaft*, ECLI:EU:C:1970:114.

336 Judgment of the CJEU of 8 December 2000, C-258/98 *Criminal proceedings against Giovanni Carra and others*, LEX No. 82834.

337 R. Grzeszczak, *"Mapa judykatury"...*, pp. 794–795.

338 E. Łętowska, *Multicentryczność współczesnego systemu prawa i jej konsekwencje*, Państwo i Prawo, State and Law 2005/4, p. 9.

339 E. Łętowska, *Multicentryczność...*, p. 4.

340 Judgment of the Constitutional Tribunal of 7 October 2021, K 3/21, LEX No. 3231776.

as Article 19(1) of the TFEU and Article 2 of the TEU, to the extent that national courts are granted the power to disregard the provisions of the Polish Constitution. As a discussion of this ruling goes far beyond the scope of this analysis, it is only necessary to point out that the question of the hierarchical precedence of norms now seems pointless and should be replaced by the question of the precedence of their application[341].

On the basis of the right to a fair trial, it is difficult to imagine a contradiction between the EU legal order and the framework provided by the Constitution, which would require the intervention of the Constitutional Tribunal with regard to acts of EU law. As stated above, and also confirmed by the Constitutional Tribunal's judgments in Cases K 18/04 and K 32/09, the standards of protection of individual rights and freedoms expressed in EU law and the Constitution of the Republic of Poland are formed on the same level, derived, moreover, from the European Convention on Human Rights.

However, the relationship between the European Convention on Human Rights and the Constitution of the Republic of Poland is different. The Convention is a multilateral international agreement which the Republic of Poland is obliged to respect as binding international law (Article 9 of the Polish Constitution). However, an important difference lies in the fact that the European Court of Human Rights' review of the observance of human rights does not consist of an assessment of domestic law, but includes an examination of the violation of human rights and freedoms framed subjectively (in relation to the individual). The judgment of the ECHR concerns the sovereign shaping of the State's obligations towards the applicant, but does not explicitly touch upon national law or acts of its application. The ECHR's review concerns the violation of human rights *in concreto*, although in certain cases (where the violation of the Convention was caused solely by a defectively formulated national law) the application of the legal norm under review *pro futuro* may lead to further violations of the Convention[342].

On the other hand, one should not lose sight of the fact that the established judicature of the ECHR, which has *erga omnes* relevance beyond the specific case and sets a pan-European standard for the protection of human rights, makes this body similar to national constitutional courts[343]. However, the precedential nature of the ECHR's case law does not have a normative effect, but an indirect effect can be observed in some cases[344].

341 R. Grzeszczak, *"Mapa" judykatury...*, p. 785.

342 E. Łętowska, *Multicentryczność...*, p. 6.

343 A. Wisniewski, *Europejski Trybunał Praw Człowieka trybunałem konstytucyjnym Europy?*, Prawo i Więź 2020/4, pp. 324–325.

344 M. Balcerzak, *The Doctrine of Precedent in the International Court of Justice and the European Court of Human Rights*, Polish Yearbook of International Law, 2004–2005, p. 138.

Under Article 46(1) of the Convention, the Contracting Parties undertake to comply with the final judgment of the Court in all cases to which they are parties. A judgment of the ECHR is therefore binding only on the State which was a party to the proceedings. The Convention does not specify the relevance of judgments rendered against third party States[345]. However, by ratifying the Convention, States Parties have undertaken to ensure that their domestic legal systems are compatible with the Convention. As a result, they are obliged to remove obstacles in the legal system which might prevent adequate compliance. It is therefore accepted that the ECHR may impose obligations on States to adopt general measures which are nevertheless declaratory in nature (leaving the State free to implement the judgment and remove the effects of the violation). State obligations may entail legislative and sometimes even constitutional changes[346], whereas ECHR judgments do not have a constitutive effect on the validity of national legislation.

There have been cases in the past where enforcement of an ECHR judgment has been refused on the basis of domestic constitutional law. Examples include the judgment of the Russian Constitutional Court of 19 January 2017 No. 1-P/2017[347] or the judgment of the Polish Constitutional Tribunal of 10 March 2022, which found the first sentence of Article 6(1) of the Convention to be in violation of a number of constitutional norms, including Articles 8, 176, 178 and 190 of the Polish Constitution. The decision followed the European Court of Human Rights' judgments in *Ástráðsson v. Iceland* and *Xero-Flor v. Poland* concerning the guarantees of impartiality and independence of the court[348]. A detailed discussion of the Tribunal's decision is beyond the scope of this work.

3.3. Access to court

The *sine qua non* of a fair trial is individual access to justice[349]. Indeed, the other aspects of the right to a fair trial are realised through access to court[350]. The right to justice implies an obligation to establish a legal regime that ensures that a case is heard by a court at the request of the person concerned[351].

The establishment of a procedure before a court which lays down requirements to be met by an individual in order to initiate the procedure (e.g. legal capacity,

345 A. Bodnar, *Zmiana konstytucji jako konsekwencja wykonania wyroku ETPCz,* Europejski Przegląd Sądowy 2010/10, pp. 43–44.

346 M.A. Nowicki, *Wokół Konwencji Europejskiej. Komentarz do Europejskiej Konwencji Praw Człowieka,* Warsaw 2021, pp. 282–283.

347 A. Wisniewski, *Europejski Trybunał...*, pp. 322–323.

348 Judgment of the European Court of Human Rights of 7 May 2021, Application No. 4907/18, LEX No. 3170326.

349 A. Łazarska, *Rzeteln proces...*, p. 260.

350 P. Grzegorczyk, K. Weitz, [in:] *Konstytucja RP...*, p. 1111.

351 Judgment of the Constitutional Tribunal of 9 June 1998, K 28/97, LEX No. 33151.

national jurisdiction, formal requirements for pleadings) is in itself a restriction of the right to court, but it is necessary in view of other values respected in a state governed by the rule of law, such as the efficient functioning of the judiciary. Restrictions must remain proportionate to the objective sought to be achieved by their introduction, i.e. the exercise of the right of access to court must not be unduly restricted. There is also a different view in the doctrine, according to which the conditions of admissibility of bringing a case before the court are not so much 'restrictions' on access to court, but rather help to shape its content and ensure its proper implementation. However, this does not mean that these conditions – even though they do not constitute restrictions on the right of access to court – are not subject to an assessment of their compliance with the Constitution[352].

At present, there are practically no situations in which the legislator explicitly closes the judicial channel, but more often the problem arises that the judicial channel is not explicitly provided for. In such situations, it should be assumed that there is a presumption of a judicial remedy, which is derived from Articles 2 and 45(1), as well as from Article 77(2) of the Constitution. Since the last of these provisions introduces the prohibition of closing the judicial channel for the pursuit of violated freedoms and rights, it should be assumed that the judicial channel exists regardless of whether the legislator has expressly provided for it in a particular case[353].

Infringement of access to court may be of a direct nature, i.e. the complete exclusion of access to justice, which is prohibited by Article 77(2) of the Constitution, or of an indirect nature, i.e. the shaping of procedural requirements in such a way as to make it excessively difficult to initiate proceedings. Access to court must mean not only the mere availability of a judicial path, but also the actual possibility of asserting one's rights. The right to access to justice cannot be a mere formality, but must be genuinely guaranteed. Access to justice must not be unduly complicated and burdened with technical difficulties and the court should be accessible to the individual without unnecessary barriers[354].

One of the limitations to which the Constitutional Tribunal draws attention is the question of economic obstacles. The Constitutional Tribunal of Poland, like the European Court of Human Rights, points out that the introduction of an obligation to pay a fee for initiating proceedings before a court is not excluded in principle. Indeed, court fees are a traditionally recognised instrument of state policy, serving, inter alia, to achieve the necessary organisational and judicial efficiency of the courts and to exclude vexatious and manifestly unfounded claims. In addition, court fees have other functions, including fiscal (to obtain at least partial compensation for the functioning of the judicial system), social (to limit litigation, to minimise incentives to protect fictitious interests or the desire to enrich oneself

---

352 P. Grzegorczyk, K. Weitz, [in:] *Konstytucja RP...*, p. 1111.
353 M. Florczak-Wątor, *Prawo do sądu...*, pp. 54–55.
354 A. Łazarska, *Rzeteln proces...*, p. 263.

unjustly at the expense of the opponent) and judicial (primarily the impact of costs on the behaviour of litigants). Undoubtedly, the principle of paid proceedings may also have a negative impact on access to court, especially if its implementation leads to excessive fiscalism, which may impede access to justice or lead to a breach of the principle of equality of the parties. For this reason, the institution of exemption from court costs, which guarantees that disadvantaged persons can obtain legal protection, is important for ensuring parties' access to justice. However, this does not mean that the Constitution requires that exemption from court costs be granted to everyone, even to the most disadvantaged. This is because in a situation where an action or defence is manifestly unfounded, it is not justified by any social or procedural reasons[355] .

Another obstacle to access to court may be excessive procedural formalism. Although there is no doubt that formalism may restrict the freedom of the content and form of procedural acts, as well as the time limits for their execution, it is an indispensable element of any court procedure, necessary for the protection of other universally respected values, such as trust in the law or legal certainty. E. Łętowska points out that procedural formalism is an indispensable element for disciplining the participants in the proceedings and an instrument for influencing the efficiency of court procedure[356]. At the same time, the legislator's freedom is not unlimited, and its principles are always determined by the principle of proportionality[357]. As a rule, procedural rigour must be applied equally to both parties to the proceedings[358]. However, the Constitutional Tribunal points out that the situation must be assessed differently when the person seeking legal protection acts alone and differently when they are represented by a professional. In the latter case, it cannot, as a rule, be said that there is an excessive restriction of the right of access to court. Indeed, the very nature of legal representation implies a legitimate assumption that the lawyer will act professionally to the best of their knowledge and with due diligence[359].

A further obstacle to the exercise of the right to court may be the temporary exclusion of the judicial route due to the obligation to exhaust pre-litigation procedures. This is the case, for example, with the various types of appeal procedure (provided for, for example, in Article 75 of the Act of 15 November 1984 - Transport Law[360]) or the demarcation procedure (Article 34 of the Act of 17 May

---

355 Judgment of the Constitutional Tribunal of 7 September 2004, P 4/04, LEX No 122364.

356 E. Łętowska, *Prawo do sądu – różnice perspektywy*, [in:] *Aurea praxis Aurea theoria. Księga pamiątkowa ku czci Profesora Tadeusza Erecińskiego. Tom II*, J. Gudowski, K. Weitz (eds.), Warsaw 2011, p. 2858.

357 J. Juchniewicz, *O granicach swobody ustawodawcy......*, p. 44.

358 P. Grzegorczyk, K. Weitz, [in:] *Konstytucja RP...*, p. 1113.

359 Judgment of the Constitutional Tribunal of 17 November 2008, SK 33/07, LEX No. 463347.

360 Journal of Laws 2020, item 8 (consolidated text).

1989 - Geodetic and Cartographic Law[361]). Such rules do not, in principle, violate the right of access to court as long as the applicable rules provide for judicial review of the decision. Compulsory pre-litigation proceedings may not, moreover, lead to a lowering of the standards provided for in Article 45(1) of the Constitution, including, in particular, an undue delay in the date on which the case is heard by the court[362].

3.4. The concept of 'court' in Article 45(1) of the Constitution of the Republic of Poland

The implementation of the right to court requires that the case be heard by a court having the characteristics specified in the Constitution, i.e. a court that is 'competent, autonomous, impartial and independent' (pol. *właściwy, niezależny, bezstronny i niezawisły sąd*). If a body does not have these characteristics, it is not a court within the meaning of Article 45(1) of the Constitution, even if the legislator designates it as such[363]. Only when a case is considered by a body possessing the characteristics referred to in Article 45(1) can the right to court be said to have been properly implemented. These requirements relate to the concept of a court as defined in Article 6(1) of the European Convention on Human Rights and partly overlap[364].

Article 45(1) of the Constitution refers to an autonomous and independent court. Although the English translation of the Polish Constitution contains the terms 'competent, impartial and independent', the official Polish version of the Constitution uses the following four adjectives: 'competent, autonomous, impartial and independent'. The Polish Constitution thus distinguishes between the independence and autonomy of the courts.

The autonomy of the courts is the organisational and functional separation of the courts from the structure of other authorities[365]. The separation of the judiciary from the other branches of government is laid down in Article 173 of the Constitution and means that the judiciary has a separate structure in the system of state institutions and that the administration of justice is not influenced by the legislative or executive branches of government. This does not mean that the judiciary is completely isolated from the other branches[366].

---

361 Journal of Laws 2020, item 1990 (consolidated text).

362 P. Grzegorczyk, K. Weitz, [in:] *Konstytucja RP...*, p. 1113.

363 M. Florczak-Wątor, [in:] *Konstytucja Rzeczypospolitej Polskiej. Komentarz*, P. Tuleja (ed.), Warsaw 2019, p. 163.

364 P. Grzegorczyk, K. Weitz, [in:] *Konstytucja RP...*, p. 1119.

365 S. Dabrowski, *Niezależność sędziowska a podział władz*, Kwartalnik Krajowej Rady Sądownictwa 2004/1, p. 15.

366 J. Sobczak, *Niezawisłość sędziowska i niezależność sądów. Problem ważny i ciągle aktualny*, Gdańskie Studia Prawnicze 2015/4, p. 84.

Judicial independence, on the other hand, means that a judge acts solely on the basis of the law, in accordance with their conscience and inner convictions. Judicial independence consists of the following elements: 1) impartiality towards the parties, 2) independence from non-judicial authorities, 3) independence from other authorities and bodies, 4) independence from the influence of political factors, 5) internal independence of the judge. The independence of the judge is closely linked to the autonomy of the courts – without an autonomous judiciary, the notion of judicial independence would remain in a formal and institutional vacuum. It should be noted that independence is not a privilege of judges[367], but their constitutional obligation. The obligation to maintain independence is addressed not only to the judge, but also to the legislature and the administration of justice[368]. The judicial independence does not only concern the function of adjudication, but extends to all other activities of the court which fall within the exercise of the office of judge, i.e. it concerns all actions of the judge related to the adjudication process. This is required by the need to ensure freedom of decision, whatever the stage of the case[369]. The guarantees of judicial independence of judges provided by the Constitution include provisions concerning the appointment of judges for an indefinite period (Article 179), the non-removability of judges (Article 180(1)), the non-transferability of judges (Article 180(2)), the principle of adequate remuneration of judges (Article 178(2)) and the immunity of judges (Article 181)[370].

Although the wording of Article 45(1) of the Constitution indicates that the court must be 'competent' – and this comes first before the requirements of independence, impartiality and independence – this concept has not yet been sufficiently clarified in constitutional judicature or doctrine. The Constitutional Tribunal has not yet ruled on the unconstitutionality of laws based on a conflict with this aspect of the right to a court. The European Convention on Human Rights and the Charter of Fundamental Rights also make no reference to this feature of the court[371]. It should be noted that the requirement of a competent court means that the legislator is obliged to regulate fully by law the issues of territorial, functional and personal jurisdiction[372]. Such an approach must be considered too narrow. The provision of Article 45(1) of the Constitution is not intended to grant an individual the right to have a case heard by a court within the limits of its jurisdiction, in the sense that a violation of the rules of jurisdiction in the particular case would lead to a violation of the constitutional right to court. Such an understanding of the right to a competent court does not seem to have any rational

367 S. Dabrowski, *Niezależność sędziowska ...*, p. 15.
368 J. Sobczak, *Niezależność sędziowska...*, p. 83.
369 J. Sobczak, *Niezależność sędziowska...*, p. 88.
370 S. Dabrowski, *Niezależność sędziowska...*, p. 16.
371 P. Grzegorczyk, K. Weitz, [in:] *Konstytucja RP...*, p. 1120.
372 P. Sarnecki, [in:] *Constitution of the Republic of Poland. Commentary*, L. Garlicki, M. Zubik (eds.), Warsaw 2016, p. 240.

support. The provisions of legislation containing procedural norms do not attach such great importance to the consequences of a breach of jurisdiction. It would be all the more incomprehensible to give the consequences of a breach of jurisdiction the rank of a breach of the Constitution. The guarantee of a competent court, on the other hand, means that the legislator is obliged to determine *ex ante* and in an abstract manner the jurisdiction of the court, so that the individual is enabled to determine in advance which court is competent to hear their case. The main purpose of this is to ensure the predictability of the courts' jurisdiction and to exclude any manipulation of jurisdiction in relation to a particular case. The jurisdiction of the court should be determined in advance in as stable and predictable a manner as possible, without the possibility of discretionary interference by the public authorities as to which court will hear a particular case[373]. A competent court does not only mean the type of specific court with territorial or functional jurisdiction. This guarantee also implies an obligation on the legislator to determine in advance, in an abstract manner, the type of body which should hear a case of a given category and at a given instance[374].

The Constitutional Tribunal also points out that the right to a competent court, as laid down in Article 45(1) of the Constitution, includes a guarantee that the case will be heard by a judge who is authorised to sit in a particular court. If a judge exceeds the scope of authority, both in terms of place and subject matter, and, for example, rules in a court which is not their seat, they become an incompetent judge (court) within the meaning of Article 45(1) of the Constitution. However, this does not mean that the act of delegating a judge from another court with their consent is unlawful from the point of view of the right to court. In fact, the act of delegation legitimises a judge to temporarily sit in a court other than their original court[375]. The above position corresponds to the standard set by the ECHR, which emphasises that the requirement of due process is an element of the right to court established by law. However, the ECHR does not oppose the delegation of a judge to perform duties in another court[376].

3.5. The right to a fair procedure

The right to court also includes the right to a fair procedure. According to the jurisprudence of the Constitutional Tribunal, the principle of procedural fairness consists mainly of the following rights: 1) the right to be heard, 2) the right to the reasoning of the decision (in order to prevent it from being arbitrary), 3) the right to predictability of the course of the proceedings[377]. A. Łazarska defines the

373 P. Grzegorczyk, K. Weitz, [in:] *Konstytucja Rzeczypospolitej Polskiej...*, p. 1121.
374 P. Grzegorczyk, K. Weitz, [in:] *Konstytucja Rzeczypospolitej Polskiej...*, p. 1122.
375 Judgment of the Constitutional Tibunal of 15 January 2009, K 45/07, LEX No. 469915.
376 P. Grzegorczyk, K. Weitz, [in:] *Konstytucja Rzeczypospolitej Polskiej...*, p. 1122.
377 E. Tkaczyk, *Konstytucyjne prawo do sądu...*, p. 41.

fairness of a trial differently, pointing out that the condition for it is transparency. This concept includes a clear, certain and predictable procedure for reaching a verdict, as well as the clarity, comprehensibility and transparency of the verdict itself. The transparency of the procedure consists of elements such as the clarity of the procedure, the publicity of the proceedings, their formalism and the obligation to state reasons for court decisions[378].

The right to be heard presupposes the existence of specific rights, such as the right to make applications and requests, to raise and comment on issues of fact and law, to be informed of the course and progress of the proceedings, to be informed of the opponent's position or of the facts established by the court, and to have the court consider the position put forward by the party[379].

A precondition for the effective exercise of the right to be heard is the internal openness of the proceedings. Internal openness means that the parties are aware of the existence and conduct of the proceedings and that they can participate in them. It implies, inter alia, the right of the parties to access the case file, the right to be informed about the progress of the case and the right to participate in the procedural activities of the court. Internal openness can be achieved primarily, but not exclusively, through the participation of the parties in the proceedings (both in public hearings and in closed sessions). The right to be heard can also be exercised in writing[380].

How these rights are exercised remains a matter of legislative discretion, taking account of their nature, but public hearings are the preferred approach to ensure the full exercise of the right to a fair trial. This does not mean, however, that a party is automatically deprived of the right to be heard simply because the court rules in closed session. This does not mean that parties may not dispense with their right to have their case heard in public. This waiver must, however, be conscious, in the sense that the party must first be given the opportunity to actually participate in the court's proceedings[381]. Accordingly, the consideration of a case in the absence of a party, without a prior hearing, does not conflict with the constitutional right to court, provided that the party was given the opportunity to participate in the hearing or to submit a written statement and that it was the party that made the decision to waive their rights.

Equality of arms requires that each party be given the same opportunities in litigation. Proceedings before the court should ensure that the parties can equally exercise their procedural rights, such as submitting requests and motions, claims and evidence[382]. In proceedings involving two opposing parties, an equal right to be heard must be granted. In this respect, the principle of equality of arms

378 A. Łazarska, *Rzetelny proces...*, pp. 327–328.
379 P. Grzegorczyk, K. Weitz, [in:] *Konstytucja Rzeczypospolitej Polskiej...*, p. 1133.
380 P. Grzegorczyk, K. Weitz, [in:] *Konstytucja Rzeczypospolitej Polskiej...*, p. 1134.
381 P. Grzegorczyk, K. Weitz, [in:] *Konstytucja Rzeczypospolitej Polskiej...*, pp. 1133–1135.
382 A. Łazarska, *Rzetelny proces...*, pp. 452–453.

is closely related to the right to be heard. However, the principle of equality of arms has a much wider dimension and also concerns the equal treatment of the parties in other respects, such as the rules on the payment of legal costs, formal requirements and the consequences of their non-compliance, or the right to be informed of the reasons for the court decision[383]. The principle of equality of arms does not mean that the proceedings must be conducted in an adversarial manner. In studies of Polish civil procedure, adversariality means that the parties, who are in an adversarial position towards each other, are responsible for gathering material for the proceedings and the court does not take any initiative. Article 45(1) of the Constitution does not provide for the right to conduct proceedings in such a manner, and it is subject to the legislator's decision whether to give the model of proceedings an inquisitorial or adversarial character, or to combine elements of both principles[384]. In the jurisprudence of the European Court of Human Rights, the adversarial principle is understood differently and means that each party has the opportunity to be informed of the opponent's position and to respond to it; only in this sense is the adversarial principle considered part of the right to a fair trial.

Another guarantee for the implementation of the principle of procedural fairness is the principle of procedural predictability. It implies the requirement of clear, legible and predetermined procedural rules applicable to individual proceedings from their start to conclusion. It is linked to the principle of procedural formalism, which is intended to protect against the exercise of judicial discretion in the course of proceedings[385]. The dispute before the court is to be resolved within the framework of a specific procedure that indicates the rules and principles of its conduct, which promotes the postulate of the fairness of the proceedings. The certainty of the procedure is intended to prevent judicial arbitrariness and acts as a safeguard. Procedural rules should be designed in a transparent and precise manner, so that the addressee is able to determine their procedural rights and obligations. A lack of such precision, but also misapplication of the rules, may limit the individual's right to a fair trial. The principle of predictability of proceedings is reinforced by the requirement laid down in Article 176(2) of the Constitution that proceedings before a court shall be governed by a statute, which, by virtue of its position in the hierarchy of sources of law, undoubtedly promotes legal certainty and stabilisation of the course of proceedings[386].

According to the Constitutional Tribunal, the written statement of reasons for judicial decisions is one of the essential elements of the right to a fair trial. It fulfils the following functions: 1) it imposes self-control on the court, as it must show that the decision is correct in substance and form and meets the requirements of justice,

---

383 P. Grzegorczyk, K. Weitz, [in:] *Konstytucja Rzeczypospolitej Polskiej...*, p. 1136.
384 P. Grzegorczyk, K. Weitz, [in:] *Konstytucja Rzeczypospolitej Polskiej...*, p. 1138.
385 P. Grzegorczyk, K. Weitz, [in:] *Konstytucja Rzeczypospolitej Polskiej...*, p. 1140.
386 A. Łazarska, *Rzetelny proces...*, pp. 328–330.

2) it documents the arguments in favour of the decision taken, 3) it is the basis for external control by courts of second instance, 4) it serves the acceptance of the decision by the party, 5) it strengthens the sense of public confidence and democratic control over the administration of justice, 6) it strengthens legal certainty[387].

The court is obliged not only to make a decision, but also to justify it in a way that allows the party to know why the decision was made. Above all, a fair process should be transparent, and the actions of the court should be understandable to its participants[388]. The duty to give reasons for decisions is also part of the right to be heard discussed above. This is because the court is obliged to take into account the positions of the parties and to refer to them. A statement of reasons which completely ignores the assessment of the arguments put forward by the parties will not fulfil its function, in particular as regards convincing the parties of the validity of the court's position. Such a statement of reasons will be superficial[389] and will not constitute a sufficient guarantee against the arbitrariness of the decision issued, and will therefore violate the party's right to a court. Undoubtedly, such a lack of reasoning is not conducive to building confidence in the judiciary. This does not mean, however, that the court is obliged to address in detail each and every argument raised by a party throughout the proceedings. It seems sufficient to refer to those arguments which are relevant to the resolution of the case. This will fulfil the function of the statement of reasons, which is to give the individual the feeling that they have been heard, because their arguments have been considered by the court before the decision is taken. Nor does the obligation to give reasons for a decision mean that the court must give reasons for every incidental decision taken in the course of the proceedings. There appears to be no breach of constitutional standards in allowing only those judgments that have been the subject of further appeal to be justified in writing. Similarly, a rule requiring the court to give reasons in writing only if a party applies for them, or the requirement to pay a court fee for such an application, does not constitute an obstacle to the right to obtain reasons for a judgment. However, the procedure must not be overly formalised or complicated in order to prevent a party from accessing the reasons for the decision[390].

3.6. The principle of openness

The openness of proceedings before a court has been written directly into the content of the right to a fair trial arising from Article 45(1) of the Constitution. The analysed provision mentions the right of everyone to 'a public hearing of

---

387 Judgment of the Constitutional Tribunal of 16 January 2006, SK 30/05, LEX No. 182438.

388 A. Łazarska, *Rzetelny proces...*, p. 370.

389 A. Łazarska, *Rzetelny proces...*, pp. 371–372.

390 A. Łazarska, *Rzetelny proces...*, pp. 369–370.

the case'. Openness of proceedings is a prerequisite for the proper functioning of the judiciary, as it is an important guarantee of the maintenance of procedural requirements, the independence and impartiality of the court, as well as the public's sense of justice[391].

In relation to the participants of the proceedings, the openness of the proceedings can be classified as internal (in relation to the participants of the proceedings) and external openness (in relation to the public). The question arises whether the principle of openness expressed in Article 45(1) concerns only external openness or whether the constitutional standard also covers internal openness[392]. P. Grzegorzyk and K. Weitz point out that this clearly defined element of the right to justice concerns only external openness and not internal openness, which in turn is an element of the right to be heard. It thus concerns only the openness of the proceedings in relation to third parties outside the proceedings[393]. However, some authors, including A. Kościółek, understand the constitutional principle of openness in a broader sense, as openness not only towards third parties, but also towards the parties to the proceedings themselves. It should be noted that the provision of Article 45(1) of the Constitution does not contain any indications as to the scope of the concept of openness, and therefore there is no obstacle to a broad understanding of openness (both in its external and internal aspects). Internal openness is not only an element of the principle of procedural fairness, but also a value in itself. Such a position is not an obstacle to the recognition of links between the principle of internal openness and the right to be heard[394].

The publicity of a case consists of three elements: the openness of the court hearings (and in particular of the trial), the openness of the court proceedings (and therefore the possibility of obtaining information about the proceedings and their progress) and the public announcement of the decision[395].

The publicity of court hearings implies, first and foremost, an obligation to ensure that the public has the opportunity to attend court proceedings[396]. However, the position that the case is public only if the court hears the case in a trial, but not if the law provides that the case may be heard in closed session, is unacceptable. If accepted, the constitutional requirement of openness would be determined by the ordinary legislature in deciding whether a particular category of case should be heard in public or adjudicated *in camera*. The requirement of openness provided for in Article 45(1) of the Constitution should be interpreted as the obligation to ensure that court proceedings, regardless of their nature, are open to the public.

---

391 P. Sarnecki, [in:] *Konstytucja...*, p. 241.

392 A. Kościółek, *Zasada jawności w sądowym postępowaniu cywilnym*, Warsaw 2018, p. 39.

393 P. Grzegorczyk, K. Weitz, [in:] *Konstytucja Rzeczypospolitej Polskiej...*, pp. 1140–1141.

394 A. Kościółek, *Zasada jawności...*, pp. 40–41.

395 P. Grzegorczyk, K. Weitz, [in:] *Konstytucja Rzeczypospolitej Polskiej...*, p. 1141.

396 Judgment of the Constitutional Tribunal of 11 June 2002, SK 5/02, LEX No. 54901.

However, this does not mean that every court session must be open to the public, as the principle of openness may be subject to certain restrictions[397].

The principle of openness of the proceedings also implies the right of third parties to be informed of pending proceedings. However, this does not imply an obligation to provide information to the same extent as for the parties. The scope of the information provided may be defined relatively narrowly and should be limited to access to basic information concerning the dates of hearings or the decision made. In any case, the constitutional principle of openness does not imply that outsiders have the right to inspect the case file, as in many cases this could violate the parties' right to privacy (Article 47 of the Constitution) or other protected values. The postulate of openness of the proceedings in relation to third parties is sufficiently implemented, inter alia, in the court schedule[398].

According to the second sentence of Article 45(2) of the Constitution, 'judgments shall be announced publicly'. A judgment should be understood as any substantive decision on the subject of the proceedings and not in the technical-legal sense[399]. P. Sarnecki points out that the principle of public announcement of a judgment is absolute in nature and does not allow for any exceptions, and that 'announcement' should be understood as the pronouncement of the content of the judgment by the presiding judge[400]. P. Grzegorczyk and K. Weitz, on the other hand, take the opposite view, pointing out that although the basic form of publication of a judgment is its oral pronouncement at a public hearing, this is not the only form of publication that satisfies constitutional requirements. Making a judgment available for inspection in the building of the court or publishing its content in a publicly accessible register or database of judgments should also be considered sufficient[401]. The second view is to be accepted. Article 45(2), second sentence, of the Constitution does not introduce the requirement of oral announcement of a judgment. Since in certain cases it is possible to limit the openness of the proceedings, it seems permissible to limit (but not to exclude) the principle of oral announcement of the judgment in a public session. The waiver of public announcement of the judgment may be justified in civil cases that may be heard in closed sessions. The constitutional standard in this respect appears to be lower than in criminal cases[402].

Irrespective of the preferred view, however, it should be noted that the provision of Article 45(2), second sentence, of the Constitution contains a prohibition of secret sentencing without the content of the court's decision being made public, as

397 P. Grzegorczyk, K. Weitz, [in:] *Konstytucja Rzeczypospolitej Polskiej...*, p. 1142.
398 A. Kościółek, *Zasada jawności...*, p. 255.
399 P. Grzegorczyk, K. Weitz, [in:] *Konstytucja Rzeczypospolitej Polskiej...*, p. 1143 and P. Sarnecki, [in:] *Konstytucja...*, p. 242.
400 P. Sarnecki, *Konstytucja...*, p. 242.
401 P. Grzegorczyk, K. Weitz, [in:] *Konstytucja Rzeczypospolitej Polskiej...*, p. 1143.
402 P. Grzegorczyk, K. Weitz, [in:] *Konstytucja Rzeczypospolitej Polskiej...*, p. 1144.

this is a necessary element of a democratic legal state and sentencing is the implementation of the State's public function of administering justice[403].

It is a matter of debate whether the principle of openness applies only to the court of first instance or whether the appeal proceedings must also be open to the public. The standard resulting from the jurisprudence of the European Court of Human Rights allows for a departure from the principle of openness of the proceedings before the court of second instance or the court of cassation, in particular when the case involves only a legal issue and not a factual one. The question therefore arises as to whether such a solution is permissible under the Polish Constitution[404]. However, in view of the fact that the standard of a fair trial laid down in Article 45(1) of the Constitution also covers proceedings before a court of second instance[405], it does not seem reasonable to accept the general principle of excluding the openness of appeal proceedings. Thus, the requirement of openness of proceedings applies to every stage of the procedure, with the exception of judicial deliberation[406]. This does not mean that the ordinary legislator may not introduce such solutions which, taking into account the nature of the given proceedings, limit the openness of proceedings before the court of second instance in certain types of cases, taking into account, for example, the principle of the effectiveness of proceedings. The constitutional principle of the openness, like the right to a fair trial in general, is not absolute.

Article 45(2) of the Constitution of the Republic of Poland allows for the exclusion of public hearings. In the opinion of the Constitutional Tribunal, the restriction of the right to a public hearing is also permissible on the basis of general principles, i.e. those set out in Article 31(3) of the Constitution[407]. Thus, the legislator may allow the limitation of the publicity of certain types of proceedings, provided that this solution is in accordance with the principle of proportionality. On the other hand, a general exclusion of the openness of proceedings motivated solely by the need to increase their efficiency would be unacceptable[408].

As indicated above, in relation to the principle of the openness of proceedings – in addition to the general clause allowing for its restriction, which derives from Article 31(3) of the Constitution – another specific clause is provided for in Article 45(2), according to which 'Exceptions to the public nature of hearings may be made for reasons of morality, State security, public order or protection of the private life of a party, or other important private interest'. The principle of openness is limited by the need to protect other no less important values and should not be

403 P. Sarnecki, [in:] *Konstytucja...*, p. 242.
404 A. Łazarska, *Rzetelny proces...*, p. 357.
405 P. Grzegorczyk, K. Weitz, [in:] *Konstytucja Rzeczypospolitej Polskiej...*, p. 1114.
406 P. Tuleja, [in:] *Konstytucja...*, p. 162.
407 Judgment of the Constitutional Tribunal of 2 October 2006, SK 34/06, LEX No. 210785.
408 A. Łazarska, *Rzetelny proces...*, p. 358.

applied unconditionally. The limitations considered permissible by the legislator in the above-mentioned provision relate only to the exclusion of external openness. The Constitution does not contain any explicit consent to the restriction of internal openness, which does not mean that it is not potentially possible on the basis of general principles (Article 31(3) of the Constitution)[409].

The exclusion of the 'open nature of hearings' referred to in the cited provision should be interpreted in a broader sense, i.e. as an exclusion of the openness of the 'hearing of the case' and not of the mere court session. It is reasonable to adopt a uniform solution to the question of openness in its various aspects. This applies first and foremost to court hearings, but also, for example, to the possibility of obtaining information on the progress of the case. There is no reason to differentiate between the reasons for excluding the public from the trial itself and other elements of the case. The opposite view is also held, according to which the clause provided for in Article 45(2) of the Constitution applies only to the openness of court sessions, and other restrictions on openness are possible only on the basis of Article 31(3) of the Constitution[410]. This view cannot be considered valid for reasons of expediency. The exclusion of publicity for a case should also mean that no information can be obtained about the course of the trial – otherwise the protection of the values that led to the exclusion of publicity could be unduly weakened.

Although not explicitly stated in the provision of Article 45(2) of the Constitution, the basis for the exclusion of publicity can only be established by statute, as is the case with Article 31(3). The difference between the two provisions lies in the fact that Article 45(2) expressly speaks of the 'exclusion' of the openness of a hearing, rather than merely of its 'restriction'. It is therefore possible to abolish the openness of a trial altogether, even to the extent of undermining the very essence of the right to a public trial. However, taking into account the protection of civil rights requires compliance with the general principle of proportionality, understood by analogy with Article 31(3) of the Constitution[411]. P. Sarnecki takes a different view of the matter, pointing out that the exclusion of the public from a trial on the basis of Article 45(2) of the Constitution of the Republic of Poland must meet all the general requirements for the restriction of rights and freedoms, i.e. the requirement of law, proportionality, but also the requirement of preserving the essence of the right, as set out in Article 31(3) of the Constitution[412].

409 A. Kościółek, *Zasada jawności...*, p. 429, p. 431
410 P. Grzegorczyk, K. Weitz, [in:] *Konstytucja Rzeczypospolitej Polskiej...*, pp. 1143–1144.
411 P. Grzegorczyk, K. Weitz, [in:] *Konstytucja Rzeczypospolitej Polskiej...*, pp. 1144–1145.
412 P. Sarnecki, [in:] *Konstytucja...*, p. 242.

3.7. Efficiency of judicial proceedings as an element of the right to a fair trial

Article 45(1) of the Constitution of the Republic of Poland grants an individual the right to have a case heard 'without undue delay'. The prompt processing of cases is therefore an indispensable element of the constitutional right to justice, alongside openness and fairness. The problem of the length of proceedings is now one of the main problems facing the justice system[413]. The requirement to consider a case without undue delay is an expression of the elevation to constitutional status of the principles of speed, efficiency and effectiveness of proceedings[414]. Justice must not be delayed in such a way as to undermine the protection of, and confidence in, the courts[415].

The analysis of this issue should begin by defining the concept of 'efficiency' and contrasting it with the concepts of 'speed' and 'effectiveness'. Efficiency of proceedings cannot be equated exclusively with their speed, although the two concepts are undoubtedly closely related, and the speed of proceedings is a function of efficiency. Speed refers only to the duration of the procedure. Fast proceedings are characterised by a short duration[416]. Efficiency, on the other hand, is the proper organisation of the process[417]. In assessing this element, account should be taken of the adequacy, regularity and timeliness of the steps taken. These two concepts are interrelated in such a way that even proceedings which are lengthy and therefore do not meet the requirement of speediness may prove to be efficient if the timeliness and adequacy of the steps taken are considered to be correct[418]. On the other hand, even the maximum speed of a procedure will not be a proof of its efficiency if the purpose of the procedure is not achieved[419].

The concept of effectiveness of the procedure should be understood in a broader sense than that of efficiency – as the achievement of the objectives of the procedure and the fulfilment of its functions in the shortest possible time, using proportionate means[420]. In order to guarantee the right to court, it is important to ensure the speed of the proceedings and their efficiency (i.e. the way in which they are

---

413 M. Załucki, *Nowe technologie a sprawność i przyszłość sądownictwa w Polsce*, Przegląd Sądowy 2021/11–12, p. 7.

414 P. Grzegorczyk, K. Weitz, [in:] *Konstytucja Rzeczyspospolitej Polskiej...*, p. 1146.

415 Judgment of the Constitutional Tribunal of 26 February 2008, SK 89/06, LEX No. 347185.

416 S. Rożek, *Sprawność postępowania cywilnego na tle rozstrzygania sprawy spadkowych*, Warsaw 2022, pp. 11–12.

417 S. Rożek, *Sprawność...* p. 15.

418 S. Rożek, *Sprawność...*, p. 11.

419 K. Flaga-Gieruszyńska, *Problem sprawności i efektywności postępowania arbitrażowego*, Kwartalnik ADR 2011/4, p. 160.

420 P. Pogonowski, *Efektywność filarem sprawiedliwego postępowania cywilnego*, Polski Proces Cywilny 2021/3, p. 360.

organised), while preserving the primacy of the objective of these proceedings, i.e. the issuance of a correct judgment. In fact, the effectiveness of the procedure does not only consist in resolving the dispute and issuing a decision in the shortest possible time, but also in issuing a just decision after a fair procedure[421]. The effectiveness of the civil justice process is therefore a fundamental premise and a prerequisite for the fairness of a trial. Effectiveness means reconciling the aim of the procedure, which is to reach a fair decision, with the need to resolve the case in the shortest possible time. The effectiveness of judicial protection depends to a large extent on the speed with which it is granted. It is the responsibility of the court to ensure that the case is dealt with as promptly as possible, while respecting the procedural guarantees of the party[422].

In the light of the above definitions, it must be assumed that the constitutional requirement of 'a trial without undue delay' does not imply that proceedings must be prompt in every case. The speed of proceedings is not an absolute value but is only relevant if the achievement of the fundamental objective of the proceedings is ensured[423]. The Constitutional Tribunal also points this out, stressing that the principle of prompt proceedings is limited by the condition that the pursuit of a timely conclusion of proceedings may only take place if this is possible without prejudice to the fairness of the proceedings and, above all, to the principle of material truth, which prevails[424]. The Constitutional Tribunal thus gives priority to the principle of fairness of the proceedings, suggesting that the efficiency of the proceedings, however important, is of secondary importance. In other judgments, however, the Constitutional Tribunal prescribes an *optimum* between the requirements of fairness and efficiency of proceedings[425].

P. Grzegorczyk and K. Weitz disagree with the first of the Constitutional Tribunal's positions on the relationship between the principle of fairness of proceedings and their efficiency, considering it to be superficial. The authors point out that the principle of prompt consideration of a case is a constitutional right of an individual and there is no reason to treat it as weaker than other rights that constitute the right to court[426]. Proceedings before a court should also be fair, public and carried out without undue delay. Consequently, it should have been recognised that dealing with a case without undue delay does not simply mean dealing with it quickly, but dealing with it effectively, i.e. as quickly as possible,

421 P. Pogonowski, *Efektywność...*, p. 358.
422 K. Flaga-Gieruszyńska, *Influence of informatization on the effectiveness and reliability of civil proceedings on the example of Polish solutions,* Fiat Iustitia 2018/1, p. 116.
423 K. Flaga-Gieruszyńska, *Szybkość, sprawność i efektywność postępowania cywilnego - zagadnienia podstawowe,* Zeszyty Naukowe KUL 2017/3, pp. 6–7.
424 Judgment of the Constitutional Tribunal of 13 May 2002, SK 32/01, LEX No. 54065.
425 Judgment of the Constitutional Tribunal of 9 July 2002, P 4/01, LEX No. 54912.
426 P. Grzegorczyk, K. Weitz, [in:] *Konstytucja Rzeczypospolitej Polskiej...*, p. 1147.

while preserving the fairness of the proceedings and the quality of the decision which concludes them.

It is not possible to define in the abstract how long judicial proceedings should take, as this depends on many factors, such as the nature of the case, its complexity and the volume of evidence. A violation of an individual's right to a trial 'without undue delay' occurs when there are insufficient reasons for prolonging the proceedings or when these reasons are not acceptable from the point of view of effective judicial protection. Thus, an assessment of whether the constitutional standard has been met requires an examination of whether the proceedings could have been conducted in a shorter time and, if so, for what reasons (whether justified or not) this did not happen[427].

The injunction to hear cases without undue delay is addressed both to the legislature and to the State administration, and ultimately to the courts. It is the duty of the State to create the organisational, personnel and legal conditions to enable cases to be dealt with efficiently by the courts. The courts, for their part, must take care to ensure that they operate in such a way that the right to a trial without undue delay is met as far as possible[428]. The legislator's duty is to adopt, on the one hand, organisational provisions that create conditions for the optimal functioning of the judiciary and, on the other hand, procedural provisions that allow for the possible streamlining of court proceedings. An expression of the legislator's pursuit of the constitutional principle of efficiency is the Act on the Complaint of Excessive Delays in Proceedings[429].

---

427 P. Grzegorczyk, K. Weitz, [in:] *Konstytucja Rzeczypospolitej Polskiej...*, pp. 1146–1147.

428 P. Grzegorczyk, K. Weitz, [in:] *Konstytucja Rzeczypospolitej Polskiej...*, p. 1146.

429 Act of 17 June 2004 on a complaint for violation of a party's right to hear a case in pre-trial proceedings conducted or supervised by a prosecutor and court proceedings without undue delay, Journal of Laws 2018, item 75 (consolidated text).

4. Impact of selected guiding principles of civil procedure on the implementation of the right to a fair trial

4.1. Introductory remarks

In the previous considerations, the notion of the right to a fair trial was discussed, which consists of a number of rights of an individual, primarily related to the actual access to court, its organisational and constitutional formation and procedural rules that guarantee a fair hearing of the case. The source of the right to a fair trial is the Constitution of the Republic of Poland and international legal acts. However, the actual implementation, i.e. 'the transformation of the will of the legislator into the letter of positive law and its application'[430], is in the hands of the national legislator, whose task is to regulate the procedural model of proceedings before the court in such a way that the right to a fair trial is realised on the basis of a specific case examined by the court. In the area of civil proceedings, the legislator introduces guarantees for the realisation of the right to a fair trial, inter alia, by defining the main procedural rules governing these proceedings.

Procedural principles (also called rules of civil procedure[431]) should be understood as generalised ways and directions of solving basic issues of procedural law[432], which shape the structure of civil proceedings in their most essential constituent elements[433]. They are the guiding ideas (directives) of the procedure, accepted and implemented in the provisions of the Code of Civil Procedure[434], or not explicitly expressed in the provisions, but resulting from the very nature of the procedure and determining its structure[435]. The Code implements the directives that constitute the right to a fair trial through the principles of fairness, material truth, equality, publicity, rule of court instances, efficiency, adversarial proceedings[436]. The existence of a given procedural principle is assumed on the basis of an

---

430 P. Pogonowski, *Wpływ wejścia w życie Konstytucji RP z 1997 r. na sądowe postępowanie cywilne*, [in:] *Czterdziestolecie Kodeksu postępowania cywilnego. Zjazd katedr postępowania cywilnego w Zakopanem (7–9.10.2005 r.)*, Krakow 2006, p. 227.

431 A. Kościółek, *Zasada jawności...*, p. 93.

432 A. Jakubecki, *Naczelne zasady postępowania...*, p. 350.

433 A. Kościółek, *Zasada jawności...*, p. 93.

434 P. Pogonowski, *Realizacja prawa do sądu w postępowaniu cywilnym*, Warsaw 2005, p. 55.

435 A. Kościółek, *Zasada jawności...*, p. 93.

436 P. Pogonowski, *Wpływ wejścia...*, pp. 243–244.

analysis of specific legal solutions. Some principles correspond to a specific provision of the Code of Civil Procedure, which formulates the principle explicitly (e.g. Article 6 § 1 of the CCP provides for the principle of promptness of proceedings). In other cases, the existence of a procedural principle is evidenced by a series of provisions that unify certain institutions or regulate the rights and obligations of litigants. In this way, it is possible to identify partial manifestations of a certain presumption, the sum of which allows to identify a procedural principle[437] (e.g. an expression of the implementation of the principle of equality of the parties is Article 5 of the CCP concerning the provision of instructions to a party appearing without a professional representative, or a number of provisions concerning the course of the hearing, i.e. Articles 210, 212, 214 of the CCP and others)[438].

Among the procedural rules, it is possible to distinguish those which have the character of guiding principles. The 'guiding' principles, as opposed to those of a technical procedural nature, are of a general and leading nature, which manifests itself in the orientation of all the court's procedural activity towards their implementation, taking into account the court's function of protecting subjective rights[439]. Some authors, including A. Kościółek, do not attach much importance to the adjective 'guiding', pointing out that the term has little significance in the context of defining the concept of procedural principles[440]. However, one should argue for the legitimacy of distinguishing the category of guiding principles. The adjective 'guiding' (pol. naczelny) is defined in the Polish dictionary as 'coming to the fore'. This is the meaning that should be given to the concept of 'guiding procedural principles', assuming that certain principles are of fundamental, overriding importance for the civil procedural model. These will be, first and foremost, those principles that derive from the constitutional right to a fair trial, such as the principle of equality or the principle of openness. Certainly, these principles perform a significant guarantee function in civil proceedings that cannot be attributed to all procedural principles.

The (guiding) procedural principles commonly include the principles of disposition, adversary, equality of parties, oral argument, directness, concentration of trial material, procedural formalism, and the principle of truth and openness[441]. A discussion of all the guiding principles of civil procedure is beyond the scope of this study. Therefore, among the principles usually highlighted in the study of civil procedure, the principles of equality of parties, promptness and openness of proceedings have been analysed in detail below. On the one hand, this is justified by the fact that not all of the listed procedural principles are an expression of the

---

437 A. Kościółek, *Zasada jawności...*, pp. 99–100.

438 J. Bodio, W. Graliński, *Znaczenie zasady równouprawnienia strony w procesie cywilnym*, Studia Iuridica Lublinensia 2016/1, p. 258.

439 J. Bodio, W. Graliński, *Znaczenie zasady...*, p. 257.

440 A. Kościółek, *Zasada jawności...*, p. 93.

441 J. Bodio, W. Graliński, *Znaczenie zasady...*, p. 257.

right to a fair trial (e.g. the adversarial principle in the sense of responsibility for the outcome of the proceedings is not part of the right to a fair trial, as the legislator could just as well decide to give priority to the principle of inquisitiveness). Secondly, on the other hand, the implementation of the above principles is linked to the introduction of procedural institutions in the era of the COVID-19 pandemic (analysed in this work). On the other hand, these instruments do not have a decisive impact on the implementation of the other principles.

4.2. Principle of equality

The principle of equality implies that both parties to the proceedings must have the same rights and procedural guarantees, as well as the same opportunities to defend their interests[442]. The principle of the equality of the parties is not explicitly expressed in the provisions of the Code of Civil Procedure, with the exception of Article 1183 of the Code of Civil Procedure, which, however, refers to proceedings before an arbitration court[443] ('In proceedings before an arbitration court, the parties should be treated equally. Each party shall have the right to be heard and to present its claims and evidence in support thereof.'). Nevertheless, the equality of the parties is one of the fundamental principles of civil proceedings, which derives from their very nature[444], the source of which is Article 32(1) of the Constitution. The principle of equality is an integral part of the right to a fair trial stemming from Article 6(1) of the ECHR, Article 47 of the CFR and Article 45(1) of the Constitution, and constitutes an indispensable condition of procedural justice[445]. It should be recalled that the guarantees of the right to a fair trial include the right to a procedure reasonably adapted to the requirements of justice, i.e. such that the parties' procedural positions are equal. A fair trial should provide the parties with rights appropriate to the subject matter of the proceedings, which means that its rules should be adapted to the specificities of the case being heard. Since civil disputes are characterised by the equality of the parties involved, a logical consequence of this is the appropriate design of civil procedure, which presupposes the balance of the rights of the parties[446]. The principle of equality does not mean that all participants in the procedure should have the same rights and obligations, but it does presuppose differentiation of individuals according to certain rules – this principle does not exclude different treatment of parties who are different, but this differentiation must be justified and based on certain criteria[447]. Given that civil

442 J. Bodio, W. Graliński, *Znaczenie zasady...*, p. 258.

443 K. Lichoń, *Obowiązywanie zasady równości stron w postępowaniu przed sądem polubownym*, [in:] *Folia Iuridica Wratislaviensis*,, L. Górnicki (ed.), Wrocław 2013, p. 161.

444 A. Jakubecki, *Naczelne zasady...*, p. 371.

445 A. Łazarska, *Rzetelny proces ...*, p. 425.

446 Judgment of the Constitutional Tribunal of 28 July 2004, P 2/04, LEX No. 121582.

447 A. Łazarska, *Rzetelny proces...*, pp. 427–428.

cases are not identical and that their subject matter covers a wide spectrum, this determines procedural differentiation[448]. Some manifestations of privileging one of the parties can be seen, for example, in the special proceedings in the field of labour and social security law (Articles 462, 464, 466, 467, 4771 of the CCP). The legislator grants special procedural rights to a certain category of subjects, considering them to be the 'weaker party', regardless of whether the situation of a given subject in a particular case actually requires the granting of such protection[449].

The principle of equality in the Code of Civil Procedure consists of two aspects: equality of arms, i.e. equal opportunities for the parties to use procedural means, and the right to be heard, i.e. the opportunity to present one's position and claims (equally)[450] .

The equality of the parties is guaranteed by the fact that civil proceedings are based on the adversarial principle, in which the parties conduct a dispute with equal opportunities to present claims and evidence[451]. The principle of equality is implemented in the Code of Civil Procedure by allowing the parties to express their views on the opponent's position by means of a statement of defence (Art. 205^1 of the CCP), objections against a payment order (Art. 505 of the CCP, Art. 493 of the CCP), opposition to a default judgment (Article 344 of the CCP), reply to an appeal (Article 373^1 of the CCP), reply to a complaint (Article 395 § 1 of the CCP). During the hearing, both parties – first the plaintiff and then the defendant – present their positions in a verbal presentation (Article 210 § 1 of the CCP). The guarantee that both parties' positions will be presented at the hearing is provided by the provision of Article 211 of the CCP, which stipulates that, in the absence of a party at the hearing, the presiding or the reporting judge shall present the conclusions, statements and evidence of the party entered in the case file.

A manifestation of the legislator's desire to preserve the principle of the fairness of the proceedings, also in terms of the equality of the parties, are two provisions introduced by the 2019 amendment to the CCP[452], regulated in Article 156^1 of the CCP and Article 156^2 of the CCP. The first provision is concerned with informing the parties of the probable outcome of the case in the light of the statements and evidence presented so far. The second, on the other hand, provides for the parties

448 A. Łazarska, *Rzetelny proces...*, pp. 430–431.

449 The tendency to strengthen the procedural position of certain groups of entities is also evident in the Amending the Act – Code of Civil Procedure and certain other acts. The legislator introduced as of 1 July 2023 of a new type of separate proceedings, i.e. proceedings with the participation of consumers. The justification of the draft (p. 3) indicates that the scope of protection of consumer rights needs to be increased. Parliamentary Paper No. 2650, https://www.sejm.gov.pl/sejm9.nsf/druk.xsp?nr=2650.

450 J. Bodio, W. Graliński, *Znaczenie zasady...*, p. 257.

451 A. Łazarska, *Rzetelny proces ...*, p. 453.

452 Act of 4 July 2019 amending the Act – Code of Civil Procedure and certain other acts, Journal of Laws 2019, item 1469.

to be warned of the possibility that a decision may be taken on a legal basis other than that previously indicated by one of the parties. The premise of both these provisions is that the court should not give an unexpected judgment based on a position which the party has not yet considered and to which the court has not drawn the parties' attention in the course of the proceedings[453]. The obligations of the court set out in Articles 156[1] and 156[2] of the CCP constitute the implementation of the party's right to predictability of the decision and thus serve to guarantee the effective implementation of the right to a fair trial[454]. The importance of these two provisions for the principle of equality of the parties should also be noted. These provisions have a significant impact on the implementation of the right to be heard and the principle of equality of arms. The prohibition on surprising the parties with the decision and the information obligations of the court in this respect allow both parties to take into account the view expressed by the court and to prepare adequately for the presentation of their procedural position. The purpose of the court's action is to ensure that the parties are heard and that their views are taken into account and to avoid a situation in which the parties are surprised by a decision which they could not have foreseen, even with due diligence[455]. On the other hand, it is pointed out that the instruction referred to in Article 156[1] of the CCP must not go beyond the average measure, beyond which the parties may consider that the court has violated the principle of equality. Indeed, a party may feel aggrieved by the manner in which the presiding judge conducts the proceedings and consider that the court is not impartial in the case[456].

The principle of equality of arms is also reflected in the provision of Article 232 of the CCP, according to which, as a general rule, it is the duty of the parties to produce evidence to prove the facts from which they derive legal effects. The parties are in charge of the proceedings and are responsible for their outcome. It is not the role of the court to conduct an inquiry to discover evidence to supplement or clarify the claims of the parties. Nor is the court obliged to admit evidence of its own initiative[457]. On the basis of the second sentence of Article 232 of the CCP, although the court may admit evidence not submitted by a party, a restrictive interpretation of this provision is generally accepted, according to which the court's evidentiary initiative must be limited, since its abuse could lead to a

453 H. Pietrzkowski, *Metodyka pracy sędziego w sprawach cywilnych*, Warsaw 2021, p. 57.

454 Resolution of the Supreme Court of 17 February 2016, III CZP 108/15, LEX No. 1977618.

455 I. Gromska-Szuster, [in:] *Kodeks postępowania cywilnego. Komentarz. Tom I*, T. Wisniewski (ed.), Warsaw 2021, p. 684.

456 K. Gajda-Roszczynialska, [in:] *Kodeks postępowania cywilnego. Koszty sądowe w sprawach cywilnych. Dochodzenie roszczeń w postępowaniu grupowym. Przepisy przejściowe. Komentarz do zmian,* T. Zembrzuski (ed.), Warsaw 2020, p. 369.

457 J. Paszkowski, [in:] *Kodeks postępowania cywilnego. Komentarz. Tom I,* T. Szanciło (ed.), Warsaw 2019, p. 895.

violation of the principle of equality. The court should intervene in the search for evidence only in exceptional cases[458].

The formal aspect of the principle of equality of the parties, which grants them formal equality in the use of the same procedural means, does not always guarantee the actual equality of the parties (material aspect)[459]. In some cases, a situation may arise in which, due to sociological, psychological or economic conditions, the real equality of the parties is disturbed. A party who does not have the capacity to conduct the proceedings independently or who is burdened with difficulties in doing so is called an unmanageable party[460]. The legislator's role is to ensure that the procedural rules provide solutions that mitigate the effects of the inequality caused by the party's inability to present its case or defend its interests properly.

Instruments to mitigate the inequality of the parties are the possibility of requesting the appointment of a public lawyer (Article 117 et seq. of the CCP) and the exemption from court costs (regulated outside the CCP). It is recognised in the jurisprudence that the court should appoint a legal representative for a party if it considers his participation necessary and the case is factually or legally complicated, or if the party shows an inability to make use of the legal possibilities of conducting the proceedings[461]. The right to request the appointment of a court-appointed lawyer is undoubtedly one of the tools for levelling the conditions for litigants. The same should be said of the possibility of applying for exemption from court costs, which is a means of ensuring equality of arms for a party who, for economic reasons, is unable to participate in the proceedings under the same conditions as the opposing party.

The instructions given by the court also serve to reduce inequalities regarding the procedural situation of the parties. Pursuant to Article 5 of the CCP, where reasonably required, the court may give necessary advice on procedural actions to the parties to and participants in proceedings that are not represented by a professional. If one of the parties is represented by a professional representative and the other party acts alone, an imbalance between the parties may arise. In such cases, the court may give the necessary instructions to that party, but only 'if reasonably required'. This provision does not introduce a general obligation to give instructions in every case where a person appears in court without a representative. However, the court is obliged to give instructions where there is a need to avoid inequality between the parties to the proceedings, in particular where a party is unable to understand the substance of the proceedings and therefore to take appropriate procedural steps[462]. The scope of the duty to provide advice extends

458 J. Misztal-Konecka, *O obowiązywaniu zasady kontradyktoryjności w postępowaniu nieprocesowym: przyczynek do dyskusji*, Zeszyty Prawnicze 2016/3, p. 157.

459 A. Skorupka, *Realizacja zasady równości w aspekcie materialnym na przykładzie osób niewidomych*, Polski Proces Cywilny 2018/3, p. 149.

460 A. Łazarska, *Rzetelny proces...*, pp. 438–439.

461 Decision of the Supreme Court of 11 January 2022, II USK 596/21, LEX No. 3342281.

462 Decision of the Supreme Court of 19 February 2021, I USK 89/21, LEX No. 3122707.

only to the necessary steps to be taken in the course of the proceedings and not to instructing a party as to all possible conduct to adopt in a given situation. The duty to advise does not extend to warning a party against reckless conduct or lack of regard for his own interests[463]. The purpose of giving the necessary instructions is to guarantee the parties a fair trial based on the principles of procedural fairness, including the principle of equality of arms, and not to 'lead by the hand' during the trial a party that does not show concern for its own interests. The provision of Article 212 § 2 of the CCP corresponds to Article 5 of the CCP, according to which the presiding judge may, if there is a justified need, give the necessary instructions to the parties at the hearing and, depending on the circumstances, draw attention to the advisability of appointing a legal representative. Contrary to Articles 5 and 212 of the CCP, the obligation to give instructions to a party who is not represented by a professional lawyer is provided for in Article 210 § 2^1 of the CCP, which in any event orders that instructions be given at the hearing on the content of Article 162 § 1, Article 205^{12} § 2, Article 229 and Article 230 of the CCP. In addition, both parties shall be served with the instructions referred to in Article 205^2 of the CCP. The obligation to give instructions on the available legal remedies is also provided for in Article 327 §§ 1 and 4 of the CCP, Article 343 § 1 of the CCP, Article 357 § 2 of the CCP.

4.3. Principle of promptness

The right to have a case heard within a reasonable time, which derives from Article 45(1) of the Constitution, Article 6(1) of the ECHR and Article 47(2) of the Charter of Fundamental Rights, is reflected in the Code of Civil Procedure in the form of the principle of promptness expressed in Article 6 of the CCP. According to the provision referred to in paragraph 1, the court should prevent any delay in proceedings and endeavour to decide a case at the first hearing if this can be done without detriment to the clarification of the case. Paragraph 2, on the other hand, stipulates that shall provide all the facts and evidence without delay so as to enable the proceedings to be conducted promptly and efficiently. Even a brief analysis of the cited provision leads to the conclusion that the obligation to avoid protraction of proceedings has been imposed by the legislator on the court, whose role in this respect is paramount. However, it is important to remember that the legislator also imposes on the parties concerned obligations aimed at ensuring an efficient and speedy examination of the case. In practice, the parties also have a significant influence on the course of the proceedings (including their duration), as they often delay the submission of procedural documents for various reasons[464], thus contributing to the length of the proceedings. The provision of Article 6 of the CCP

463 P. Feliga, [in:] *Kodeks postępowania cywilnego. Komentarz. Tom I,* T. Szanciło (ed.), Warsaw 2019, pp. 34–35.
464 A. Jakubecki, *Naczelne zasady...*, p. 376.

assumes that the way to implement the principle of promptness is through proper cooperation between the court and the parties[465].

In recent years, the main objective of the successive amendments to the Code of Civil Procedure has been to expedite civil proceedings. In order to achieve this objective, it is necessary to strike a balance between the values that the Code is intended to uphold – solutions that satisfy the postulate of speed of proceedings, although this should not be the case in principle, are very often associated with certain limitations of other procedural principles and guarantees[466]. Due to the fact that the legislator's attention in recent years has been focused on solutions aimed at expediting proceedings, the subject matter relating to the implementation of the principle of promptness is extremely extensive. Selected provisions implementing the principle of promptness on the basis of the Code of Civil Procedure are discussed below.

The postulate of expediting proceedings is realised primarily by the principle of concentration of the procedural material, which consists in the possibility of limiting the course of civil proceedings through a system of preclusion. Preclusion can be implemented in a model of discretionary power of the judge or in a model of contingency. In the former, the court has the power to overrule and disregard the circumstances and evidence presented by the parties if it considers that a party has presented them late with a view to delaying the proceedings. The contingency model means that a party is obliged to put forward all the defences it is able to raise at the same time, even if the use of one of them renders others unnecessary[467].

The main purpose of the principle of preclusion of evidence is to discipline the parties in order to meet the need for speed and efficiency. The idea is to induce the parties to submit the necessary statements and evidence at the earliest possible stage of the proceedings in order to ensure that the court has access to all the material in the case and to enable it to reach a correct decision as quickly as possible[468]. However, preclusion should not be applied in an overly formalistic manner at the expense of the possibility of resolving the case on the merits. A party should have the opportunity to raise claims covered by issue preclusion or to provide evidence if it appears that it could not have done so earlier[469]. An overly strict approach to the exclusion of procedural material may lead to an erroneous judgment where the allegations and evidence omitted by the court would have been decisive for the

465 P. Feliga, [in:] *Kodeks postępowania cywilnego...*, p. 38.

466 J. May, *Rozwiązania usprawniające proces cywilny (zagadnienia wybrane)*, [in:] *Postępowanie cywilne w dobie przemia*, I. Gil (ed.), Warsaw 2017, p. 143.

467 A. Łazarska, *Rzetelny proces...*, pp. 388–389.

468 K. Gajda-Roszczynialska, *System koncentracji materiału procesowego po zmianach wprowadzonych na mocy ustawy z 4.07.2019 r. o zmianie ustawy – Kodeks postępowania cywilnego oraz niektórych innych ustaw w postępowaniu zwyczajnym*, Polski Proces Cywilny 2020/1, p. 70.

469 Judgment of the Supreme Court of 5 December 2007, I CSK 295/07, LEX No. 382064.

outcome of the case[470]. At the same time, it should be remembered that Article 6 of the CCP requires that proceedings be conducted efficiently and expeditiously, but 'without detriment to the clarification of the case'. The need for a prompt procedure must not lead to simplifications to the detriment of the truth and the resolution of the case[471].

The system of concentration of trial material under the Code of Civil Procedure has been significantly reshaped by the 2019 amendments. Prior to the entry into force of this Act, this issue was primarily governed by Article 207 § 6 of the CCP, according to which the court disregarded late claims and evidence, unless the party proved that it had not submitted them in the statement of claim, statement of defence or other preparatory pleading through no fault of its own, or that taking into account late claims and evidence would not cause a delay in the recognition of the case, or that there were other exceptional circumstances. This system was dominated by the contingency model, according to which a party was obliged to identify all arguments and evidence in the first statement of case and the court was obliged to disregard those which were submitted late ('the court shall disregard'). This system was supplemented by the principle of the discretion of the judge, which allowed the omission of late arguments and evidence if the court considered that the party had failed to submit them through no fault of its own, or if their inclusion would not lead to a delay in the examination of the case, or if there were other special circumstances.

At present, issues relating to the concentration of evidence are governed by Chapter 2a Organisation of proceedings, which is included in Section II of Title VI Proceedings at first instance (Articles 205^1 et seq. of the CCP). The first of the changes introduced to expedite the examination of the case is the obligation to file a statement of defence (Article 205^1 § 1 of the CCP). Previously, filing a statement of defence was a right, not an obligation (repealed Article 207 of the CCP), and if the defendant did not include all the claims and evidence in their statement of defence, the court was obliged to disregard them at a later stage of the proceedings. The legislator did not provide for such strictness in the amended provisions of the CCP. Currently, the failure to include all claims and evidence in the first statement of defence does not result in the loss of the right to submit them at later stages of the proceedings[472]. The obligation to lodge a statement of defence – although the failure to do so does not currently lead to the exclusion of claims and evidence – is a solution that contributes to improving the efficiency of proceedings. The defendant is obliged to respond to the claimant's submissions at an early stage of the proceedings, which allows for an appropriate organisation of the proceedings adapted to the position of both parties. Failure to file a statement of defence

470 A. Łazarska, *Rzetelny proces...*, p. 390.
471 H. Dolecki, T. Radkiewicz, [in:] *Kodeks postępowania cywilnego. Komentarz. Tom I*, T. Wisniewski (ed.), Warsaw 2021, p. 105.
472 P. Feliga, [in:] *Kodeks postępowania...*, p. 788.

has another important effect, namely the possibility of issuing a default judgment in a closed session (Article 339 § 1 of the CCP). Previously (before the amendment in 2019), a default judgment could only be issued at a public trial. The introduced solution undoubtedly contributes to the implementation of the principle of promptness, as it allows to terminate the proceedings as soon as it is established that the defendant, despite having been duly served with a copy of the statement of claim and being obliged to file a reply to the claim, is not interested in participating in the proceedings. It should also be noted that if the case is referred to trial and the defendant does not appear at the hearing scheduled for that trial or does not take part in it despite his physical presence, a judgment by default is mandatory (Article 340 § 1 of the CCP).

The principle of concentration of procedural material is reflected in the wording of Article 205^3 of the CCP. According to § 1, the presiding judge may order the exchange of further pleadings, determining the order and deadlines for their submission, as well as the circumstances to be explained. It is important to note that, from the point of view of the provision in question, the order for the exchange of preparatory pleadings should be made 'in justified cases'. This concept should be understood through the prism of the purpose of the pre-trial briefs, which is to prepare the case for judgment (Article 127 § 1 of the CCP)[473]. The exchange of further pre-trial briefs will therefore be desirable where it can contribute to a more efficient determination of the case by the court. The legislator indicates that this will be the case in particular in complex cases. In other cases, where the circumstances of the case do not require it, the lodging of consecutive pre-trial pleadings may contribute to prolonging the proceedings (because of the time taken for several but unnecessary exchanges of correspondence between the parties). For this reason, Article 205^3 § 5 of the CCP provides that the presiding judge shall order the return of a pleading which has been lodged without an order from the presiding judge for the exchange of pre-trial briefs.

Another manifestation of the concentration of procedural material is the provision of Article 205^3 § 2 of the CCP, according to which the presiding judge may oblige a party to set out in a pre-trial brief all the claims and evidence relevant to the resolution of the case. The risk of failing to comply with this obligation is the loss of the right to refer to it later in the course of the proceedings. In such a case, the statements and evidence submitted in breach of this obligation will be disregarded, unless the party proves that it was not possible to refer to them in the written statement or that the need to refer to them arose subsequently. This provision refers to the previously discussed provision of the repealed Article 207 § 6 of the CCP. The difference, however, is that in the previous regime, preclusion of claims and evidence always applied if the party failed to include all claims and evidence in the statement of claim or statement of defence. At present, however, pursuant to Article 205^{12} § 2 of the CCP, a party may refer to claims and evidence

473 P. Feliga, [in:] *Kodeks postępowania...*, pp. 793–794.

in support of its motions or in rebuttal of the opposing party's motions and claims until the end of the trial, unless the presiding judge has ordered the party to submit them in a pre-trial brief on penalty of excluding them at a later stage of the proceedings, or unless a pre-trial hearing has been scheduled. The timing of the concentration of trial material will therefore vary depending on whether the presiding judge convenes a pre-trial hearing or requires a party to submit all claims and evidence in a pre-trial brief on penalty of excluding them at a later stage or, without taking the above steps, refers the case to trial[474]. The 2019 amendment has therefore increased the organisational powers of the presiding judge, whose discretion now determines at what stage the exclusion of new claims and evidence occurs.

The streamlining of civil proceedings is the main motive of the 2019 amendment, which is to be implemented in particular by changing the rules of organisation of proceedings. The literature on civil procedure has repeatedly emphasised the crucial importance of the preparatory phase for the proper clarification of the case, identifying the lack of adequate regulation of the preparatory phase as a significant shortcoming in the regulation of civil procedure[475]. The flagship institution introduced by the 2019 amendments, which is intended to ensure the objective of speeding up the consideration of cases, is the pre-trial hearing[476]. The main purpose of the pre-trial hearing is to obtain from the parties, at an early stage of the proceedings, information relevant to the resolution of the case, to establish the merits of the case, to focus the evidence and to critically analyse it for its relevance to the resolution of the case. The purpose of the pre-trial hearing is, if the dispute cannot be resolved by settlement, to establish a trial schedule so that the trial can be held on a single date[477]. The above-mentioned aspirations are explicitly expressed by the legislator in the wording of Article 205^5 § 1 of the CCP.

A pre-trial hearing may be scheduled after the statement of defence has been lodged or after the deadline for its lodgement has expired unless a default judgment has been rendered. The date of the first pre-trial hearing should not be later than two months after the statement of defence has been lodged or the deadline for it has expired (Article 205^4 §§ 1 and 2 of the CCP). This time limit is merely indicative and, although the court should endeavour to comply with it, exceeding it does not entail any negative procedural consequences. In view of the court's obligation to seek a prompt resolution of the case, the introduction of a time limit within which a preparatory hearing should be held is to be assessed positively. Since the purpose of this institution is to concentrate the procedural material at the earliest possible stage of the proceedings, it is desirable that it be held as soon as possible.

---

474 K. Gajda-Roszczynialska, *System koncentracji...*, p. 72.

475 E. Gapska, *Przygotowanie rozprawy cywilnej – niewykorzystana szansa,* [in:] *Postępowanie cywilne w dobie przemian*, Warsaw 2017, pp. 115–116.

476 A. Machnikowska, *Organizacja procesu cywilnego przed sądem pierwszej instancji z perspektywy posiedzenia przygotowawczego*, Palestra 2019/11–12, p. 53.

477 A. Machnikowska, *Organizacja procesu...*, p. 60.

If the preparatory hearing does not lead to a settlement of the dispute, a trial plan is drawn up, which must include decisions on the evidentiary submissions of the parties and the order in which evidence is to be taken (Article 205^{9} § 1 of the CCP). The trial plan may also contain other elements mentioned in Article 205^{9} § 2 of the CCP, in particular the precise definition of the parties' claims and objections, the determination of the disputed and uncontested facts between the parties, and even the date for the closure of the trial and the pronouncement of the judgment. It is important from the point of view of concentration of procedural material and speed of proceedings that the trial plan, which is approved by the court (Article 205^{10} § 3 of the CCP), is binding on the parties in the course of further proceedings and, as a rule, remains unchanged. The trial plan can only be changed by court order and only if it has become obsolete. On the other hand, a new trial plan may be drawn up only 'if there is a compelling need' (Article 205^{11} of the CCP). An amendment of the trial plan is justified if the current schedule no longer ensures the efficient organisation of the proceedings, while at the same time the amendments are minor and do not render the entire trial plan obsolete, with changes to the trial dates being made by decision of the presiding judge. If the trial schedule becomes obsolete in whole or in substantial part, a new trial plan must be prepared. This may be the case, for example, if the subject matter of the case changed (Articles 194–196 of the CCP)[478]. After the approval of the trial plan, the parties may no longer submit new claims and evidence, and those submitted later must, as a rule, be disregarded, unless the party can show that it was impossible to submit them or that the need to submit them arose later (Article 205^{12} § 1 of the CCP). The pre-trial hearing and the trial plan are therefore important instruments for implementing the principle of concentration of material in the case and for determining the organisation of the entire case at an early stage. The approval of the case schedule prevents the parties from submitting new requests for evidence and from raising new claims, which obviously has an impact on the efficiency of the proceedings and prevents the parties from trying to prolong the proceedings. A pre-trial hearing, the main purpose of which is to decide on the requests for evidence submitted, also makes it possible to disregard evidence that is not material to the outcome of the case, thus limiting the amount of evidence and reducing the time taken to hear the case.

The acceleration of the examination of the case is also favoured by the provisions of Article 205^{7} of the CCP concerning the adjournment of the pre-trial hearing. The possibility of adjourning the pre-trial hearing is regulated in the cases strictly specified in the said article, and in other cases it is not allowed (§ 4). The postponement of the pre-trial hearing is obligatory if the parties are referred to mediation (§ 1). An optional adjournment, on the other hand, is only possible 'if necessary', and in particular if: 1) there is a prospect of an amicable settlement of the case, 2) there is a need to clarify relevant circumstances, 3) in case of excused absence

478 P. Feliga, [in:] *Kodeks postępowania...*, pp. 821–822.

of a party, 3) at the joint request of the parties (whereby a pre-trial hearing may only be adjourned twice at the joint request of the parties, each time for a specified period not exceeding three months).

Although it follows from the wording of Article 205^4 § 1 of the CCP that the convening of a pre-trial hearing is mandatory ('the presiding judge shall convene'), the law allows for the possibility of dispensing with the pre-trial hearing and giving the case another appropriate course (Article 205^4 § 3 of the CCP). This is possible if the circumstances of the case indicate that holding a pre-trial hearing will not contribute to a more efficient examination of the case. The aim of this solution is to make the rules governing the organisation of proceedings more flexible and to adapt them to the needs arising from the current workload of judges[479].

The question arises in which situations (and in which cases) the holding of a pre-trial hearing may contribute to a more efficient examination of the case and when it may have the opposite effect. Certainly, a pre-trial hearing will have a positive effect on the efficiency of the proceedings if the outcome is a settlement and the proceedings are consequently discontinued (Article 355 of the CCP). This forum favours an amicable settlement of the dispute, which is influenced by several factors. The preparatory hearing facilitates an informal 'discussion between the court and the parties', which not only increases the court's efficiency in the area of mediation, but also helps to change the image of the court as a party-friendly institution[480]. The rules on *in camera* hearings apply to the pre-trial hearing (Article 205^5 § 2 of the CCP), so that only the summoned participants have access. Thus, there is no risk of third parties being present at possible settlement discussions whose appearance would negatively influence the process of reaching a common position on the settlement. The compulsory presence of the parties and their lawyers at the hearing (Article 205^5 § 5 of the CCP) also serves the amicable settlement of the dispute – the absence of one of the parties at the hearing would undoubtedly make it impossible to reach a settlement, while the simultaneous presence of the parties makes it easier for the presiding judge to urge the conclusion of a settlement. Another solution for settlement during the pre-trial hearing is the prohibition to include in the hearing minutes statements made by the parties attempting to settle the dispute. Furthermore, during the proceedings before the court, any reference to settlement proposals or other statements is inadmissible. The course of the pre-trial hearing is not recorded by means of audio or video recording devices, nor may it be recorded by the parties (Article 205^7 of the CCP).

Apart from the case where the case is closed at the pre-trial stage by a settlement, it appears that the preparation of a trial plan will speed up the examination of a case where it can be established at an early stage that the case is factually or legally complex or that an extensive evidentiary procedure will be necessary. In such cases, the preparation of a trial plan will make it possible to

479 A. Machnikowska, *Organizacja procesu...*, p. 61.
480 A. Machnikowska, *Organizacja procesu...*, p. 63.

organise the proceedings efficiently and even to set specific dates for procedural steps to be taken. The drawing up of a trial plan and its *ex officio* notification to the parties (Article 205^{10} § 5 of the CCP) replaces the need for notification of the dates of hearings and other actions covered by the plan, as well as summons to specific duties. This reduces the time required for service, which is often a factor in prolonging proceedings (according to Article 149 § 2 of the CCP, a summons for a hearing should be served at least one week before its date, plus the time required to prepare a written summons and deliver it by post). The preparation of a trial plan in cooperation with the parties present at the hearing will also make it possible to identify which facts are undisputed between the parties (and therefore do not require the taking of evidence at all), which evidence is essential for the outcome of the case and which evidence should be disregarded. The preparation of a trial plan makes it possible to determine precisely the facts on which the evidence it contains is to be based, which in turn makes it possible to conduct the trial more efficiently. The trial plan is an instrument which makes it possible to limit the scope of the taking of evidence while ensuring that all relevant circumstances of the case are clarified. It should therefore be considered as an important tool for improving the efficiency of the proceedings.

On the other hand, a preparatory hearing will not have the intended effect of expediting proceedings in all categories of cases. Where the decision can be taken at the first hearing scheduled for trial, or even at a closed hearing, the scheduling of a pre-trial hearing will be unnecessary and will contribute to prolonging the duration of the proceedings. So far, it has not been possible to reach a judgment at a pre-trial hearing, which means that even after all the relevant circumstances of the case have been clarified at the closed hearing, it is still necessary to set a trial date. However, after the amendment of the Code of Civil Procedure from July 2023, the court may issue a judgment in closed session if the dispute could not be resolved in the course of the pre-trial hearing and the conditions for adjudicating the case in the manner provided for in Article 148^1 § 1 of the CCP are met. In such a case, the provision of Article 148^1 § 3 of the CCP does not apply and it is therefore irrelevant whether the party has requested to be heard at trial. A pre-trial hearing will also not be necessary if the parties have not presented witnesses or expert opinions, but only from documents, or if the evidence presented by witnesses can be heard during a single session scheduled for the trial. A pre-trial hearing will not serve its purpose in 'template' cases, which are heard according to a certain predetermined pattern, and in cases which are simple in terms of evidence and law and where the wait for a judgment is usually short.

This dependency seems to have been taken into account by the legislator, since in simplified proceedings there is no pre-trial hearing (Article 505^2 of the CCP). According to the legislator's intentions, the simplified procedure should be used to examine 'minor' cases that are commonplace and whose factual and legal circumstances do not give rise to any doubts[481]. At the same time, the criterion

---

481 P. Pogonowski, [in:] *Kodeks postępowania cywilnego. Komentarz. Tom I*, T. Wisniewski (ed.), Warsaw 2021, p. 1037.

for qualifying a case for simplified procedure is the value of the claim (up to PLN 20,000 – Article 505[1] of the CCP), therefore it cannot be automatically excluded that even a case with a low value of the claim will not be complex. Therefore, although pre-trial hearings are not usually held, the court may organise them in simplified proceedings if this can help to resolve the dispute more efficiently.

However, the practice so far shows that this institution is not often used by the courts. A more popular alternative is to issue orders requiring the parties to submit pre-trial briefs. It is even common for professional lawyers to request, in the statement of claim or the statement of defence, 'not to schedule a preliminary hearing, as it will not help to speed up the examination of the case'. The institution of a preliminary hearing is not actively used by the courts. From the judges' point of view, the preliminary hearing does not fulfil its purpose of expediting the examination of the case. Other means of concentrating procedural material, such as the exchange of pre-trial briefs, seem to serve this purpose better. In view of the fact that the pre-trial hearing should be a fundamental institution in the organisation of proceedings, which the legislator intended to make a significant contribution to improving the efficiency of the proceedings before the courts, it must be concluded that it is not fulfilling its function. The extent of the deviations from the holding of a pre-trial hearing, which is normally obligatory, leads to the conclusion that it is becoming a rare exception rather than the rule[482].

If no pre-trial hearing has been held and no trial plan has been drawn up, orders for the preparation of the trial are issued on the basis of the statement of claim and other pleadings (Article 208 § 3 of the CCP). In such a situation, the provision of Article 206 of the CCP obliges the presiding judge and the court to take steps to proceed with the case at the earliest possible date. As a rule, the hearing should be prepared so that the case can be decided at the first hearing scheduled (Article 206[1] of the CCP). Further hearings should only be scheduled if necessary, in particular if it is not possible to take evidence at a single hearing. The legislator indicates that if it is necessary to set several hearings, they should be held on consecutive days and, if not possible, so that the time between hearings is not excessive. The provision of Article 206[1] of the CCP is postulatory in nature. It is an interpretative directive, since it is a clear specification of the principle of hearing a case at the earliest possible date (Article 206 of the CCP)[483] and an expression of the principle of the promptness of proceedings from Article 6 of the CCP. The achievement of the stated objective will depend to a large extent on the proper organisation of the trial at its preliminary stage (whether or not a trial plan has been drawn up or the preparation of the trial has been carried out on the basis of the statement

482 J. May, *Usprawnienie i przyspieszenie procesu cywilnego: nowe rozwiązania prawne czy stare sprawdzone metody? – wybrane zagadnienia,* [in:] *Rozstrzyganie spraw cywilnych. Aktualne wyzwania i perspektywy,* M. Białecki, S. Kotas-Turoboyska, F. Manikowski, J. Słyk, E. Szczepanowska (eds.), Warsaw 2022, p. 305.

483 P. Feliga, [in:] *Kodeks postępowania...*, p. 831.

of claim and other pre-trial briefs). It should be noted, however, that even if the case is properly prepared on the basis of the principles of concentration of the case material discussed above, it will not always be possible to resolve the case at the first hearing or to schedule subsequent hearings at dates not too far apart from each other. The implementation of the principle of promptness is influenced by a number of other factors, such as the organisation of the court (e.g. accessibility of courtrooms), the workload of a particular judge with other official duties or, finally, significant staff shortages in the courts.

The objective of expediting proceedings is served by the provisions on the adjournment of court proceedings (which limit this possibility). According to Article 156 of the CCP, the court may adjourn a hearing, even at the unanimous request of the parties, only for an important reason. In addition to the unanimous request of the parties, a hearing may be adjourned if the court finds an error in the service of the written summons or if the absence of a party is caused by an extraordinary event or other irremovable obstacle (Article 214 § 1 of the CCP). The hearing shall also be adjourned if it is necessary to make subjective changes on the part of the plaintiff or defendant, if the court decides to summon or notify of pending proceedings those who have not yet acted as plaintiff or defendant (Article 215 of the CCP). The provisions in question concerning the scheduling of hearings and the possibility of their adjournment demonstrate the great importance that the legislator attaches to the principle of promptness of proceedings. In fact, the legislator limits the situations in which a hearing can be postponed at all, giving priority to the principle of deciding the case at the first scheduled hearing.

The principle of promptness in the Code of Civil Procedure is not only implemented through provisions on the concentration of procedural material. The speed of proceedings is also influenced by the way in which the parties can correspond with the court, in particular by simplifying this communication[484]. The problem of service of judicial documents is one of the factors influencing the length of court proceedings. The time that elapses between the sending of judicial correspondence and the receipt of an acknowledgement of receipt undoubtedly contributes to the length of proceedings. Solutions using IT tools, such as electronic proof of receipt (EPO), should help to speed up proceedings and reduce their cost[485]. Such an objective is also supported by the provision of Article 132 § 1^3 of the CCP on the direct service of documents in the course of proceedings between professional lawyers by electronic means[486]. The admissibility of service by electronic means is subject to the prior lodging of a consent form and the provision of contact details (e-mail address or fax number) to the court. Electronic communication, which allows a letter to be sent directly and almost in real time, is

---

484 A. Łazarska, *Rzetelny proces...*, p. 392

485 M. Zalucki, *Nowe technologie...*, pp. 9–10.

486 A. Borys, [in:] *Regulacje służące usprawnieniu cywilnego postępowania rozpoznawczego*, I. Gil (ed.), Warsaw 2020, p. 122.

undoubtedly an important means of expediting proceedings. The rationalisation of communication – although, for the reasons given, not to the same extent as electronic service – is served by the obligation of direct service of pleadings between professional lawyers (Article 132 § 1 of the CCP). Bypassing the court saves the time that would otherwise elapse between the delivery of a copy of the document to the court, the court's taking of the appropriate measures and the delivery of the document to the opposing party. The Code of Civil Procedure allows electronic service not only between lawyers but also between the court and a party (Article 131^1 of the CCP)[487]. Service by means of an electronic communication system is deemed to have been effected if the addressee has deposited a letter by means of such a system or has chosen this method of depositing documents. In some proceedings, it is compulsory to submit a document by means of the electronic communication system (e.g. in electronic payment order proceedings – Article 505^{31} § 1 of the CCP).

Another important instrument for improving the course of proceedings is the possibility of simplified summons to the parties, witnesses, experts and other persons, provided for in Article 149^1 of the CCP. This provision introduces an exception to the principle of official service and provides that the court may issue the summons 'in the manner it considers most expedient' if it determines that this is necessary to expedite the examination of the case. As a condition of effectiveness and as a guarantee for the person summoned, it is required that there is no doubt that the summons has reached the recipient within the time limits laid down for traditional summonses.

The prevention of the prolongation of the proceedings is carried out by means of a system of disciplining the parties[488]. In the course of proceedings, parties may use their procedural rights in a way that may destabilise the course of the proceedings[489]. This is prevented by a number of mechanisms, including the prohibition of abuse of procedural rights, which is enshrined in the provisions of the 2019 revision. According to Article 4^1 of the CCP, parties and participants in proceedings may not use a right provided for in the rules of procedure in a manner incompatible with the purpose for which it was established. The abuse of procedural rights is the exercise of procedural rights by taking actions that are formally permitted, but which, in the circumstances of a particular case, are considered to be used contrary to the intention of the legislator. It is the behaviour of a party which gives rise to the presumption that it is intended to disrupt the course of the proceedings[490].

---

487 The practical use of the institution of electronic service is further considered in the following chapters.

488 A. Łazarska, *Rzetelny proces...*, p. 394.

489 P. Feliga, [in:] *Kodeks postępowania...*, p. 27.

490 M. Białecki, *Organizacja postępowania jako próba realizacji postulatu szybatu postępowania cywilnego a nadużycie prawa procesowego przez strony i uczestników postępowania*, [in:] *Nowelizacja postępowania cywilnego. Wpływ zmian na praktykę sądową*, S. Kotas-Turoboyska, F. Manikowski (eds.), Warsaw 2021, p. 35.

Indications of abuse of procedural rights may include deliberate delay of proceedings, repeated submission of the same applications, filing of unjustified objections and appeals, challenging court decisions based on the correct application of procedural rules[491].

If it is established that a party has abused his procedural rights, the court may, after prior notice, apply in the final judgment the measures provided for in Article 226^2 § 2 of the CCP, including the imposition of a fine or the obligation to reimburse court costs to a greater extent than the result of the case would indicate, or even to reimburse court costs in full. The question arises whether, in addition to the consequences expressly provided for in Article 226^2 of the CCP, other sanctions are possible, even in the absence of a specific provision[492], e.g. in the form of disregard for a party's actions constituting an abuse of procedural rights. A. Jakubecki points out that in civil procedural law there is no general sanction for abuse of procedural rights and there are no grounds for applying the sanction of disregarding a procedural act. In fact, the legislator has refrained from adopting such a general formula. In the case of abuse of procedural rights, the only remaining possibility is the application of Article 226^2 of the CCP[493]. M. Manowska gives a similar answer to the question, pointing out that the provision of Article 4^1 of the CCP contains a general clause, which has only an auxiliary application and cannot, under any circumstances, constitute an independent legal basis for declaring a procedural act null and void. A general rule cannot create a source of direct sanction separate from those provided for by the law[494]. This position should be agreed with. The original draft of Article 4^1 of the CCP read as follows: 'The taking of an action by a party in abuse of procedural rights shall exclude the effects that the law attaches to such action'[495]. The legislator ultimately abandoned the above formula and, in addition to the provision of Article 226^2 of the CCP, which is an explicit reaction to the abuse of procedural rights by a party, introduced a series of other specific sanctions aimed at disciplining litigants.

Since a party who abuses procedural rights can in principle only be fined or ordered to pay the costs of the proceedings by the court – and this can only be imposed in the final judgment – the question arises whether this institution can really influence the efficiency of the proceedings if the instruments provided to counter abuse of procedural rights can only be applied at the end of the proceedings. It seems that this institution could have a much greater impact on the parties

---

491 G. Kamiński, *Zakaz nadużycia praw procesowych*, Warsaw 2021, p. 72.

492 K. Weitz, *Nadużycie „prawa" procesowego cywilnego*, Polski Proces Cywilny 2020/1, p. 17.

493 A. Jakubecki, *Sankcje za nadużycie uprawnień procesowych w Kodeksie postępowania cywilnego*, Palestra 2019/11–12, p. 196.

494 M. Manowska, [in:] *Kodeks postępowania cywilnego. Komentarz. Tom I*, M. Manowska (ed.), Warsaw 2021, pp. 49–50.

495 G. Kamiński, *Zakaz nadużycia...*, p. 114.

if the court were empowered to impose sanctions for abuse of procedural rights at any stage of the proceedings.

Among the instruments designed to counteract the prolongation of proceedings by the parties as a result of their dishonest or disloyal conduct, other sanctions of a pecuniary nature may also be mentioned, e.g. Article 103 of the CCP, which allows a party to be ordered to pay the costs caused by his negligent or manifestly improper conduct, Article 214 of the CCP, which provides the basis for the imposition of a fine on a party who has pleaded in bad faith untrue circumstances which have led to the adjournment of the hearing, or, finally, Article 255 of the CCP, concerning a fine for the reckless submission of allegations concerning the authenticity of a document.

The legislator has also introduced a number of specific solutions which make it possible to disregard actions taken in bad faith. Such instruments include provisions that order the dismissal of a subsequent application to recuse a judge on the same grounds (Article 53^1 of the CCP), a repeated application for free legal aid (Article 117^2 of the CCP), an application to rectify a judgment submitted for the sole purpose of delaying the proceedings (Article 350^1 of the CCP) or a complaint lodged for the sole purpose of delaying the proceedings (Article 394^3 of the CCP).

The principle of promptness of proceedings is also implemented in the provisions of the Code of Civil Procedure on the procedure of taking evidence. A significant part of the provisions of the CCP concerning the course of evidence proceedings, including the new provisions introduced by the 2019 amendment, concerns streamlining and ensuring a reasonable pace of evidence proceedings[496]. The reduction of the scope of the evidentiary procedure, which is intended to lead to its acceleration, is served by the provisions of Article 210 § 2 of the CCP and Article 230 of the CCP. Pursuant to the first of these provisions, each party is obliged to submit a response to the other party's statement of facts. The party must also state the facts that are in dispute. This provision corresponds to Article 127 § 1 of the CCP, which requires a party to state in a pre-trial brief the facts which it admits and those which it denies. In turn, Article 230 of the CCP provides for a sanction for failure to comply with the above obligation, in the form of deeming undenied facts to be admitted (and thus not requiring any proof at all, Article 229 of the CCP). The explanatory memorandum to the draft of 2019 amendment states that the above provisions are intended to counteract the unjustified expansion of the scope of the evidentiary proceedings, which constitutes a procedural obstacle. Until now, there has been a practice of 'blanket' denial of all arguments of the opponent, except for those expressly admitted, which consequently led to a widening of the scope of facts subject to evidentiary proceedings[497]. The legislator

496 P. Gil, [in:] *Regulacje służące usprawnieniu cywilnego postępowania rozpoznawczego*, I. Gil (ed.), Warsaw 2020, p. 146.

497 Explanatory Memorandum to the Government's Bill on Amendments to the Civil Procedure Code and Certain Other Acts, Parliamentary Paper No. 3137, p. 53.

places the burden on the parties to define precisely which facts in dispute are to be covered by the evidentiary procedure, which presumably has the effect of reducing its duration. However, it is not only the parties who are obliged to ensure that the taking of evidence relates only to facts which are relevant to the case. The court also has appropriate means at its disposal to disregard evidence which is intended to prove an undisputed or irrelevant fact (Art. 235^2 § 1 of the CCP, which does not serve to prove a given fact (point 3), which only serves to prolong the proceedings (point 5), or which does not comply with the requirements of Article 235^1 of the CCP (point 6), which obliges a party to designate evidence in such a way that it can be taken and to specify the facts to be proved).

The activation of the parties in the course of evidentiary proceedings and, at the same time, the implementation of the postulate of cooperation between the court and the parties resulting from Article 6 § 2 of the Code of Civil Procedure is served by the provision of Article 242^1 of the Code of Civil Procedure, according to which a party who has requested that a witness, expert or other person be summoned to a hearing shall make efforts to ensure that said person appears at the appointed time and place and, in particular, shall notify them of the obligation to appear. The explanatory memorandum to the draft of 2019 amendment indicates that this provision makes the party jointly responsible for the proper conduct of the taking of evidence. The purpose of the provision, which does not provide for a formal sanction for failure to comply with the obligation, is to shape the appropriate attitude of the parties, who, together with the court, should cooperate in ensuring the efficient conduct of the proceedings[498]. It is pointed out, however, that the provision of Article 242^1 of the CCP must be understood in such a way that a party's failure to comply with its obligations may be sanctioned as an act aimed at prolonging the proceedings, e.g. under Article 103 of the CCP[499]. It also appears that the court could disregard witness evidence if a party deliberately fails to comply with its obligations under Article 242^1 CCP. The basis for such action would then be Article 235^2 § 1 point 5 of the CCP, which relates to evidence intended to prolong proceedings.

Another manifestation of the principle of promptness in the evidentiary phase of the proceedings is the possibility, provided for in Article 242 of the CCP, for the court to set a time limit after which evidence may be taken only if it does not cause further delay in the proceedings. Its application is subject to a finding that circumstances have come to light which create 'obstacles of undetermined duration' to the taking of evidence. This mechanism is intended to discipline the parties and is a measure against the protraction of proceedings. This provision is

498 *Ibid*, pp. 55–56.

499 K. Górski, [in:] *Kodeks postępowania cywilnego. Komentarz. Tom I*, T. Szanciło (ed.), Warsaw 2019, p. 931.

an option and not an obligation for the court, but it should be borne in mind that it is for the court to organise the proceedings in such a way as to ensure the right of the parties to be heard without undue delay[500]. This provision should be applied in accordance with its purpose, which is to ensure the efficiency of the proceedings, and not, for example, because of the complexity of the evidence or considerations of procedural economy.

The principle expressed in Article 6 of the CCP is implemented by the provision introduced by the Act of 10 July 2015 amending the Civil Code, the Code of Civil Procedure and certain other acts[501], and concerning the possibility of hearing the case *in camera* (Article 148^1 of the CCP). According to the intention of the legislator, this provision should contribute to the streamlining of proceedings in cases where the court deems it unnecessary to hold a trial[502]. Acceleration of proceedings is also served by the principle introduced by the 2019 amendment, expressed in Article 148 § 3 of the Code of Civil Procedure, that court orders may be issued by the court in closed session. However, as both provisions are part of the implementation of the principle of promptness and constitute an important exception to the principle of openness of proceedings, they will also be analysed in the next part of the chapter.

The analysis of the above-mentioned provisions of the Code leads to the conclusion that the legislator has recognised the problem of the excessive length of proceedings and, in response, has introduced a number of solutions aimed at expediting the proceedings before the courts. A special effort of the legislator in this area can be seen in the amendment to the Code of Civil Procedure of 2019, which introduces a number of mechanisms discussed above, such as: a general prohibition of the abuse of procedural rights and a simplified procedure for such abuse, the introduction of the preparatory phase of the proceedings and the concentration of evidence, the strengthening of the leading role of the presiding judge, especially in the aspect of the preparatory phase of the trial[503]. Due to the large number of provisions in the Code of Civil Procedure aimed at implementing the principle of expediency, a detailed discussion of each of them would be difficult and would go beyond the scope of this work. The main institutions aimed at accelerating court proceedings have been discussed above.

---

500 A. Łazarska, [in:] *Kodeks postępowania cywilnego. Komentarz. Tom I,* T. Szanciło (ed.), Warsaw 2019, p. 930

501 Journal of Laws 2015, item 1311.

502 H. Sarżyński, *Zmiany w art. 148^1 k.p.c. jako środek przyspieszający postępowanie, kosztem zasady jawności i kontradyktoryjności,* [in:] *Postępowanie cywilne w dobie przemianności,* Warsaw 2017, p. 299.

503 N. Boluk, B. Karolczyk, [in:] *Postępowanie cywilne po nowelizacji,* B. Karolczyk (ed.), Warsaw 2020, pp. 31–32.

4.4. Principle of openness of proceedings

The principle of openness is enshrined in Article 42 § 2 and 3 of the Act of 27 July 2001 – Law on the Organisation of Common Courts[504], which stipulates that the courts shall hear and decide cases in open proceedings, and that the hearing of a case in closed proceedings or the exclusion of openness is permitted only in accordance with the provisions of a statute. The principle of openness of proceedings, both in its external and internal aspects, is directly expressed in Article 9 of the Code of Civil Procedure. According to the wording of § 1 of this article, 'except as otherwise provided by a specific regulation, cases shall be heard in open court. The parties and participants in the proceedings shall have the right to inspect the case file and to obtain copies, duplicates or extracts thereof'.

At this point, it should be recalled that the principle of external openness, also referred to as the public nature of the proceedings, means openness to third parties (including representatives of the mass media) who are not active participants in the proceedings, but only passive observers[505]. Internal openness, on the other hand, refers to the openness of the process towards the parties and participants in the proceedings[506].

The basic manifestation of external openness is the possibility for the public and media representatives to attend court hearings. Hearings, both in trials and in other proceedings governed by the Code of Civil Procedure, are divided into public and closed hearings. In turn, public hearings are divided into hearings for the substantive determination of the case (trial) and other hearings for the performance of procedural acts, such as the taking of evidence before the summoned court (Article 238 of the CCP). Closed hearings usually concern formal and ancillary matters[507]. The Supreme Court, in its ruling of 26 January 2012[508] has indicated otherwise, accepting that in non-contentious proceedings there is no category of public hearings and that the court may hear the case either in a trial or in a closed session. In the opinion of the Supreme Court, the 'hearing of the participants in a court session' referred to in Article 514 of the CCP should be understood as an *in camera* session, because the way to speed up and simplify the proceedings in the absence of a hearing – which is clearly the purpose of the introduction of this provision – cannot be to hold an open session, which is practically no different from a trial. The above position is criticised by K. Górniak, who points out that there are no grounds for the proposed interpretation of Article 514 of the CCP. In non-contentious proceedings, the principle of openness applies to the same extent as in contentious proceedings, and therefore it should be assumed that despite the

504 Journal of Laws 2020, item 2072 (consolidated text).
505 A. Kościółek, *Zasada jawności...*, p. 164.
506 A. Kościółek, *Zasada jawności...*, p. 321.
507 H. Pietrzkowski, *Metodyka pracy sędziego...*, p. 451.
508 Resolution of the Supreme Court of 26 January 2012, III CZP 83/11, LEX No. 1102775.

fact that a hearing has not been convened, the court may take measures in an open session[509]. An example of the court acting in open session in a non-contentious procedure (but not a trial) is the procedure for the opening and announcement of a last will and testament (Article 649 of the CCP)[510].

According to Article 148 § 1 of the CCP, in the absence of a specific regulation to the contrary, hearings shall be held in open court and cases shall be heard in a trial. On the other hand, the court may refer a case to an open court and schedule a trial even if the case should be heard *in camera* (Article 148 § 2 of the CCP).

In non-contentious proceedings, unlike in contradictory cases, the rule is that cases are heard without a public hearing being scheduled. According to Article 514 § 1 of the Code of Civil Procedure, hearings shall be held whenever the law so provides. Otherwise, hearings may be scheduled whenever the court considers it appropriate in the circumstances. A compulsory hearing is provided for, for example, in Article 555 of the CCP (in cases of incapacity) or in Article 669 of the CCP (in cases of declaration of inheritance).

Prior to the entry into force of the 2019 amendment, the rule in contradictory cases was that the case was heard in open court, while closed hearings could only be held in cases provided for by special provisions (e.g. when it was necessary to reject a claim – Article 199 § 3 of the CCP, to transfer a case to a court of competent jurisdiction – Article 200 § 1 of the CCP, or in incidental matters, e.g. to impose a fine – Article 123 of the CCP). As a result of the above-mentioned amendment, Article 148 § 3 of the CCP has been added, according to which the court may take a decision (order) in a closed session. This provision applies to any decision, including order on the merits[511], unless a specific provision provides for the case to be heard in public.

Another exception to the principle of a public hearing of the case is provided for in Article 148^1 of the CCP (the provision entered into force on 8 September 2016), which allows a judgment to be rendered in a closed session if the defendant has admitted the claim or if, after the parties have filed pleadings and documents, including the filing of charges or objections to the order for payment or objections to a default judgment, the court, taking into account the sum of the arguments and evidence presented, finds that it is not necessary to hold a trial. At the same time, the legislator has stipulated in § 3 of the said article (in the version in force as of 1 July 2023) that the examination of the case in closed session is inadmissible if in the first pleading a party has requested to be heard in person at the trial or a special regulation provides for such an obligation, unless the defendant has acknowledged the claim. Previously, it was sufficient for a party to request a trial in the first

509 K. Górniak, *Jawność posiedzeń sądowych w postępowaniu nieprocesowym*, Przegląd Sądowy 2017/11–12, pp. 63–64.

510 T. Żyznowski, [in:] *Kodeks postępowania cywilnego. Komentarz. Tom I*, T. Wisniewski (ed.), Warsaw 2021, p. 575.

511 I. Gromska-Szuster, [in:] *Kodeks postępowania cywilnego…*, p. 658.

pleading. At present a party has to request to be heard. The above provision does not apply in simplified proceedings where the value of the claim does not exceed PLN 4,000. In such cases, a judgment may be rendered in closed session regardless of the parties' request (Article 505^{1a} of the CCP).

The appeal procedure also provides for the possibility of hearing the case *in camera*. According to the wording of Article 374 of the CCP, the court of second instance may examine a case *in camera* if a trial is not necessary. The examination of a case *in camera* is inadmissible if a party has requested a hearing in the complaint or in the response to the complaint, unless the complaint or the complaint has been withdrawn or the case has been rendered invalid.

The above provisions reflect a certain tendency on the part of the legislator to move away from the principle of the oral nature of proceedings[512]. The oral nature of the procedure is directly linked to the principle of openness[513]. Thus, the changes introduced will gradually lead to the abolition of the external openness of many court proceedings[514]. In this context, a further correlation can be observed. Where the legislator has departed from the principle of openness, it has done so in most cases with the aim of streamlining the procedure. Thus, in many cases, such as Article 148^1 of the CCP, the implementation of the principle of openness of proceedings gives way to the demand for acceleration of proceedings.

The rules governing access to court hearings are set out in Article 152 of the CCP. In principle, all persons of age have access to the courtroom. The provision introduces the additional condition that they must not be armed. However, the age requirement does not apply to participants in the proceedings (parties, interveners, legal representatives, lawyers and summoned persons), but only to members of the public who wish to attend the court session. However, this age requirement is not absolute, as the presiding judge may allow minors to attend the court session. The right of public access to court hearings applies only to public sessions (i.e. trials and other public hearings), while access to closed sessions is granted only to persons who have been summoned (Article 152 § 4 of the CCP). It follows from the above that the hearing of a case in closed session constitutes a significant limitation of openness, both externally and internally. This is because, as a rule, the participants in the proceedings are not allowed to enter the closed session of the court.

A further restriction on the openness of proceedings is the provision contained in Article 152 § 4 of the CCP, according to which persons who are in a condition incompatible with the dignity of the court may not be present at the court's proceedings. The term 'incompatible with the dignity of the court' has not been defined by the legislator, but it should be assumed that it refers primarily to persons who are under the influence of alcohol or other drugs with similar effects, as

512 M. Dziurda, *Czy nadchodzi zmierzch zasady ustności w postępowaniu cywilnym?*, Polski Proces Cywilny 2022/1, p. 136.

513 A. Łazarska, *Rzetelny proces...*, p. 351.

514 I. Gromska-Szuster, [in:] *Kodeks postępowania cywilnego...*, p. 659.

well as to persons whose clothing is untidy or incomplete. The provision applies not only to members of the public but also to participants in the proceedings[515]. The possibility of excluding the public or participants in the proceedings from the courtroom, which has a direct bearing on the realisation of the openness of the proceedings, is provided for in Article 48 of the Law on the Organisation of Common Courts. Pursuant to § 2 of the aforementioned Article, the court may exclude a person from participating in the proceedings. However, the provision introduces an additional condition, according to which the participant in the proceedings must be informed in advance of the legal consequences of his absence from court proceedings. Paragraph 3, on the other hand, allows the public to be removed from the courtroom for misbehaviour. Obviously, the removal of the public or participants in the proceedings from the courtroom constitutes a permissible interference with the principle of openness, without infringing the constitutional right to court, since this serves to protect other values, e.g. the authority and integrity of the courtroom[516]. However, this power should only be exercised by the presiding judge and the court when it is necessary and aimed at genuinely protecting the stated values.

An additional guarantee of the openness of the proceedings is the obligation to draw up a record of the public hearing, which is usually made by means of an audio and video recording device (Article 157 of the CCP). Parties and participants in the proceedings have the right to receive a video and audio recording, unless there is an important public or private interest to the contrary (Article 9 § 2 of the CCP). Thus, even if a party did not attend the public hearing, they have the right to receive the recording, thus obtaining knowledge of the proceedings.

The rules for excluding public hearings are contained in Article 153 of the Code of Civil Procedure. The court shall, acting *ex officio*, order that all or part of a hearing be held *in camera* if the public hearing of the case threatens: 1) public order; 2) good morals; or 3) if protected classified information is likely to be disclosed. In addition, at the request of a party, the public hearing of the case may be excluded if: 1) circumstances constituting a trade secret may be disclosed, 2) if the reasons given by the party are considered justified by the court, 3) if details of family life are to be discussed.

Comparing the list of grounds justifying the exclusion of public hearings with the content of the provision of Article 6(1), second sentence, of the ECHR, which also contains grounds for the exclusion of public hearings before the court, it should be noted that the first two grounds of Article 153 of the CCP (public order and morality) are also mentioned in the cited provision of the Convention. The ground of 'protection of classified information', on the other hand, seems to

---

515 E. Stefańska, [in:] *Kodeks postępowania cywilnego. Komentarz. Tom I,* M. Manowska (ed.), Warsaw 2021, pp. 538–539.

516 J. Kremer, [in:] *Prawo o ustroju sądów powszechnych. Komentarz,* A. Górski (ed.), Warsaw 2013, p. 210.

correspond to 'state security in a democratic society'. The cases in which classified information is given a special security classification are indicated in Article 5 of the Law of 5 August 2010 on the Protection of Classified Information[517]. This provision mainly concerns information, the disclosure of which may endanger internal security, defence, the constitutional order of the Republic of Poland, public officials or state witnesses, disrupt the functioning of state bodies or seriously endanger the economic interests of the Republic of Poland.

When analysing the grounds contained in Article 153 of the CCP for excluding the public from a hearing at the request of a party, it should be noted that the Code's 'disclosure of a party's family life' falls within the premise of 'protection of a party's private life', which derives from both the European Convention on Human Rights and the Polish Constitution. However, two other prerequisites, i.e. the protection of trade secrets and 'legitimate reasons of a party', may raise doubts as to the implementation of the constitutional and European standard.

The legal definition of a trade secret is contained in Article 11(2) of the Act of 16 April 1993 on Unfair Competition[518]. According to this provision, a trade secret is understood to be technical, technological, organisational information of the company or other information having economic value, which, as a whole or in a particular context and collection of its elements, is not generally known or easily accessible to persons who normally handle this type of information, provided that the person authorised to use or dispose of the information has taken measures with due diligence to keep it confidential.

While it can be assumed that the need to protect trade secrets falls within the category of 'other important private interests' referred to in Article 45(2) of the Constitution[519], the problem arises as to how to qualify the protection of business secrets on the basis of the second sentence of Article 6(1) of the ECHR. The quoted provision of the Convention allows for the exclusion of disclosure, inter alia, 'in special circumstances, to the extent deemed absolutely necessary by the court, where disclosure would be prejudicial to the interests of justice'. There is no doubt in principle that the need to protect an important trade interest may constitute a 'special circumstance' allowing the court to decide *in camera* that disclosure is necessary. The question, however, is whether in such a case the condition of counteracting an impairment of the interests of justice is met. The interest of justice is a general clause with a vague meaning. The term 'interest' is defined as 'benefit, advantage'. In turn, the term 'administration of justice' means the totality of the court's procedural activities carried out in the public interest[520]. The interest of the administration of justice will therefore refer to a certain benefit to be derived from it. Obviously, it is not the benefit as such that is at stake, but rather the fulfilment,

517 Journal of Laws 2019, item 742 (consolidated text).
518 Journal of Laws 2020, item 1913 (consolidated text).
519 A. Kościółek, *Zasada jawności...*, pp. 528–529.
520 Resolution of the Supreme Court of 27 September 1980, U 1/80, LEX No. 19661.

understood in the abstract, of the objective set for the administration of justice, and thus, in simple terms, the delivery of a judgment in accordance with the actual circumstances, under the conditions of its proper functioning. The concept of the 'interest of justice' is similar to the concept of the 'welfare of justice' used in the CCP, which S. Kotas-Turoboyska defines as the effort to ensure the proper legitimacy of the court in the perception of the public and in the assessment of the parties to the proceedings, thus building prestige and trust in the administration of justice[521]. From the point of view of achieving the objectives of the proceedings, the search for the material truth is important. This requires that the parties disclose information about the facts of the case truthfully and without concealing any facts (Article 3 of the CCP). However, in the course of the proceedings, a party may fear disclosure of a trade secret and wish to protect it from unauthorised use. Therefore, they may refuse to disclose to the court circumstances relevant to the resolution of the case, the disclosure of which would jeopardise the trade secret. It is in the interest of justice for a party to disclose the necessary facts to enable a proper decision to be made in the case, but this will be hindered if the party fears that its trade secrets will be disclosed to third parties. The court's search for the truth therefore justifies the protection of trade secrets. It is unacceptable for the conduct of the proceedings before the court to cause prejudice to one of the parties. From this point of view, it is also in the interest of justice to protect a legitimate private interest. Furthermore, the disclosure of trade secrets could lead to a loss of confidence in the judiciary and thus harm it.

It should also be noted that there is no particular justification for subjecting trade secrets to public scrutiny. The exclusion of publicity of the proceedings, to the extent that trade secrets may be disclosed, therefore appears to be a proportionate restriction that does not violate the essence of the right to publicity of proceedings. Consequently, the assessment that Article 153 § 1^1 of the CCP does not violate the Convention right to a public hearing guaranteed by Article 6(1) of the ECHR should be accepted.

Notwithstanding the above, it should be recalled that the mere fact that there is material of a confidential nature in the file does not automatically justify the closure of the entire trial to the public[522]. Exclusion of the public should only take place when it is necessary to protect other values. The openness of the proceedings should therefore be limited only to the extent that the examination of the case concerns sensitive issues (it may be sufficient, for example, to limit access to the file or to exclude the public only partially from the hearing).

---

521 S. Kotas-Turoboyska, *Pojęcie dobra wymiaru sprawiedliwości w rozumieniu art. 44^1 k.p.c.*, [in:] *Rozstrzyganie spraw cywilnych. Aktualne wyzwania i perspektywy*, M. Białecki, S. Kotas-Turoboyska, F. Manikowski, J. Słyk, E. Szczepanowska (eds.), Warsaw 2022, p. 204.

522 M. A. Nowicki, *Wokół Konwencji* ..., p. 710.

Secondly, it is necessary to refer to the requirement of a 'legitimate reason stated by a party' laid down in Article 153 § 2 of the CCP. This provision is not mentioned in the Convention or in the Constitution. When deciding whether the reason given by a party is justified, the court must take into account the provisions that are higher in the structure of legal sources, i.e. acts of international law and the Constitution. Therefore, when assessing whether it is permissible to exclude publicity of the proceedings at the request of a party, the court should consider as justified only such reasons which fall within the catalogue of premises set out in the second sentence of Article 6(1) of the ECHR and Article 45(2) of the Constitution. Only such an understanding of the provision of Article 153 § 2 of the CCP will not raise doubts as to its constitutionality (and compliance with the Convention)[523]. However, since the 'justifiable reasons' in Article 153 § 2 of the CCP must be interpreted through the prism of the requirements contained in the Convention and the Constitution, the question arises as to the meaning of this basis for the exclusion of publicity in the CCP. The Constitution, in Article 45(2), provides for the exclusion of publicity on the grounds of morality, state security and public order, as well as on the grounds of the protection of the private life of the parties or an important private interest. The first four grounds are expressly repeated in Article 153 of the CCP. Only 'important private interest' is not explicitly mentioned in the provisions of the Code of Civil Procedure. It therefore appears that legitimate reasons invoked by a party can only refer to 'important private interest'. The wording used in Article 153 § 2 of the CCP is, to say the least, unfortunate. A much better approach would be to simply repeat the wording used by the legislator in Article 45(2) of the Constitution. In that case, there would be no room for interpreting a provision of statutory rank in contradiction with the Constitution of the Republic of Poland.

The openness of judicial proceedings is not limited to the openness of the hearings, but also concerns the openness of the examination of the case, which means that the parties and, to a limited extent, other persons have the right to obtain information about the proceedings. In this context, the most important manifestation of the openness of proceedings is the right of access to the case file[524]. The general rule governing access to the case file is contained in Article 9 of the CCP, § 1 of which provides that the parties and participants in the proceedings have the right to inspect the case file and to obtain copies, duplicates or extracts thereof. In non-contentious proceedings, the matter is governed by Article 525 of the CCP, according to which the case file is accessible to the participants in the proceedings and, with the consent of the presiding judge, to anyone who sufficiently justifies the need to inspect the file. Under the same rules, it is possible to make and receive copies and extracts from the file and to receive audio and video

523 A. Kościółek, *Zasada jawności...*, p. 529.
524 A. Kościółek, *Zasada jawności...*, p. 332.

recordings. In non-contentious proceedings, due to their specific nature, the circle of persons entitled to inspect the file is wider. In the case of a contentious proceedings, in principle only the parties to the proceedings are entitled to access the case file.

The rules governing the inspection of files and the obtaining of documents from them are governed by the provisions of Articles 126 et seq. of the Regulation on the Rules of Procedure of Common Courts[525]. The persons referred to in Articles 9 and 525 of the CCP have the right to inspect the file and photograph it (§ 129), as well as to examine the image or sound recording of a hearing or other act of the court (§ 130). It is also possible to send the file to the district court competent for the place of residence of the party, in order to facilitate the inspection of the file and the making of copies (§ 136(1)). Access to the file by a party in custody is also provided for by ordering that the file be sent to the relevant prison or detention centre (§ 136 (2)).

A party interested in obtaining information on the progress of proceedings does not always have to seek direct access to the case file in the courthouse. The principles of providing access to information on cases are regulated by the provisions of § 123 et seq. of the Regulation on the Rules of Procedure of Common Courts. Pursuant to § 123, court clerks shall, as a rule, provide interested parties by telephone with information on the date and manner of resolution of the case, identical to that contained in the court docket. In addition, a party or any other participant in the proceedings may obtain information on the progress of the proceedings by electronic means, without the necessity of appearing in person at the court, after fulfilling the conditions set forth in § 124(1) of the Regulation concerning the requirement of identification.

A further reinforcement of the internal openness of the procedure, in terms of access to information on the progress of the case, is the Information Portal, an ICT system for access to information on the progress of the case, through which a party can access data such as: the progress of the case, actions taken by the court, dates of scheduled hearings, documents generated by the court in electronic form[526]. Pursuant to § 132 of the Regulation, it may provide access to data on the case, the content of the minutes, court and procedural documents for parties, participants and their representatives and attorneys through accounts in the ICT system. The purpose of the Information Portal is to improve access to the case, including information on the status of the case, actions taken, and the content of documents issued by the courts. Thus, through this system, the right of access

525 Ordinance of the Minister of Justice of 18 June 2019 Rules of Procedure of Common Courts, Journal of Laws 2021, item 2046 (consolidated text).

526 S. Kotecka-Kral, *Informatyzacja działalności korporacji prawniczych na przykładzie postępowania cywilnego,* [in:] *Prawo nowych technologii*, K. Flaga-Gieruszyńska, J. Gołaczyński (eds.), Warsaw 2021, p. 213.

to information on the case provided for in Article 9 of the CCP is implemented. A very important functionality of the Portal is the e-Protocol module, thanks to which a party can access the minutes of the hearing recorded by means of video and audio recording[527]. A party not present at the hearing can thus follow the proceedings in detail. It should also be noted that the functioning of the Information Portal not only contributes to the implementation of the principle of (internal) openness, but also affects the efficiency of the procedure, since it makes it possible to quickly obtain important information on the progress of the proceedings instead of using traditional (and more time-consuming) methods of communication with the court[528].

External openness in the conduct of proceedings is ensured by the court docket, which provides basic information about the case[529]. The court docket is a list of the hearings scheduled for a given day. The scope of the information to be provided on the cause sheet is specified in § 93 the Regulation. The docket contains the names of the judges and lay judges, the file numbers of the cases scheduled to be heard on a given day, an indication of the hours at which the cases are scheduled, the names and surnames, the names or company names of the parties or participants in non-contentious proceedings. Where witnesses, experts or interpreters are summoned to a hearing or a hearing, their names and the time of the hearing or hearing shall be indicated on the docket. The information contained in the docket may be subject to the restrictions listed in § 93(3) and (4) of the Regulation. This is the procedure in cases involving the custody of minors which are heard *in camera*, in which case the data of the minor shall not be included in the docket. The president of the court division, or the presiding judge may also decide not to disclose the names of the parties or of the persons summoned for reasons of protection of morals, national security or public order, or for reasons of protection of private life or other important private interests. Also, the docket published on the website of the court does not contain any personal data (§ 94(2) of the Regulation).

Since court hearings are a manifestation of the implementation of the principle of openness, the question arises as to whether restrictions on the openness of proceedings should be regulated by an act of sub-statutory rank (i.e. in the Regulation)[530]. It seems doubtful whether, in the light of Article 31(3) of the Constitution, it is permissible to regulate this issue by means of an ordinance of the Minister of Justice, since restrictions on the exercise of constitutional freedoms and rights may be established only by statute.

---

527 T. Januszkiewicz, [in:] *Jawność i jej ograniczenia. Tom VIII. Postępowania sądowe*, J. Gołaczyński, G. Szpor (eds.), Warsaw 2015, p. 211.

528 S. Kotecka, [in:] *Jawność i jej ograniczenia. Tom VIII. Postępowania sądowe*, J. Gołaczyński, G. Szpor (eds.), Warsaw 2015, pp. 42–43.

529 A. Kościółek, *Zasada jawności...*, p. 218.

530 A. Kościółek, *Zasada jawności...*, p. 218.

In addition to the principle of the openness of court proceedings, and public access to the case, the constitutional and Convention standard also includes the principle of the public announcement of court judgments. In accordance with the CCP, the principle of public announcement of judgments is provided for in Article 326 § 2 and 3 of the CCP, which stipulates that the announcement of a judgment shall be made at a public hearing and by reading out the operative part of the judgment. Following the announcement of the judgment, the presiding judge or the reporting judge shall orally state the main reasons for the decision or announce a full statement of reasons.

There are different opinions in civil procedure theory as to what is to be understood by the 'announcement of a judgment'. On the one hand, the literal content of the provision of Article 326 § 3 of the CCP is referred to, and it is argued that the announcement relates only to the operative part of the judgment, whereas the oral announcement of the reasons for the decision is a separate activity of a subsequent nature. The opposite view considers that the act of announcing the judgment consists, firstly, in reading the operative part of the judgment and, secondly, in giving reasons for the judgment[531]. The second position is shared by the Supreme Court[532], which explicitly states that the main reasons for the decision are part of the announcement of the judgment. This position should be upheld, as it is in line with the case law of the ECHR, which, as already indicated in the previous considerations, has pointed out that the obligation to announce the judgment should also include a statement of reasons for the decision, and that the mere reading of the operative part of the judgment is not sufficient to comply with the principle of publicity[533].

The Code of Civil Procedure provides for exceptions to the principle of public notification of judgments. The first of these follows from the content of Article 326 § 4 of the CCP, according to which the reading of the operative part and the statement of the essential reasons for the decision may be dispensed with if no one (including the public) appears at the announcement of the judgment. The waiver of the public announcement of the judgment in the present case does not give rise to any doubts. Since the parties and members of the public did not appear at the announcement of the judgment, there can be no question of a violation of their right to a public hearing in this case. However, the above observation remains valid in so far as the parties were objectively able to attend the hearing scheduled for the announcement of the decision, the basic condition for which was the possibility of being informed of the time and place of the announcement of the judgment. Pursuant to Article 326 § 2 of the CCP, the absence of the parties does not prevent

531 A. Kościółek, *Zasada jawności...*, pp. 302–303.
532 Resolution of the Supreme Court of 22 February 2007, III CZP 160/06, LEX No. 224581.
533 Judgment of the European Court of Human Rights of 17 January 2008, Application No. 14810/02.

the announcement of the judgment. If the judgment is announced immediately after the hearing is closed (Article 326 § 1 of the CCP), i.e. at the same session at which the hearing was closed and the date of which was notified to the party, it should be assumed that the party was given the opportunity to participate in the announcement of the judgment. In such a case, the party was informed of the date of the hearing and could therefore expect that the announcement of the judgment might take place. Doubts may arise, however, if a party did not attend the session at which the hearing was closed and the court, pursuant to Article 326 § 1 of the CCP, postponed the announcement of the judgment to another date. In such a case, the court does not notify the absent party of the date of the hearing by means of a written summons, even if the date of the announcement of the judgment has been postponed further[534]. It can be assumed that a party who deliberately withdraws from the hearing should take into account that the trial may be closed and the announcement of the decision may be postponed to another date. It is also important that a party interested in the progress of the case can easily obtain information about the planned date of publication of the judgment.

A permissible exception to the public announcement of the decision, but only with regard to the statement of reasons for the decision, is provided for in Article 326 § 3 of the CCP, which allows an exception to the announcement of the reasons for the decision in a case that has been heard behind closed doors. In such a case, however, it is not possible to refrain from reading the operative part of the judgment itself.

By their very nature, cases decided in closed session (e.g. pursuant to Article 148^1 of the CCP or in the case of a default judgment – Article 339 § 1 of the CCP) are not subject to public announcement of the judgment. In such cases, the provisions of the CCP do not provide for a public hearing to announce the judgment. However, as a general rule, the court shall *ex officio* notify all parties of a judgment rendered *in camera* (Article 327 § 3 of the CCP and Article 343 § 1 of the CCP).

Pursuant to Article 357 § 2 of the CCP, the court shall also *ex officio* serve the parties with decisions taken in closed session, unless a special provision stipulates otherwise. An example of a special provision is Article 357 § 4 of the CCP, according to which decisions which exclusively concern other persons shall not be served on the parties. This applies, for example, to an order imposing a fine on a witness. Another example of a decision that is not served on all parties is a decision rejecting an application for security (under Article 740 § 1 of the CCP, it is served only on the applicant). Although both provisions are a certain manifestation of the limitation of the principle of openness towards the parties, their functions are fundamentally different. The former is concerned with the principles of procedural economy and the avoidance of service on the parties of orders which in no way

534 Judgment of the Supreme Court of 25 April 2008, II CSK 613/07, LEX No. 420867.

affect their rights and obligations. The purpose of Article 740 § 1 of the CCP, on the other hand, is to fulfil the function of the security and injunction procedure and to give the creditor a real possibility of enforcing the injunction. The fact that the obligor is informed of the injunction prior to its execution could affect its effectiveness[535] (the situation in which the court of appeal changes the decision of the court of first instance on the refusal to grant an injunction). Such a partial (temporary) restriction of the principle of publicity is thus aimed at protecting other values considered important by the legislator. In this case, it is the need to ensure the effective enforcement of the court's decision.

535 D. Zawistowski, [in:] *Kodeks Postępowania Cywilnego. Komentarz. Tom IV*, T. Wisniewski (ed.), Warsaw 2021, p. 78.

5. The COVID-19 pandemic as a premise for the limitation of civil rights and freedoms

5.1. Declaration of the state of epidemic and the state of epidemic threat on the territory of the Republic of Poland

The dynamic increase in the number of SARS-CoV-2 infections worldwide and the declaration of the COVID-19 pandemic by the World Health Organisation on 11 March 2020[536], as well as the first cases of the disease in Poland, have prompted public authorities to take measures to counter the spread of the coronavirus.

Accordingly, on the basis of the Ordinance of the Minister of Health of 13 March 2020[537], the state of epidemic threat was declared on the territory of the Republic of Poland as of 14 March 2020. Later, on 20 March 2020, by the Ordinance of the Minister of Health of 20 March 2020, the state of epidemic was declared on the territory of Poland[538]. The epidemic state was in force until 16 May 2022[539]. From 16 May 2022 to 1 July 2023 the state of epidemic threat was again declared[540].

The declaration of the state of epidemic and the epidemic threat throughout the country was based on Article 46(2) of the Act of 5 December 2008 on the Prevention and Control of Human Infections and Infectious Diseases[541] (the Epidemic Control Act). According to the wording of the above-mentioned provision, if an epidemic threat or an epidemic occurs in the territory of more than one voivodship, the Minister of Health, in agreement with the Minister of Public Administration, shall, on the proposal of the General Sanitary Inspector, issue an ordinance declaring an

536 P. Kowalski, [in:] *Pandemic COVID-19 a prawa i wolności obywateli*, T. Gardocka, D. Jagiełło (eds.), Warsaw 2020, p. 1.

537 Ordinance of the Minister of Health of 13 March 2020 on the declaration of the state of epidemic threat in the territory of the Republic of Poland, Journal of Laws of 2020, item 433.

538 Ordinance of the Minister of Health of 20 March 2020 on the declaration of the state of epidemic in the territory of the Republic of Poland, Journal of Laws of 2020, item 340.

539 Ordinance of the Minister of Health of 12 May 2022 on the revocation of the epidemic state in the territory of the Republic of Poland, Journal of Laws 2022, item 1027.

540 Ordinance of the Minister of Health of 12 May 2022 on the declaration of the state of epidemic threat in the territory of the Republic of Poland, Journal of Laws 2022, item 1028.

541 Journal of Laws 2022, item 1657 (consolidated text).

epidemic threat or an epidemic state. The legal definition of an epidemic state is set out in Article 2(22) of the Epidemic Control Act. An epidemic state is a legal situation introduced in a given area in connection with the outbreak of an epidemic in order to take anti-epidemic and preventive measures, as defined by law, to minimise the effects of the epidemic. A state of epidemic threat, on the other hand, is a legal situation introduced in a given area in connection with the risk of an epidemic in order to take the preventive measures laid down by law (Article 2(23) of the Epidemic Control Act).

The difference between the two states therefore comes down to whether there is an epidemic in the area or merely a risk of an epidemic. Furthermore, in a state of epidemic, measures are taken to minimise the effects of the epidemic, whereas in a state of epidemic threat measures are of a preventive nature. According to Article 2(9) of the Epidemic Control Act, an epidemic is to be understood as the occurrence of infections or outbreaks of infectious diseases in a given area in a significantly higher number than in the previous period, or the occurrence of infections or infectious diseases that were not previously present. It follows from the above definition that a 'significant' increase in the incidence of COVID-19 should lead to the cancellation of the state of epidemic threat and the introduction of a state of epidemic in its place. However, the legislator does not specify what is meant by a 'significant' increase or an 'earlier period', leaving it to the competent sanitary inspector to assess the need to apply for the declaration of a state of epidemic.

As L. Bosek points out, *de lege ferenda* the definition of an epidemic needs to be corrected, as the concept is too broad and covers both particularly dangerous mass outbreaks of serious infectious diseases and seasonal outbreaks (the definition includes, for example, seasonal influenza, which raises justified doubts)[542]. In the author's opinion, the objective indicator for the introduction or lifting of a state of epidemic should be the high mortality rate, not the contagiousness of the infectious disease itself. The absence of casualties in the long term should, in turn, lead to the lifting of the state of epidemic. From the definition of the epidemic state contained in Article 2(22) of the Epidemic Control Act, it is possible to derive the prohibition of a blanket declaration of the state of epidemic, as well as its non-cancellation in a situation where there are no factual grounds for assuming that the threat still exists[543]. The reason for this is that epidemic states are introduced in order to take measures against epidemics and to minimise the effects of an epidemic, so that the end of the risk should obviate the need for this special legal regime.

At the same time, the Epidemic Control Act does not provide clear guidelines for the lifting of the epidemic or epidemic threat status. In particular, the Act does not introduce an obligation to revoke the state of epidemic or epidemic threat, which raises fundamental doubts, as the discretion of the authority (the Minister

542 L. Bosek, *Stan epidemii. Konstrukcja prawna,* Warsaw 2022, p. 182.
543 L. Bosek, *Stan epidemii...*, pp. 184–185.

of Health or the Council of Ministers, which can also revoke the ordinance on the introduction of the state of epidemic on the basis of Article 149(2) of the Constitution) should be subject to clear legal limitations[544]. The Act also does not require that the duration of a state of epidemic or epidemic threat, with the possibility of its prolongation, be determined in advance.

It should also be noted that the state of epidemic and the state of epidemic threat are declared throughout the country by the Minister of Health at the request of the General Sanitary Inspector. The Minister of Health always acts upon a request and cannot declare an epidemic or an epidemic threat on his own initiative. However, the Minister of Health is not bound by the classification of a given situation by the General Sanitary Inspector[545]. The ordinance of the Minister of Health is issued in agreement with the Minister of Public Administration, which means that, in the context of administrative cooperation, the two bodies must agree on the content of the ordinance (agreement on the content of the normative act – § 74(1) of the Ordinance of the Prime Minister of 20 June 2002 on 'Principles of Legislative Techniques'[546]). The procedure for revoking a state of epidemic or epidemic threat is similar. The issuance of an ordinance by the Minister of Health requires, firstly, a request from the General Sanitary Inspector and, secondly, cooperation with the Minister of Public Administration.

As an aside, it should be noted that if an epidemic threat or epidemic occurs on the territory of only one voivodship, the voivode, upon the request of the Voivodship Sanitary Inspector, declares and revokes the epidemic threat or epidemic state by means of a decree (Article 46(1) of the Epidemic Control Act). If a state of epidemic affects the territory of more than one voivodship, two voivods may not simultaneously declare a state of epidemic or epidemic threat for the territory of each voivodship separately. In such a case, the Minister of Health shall have the exclusive power to issue an ordinance pursuant to Article 46(2) of the Act[547].

The declaration of the state of epidemic threat or the state of epidemic in the country authorises the Minister of Health, in accordance with Article 46(4) of the Epidemic Control Act to issue certain orders and prohibitions, including, for example, temporary restrictions on movement, the prohibition of public gatherings or the obligation to carry out preventive vaccinations. A similar authorisation for the Council of Ministers to issue specific orders and prohibitions in the event of the state of epidemic and epidemic threat is contained in Articles 46a and 46b of the Epidemic Control Act. At the same time, it was pointed out that such a

544 L. Bosek, *Stan epidemii...*, p. 203.

545 L. Bosek, [in:] *Ustawa o zapobieganiu oraz zwalczaniu zakażeń i chorób zakaźnych u ludzi. Komentarz.*, L. Bosek (ed.), commentary to Article 46, Nb 21, Legalis.

546 Journal of Laws of 2016, item 283 (consolidated text), hereinafter referred to as the 'Principles of Legislative Techniques'.

547 M. Radajewski, *Stan zagrożenia epidemicznego oraz stan epidemii jako formy prawne ochrony zdrowia publicznego,* Przegląd Legislacyjny 2021/4, p. 63.

blanket delegation constitutes a violation of Article 92(1) of the Constitution of the Republic of Poland and cannot be the basis for restricting civil rights and freedoms, which should be the domain of the statute[548]. It was also argued that although ordinances can be used to interfere with certain constitutional rights and freedoms, most of the restrictions adopted in relation to the COVID-19 pandemic did not have a sufficient legal basis[549].

The epidemic situation in the country required far-reaching changes to the legal system, including legislation other than that mentioned above. In fact, the existing legislation proved to be inadequate in the face of the COVID-19 pandemic. In the early days of the pandemic, significant shortcomings in the existing legal framework became apparent[550]. Of particular note is the Act of 2 March 2020 on Special Solutions Related to the Prevention and Control of COVID-19, Other Infectious Diseases and Crisis Situations Caused by Them[551] (the COVID-19 Special Act). The subject of the Act (Article 1(1)) is the principles and procedures for preventing and combating the SARS-CoV-2 virus infection and the spread of COVID-19 disease, the duties of public administration bodies in this respect, the rights and duties of providers and recipients of health care and other persons residing in the territory of the Republic of Poland, as well as the principles of covering the costs of the above tasks. In addition, the Act regulates a number of issues relevant to the conduct of civil proceedings in the event of an epidemic or the threat of an epidemic.

On 31 March 2020, the Law on Amendments to the Act on Special Solutions Related to the Prevention and Control of COVID-19, Other Infectious Diseases and Crisis Situations Caused by Them and Certain Other Acts was adopted[552]. This law, known as the Crisis Shield, introduced amendments to 64 laws, including the amendment of the COVID-19 Special Act[553]. The above-mentioned Act added, inter alia, Article 15zzs of the COVID-19 Special Act concerning the suspension of procedural and material time limits in court proceedings and Article 15zzu concerning the suspension of the execution of enforcement orders for the eviction of residential premises, which will be further considered in this work.

A further amendment to the COVID-19 Special Act took place within the framework of the so-called Crisis Shield 2.0.[554], i.e. the Act of 16 April 2020 on Specific Support Instruments in Connection with the Spread of the SARS-CoV-2 virus[555].

548 P. Tuleja, *Pandemia COVID-19 a konstytucyjne stany nadzwyczajne,* Palestra 2020/9, p. 14.
549 M. Radajewski, *Stan zagrożenia epidemicznego...*, pp. 74–75.
550 M. Radajewski, *Stan zagrożenia epidemicznego...*, p. 80.
551 Journal of Laws 2021, item 2095 (consolidated text), hereinafter also referred to as the 'COVID-19 Special Act'.
552 Journal of Laws 2020, item 568.
553 P. Kowalski, [in:] *Pandemia COVID-19...*, pp. 2–5.
554 P. Kowalski, [in:] *Pandemia COVID-19...*, p. 5.
555 Journal of Laws 2020, item 695.

Pursuant to Article 73(46) of this Act, the aforementioned Articles 15zzs and 15zzu of the COVID-19 Special Act were amended, as well as 60 other laws.

The so-called Crisis Shield 3.0, i.e. the Act of 14 May 2020 On Amendments of Certain Laws on Protective Measures in Connection with the sSpread of the SARS-CoV-2 virus[556] contained a new amendment to the COVID-19 Special Act. Under this Act, the provision of Article 15zzs was repealed (Art. 46(20)) and, inter alia, the following Articles were added (Article 46(21)): Article 15zzs[1] (concerning remote hearings and hearings *in camera*), Article 15zzs[2] (concerning closed hearings), Article 15zzs[3] (concerning hearings *in camera*). Pursuant to Article 2 of this Law, Article 952[1] § 5 of the Code of Civil Procedure was also added, which provides for the prohibition of holding public auctions of residential premises.

The COVID-19 Special Act was subsequently amended several times. From the point of view of the subject of this study, another significant amendment was the introduction of Article 15zzs[9] (the provision mainly concerned the service of court documents through the Information Portal) and a significant change in the wording of Article 15zzs[1], made pursuant to the Act of 28 May 2021 amending the Code of Civil Procedure and certain other acts[557].

In the academic debate, it has been argued that the series of special laws and other sub-statutory acts (from March to August 2020, 11 laws directly related to COVID-19, 9 Ordinances of the Minister of Health and 24 Ordinances of the Council of Ministers[558]) adopted in the era of the COVID-19 pandemic do not meet the standards of proper legislation, mainly due to the chaotic and vague nature of the regulations, the inclusion in these legal acts of some provisions that have no temporal or substantive link to the COVID-19 pandemic[559], and the frequent amendments that enter into force, often on the day of their announcement or a few hours after their announcement[560]. However, the main objections to the legislation during the pandemic related to the introduction of specific orders and prohibitions, often restricting fundamental individual rights and freedoms by regulation, on the basis of blanket authorisations contained in the amended articles 46a and 46b of the Epidemic Control Act[561]. As these restrictions mainly concerned movement bans, quarantine obligations or restrictions on business activities, the question of the legality of these provisions is beyond the scope of this study.

A number of objections were also raised against the COVID-19 Special Act. Among other things, it has been pointed out that in the successive explanatory memoranda to the draft, the legislator did not devote sufficient space to explaining

556 Journal of Laws 2020, item 875.
557 Journal of Laws 2021, item 1090.
558 H. Izdebski, [in:] *Pandemia COVID-19 a prawa i wolności obywatela*, T. Gardocka, D. Jagiełło (eds.), Warsaw 2020, pp. 32–33.
559 H. Izdebski, [in:] *Pandemia COVID-19...*, pp. 29–30.
560 H. Izdebski, [in:] *Pandemia COVID-19...*, p. 34.
561 S. Trociuk, *Prawa i wolności w stanie epidemii*, Warsaw 2021, pp. 15–16.

the application of alternative measures and to considering the impact of the provisions, which would have made it possible to choose more optimal solutions[562].

5.2. The principle of proportionality in the context of the timeframe of restrictions of the right to a fair in the era of the COVID-19 pandemic

It has been argued in judicial studies that the state of epidemic proclaimed on the territory of the Republic of Poland has the characteristics of a state of natural disaster within the meaning of Article 232 of the Polish Constitution. The Council of Ministers, by approving the state of epidemic declared by the Minister of Health's ordinance, deliberately refrained from formally introducing the state of natural disaster, considering that the available ordinary constitutional means would be sufficient to combat the pandemic[563]. It has been pointed out that the authorities are acting according to the rules provided for a state of emergency, but without its formal introduction[564]. P. Tuleja calls such a situation a 'hybrid state of emergency'[565]. M. Radajewski notes, however, that although the COVID-19 pandemic meets the definition of a natural disaster, it should be remembered that the measures to combat an infectious disease epidemic can only take the form of a constitutional state of emergency as a last resort, when ordinary constitutional measures are not sufficient. Under the conditions of the normal functioning of the State, the legislature has at its disposal specific institutions for the prevention and control of epidemics, namely the possibility of declaring a state of epidemic and a state of epidemic threat, which the Government decided to introduce instead of a state of natural disaster following the outbreak of the COVID-19 pandemic[566].

This choice of legal means to combat the epidemic establishes that extraordinary circumstances cannot be invoked to justify solutions that restrict individual rights and freedoms. Since ordinary constitutional measures were deemed sufficient, there is no justification for extraordinary restrictions on civil rights. Consequently, when deciding not to declare the constitutional state of emergency, the authorities must take into account the requirement laid down in Article 31(3) of the Constitution to introduce restrictions in the form of a statute, the need to comply with the principle of proportionality and the prohibition of infringing the essence of the rights and freedoms subject to restriction[567]. A similar view was

562 H. Izdebski, [in:] *Pandemia COVID-19...*, p. 46.
563 S. Trociuk, *Prawa i wolności...*, pp. 12–13.
564 S. Czarnow, *Między stanem epidemii a stanem klęski żywiołowej – COVID-19 a niektóre prawa człowieka*, Radca Prawny. Zeszyty Naukowe 2021/3, p. 13.
565 P. Tuleja, *Pandemia COVID-19 a konstytucyjne...*, p. 15.
566 M. Radajewski, [in:] *Pandemia COVID-19 a prawa i wolności obywatela*, T. Gardocka, D. Jagiełło (eds.), Warsaw 2020, p. 88.
567 S. Trociuk, *Prawa i wolności...*, pp. 12–13.

expressed by P. Tuleja, who argued that the absence of a declaration of a state of emergency meant that the authorities could not invoke the principle of proportionality of intervention to the degree of threat, which is derived from Article 228(5) of the Constitution, and were bound by the limitation clauses set out in Article 31(3)[568].

Pursuant to Article 31(3) of the Constitution of the Republic of Poland, restrictions on the exercise of constitutional freedoms and rights may be imposed only if they are necessary in a democratic state. Such limitations must be useful for achieving the objective pursued, be restrictive to the extent necessary and the benefits derived from them must be in proportion to the burdens imposed on citizens. Among the available means, the one that is least burdensome to the individual must be chosen, not the one that achieves the objective as quickly as possible[569].

As stated above, restrictions on the exercise of constitutional rights and freedoms can only be established by statute. This means that the law must determine the basic elements of the restriction of a given right or freedom. However, the above does not preclude the inclusion in a statue of an authorisation for the competent body to issue an ordinance regulating in detail certain issues relating to the restricted rights and freedoms. In this case, the completeness and detail of the statutory regulation must be considerably increased, while the ordinances should only regulate technical issues that are not of fundamental importance from the point of view of a given right or freedom[570]. The Constitutional Tribunal, in explaining the meaning of the principle of the exclusivity of the statute in limiting constitutional rights and freedoms contained in Article 31(3) of the Constitution, has pointed out that it does not exclude the delegation of certain matters relating to the implementation of constitutional rights and freedoms to be regulated by ordinance. However, only such matters may be delegated for regulation by ordinance which are not of significant importance for the exercise of human rights and freedoms, while the authorisation to issue an ordinance must meet the requirements set out in Article 92 of the Constitution, i.e. it must be detailed and issued for the purpose of implementing the statue, as well as specifying the body competent to issue the ordinance, the scope of the matters delegated for regulation and guidelines concerning the content of the act. The act must regulate exhaustively and completely all important issues relevant to the exercise of rights and freedoms[571].

There is no doubt that the consideration of the protection of citizens' health and the need to combat the COVID-19 pandemic required the legislator to take appropriate legislative measures that also affect the functioning of the judiciary,

---

568 P. Tuleja, *Pandemia COVID-19 a konstytucyjne...*, p. 16.

569 M. Florczak-Wątor, *Niekonstytucyjność ograniczeń praw i wolności jednostki wprowadzonych w związku z epidemią COVID-19 jako przesłanka odpowiedzialności odszkodowawczej państwa,* Państwo i Prawo 2020/12, p. 17.

570 S. Czarnow, *Między stanem epidemii...*, pp. 20–21.

571 Judgment of the Constitutional Tribunal of 8 July 2003, P 10/02, LEX No. 80205.

including the implementation of the right to a fair trial. The protected value of health (both public and individual) is of at least equal, if not greater, importance than the right to a fair trial. Article 31(3) of the Constitution includes health among the values for the protection of which measures may be taken that restrict individual rights and freedoms. This leads to the conclusion that interference with the constitutionally protected right to a fair trial in connection with the COVID-19 pandemic may have been justified by the need to protect health.

The limitations discussed in the following chapters, which affect the conduct of civil proceedings in the COVID-19 pandemic era, are in the vast majority laid down in statutory law. The usefulness and indispensability of the provisions contained (mainly) in the COVID-19 Special Act will be considered in later chapters. At this point, however, attention must be paid to the proportionality of these restrictions in terms of their temporal validity.

The common element of most of the legal institutions discussed in the following chapters is their duration, which is expressed in the following wording 'during the period of the state of epidemic threat or the state of epidemic declared due to COVID-19 and within one year from the revocation of the last of them (...)'. Such a solution was adopted, inter alia, in Articles $15zzs^1$ and $15zzs^9$ of the COVID-19 Special Act. On the other hand, in the now repealed Article 15zzs, the legislator decided to define the duration of the provision slightly differently ('during the period of the state of epidemic emergency or the state of epidemic declared due to COVID'), abandoning the additional period of one year after the end of the last of these states (and omitting the reference to '19', which in itself shows a lack of attention to the rules of proper legislation). In Article 952^1 § 5 of the Code of Civil Procedure (added as part of one of the 'anti-pandemic' laws and subsequently repealed retroactively as of 24 February 2022), the legislator used the phrase 'during the period of the state of epidemic threat or state of epidemic and 90 days after its end', omitting the condition that the epidemic must be caused by COVID-19. On the other hand, Article $15zzs^2$ of the COVID-19 Special Act does not specify the period of validity at all, which should be interpreted as meaning that the provision remains in force until it is derogated from by law, regardless of whether the state of epidemic or epidemic threat is lifted.

In the light of the foregoing, it is necessary to consider, firstly, whether the determination of the duration of the said provisions by reference by the legislator to the relevant Ordinance of the Minister of Health on the declaration and lifting of the state of epidemic threat or state of epidemic fulfils the condition of being 'established only by statute' resulting from Article 31(3) of the Constitution. Secondly, it is necessary to determine whether such a definition of the temporal scope of application of these provisions satisfies the requirement of indispensability, since no specific end date for the duration of an epidemic state is explicitly set. Thirdly, it is necessary to answer the question of whether the lack of a link between the scope of application of the temporal restrictions in question and the actual course of the COVID-19 pandemic satisfies the requirements of proportionality, in particular taking into account the fact that the legislator does not differentiate the solutions introduced with regard to the current epidemic situation (number of cases) or even between the epidemic state and the state of epidemic threat.

As mentioned above, the legislator does not provide for a time limit on the state of epidemic or epidemic threat, which leads to the conclusion that they are introduced for an indefinite period ('until revoked'). In order to terminate them, it is necessary to take a conventional action in the form of revoking the respective state by means of an ordinance[572]. As a result, it is not possible to determine when a state of epidemic or epidemic threat will be lifted. As the Epidemic Control Act does not provide for the obligation to review the validity of the state of epidemic or epidemic threat, its duration may be indefinite and depends on the adoption of appropriate measures by the General Sanitary Inspector, on whose initiative the Minister of Health may revoke the state of epidemic or epidemic threat.

This, in turn, leads to the conclusion that the period of application of the aforementioned provisions of the COVID-19 Special Act depends on the issuance of an ordinance on the lifting of the state of epidemic and epidemic threat and, in some cases, on the expiration of an additional period. The actual derogation of a provision of the statute is, in the present case, linked to the adoption of a sub-statutory act.

Contrary to the view presented above, it may be noted that the temporal scope of the provisions of Articles 15zzs, $15zzs^1$ and $15zzs^9$ of the COVID-19 Special Act is not strictly linked to the state of epidemic (epidemic threat), but to another event, namely the lapse of one year from the lifting of the last of these states. Therefore, it can be argued that it is not the promulgation of an ordinance that determines the expiry of a statute (which seems unacceptable in view of the constitutional hierarchy of sources of universally binding law), but it is the statute itself that determines the duration of its validity, making it dependent on the lifting of the state of epidemic or epidemic threat.

Prima facie, this position seems justified in the light of the rules adopted in the Rules of Legislative Technique. According to § 29b(1) of the Rules, the duration of a regulation shall be determined in particular by: 1) a reference to the calendar year or years; 2) an indication of the beginning and end of the validity of the regulation, expressed in calendar days; 3) an indication of the number of weeks, months or years that have elapsed since the date of entry into force of the act or its individual provisions. The phrase 'in particular' in paragraph 1 suggests that the above enumeration constitutes an open catalogue and, secondly, that the above forms are the legislator's preferred means of introducing the duration of provisions laid down in episodic provisions. However, according to the wording of Section 29b(2), in the case of episodic regulations, the beginning and end of a regulation may not depend on the occurrence of a future event, unless this is necessary in view of the scope of the regulation of the act or its individual provisions, and the date of the occurrence of the future event can be determined beyond doubt and is officially announced.

572 M. Radajewski, *Stan zagrożenia epidemicznego...*, p. 82.

The act should specify the form in which the date of the occurrence of the future event is to be officially announced and the authority responsible for this.

It should be noted, however, that the above-mentioned provisions of the COVID-19 Special Act do not refer to a time limit as a future event, but to a condition, i.e. a future and uncertain event. Indeed, it is not possible to determine *a priori* when the last of the anti-epidemic conditions will be lifted, and therefore the end date of the provision cannot be determined either. As M. Florczak-Wątor points out in relation to the Ordinance on the declaration of the state of epidemic, a provision that is valid 'until further notice' cannot be regarded as a temporal provision, as this would require the determination of a clear time frame, in particular the end date of a given provision[573]. None of the above-mentioned provisions of the COVID-19 Special Act provide such a framework.

However, it must be considered whether the regulations in question have the character of episodic regulations within the meaning of § 29a of the Rules of Legislative Technique. According to the cited provision, episodic regulations include those which introduce derogations from certain provisions and whose duration is clearly defined. With regard to the provisions of Articles 15zzs, 15zzs1 and 15zzs9 of the COVID-19 Special Act, it should be emphasised that the occurrence of the event on which the validity of the provision depends (one year after the last of the epidemic states has been lifted) does not lead to its repeal and removal from the legal order. On the other hand, the occurrence of this event renders obsolete the precondition for the application of the regulation. Formally, therefore, the regulations are still part of the statutory legal order, but their applicability ceases one year after the last of the anti-epidemic states referred to in Article 46 of the Epidemic Control Act has been lifted. In the event that the state of epidemic or the state of epidemic threat were to be proclaimed again after the expiry of one year from the date on which the epidemic state or the state of epidemic threat was lifted, the provisions of Articles 15zzs, 15zzs1 and 15zzs9 of the COVID-19 Special Act would be applicable again, without the need for them to be enacted again. Consequently, it must be assumed that the regulations in question do not have an explicitly stated period of validity, but contain a condition for application that is dependent on the occurrence of a specific event (declaration of the state of epidemic or epidemic threat). The regulations in question are therefore not episodic regulations within the meaning of the Rules of Legislative Technique.

It is therefore necessary at this point to revise the original assertion that the binding force of the specified provisions of the COVID-19 Special Act is determined by the adoption of a sub-statutory legal act. On the other hand, there should be no doubt that the court's obligation to apply these provisions (the existence of the prerequisite for their application) is linked to the issuance of the relevant regulation. Therefore, if the regulation does not lead to the repeal of a provision of a statute by means of an ordinance, there is no reason to assume a contradiction in

573 M. Florczak-Wątor, *Niekonstytucyjność ograniczeń...*, p. 13.

terms of the hierarchical order of sources of law. Indeed, there appears to be no obstacle to a statute specifying the conditions for the application of a given provision by reference to a sub-statutory act.

However, the question then arises as to whether it is acceptable for the state of epidemic or epidemic threat to be declared for an indefinite period 'until further notice', without the competent authorities being formally obliged to review the validity of maintaining this state. It should be recalled that the state of epidemic threat on the basis of COVID-19 was declared for the first time on 14 March 2020, then the state of epidemic lasted from 20 March 2020 until 16 May 2022, and then the epidemic threat was again in force from 16 May 2022 until 1 July 2023. As mentioned above, the legislator did not provide for an end date for the anti-epidemic states, which is probably related to the fact that the dynamic development of an epidemic (including COVID-19) makes it impossible to predict how long it may last on the territory of Poland.

Having stated the above, the legislator has also not explicitly provided for an obligation to periodically review the legitimacy of the continued maintenance of anti-epidemic states. However, this does not mean that there is no such obligation on the part of the public authorities. This is primarily due to the fact that the main purpose of declaring a state of epidemic or a state of epidemic threat is to establish specific restrictions on rights and freedoms in order to combat the spread of an epidemic[574]. The existence of the state of epidemic, let alone the epidemic threat, does not in itself justify a restriction of a particular right or freedom. Restrictions imposed by the legislator must be for the specific purpose of combating or preventing an epidemic. Consequently, the authorities must constantly monitor whether the factual situation justifies the continuation of the state of epidemic or the epidemic threat. There is also a constitutional justification for the above. Article 7 of the Constitution establishes the principle of legality, which the authorities are obliged to respect, while Article 31(3) of the Constitution establishes the principle of indispensability when restricting the exercise of constitutional rights and freedoms. In the light of the above principles, it is unacceptable to maintain a situation in which restrictions are imposed on individuals that are not justified by the real need to prevent the epidemic.

Chapter XI of the Constitution of the Republic of Poland implies the principle of periodicity of states of emergency, which implies the order to abolish specific solutions after the end of the threat[575]. It should be noted, for example, that a state of natural disaster (Article 232 of the Constitution) may be declared for a limited period of time, not exceeding 30 days, and may be prolonged, if necessary, with the consent of the Parliament (Sejm). It seems that similar rationing should also be applied in the case of states of epidemic and epidemic threat, which do not have a direct constitutional basis. Otherwise, the authorities may decide to bypass the

---

574 M. Radajewski, [in:] *Pandemia COVID-19 a prawa...*, p. 89.
575 P. Tuleja, *Pandemia COVID-19 a konstytucyjne...*, p. 7.

provisions on states of emergency and make use of the more flexible and, at the same time, temporary statutory anti-epidemic states. There must be agreement with the position that the time frame for the application of restrictions should be a matter for the law. As the Constitution prescribes such a time frame in relation to states of emergency, it should be specified all the more in the case of a state of epidemic. J. Roszkiewicz, using the example of restrictions on economic freedoms during the COVID-19 pandemic, points out that it is essential that a statutory delegation determine the maximum time frame for the functioning of the restrictions, with the possibility of their extension by means of a subsequent regulation[576].

It is worth noting that despite a significant decrease in new coronavirus infections between June 2021 and October 2021 (between waves III and IV of COVID-19)[577], the authorities decided to lift the epidemic state only in May 2022, almost two months after the end of wave V and after the lifting of most of the restrictions related to quarantine and isolation and mouth and nose covering (except in medical facilities and pharmacies) in March 2022[578]. The abolition of the state of epidemic and the introduction of a state of epidemic threat in its place raised doubts about the legitimacy of continuing to maintain the civil procedural restrictions in courts. Reservations in this regard were expressed, inter alia, by the Ombudsman, who wrote to the Minister of Justice asking whether further restrictions to the principle of openness of proceedings and the maintenance of the principle of single-member courts were necessary in their current form. The Ombudsman pointed out that the continuation of the current restrictions on the functioning of the courts should be reviewed in the light of the need to protect public health[579].

The dissociation of the restrictions affecting civil proceedings in the COVID-19 Special Act from the actual course of the pandemic, as seen in the above example, calls into question their proportionality in the context of the principle of necessity. Despite the ever-changing reality of the level of risk of the spread of COVID-19, the legislator has kept the restrictions directly affecting the right to a fair trial at the same level for more than three years. This, in turn, supports the assumption that the continuation of a legal regulation that is not necessary for the protection of health is contrary to the principle of proportionality as set out in Article 31(3) of

576 J Roszkiewicz, *Granice ograniczeń wolności gospodarczej wprowadzonych w celu przeciwdziałania epidemii (uwagi na tle orzecznictwa sądów administracyjnych)*, Zeszyty Naukowe Sądownictwa Administracyjnego 2022/2, p. 43–44.

577 Statistics covering the daily increase in infections from March 2020 are available at www.koronawirusunas.pl, accessed 8 October 2022.

578 Ordinance of the Council of Ministers of 25 March 2022 on the establishment of certain restrictions, orders and prohibitions in connection with the occurrence of an epidemic threat, Journal of Laws 2022, item 679.

579 The Ombudsman's speech of 30 May 2022, available on the RPO's website: https: // bip.brpo.gov.pl/sites/default/files/2022–05/Do_MS_sady_dostep_30.05.2022_1.pdf, accessed 8 October 2022.

the Constitution. Public authorities, bound by the prohibition of excessive interference with constitutional rights and freedoms of the individual, should constantly monitor the necessity of maintaining restrictions affecting the realisation of the right to a trial.

There is also no justification for applying the same restrictions to civil proceedings both in a state of epidemic and in a state of epidemic threat. It should be recalled that the state of epidemic is declared in connection with the occurrence of an epidemic in a given territory in order to take certain anti-epidemic and preventive measures to minimise the effects of the epidemic. A state of epidemic threat is a situation in which an epidemic is not present but there is a risk of an epidemic. It appears that the application of the restrictions specific to an epidemic situation, even during an epidemic threat (which is clearly characterised by a lower public health risk), may be considered excessive.

L. Bosek also sees a contradiction with the constitutional principle of proportionality. The author notes that the construction of the extended validity of procedural restrictions in force after the end of the pandemic, and even after the lifting of the state of epidemic, deserves critical assessment. These regulations, even if they are considered to be in accordance with the right to a fair trial as stipulated in Article 45(1) of the Constitution (which, in the author's opinion, is doubtful due to the lack of sufficient justification in the values stipulated in Article 31(1) of the Constitution), should be subject to change[580]. A similar view is expressed by K. Gajda-Roszczynialska, who aptly notes that the general purpose of emergency measures is to return to normality and that special regulations should be lifted immediately after the end of the state of epidemic. The temporary nature of the restrictions means that emergency measures can only be in place until the state is in an exceptional situation and should be lifted as soon as the exceptional situation ends. Such regulations should always be introduced for a limited period of time, with the possibility of renewal if necessary. The fact that the legislator in the provisions under review makes the possibility of applying special measures dependent on the occurrence of the state of epidemic or epidemic threat, and within one year of the lifting of the latter, carries the risk of raising an effective allegation of a violation of Article 45(1) in conjunction with Article 31(3) of the Constitution[581]. A. Machnikowska also points out that special provisions based on the threat of an epidemic are to remain in force even after the epidemic has ended, which leads to ignoring the necessity principle, which is one of the constitutional standards for empowering state bodies to restrict citizens' freedoms and rights[582].

---

580 L. Bosek, *Stan epidemii...*, pp. 249–250.

581 K. Gajda-Roszczynialska, *Przebudowa wymiaru sprawiedliwości w czasach pandemii COVID-19 ze szczególnym uwzględnieniem postępowania cywilnego,* Polski Proces Cywilny 2022/1, pp. 18–19.

582 A. Machnikowska, *Zasada jawności w postępowaniu procesowym – modernizacja czy marginalizacja? Wybrane zagadnienia,* Polski Proces Cywilny 2022/1, p. 81.

The solution adopted in the provisions of Articles 15zzs[1] and 15zzs[9] of the COVID-19 Special Act, according to which these regulations also apply in the period of one year after the lifting of the last epidemic state, raises even greater doubts in this respect. The lifting of an epidemic state, as defined in Article 2(23) of the COVID-19 Special Act, means that there is no danger of an epidemic in a given area. The absence of an epidemic threat should lead to the conclusion that there is no need for regulations aimed at combating epidemics, which at the same time lead to the restriction of civil rights and freedoms. M. Krakowiak points out, on the basis of the regulation on remote court hearings from Article 15zzs[1] of the COVID-19 Special Act, that such a solution should be considered legitimate due to the dynamic nature of the epidemic situation. The possibility for courts to continue to use the special provision for remote hearings may be a procedural means of a gradual return to traditional hearings[583].

However, such an approach cannot be endorsed. As stated above, it is widely accepted in the literature that the exceptional measures adopted in the context of the need to combat an epidemic should apply only during the period of the epidemic, or at least during the real threat of its occurrence. The use of special provisions adopted during the pandemic is not justified after the pandemic has ended. Indeed, there is no justifiable reason why the legislator should choose to restrict the rights and freedoms of citizens, including the right to a fair trial, during a period when no special measures are required. It should be borne in mind that the state of epidemic or epidemic threat is, by its very nature, associated with a certain rationing of these rights and freedoms. It is not justifiable to accept the view that these restrictions may last longer than is strictly necessary, even if this is to ensure a smooth transition between the operation of justice under special conditions and the normal situation. The legislator must not adopt rules that restrict individual rights and freedoms 'in advance'. At the same time, it must be borne in mind that, in the event of the emergence of the state of epidemic or epidemic threat may be reintroduced at the request of the competent authorities in order to reinstate the necessary solutions. The provisions of the COVID-19 Special Act should not be used to permanently change the model of civil procedure or the organisation of the judiciary, but should be aimed at overcoming the pandemic situation[584]. If the legislature intends to make certain changes permanent, it should do so by amending the relevant procedural legislations.

It was noted above that the content of the part of the provisions of the COVID-19 Special Act concerning civil proceedings (the aforementioned Articles 15zzs, 15zzs[1] and 15zzs[9]) is shaped by reference to the relevant regulations of the Minister of Health concerning the declaration and revocation of a state of epidemic a state

583 M. Krakowiak, *Rozprawa elektroniczna w polskim postępowaniu cywilnym,* [in:] *Rozstrzyganie spraw cywilnych,* [in:] *Rozstrzyganie spraw cywilnych,* M. Białecki, S. Kotas-Turoboyska, F. Manikowski, E. Szczepanowska (eds), Warsaw 2022, p. 221.

584 K. Gajda-Roszczynialska, *Przebudowa wymiaru sprawiedliwości...*, p. 19.

of epidemic threat. It has been argued that although these regulations, as sub-statutory legal acts, do not affect the derogation of the provisions of the COVID-19 Special Act, they are important for determining the temporal scope of these provisions. Pursuant to Article 178(1) of the Constitution, judges are independent in the performance of their duties and are subject only to the Constitution and the law. The subordination of the judiciary to the law is, however, limited to the Constitution and the statutes. In the exercise of judicial power, judges are obliged to apply these legal acts, even if they are directly or indirectly contradicted by sub-statutory legal acts (including ordinances)[585]. Therefore, the ordinary courts may carry out an incidental assessment of the legality of ordinances, including those issued on the basis of the authorisation contained in Article 46 of the Epidemic Control Act[586]. However, this control does not lead to the removal of a certain rule from the legal order, but to the refusal to apply it in a given case because it contradicts acts of a higher rank.

In the light of the above, the question arises as to whether a court of general jurisdiction may refuse to apply the provision of the COVID-19 Special Act, taking the view that the actual epidemic situation, despite the state of epidemic maintained by the authorities, does not require the consistent application of restrictions affecting the exercise of the right to a fair trial, and that the maintenance of the relevant provisions of the COVID-19 Special Act leads to a disproportionate violation of Article 45(1) of the Constitution. The question thus raised must be answered in the negative. Even if the court were to find a contradiction between the provisions of the ordinance on the declaration of a state of epidemic and Article 45(1) of the Constitution, it would be inadmissible to refuse to apply the provisions of the COVID-19 Special Act, as this would result in an incidental assessment of the legality not of the ordinance itself, but of the provisions of statutory rank. In this regard, it is necessary to support the position that the duty of a judge to be bound by the Constitution and the statutes implies a prohibition of an incidental review of the constitutionality of statutes, even if, based on an inner conviction, doubts arise as to their conformity with the Constitution of the Republic of Poland[587]. This assessment is not affected by the obligation of direct application of the Constitution of the Republic of Poland, as laid down in Article 8(2) thereof.

At the same time, it does not appear that the ordinary court has the power to assess the decisions of the public authorities on the legality of the introduction or revocation of the relevant anti-epidemic state, which falls within the competence of the responsible minister acting at the request of the General Sanitary Inspector. If the court perceives a possible contradiction between the provisions of

---

585 P. Karlik, P. Wiliński, [in:] *Konstytucja RP. Tom II. Komentarz do art. 87–243,* M. Safjan, L. Bosek (eds.) Warsaw 2016, Commentary to Article 178, Nb 64, Legalis.

586 M. Radajewski, *Stan zagrożenia epidemicznego...*, p. 69.

587 P. Karlik, P. Wiliński, [in:] *Konsytucja RP...*, Nb 62, Legalis.

the COVID-19 Special Act and the Constitution of the Republic of Poland (in particular, Article 45(1) in conjunction with Article 31(3)), it is obliged to interpret the provision of the Act about which it has raised doubts in such a way as to ensure the fullest possible implementation of the constitutional standard of the right to a fair trial. It should be emphasised once again that the principle of proportionality of restrictions on the exercise of constitutional rights and freedoms applies not only to the legislator at the stage of adoption of the law, but also to the courts at the stage of its application. Should it prove impossible to reconcile a provision of a statute with the norms of a higher order, a common court shall exercise the right provided for in Article 193 of the Constitution to refer the relevant legal question to the Constitutional Tribunal.

Without assessing at this point the legitimacy of the solutions adopted in the civil procedural provisions of the COVID-19 Special Act (which will be considered in the following chapters), the question of the temporal validity of these provisions must be answered in the negative. Undoubtedly, the obligation to apply these provisions irrespective of the actual threat of an epidemic, even after the formal lifting of the state of epidemic and epidemic threat, raises justified doubts in the context of compliance with the constitutional principle of proportionality. *De lege ferenda* amendments should be postulated on two fundamental issues related to the subject matter under discussion. First and foremost, it seems justified to include in the legal authorisation contained in Article 46 of the Epidemic Control Act the obligation to specify the period for which the state of epidemic or state of epidemic threat is introduced, following the example of constitutional states of emergency. The anti-epidemic state may be prolonged by the competent authority for other specified periods in accordance with the actual needs related to the course of the epidemic. The introduction of the possibility for the Minister of Health to declare a state of epidemic or epidemic threat, without the simultaneous obligation to examine whether the premises for its introduction are still valid, seems unjustified.

The provisions of Articles 15zzs^{1} and 15zzs^{9} of the COVID-19 Special Act should be amended to limit their scope of application to the state of epidemic only. Since most of the epidemiological restrictions have been lifted in the state of epidemic threat, there is no clear basis for maintaining provisions regulating civil proceedings in a special way. Even more so, there is no justification for the obligation to apply these provisions during the year following the lifting of the last of the epidemic states, when the COVID-19 threat no longer exists.

5.3. Impact of the COVID-19 pandemic on civil proceedings in the Member States of the European Union

5.3.1. Introductory remarks

The spread of COVID-19 across Europe made it necessary to introduce legal measures to combat the pandemic in other EU Member States. States of emergency or other emergency measures were introduced in a number of European countries.

States of emergency were declared in the Czech Republic, Portugal, Romania and Lithuania, Spain, Estonia and Hungary. A public health emergency was declared in France and a state of crisis in Luxembourg. In other European countries, the crisis associated with the development of the pandemic did not require a constitutional state of emergency. In Germany, pandemic measures were based on existing legislation. In Belgium and Austria, on the other hand, COVID-19 counter-pandemic legislation was adopted[588].

A number of legal solutions affecting the conduct of civil proceedings have been adopted in the Member States of the European Union, including the introduction of remote court hearings (via videoconferencing), the suspension of procedural deadlines and statutes of limitation, the suspension of public auctions of real estate and the enforcement of evictions, as well as instruments related to electronic communication with the courts. In some countries, e.g. Germany, Sweden, Finland, no new regulations on the conduct of civil proceedings have been introduced, as the existing provisions are considered sufficient to counteract the effects of the pandemic. In Sweden and Finland, the use of electronic communication tools allowing remote participation in proceedings has been intensified[589]. Similarly, in Lithuania, no new procedural rules were introduced as the existing instruments were considered sufficient, although in practice the courts were suspended during the first weeks of the lockdown[590].

The following is a selection of legislation in the Member States of the European Union in the above-mentioned areas of civil procedure. Most of the information collected has been made available by the EJN[591] via the European e-Justice portal[592]. Information on the measures adopted in each Member State in relation to the COVID-19 pandemic was provided by the relevant EJN contact point. Otherwise, the following information was obtained from the government websites of the Member States concerned and from the available literature. The legal

588 A. Stawicka, R. Stawicki, *Pandemia COVID-19. Sytuacja w wybranych krajach europejskich,* Raport Biura Analiz, Dokumentacji i Korespondencji Kancelarii Senatu (Report of the Office of Analysis, Documentation and Correspondence of the Senate Chancellery), Warsaw 2020, p. 9.

589 A. Sanders, *Video-Hearings in Europe Before, During and After the COVID-19 Pandemic,* International Journal for Court Administration 2020/12, p. 5.

590 V. Mikėlenas, *A Lithuanian Experience of Coronavirus and the Law,* [in:] *Coronavirus and the law in Europe,* E. Hondius, M. Santos Silva, A. Nicolussi, P. Salvador Coderch, C. Wendehorst, F. Zoll (eds.), Cambridge 2021, p. 214.

591 European Judicial Network in civil and commercial matters, established by EU Council Decision of 28 May 2001 (2001/470/EC), OJ EU. L 174 of 27 June 2001, consisting of national judicial authorities which, through contact points, facilitate cooperation between the Member States of the European Union in cross-border cases.

592 www.e-justice.europa.eu.

solutions analysed were those adopted in Austria, Belgium, Bulgaria, Croatia, Cyprus, France, Germany, Italy, Latvia, Lithuania, Luxembourg, the Netherlands, Romania, Slovenia and Spain.

5.3.2. Remote court hearings

In Spain, remote hearings were already used in civil and criminal cases before the pandemic. It was only possible to participate in a court hearing by videoconference, and only in cases specified by the law. Authorisation to participate in a hearing by videoconference was granted by the court when it was necessary for reasons of public order, economy of proceedings or security, or when it would be difficult or harmful for the person concerned to attend the hearing in person at the courthouse. Following the COVID-19 pandemic, the conditions for the admissibility of a remote hearing were extended and the principle of the priority of the remote mode was introduced[593].

Article 14 of Law No. 3/2020 of 18 September 2020 on Procedural and Organisational Measures to Combat COVID-19 and its Effects on the Administration of Justice[594] established that by 20 June 2021, in civil proceedings, all procedural acts, including hearings, should be conducted by videoconference, provided that the court has the appropriate technical means. This provision (paragraph 5) also provided for the obligation to take the necessary measures to guarantee the rights of all parties when using videoconferencing. The court could decide on the compulsory presence in the courthouse of those parties whose presence it deemed necessary (paragraph 6). It is important to note that Article 15 of the above-mentioned Act provided for public access to the courtroom during all oral proceedings – the court could order the public to attend the hearing in the courtroom, taking into account the need to ensure health protection, or it could authorise the transmission of the hearing by videoconference.

The Standing Committee of the Spanish General Council of the Judiciary has approved a document containing guidelines for the conduct of remote meetings[595]. The guidelines in question provide for the obligation to ensure the protection of the confidentiality of data (point 36) by using technical means to prevent the recording of the hearing (apart from the official recording made by the authorised body).

593 K. Jarzmus, [in:] *Nowe technologie. nowa Sprawiedliwość. Nowe pytania. Wdrażanie nowych technologii w wymiarze sprawiedliwości*, Raport Helsińskiej Fundacji Praw Człowieka, P. Kładoczny, K. Wiśniewska (eds.), Warsaw 2021, p. 121.

594 https://www.boe.es/buscar/act.php?id=BOE-A-2020–10923 (in Spanish, own translation), access: 5 August 2024.

595 Guide to conducting remote judicial proceedings, May 2020 (Guía para la celebración de actuaciones judiciales telemáticas), https://www.poderjudicial.es/cgpj/en/Services/Information-COVID-19/Guides-and-Protocols/Guia-para-la-cele bracion-de-actuaciones-judiciales-telematicas (in Spanish, own translation), access: 5 August 2024.

For their part, the professional lawyers were obliged to take the necessary measures to ensure that their participation in the court session took place in a place that guaranteed compliance with these standards, using appropriate technical means. The court was required to verify that the above requirements were met, both before and during the hearing. On the other hand, the Guidelines ensured that court hearings were open to the public (paragraphs 39–41). The participation of the public in the courtroom or in another room of the court was considered to be the most appropriate way to ensure the openness of the proceedings, while pointing out that the necessary measures should be taken to prevent members of the public from recording the proceedings. Where it was not possible for the public to attend the hearing in the courthouse, access to the hearing by videoconference had to be provided by means of a password or an invitation sent after the person concerned had been verified and informed that no recording of the hearing was permitted. The parties had to be informed of the public's participation in the hearing. In addition, information on the date, time and nature of the proceedings had to be posted on a virtual notice board so that it could be viewed by third parties. The Guidelines also set out detailed technical conditions to be met by the remote meeting and the procedure for verifying compliance (paragraphs 51 et seq.).

Since 2001, German legislation has provided for the possibility of conducting the hearing by means of direct video and audio transmission (§ 128a of the Code of Civil Procedure). The parties or their representatives may participate in the remote hearing with the permission of the court, granted upon request or *ex officio*. Witnesses, experts and parties may also be present outside the courtroom during the hearing with the permission of the court. Video and sound are then transmitted directly into the courtroom and to the place where these persons are present[596]. No additional procedural rules were introduced in connection with the COVID-19 pandemic, as the existing procedural laws provided the German courts with a wide range of tools to respond flexibly to the epidemic situation, including written procedures, waivers, and the taking of evidence by videoconference[597].

Italian law allowed evidence in civil proceedings to be taken by videoconference. However, there was no general rule introducing remote hearings[598]. This situation changed with the introduction of Article 83(7 f) of the Decree Law No. 18 of 17 March 2020[599], according to which court hearings that do not require the personal presence of the parties may be held remotely. The hearing was to be held in the presence of the judge in the courthouse in such a way as to ensure the effective

596 M. Krakowiak, *Rozprawa elektroniczna...*, p. 214.
597 Information provided by the European Judicial Network in Civil and Commercial Matters, available at www.e-justice.europa.eu, as of 25 July 2022.
598 M. Krakowiak, *Rozprawa elektroniczna...*, p. 215.
599 https://def.finanze.it/DocTribFrontend/getAttoNormativoDetail.do?ACTION=getSommario&id={CADE4535-01D4-4283-8D59-2D08D563CE69} (in Italian, own translation), access: 5 August 2024.

participation of the parties. The provision stipulates that the place from which the lawyers are connected is considered to be the courtroom and that a remote meeting is equivalent to a traditional meeting. In doing so, the Italian legislator presumed that a party could only participate in a remote meeting from the same place as their lawyer[600]. The question of the external openness of proceedings in Italian law must be addressed. According to Article 84 of the Implementing Rules of the Italian Code of Civil Procedure, preparatory (preliminary) hearings and the taking of evidence are not public. As a general rule, therefore, civil hearings are not open to the public, except at the stage of the presentation of final positions. During the pandemic, no measures were adopted to guarantee public access to court hearings[601], which resulted in a restriction of the principle of openness.

In Latvia, on the basis of the Decree of the Council of Ministers of 6 November 2020 on the proclamation of a state of emergency, the Minister of Justice issued Guidelines for the Organisation of the Work of District (City) Courts and County Courts in a State of Emergency[602]. The document recommends that civil proceedings should be conducted in writing if the court considers this acceptable and does not result in a breach of the rights of the parties. Where it is not possible to hold a hearing in writing (i.e. where a hearing is necessary, there is an urgent need to hear the case or there is a serious risk that the rights of a party will be prejudiced), the hearing should be held remotely. If it is not possible to hold the hearing remotely, the hearing may be held in the courthouse with the necessary precautions. In the case of remote hearings, the clerk of the court shall constantly monitor the quality of the sound transmitted to the participants. If this proves unsatisfactory and the remedial measures taken have been ineffective, a transcript of the recording is made and made available to the parties so that they can review and comment on the proceedings in writing. Members of the public (including representatives of the media) may attend public court hearings, provided they notify the court's press office of their intention to do so. In cases where this is not possible for epidemiological reasons, information on the possibility of remote connection is sent to interested parties who have made a request in advance.

In Romania, during the state of emergency, court hearings were to be held, if possible, by videoconference (pursuant to Article 42(3) of the Presidential Decree No. 195 of 16 March 2020 on the introduction of a state of emergency on the

600 K. Jarzmus, [in:] *Nowe technologie...*, p. 124.

601 K. Jarzmus, [in:] *Nowe technologie...*, pp. 118–119 and the 18 December 2020 response by D. Ferrero, I. D'Anselmo (Italy) to a questionnaire provided by the Helsinki Foundation for Human Rights, available at: https://www.hfhr.pl/wp-content/uploads/2021/05/Italy_CC_Clean.pdf, accessed 3 October 2022.

602 https://www.ta.gov.lv/lv/jaunums/vadlinijas-rajona-pilsetu-un-apgabaltiesu-darba-organizesanai-arkartejas-situacijas-laika-no-2020gada-9novembra-precizetas-uz-2021gada-15martu (in Latvian, own translation), access: 5 August 2024.

territory of Romania[603]). The state of emergency in Romania started on 16 March 2020 and ended on 15 May 2020.

In Lithuania, no specific solutions affecting the conduct of civil proceedings have been adopted. The Lithuanian Judicial Council made recommendations on the organisation of court work, but their implementation was left to the discretion of the court presidents. In particular, it was recommended that civil proceedings should be conducted as far as possible in writing. In cases where a hearing was necessary and the parties were willing to attend, hearings were adjourned. The holding of hearings in the courthouse was limited to urgent cases, with remote hearings being the recommended form (if the court had the technical capacity to hold them). Remote hearings in civil cases were introduced into the Lithuanian legal system as early as 2011[604], but were not used on such a large scale before the pandemic, mainly due to insufficient technical and organisational facilities of the Lithuanian courts[605].

In the Netherlands, court buildings were not accessible to the public between 17 March and 11 May 2020 (this did not apply to the hearing of urgent cases). From 24 March 2020, the possibility of holding a hearing entirely by electronic means was introduced if it was not possible to attend the court building in person due to COVID-19. As a rule, however, hearings should be held in person. The decision on the conduct of the hearing was made by the court on a case-by-case basis. During the period of restrictions, the courts remained closed to the public, except in cases of significant public interest. The court could also ask the Judicial Council to set up a streaming service to broadcast the hearing if it was in the public interest. However, the judicial authorities were obliged to take steps to increase the number of judgments published online. All restrictions on access to the judiciary were lifted on 23 March 2022, but the ability to hold remote court hearings was retained[606].

In Slovenia, in the period from 29 March to 1 July 2020, court hearings were held under precautionary measures, but it was recommended that they be held by videoconference if technically possible. On the basis of Article 5 of the Act of 20 March 2020 on Provisional Measures in the Judicial, Administrative and Other Public Spheres to Limit the Damage Caused by the Spread of the SARS-CoV-2 Virus[607], it was permissible to exclude the public from the hearing for health protection reasons.

603 https://legislatie.just.ro/Public/DetaliiDocumentAfis/223831 (in Romanian, own translation), access: 5 August 2024.

604 A. Sanders, *Video-Hearings...*, p. 6.

605 V. Mikèlenas, *A Lithuanian Experience...*, p. 214.

606 https://www.rechtspraak.nl/online-zittingen-en-overleggen (in Dutch, own translation), access: 5 August 2024.

607 http://www.pisrs.si/Pis.web/pregledPredpisa?id=ZAKO8183 (in Slovenian, own translation), accessed 3 October 2022.

The Austrian legislator has adopted the Federal Law on COVID-19 Accompanying Measures in Justice[608]. Pursuant to § 3 of the said Act, until 31 December 2022, the court may, with the consent of the parties, hold a hearing without the personal presence of the parties or their representatives, using appropriate means of communication providing for video and audio transmission. A party may object to the holding of a remote hearing within the time limit set by the court. A party, a witness, an expert or an interpreter, as well as any other person involved in the proceedings, may also request that a remote hearing be held if there is an increased risk of COVID-19. The consent of the parties is not required for a remote hearing in housing, care and adult protection cases, which would have to take place outside the court premises (e.g. in a relevant treatment facility) if the health of the hearing participant or a third party would be seriously endangered. It is noteworthy that in Austria immediate steps have been taken to improve the functioning of the technical infrastructure to ensure that videoconferencing is possible[609].

5.3.3. Suspension of time limits

In Spain, the second supplementary provision of the Royal Decree 463/2020[610] suspended the running of procedural time limits throughout the country as of 14 March 2020[611]. However, the court could agree to continue the proceedings if this was necessary to avoid irreparable damage to the rights and legitimate interests of the parties. The time limits would be back in force from the date of expiry of the Decree. This provision was repealed by the Royal Decree No. 537/2020 of 22 May 2020 with effect from 4 June 2020[612].

In Cyprus, all procedural and judicial time limits have been suspended between 16 March and 30 April 2022, with the exception of those relating to applications for interim injunctions in urgent cases and appeals against the court's decision to accept a bid at a public auction of real estate.

Similar solutions have been adopted in Italian law. Under Article 83(2) of the Decree Law No 18 of 17 March 2020, all time limits in civil and criminal proceedings

608 https://www.ris.bka.gv.at/GeltendeFassung.wxe?Abfrage=Bundesnormen&Gesetzesnummer=20011087 (in German, own translation), accessed 3 October 2022.

609 Table 'Use of digital tools by justice authorities', available on the e-Justice portal, https://e-justice.europa.eu/37147/PL/impact_of_covid19_on_the_justice_field#tocHeader2, accessed 3 October 2022.

610 Royal Decree No. 463/2020 of 14 March 2020 imposing a state of alert for the management of the health emergency caused by COVID-19 (in Spanish, own translation), https://www.boe.es/buscar/act.php?id=BOE-A-2020-3692, access: 5 August 2024.

611 COVID-19 crisis response report available on the website of the Spanish General Council of the Judiciary (in Spanish, own translation), https://www.poderjudicial.es, accessed 2 October 2022.

612 Royal Decree No. 537/2020 of 22 May 2020, https://www.boe.es/buscar/act.php?id=BOE-A-2020-5243#a8 (in Spanish, own translation), access: 5 August 2024.

were suspended from 9 March to 15 April 2020. In addition, all court hearings were adjourned until after 15 April 2020 (paragraph 1). However, the above provision did not apply to family and guardianship matters, including adoption, maintenance, compulsory treatment, injunction and election proceedings. Pursuant to Article 36 of the Decree Law No 23 of 8 April 2020, the suspension of time limits was subsequently extended until 11 May 2020[613].

In Belgium, limitation periods and procedural time limits (including time limits for appeals), the expiry of which could result in the loss of a right or other negative consequences for a party and which expired between 8 April and 17 May 2020, were extended until 17 June 2020. On the other hand, hearings in civil cases whose dates fell between 10 April and 17 June 2020 were cancelled. In these cases, a default judgment could be given on the basis of written submissions only, unless a party objected. In that case, the court was obliged to postpone the hearing of the case.

In Bulgaria, a state of emergency was declared under the Law on Measures and Actions Taken under the State of Emergency Declared by the Decision of the National Assembly of 13 March 2020 and on Countering the Effects of a Pandemic, which was initially intended to last from 13 March to 13 April 2020, but was subsequently extended to 13 May 2020. During the state of emergency, all procedural time limits were suspended, with the exception of cases concerning, inter alia, protective measures relating to the exercise of parental authority and cases falling within the scope of the Family Violence Protection Act, injunction proceedings and the preservation of evidence. Statutory time limits that expired during the state of emergency were extended by one month from the date of the end of the state of emergency. The statute of limitations was also suspended.

In Romania, on the basis of Article 41 of the Presidential Decree No. 195 of 16 March 2020, procedural deadlines and limitation periods were suspended from 16 March to 15 May 2020. The activity of the courts in all civil cases was suspended, except for urgent cases. The determination of which cases are urgent was left to the authorities of the Supreme Court of Cassation[614].

In Slovenia, the Act of 20 March 2020 on temporary measures in the judicial, administrative and other public fields to limit the damage caused by the spread of the SARS-CoV-2 virus entered into force on 29 March 2020[615]. As of 29 March 2020, all procedural (except for urgent cases specified in separate legislation) and

---

613 https://def.finanze.it/DocTribFrontend/getAttoNormativoDetail.do?ACTION=getSommario&id=%7B7B68E1A7-5491-47CB-B855-96BDEA610D75%7D (in Italian, own translation), access: 5 August 2024.

614 C. Alunaru, L. Bojin, *Coronavirus and the law in Romania,* [in:] *Coronavirus and the law in Europe,* E. Hondius, M. Santos Silva, A. Nicolussi, P. Salvador Coderch, C. Wendehorst, F. Zoll (eds.), Cambridge 2021, p. 190.

615 http://www.pisrs.si/Pis.web/pregledPredpisa?id=ZAKO8183 (in Slovenian, own translation), access: 5 August 2024.

material legal time limits were suspended. These measures remained in force until 1 July 2020.

In Germany, no new measures have been adopted to suspend the time limits in civil proceedings. The existing rules provide for the possibility of flexible extension of time limits, suspension of proceedings and reinstatement of time limits, all of which were used during the COVID-19 pandemic. The Czech Republic, Ireland, Lithuania, Hungary, the Netherlands, Denmark, Estonia, Greece, Sweden and Finland have also not adopted specific solutions for the suspension of time limits[616].

5.3.4. Eviction orders and public auctions of real estate and property

Pursuant to Article 1 bis of the Royal Decree Law No. 11/2020 of 31 March 2020 on the adoption of additional social and economic emergency measures against COVID-19[617], Spain has suspended the execution of evictions of economically disadvantaged persons until 31 December 2022. The provision only applied to landlords who are legal or natural persons with more than ten units. The suspension of evictions could only take place at the request of the debtor after verification of their economic hardship. The suspension of eviction was decided by the court after considering the circumstances of the specific case. If the request was granted, the competent public administration authorities were obliged to take appropriate measures to satisfy the housing needs of the debtor, and after the adoption of such measures, the court, within three days from the notification by the authority, took a decision to approve the lifting of the suspension of eviction and to initiate enforcement proceedings. The provision also provided for negative grounds for granting protection to the debtor, including the existence of a well-founded suspicion that the premises are being used for illegal activities, the use of threat or violence to obtain possession of the premises, and if the possession took place after the entry into force of the Royal Decree.

In Austria, the possibility has been introduced to stop the forced auction of a property at the request of the debtor if the debtor finds himself in a more difficult economic situation due to the COVID-19 pandemic and becomes homeless as a result of the eviction.

In Bulgaria, according to the aforementioned Law of 13 March 2020, following the end of the state of emergency, which lasted until 13 May 2020, all public auctions and forced seizures of assets against individuals were suspended for a period of two months from that date.

616 https://e-justice.europa.eu/37147/PL/impact_of_covid19_on_the_justice_field, accessed 2 October 2022.

617 https://www.boe.es/buscar/act.php?id=BOE-A-2020-4208 (in Spanish, own translation), access: 5 August 2024.

Similar solutions are provided for in Croatian law. Due to the COVID-19 pandemic, all electronic auctions in enforcement and bankruptcy proceedings have been postponed, with the exception of those for which the bidding period started on 24 March 2020.

In Luxembourg, the enforcement of eviction orders in residential tenancy cases has been suspended. The time limits for execution and forced auctions have also been suspended.

5.3.5. Electronic communication tools

In some Member States, given the risk of COVID-19 spreading through the postal circulation of judicial correspondence, a number of measures have been taken to facilitate communication between parties and the judiciary by electronic means.

In France, during the state of emergency, parties were notified of court judgments by any means of communication, in particular by e-mail or telephone, and such judgments were not considered to have been served.

Lithuania also adopted solutions for electronic communication with the court. Direct service was suspended and court orders on procedural matters were served electronically, mainly through the court information system. In exceptional cases, correspondence was sent by e-mail and post to parties who did not have access to this system.

In Romania, Article 42(3) of the Presidential Decree No. 195 of 16 March 2020 introduced electronic communication between courts and parties during the state of emergency. The submission of pleadings by the parties was exclusively electronic. The service of pleadings was also carried out by fax, e-mail or any other means of communication ensuring the transmission of the text and the acknowledgement of receipt.

The Netherlands has introduced the possibility of communicating directly with the judiciary via secure mailboxes (Secure Mail)[618]. On 15 October 2020, the Decree on the rules of electronic procedure in civil and administrative law[619] was adopted (to enter into force on 1 January 2021). According to the provisions of this law, a document sent electronically through a Secure Mail box is considered to be signed by hand within the meaning of the Code of Civil Procedure if the document was signed by hand before being uploaded to the relevant system (Article 5 of the Decree). Sending and receiving documents in this way is voluntary.

618 https://www.rechtspraak.nl/veilig-mailen-met-de-rechtspraak (in Dutch, own translation), access: 5 August 2024.

619 https://wetten.overheid.nl/BWBR0044275/2021-01-01 (in Dutch, own translation), access: 5 August 2024.

Croatia has an ePremet (eCaseFile) system that allows parties to access information about the case, but does not have the functionality to view the content of court documents. During the COVID-19 pandemic, letters to the court could only be sent by professional lawyers, experts, appraisers, court administrators and legal entities. Communication with the parties is carried out as far as possible by electronic means[620].

620 Table 'Use of digital tools...'.

6. Remote court hearings

6.1. Introductory remarks

The first manifestations of the computerisation of civil proceedings appeared in the Code of Civil Procedure as early as 2008, with the introduction of Article 235 §§ 2 and 3 of the CCP, which allows the taking of evidence by means of technical devices that enable this action to be carried out remotely, if the nature of the evidence does not oppose it. However, the academic circle had already been calling for the possibility of hearing witnesses at a distance[621]. Subsequently, with the Act of 10 July 2015[622], Article 151 § 2 of the CCP was introduced, according to which a public hearing may be held with the use of technical devices enabling it to be conducted remotely. In this case, the participants of the proceedings may attend the court session while being in the building of another court. The legislator did not leave it to the participants of the remote hearing to decide where they would like to be connected to the courtroom where the hearing is taking place. Due to logistical problems, mainly related to the low availability of courtrooms, this mode has not been widely used. In fact, it has been noted that this mode has not been used by any court in Poland since the provision came into force in 2016[623].

A far-reaching change necessary due to the epidemic situation in the country, which threatened the safe functioning of the courts, was the introduction into the legal system of remote hearings, i.e. hearings by means of technical devices allowing direct transmission of video and audio, as of 16 May 2020[624]. The introduction of remote hearings was dictated by the need to reduce direct human contact, which in the case of stationary sessions often consisted of spending hours in a closed courtroom without access to fresh air, potentially facilitating the transmission of the coronavirus if an infected person attended the hearing. At the same

---

621 M. Krakowiak, *Rozprawa elektroniczna...*, p. 213 and A. Kościółek, A. Arkuszewska, *Remote court hearings - evolution or revolution,* [in:] *Zdalne posiedzenia sądowe – ewolucja czy rewolucja,* [in:] *Prawo Nowych Technologii. Księga jubileuszowa z okazji jubileuszu 20-lecia działalności Centrum Badań Problemów Prawnych i Ekonomicznych Komunikacji Elektronicznej i Studenckiego Koła Naukowego – Blok Prawa Komputerowego,* J. Gołaczyński (ed.), Warsaw 2022, p. 63.

622 Act amending the Act - Civil Code, the Act - Civil Procedure Code and certain other acts, Journal of Laws 2015, item 1311.

623 J. Gołaczyński, M. Dymitruk, *Rozprawa zdalna i doręczenia elektroniczne w dobie pandemii COVID-19 po wejściu w życie nowelizacji z 28.5.2021 r.*, Monitor Prawniczy 2021/13, pp. 685–686.

624 Pursuant to Article 46 of the Act of 14 May 2020 amending certain laws with respect to protective measures in connection with the spread of the SARS-CoV-2 virus (Journal of Laws of 2020, item 875).

time, the legislation in force (Article 151 § 2 of the CCP) did not contain sufficient instruments to enable a remote hearing to be held without the presence of the participants in the courthouse[625]. According to the wording of Article 15zzs[1] (1) of the COVID-19 Special Act (in the version in force from 16 May 2020), a trial or public hearing shall be held with the use of technical devices enabling it to be held remotely with simultaneous transmission of video and audio, except that the persons participating in it need not be present in the court building, unless holding a hearing or public session without the use of the aforementioned devices would not cause an undue risk to the health of the persons participating in it. The above provision allowed the participants in the hearing (with the exception of the members of the panel) to attend the hearing anywhere outside the courthouse and to be remotely connected to the courtroom. It was only in special circumstances that the president of the court could order the participation of the members of the panel, with exception of the president and the clerk, in a remote meeting outside the court building, but this did not apply to the session at which the trial was to be closed. As a general rule, therefore, the presence of the members of the panel in the courthouse was required and the exceptions to this rule were strictly defined.

The categorical wording of the provision ('shall be held') implied an obligation on the part of the court to hold every public hearing remotely, while providing for the possibility to derogate from this rule if the conditions set out in the provision were met[626]. In practice, however, the provision of Article 15zzs[1](1) of the COVID-19 Special Act was not considered to be very restrictive, but rather a reasonable alternative to in-person hearings that improved access to justice in the era of coronavirus[627]. This meant that while there was a presumption in favour of a remote hearing, the court could dispense with this form if an in-person hearing would not pose an undue risk to the health of the participants[628].

Some comments of a terminological nature should be made at this point. The provision of Article 15zzs[1] of the COVID-19 Special Act uses the phrase 'remote trial or hearing'. It should be recalled that public hearings of the court are divided into a trial and other hearings. The trial is for the substantive determination of the case, while public hearings are for the conduct of other procedural activities[629]. In view of the above, it can be concluded that the legislator's use of the term 'trial or public hearing' in the text of Article 15zzs[1] of the COVID-19 Special Act is inaccurate. A public hearing also includes a trial (which is a type of public hearing). The

625 K. Klimas, [in:] *Postępowanie cywilne w czasie pandemii. E-doręczenia, rozprawa zdalna, posiedzenie niejawne, składnie pism procesowych*, J. Gołaczyński (ed.), Warsaw 2022, pp. 108–109.

626 J. Litowski, *Ograniczenie jawności postępowania cywilnego z uwagi na stan epidemii wywołany wirusem COVID-19*, Monitor Prawniczy 2021/2, p. 70.

627 A. Machnikowska, *Zasada jawności...*, p. 110.

628 J. Gołaczyński, M. Dymitruk, *Rozprawa zdalna...*, p. 687.

629 H. Pietrzkowski, *Metodyka pracy sędziego...*, p. 451.

legislator should therefore only use the term 'public hearing', which is intended to cover both a trial and other public hearing held remotely.

6.2. Remote court hearings after 3 July 2021

With effect from 3 July 2021[630], Article 15zzs^1 of the COVID-19 Special Act has been significantly amended. The content of Article 15zzs^1 has been expanded by adding four sections (previously the Article contained only three points). The previous contents of sections 1 and 2 have been moved to section 1, points 1–4 has been added, as well as three other sections containing contents not previously regulated in the COVID-19 Special Act[631]. The issue of remote hearings is now dealt with in points 1 and 2 of section 1. According to the amended wording of Article 15zzs^1(1) point 1 of the COVID-19 Special Act, during the period in which the state of epidemic threat or the state of epidemic declared on the basis of COVID-19 is in force and within one year of the lifting of the latter, in cases heard in accordance with the provisions of the Code of Civil Procedure, a trial or a public hearing shall be held by means of technical devices that enable it to be held at a distance with simultaneous transmission of image and sound (remote hearing), with the proviso that the persons participating in it, including the members of the panel, do not have to be present in the courthouse. On the other hand, according to the wording of Article 15zzs^1(1) point 2, the holding of a remote hearing may be dispensed with only if the public hearing of the case is necessary and its holding in the court building does not constitute an undue risk to the health of the persons participating in it.

First of all, it is important to note the distinctive term of the provision of Article 15zzs^1(1) point 1 of the COVID-19 Special Act, which provides for the obligation to hold remote hearings[632]. It should apply not only during a state of epidemic or epidemic threat, but also for one year after the last state of epidemic or epidemic threat has been lifted. In practice, it is impossible to determine when the state of epidemic or epidemic threat will be lifted and, consequently, when the obligation to hold remote hearings will cease. While such a solution is seen as a threat to the principle of necessity under Article 31(3) of the Constitution[633] (which has been discussed earlier), it should be recalled that some members of the doctrine have argued in favour of its legitimacy, pointing out that the dynamic nature of the epidemic situation requires the continued use of remote hearings and the gradual restoration of traditional court sessions[634].

---

630 By virtue of Article 4 of the Act of 28 May 2021 amending the Act - Code of Civil Procedure and certain other acts (Journal of Laws 2021, item 1090).

631 J. Litowski, *Zakres zmian art. 15zzs[1] ustawy z 2.3.2020 r. – uwagi na tle stanu prawnego obowiązującego od 3.7.2021 r.*, Monitor Prawniczy 2022/2, p. 72.

632 J. Litowski, *Zakres zmian…*, p. 72.

633 K. Gajda-Roszczynialska, *Przebudowa wymiaru…*, p. 19 and A. Machnikowska, *Zasada jawności…*, p. 81.

634 M. Krakowiak, *Rozprawa elektroniczna …*, p. 221.

The wording of Article 15zzs^1(1) point 1 of the COVID-19 Special Act leaves no doubt that the remote hearing is mandatory and that the waiver of this form in favour of a physical hearing is subject to the fulfilment of strict conditions[635]. This provision has introduced an additional requirement for the waiver of the remote meeting compared to the previously applicable Article 15zzs^1.

Until 3 July 2021, as previously signalled, the law introduced a presumption in favour of a remote form of hearing, which could be waived by the presiding judge on the basis of a discretionary decision, if the presiding judge was satisfied that a physical hearing would not pose an undue risk to the health of the participants. After the amendment, which entered into force on 3 July 2021, Article 15zzs^1(1) point 2 of the COVID-19 Special Act made it possible to waive a remote hearing only if it was necessary to hear the case in a trial or public hearing and holding it in the courthouse would not cause an undue risk to the health of the participants. The provision has thus been enriched by the additional premise of the 'necessity' of holding a public hearing.

The wording of the above requirement must be considered unfortunate at the very least. The necessity (obligation) to hold a hearing follows directly from the provision of Article 42 § 2 and 3 of the Law on the Organisation of Common Courts, according to which the courts recognise and decide cases in open proceedings, and the hearing of a case in closed session is allowed only exceptionally on the basis of a statutory provision. This principle is reflected in Article 148 § 1 of the Code of Civil Procedure, according to which court hearings are open and the court recognises cases in open court, unless a specific provision provides otherwise. The simple conclusion to be drawn from the above provisions is that, as a general rule, the court is obliged to give a decision after a public hearing in every case, and that any exceptions require the existence of an express provision of statutory rank. The referral of a case for a hearing is therefore, in principle, always 'necessary'.

In the context of the above, it seems that the premise of the 'necessity of holding a public hearing or trial', despite its imprecise formulation, should be understood differently than according to its literal wording. J. Litowski notes that 'necessity' in this case should be understood as the expediency (actual need) to hold a hearing or public trial[636], and not as a normative requirement (duty). In turn, M. Krakowiak points out that the premise of 'necessity' means that there must be direct contact between the court and the parties (participants in the proceedings) or other persons[637]. It is necessary to agree with the above and to supplement the presented positions with the statement that it is a necessity to hold an in-person hearing and not a public hearing at all. The need to hold a conventional public hearing arises when the refusal to hold such a hearing prevents or impedes the proper achievement of the objectives of the proceedings, which include the full determination

---

635 K. Klimas, [in:] *Postępowanie cywilne...*, p. 117.
636 J. Litowski, *Zakres zmian...*, p. 74.
637 M. Krakowiak, *Rozprawa elektroniczna...*, p. 225.

of the facts of the case and the issuance of a substantively correct judgment. The need for a public hearing also arises where, in the absence of such a hearing, the party runs the risk of being deprived of the opportunity to defend its rights[638]. This will mainly concern situations where it is necessary for the court to have personal contact with the evidence or the participants in the proceedings. Examples include the need to appear in person to conclude a settlement, to make a statement before the court on the acceptance or rejection of the inheritance, or the need to bring a witness or debtor before a court by force.

The need for an in-person hearing may also arise from the need to respect the principle of directness in cases where personal contact between the members of the panel and the evidence will be necessary. According to A. Kościółek, the conduct of an evidentiary hearing at a distance does not violate the principle of directness, but only requires its redefinition. In the case of the use of technical devices that allow for the performance of this activity at a distance, there is a separation of the place of performance of the evidence between the seat of the court and the place where the source of the evidence is located. The use of modern techniques for the direct transmission of images and sound makes it possible to maintain this personal contact with the parties, witnesses, experts or material evidence and thus to make personal observations by the judge, which is the essence of the principle of directness[639]. The above statement can only be partially accepted. Indeed, in some cases, a remote hearing by means of videoconferencing may lead to a weakening of the principle of directness, due to the reduced ability to perceive the reactions of the persons questioned by means of direct video and audio transmission. A traditional hearing may also be necessary in cases of digital exclusion of participants, i.e. lack of skills or ability to use the IT tools necessary to connect to the court[640].

However, it is difficult to agree with the statement that the reason for refusing to hold a remote hearing is the technical impossibility of conducting it on the part of the court or the participants. Such an understanding of the premise of 'necessity' seems inappropriate. In fact, the legislator requires courts to hold remote hearings as a general rule. If this is the case, it must be concluded that the obligation to create the technical conditions necessary for the holding of remote hearings rests with the courts (their administration) and that the lack of adequate technical possibilities is not a sufficient justification to allow this form to be abandoned. In the event that it is not possible for the participants to participate in the remote session, the legislator prescribes that such participation shall be provided in the courthouse (Article 15zzs[1](2) of the COVID-19 Special Act). In such a case, a party or a summoned person who has declared the need to do so shall take part in the remote hearing by means of devices enabling direct transmission of video and audio in

---

638 J. Litowski, *Zakres zmian…*, p. 74.
639 A. Kościółek, *Elektroniczne czynności procesowe w sądowym postępowaniu cywilnym*, Warsaw 2012, pp. 301–302.
640 K. Klimas, [in:] *Postępowanie cywilne…*, p. 120.

the court building, but outside the courtroom where the court panel is present. The lack of need for a public hearing is, moreover, only one of the two conditions that must be cumulatively fulfilled in order for an in-person hearing to be possible.

The second condition for dispensing with a remote hearing is that holding the hearing in the courthouse would not present an unreasonable risk to the health of the participants. The assessment of the fulfilment of the above condition is left to the presiding judge, who should take into account the excessive risk of coronavirus infection and not the general health of the person concerned[641]. The current epidemic situation in the country and in the region where the court is located, the protective measures taken in the courthouse, the expected number of persons attending the hearing[642], but also the expected duration of the hearing or the size of the courtroom, including the distance between the participants in the hearing, will be the main criteria to be taken into account by the presiding judge. It should be emphasised that the provision states that the absence of an 'unreasonable' risk is a prerequisite for not holding a remote hearing. Therefore, it is impossible to agree with J. Litowski, who points out that only the certainty of the absence of danger allows the hearing to be held in the traditional manner, while any doubt should lead to the holding of a remote hearing[643]. It should be noted that despite the dynamically changing epidemic situation in the following months, even with a low number of cases, coronavirus infection was still a real threat. Therefore, the assumption that a remote meeting can only be dispensed with when there is certainty that there is no risk of infection would lead to the conclusion that in the vast majority of cases there was no possibility of holding a traditional hearing.

In the explanatory memorandum to the bill amending Article 15zzs[1] of the COVID-19 Special Act, it is stated that the aim of the regulation is to take into account the safety of participants in proceedings and judicial staff and to prevent the paralysis of the judiciary[644]. It must therefore be assumed that the *ratio legis* of the compulsory remote hearings introduced as of 3 July 2021 and the tightening of the grounds for waiving them were intended to protect the health of the participants in the hearing as well as public health by preventing the spread of the coronavirus. It should be noted, however, that this objective was already pursued by the provision of Article 15zzs[1](1) of the COVID-19 Special Act in its previous wording. Indeed, this provision allowed for the possibility to dispense with the holding of a remote hearing if a stationary hearing would not pose an undue risk to the health of the participants. This reasoning has been repeated in the amended version of Article 15zzs[1](1).

---

641 J. Litowski, *Ograniczenie jawności...*, p. 72.
642 M. Krakowiak, *Rozprawa elektroniczna ...*, pp. 224–225.
643 J. Litowski, *Ograniczenie jawności...*, p. 72.
644 Government Bill to amend the Act - Code of Civil Procedure and certain other Acts, parliamentary paper no. 899, https://www.sejm.gov.pl/sejm9.nsf/druk.xsp?nr=899.

In view of the foregoing, the question arises as to whether the introduction of an additional condition in the form of 'the need to hold a public hearing' was necessary and, moreover, whether it achieves the objective of health protection stated by the legislator and whether this objective is real. Indeed, it is questionable how the amendment of the provision by adding the prerequisite in question to the content of Article 15zzs^1(1) of the COVID-19 Special Act achieves the objective of health protection, when the previous wording of the provision already included the epidemic premise (excessive health risk). It is therefore necessary to determine whether the amendment is purely editorial or whether the legislator's intervention is intended to pursue a different objective, which is not mentioned in the explanatory memorandum of the draft. In particular, the question arises as to whether the legislator's aim was not to shift the boundary between the forms of holding court hearings and, consequently, to reverse the principle according to which the primary form of the court's operation is a stationary hearing and a remote hearing is only an exception[645].

An attempt to respond to the above doubts should begin by noting that the government's explanatory memorandum to the draft states that absolute priority should be given to a remote hearing, and in the clash between two constitutional values – openness of proceedings and the right to hear a case without undue delay – there is no doubt as to which should be given priority[646]. Although it is not explicitly stated, it is obvious that the principle of procedural efficiency is more important to the authors of the amendment, which justifies even solutions that affect the limitation of the principle of openness. In the light of the above, it appears that the real purpose of the amendment was not so much to protect the health of participants in court hearings, but to speed up civil proceedings in the era of the COVID-19 pandemic. As indicated earlier, if the sole purpose of the provision of Article 15zzs^1 of the COVID-19 Special Act was to protect health, then the introduction of an additional premise would be unnecessary, since this purpose was explicitly expressed in the previous wording of the Act.

It has been pointed out that Article 15zzs^1 of the COVID-19 Special Act has become more categorical[647] after the amendment of 28 May 2021. However, one cannot agree with the statement that this change should be considered only in editorial terms. An analysis of the explanatory memorandum of the draft leads to the conclusion that the legislator's intention was to clearly reverse the relationship between traditional and remote court hearing. The amendment of 28 May 2021 was intended to break with the previous approach, according to which a remote hearing was a convenient alternative to a traditional session[648], and the choice of

645 T. Zembrzuski, *Ograniczenia jawności postępowania w sprawach cywilnych w dobie pandemii – potrzeba chwili czy trwałe rozwiązanie?*, Forum Prawnicze 2021/3, p. 6.
646 Parliamentary paper No. 889.
647 M. Krakowiak, *Rozprawa elektroniczna* ..., p. 117.
648 A. Machnikowska, *Zasada jawności*..., p. 110.

the appropriate form was left to the discretion of the presiding judge, who was not constrained by overly strict conditions for waiving a remote hearing. Instead, the legislator introduced a rigid rule that all court hearings should be held remotely, except in those situations where it was absolutely necessary to hold a traditional hearing.

Thus, the real purpose of the amendment was to speed up the civil proceedings, which is particularly evident given that the premise of the 'need for a remote hearing' remains disconnected from the actual development of the pandemic. In the light of Article 15zzs^1(1) of the COVID-19 Special Act, the holding of a remote hearing is obligatory even if it is considered that there is no epidemic threat. In such a case, it cannot be considered justified on health protection grounds if the holding of an in-person hearing does not depend solely on the course of the pandemic. Both conditions ('necessity' and epidemic) for holding an in-person hearing must be met cumulatively. It should be noted that the obligation to quarantine and isolate in the case of coronavirus infection and the obligation to cover the mouth and nose have been abolished as of 28 March 2022[649], and the state of epidemic has been abolished as of 16 May 2020 and replaced by the state of epidemic threat[650]. From the above, it should be concluded that holding a court session in a court building from May 2022 has not caused an excessive epidemic risk (although the epidemic situation in the country should be assessed as dynamic and infections could be expected to increase again in the future). Nevertheless, the obligation to hold remote sittings remained in force until March 2024.

6.3. Conducting a remote hearing

Article 15zzs^1(1) of the COVID-19 Special Act provides that the hearing may be held at a distance 'by means of technical equipment enabling it to be held at a distance with simultaneous direct video and audio transmission'. The participants in the hearing, including the members of the panel, do not have to be present in the courthouse. The legislator has not introduced any restrictions in this respect, which means that the participants in the hearing may be connected to the court anywhere, not excluding the possibility of being outside the country[651]. It should be noted, however, that the solemnity of an official act such as a court hearing requires that the participant should not be in a place (and situation) that is incompatible with this, e.g. in a crowded railway station or while travelling by car. The

---

649 Ordinance of the Council of Ministers of 25 March 2022 on the establishment of certain restrictions, orders and prohibitions in connection with the occurrence of an epidemic threat (Journal of Laws 2022, item 679).

650 Ordinance of the Minister of Health of 12 May 2022 on the cancellation of an epidemic state in the territory of the Republic of Poland (Journal of Laws 2022, item 1027).

651 K. Klimas, [in:] *Postępowanie cywilne...*, p. 113.

participant should ensure that the place where they are located guarantees the proper order and formal nature of the court hearing.

The wording of the provision in question indicates that a remote hearing must take place with direct transmission of both video and audio. It is therefore unacceptable to hold a hearing with only audio transmission and no video transmission. This is due to the need for the court to verify the identity of the persons participating in the hearing and, in many cases, to verify that a participant in the hearing is not in a situation where their statements are influenced by other persons, which is important when assessing the credibility of persons questioned by the court. Direct video and audio transmission is also intended to create conditions comparable to a traditional hearing in a courtroom[652]. Moreover, this requirement is of considerable importance for the preservation of the principle of directness. Allowing a hearing to be conducted remotely by means of audio transmission alone would therefore lead to a situation in which the direct contact between the court and the participants in the hearing is weakened. K. Klimas rightly points out that it is inadmissible, even after verification of the identity of the persons participating in the hearing, to have only a view from the camera used by the participant due to poor connection quality if the transmission of image and sound is impaired. If there are technical problems preventing the simultaneous transmission of video and audio, the hearing should be adjourned. On the other hand, it would not be acceptable to dispense with the transmission of video, even if this would lead to an improvement in the quality of the audio[653].

The provision of Article 15zzs[1] of the COVID-19 Special Act does not provide any further guidance on how to conduct a remote session. In particular, the legislator has not provided for the competence to issue implementing regulations that would regulate the procedure for holding court hearings in this form. M. Krakowiak points out[654] that, in this situation, it is necessary to refer to the provisions of the Ordinance of the Minister of Justice of 24 February 2010 on devices and technical means enabling the taking of evidence at a distance in civil proceedings[655], issued on the basis of the statutory authorisation contained in Article 235 § 3 of the CCP. In § 2(1), the Ordinance provides that the taking of evidence at a distance is to be carried out using analogue or digital technical devices that enable telecommunication transmission within the meaning of Article 2(27a) of the Act of 16 July 2004 – the Telecommunications Act[656], and in particular using devices that allow two-way communication in real time, enabling the transmission of sound or image and sound between the participants in a procedural act. However, the Ordinance does not provide for a detailed procedure for conducting remote evidence.

652 K. Klimas, [in:] *Postępowanie cywilne...*, p. 116.
653 K. Klimas, [in:] *Postępowanie cywilne..*, pp. 116–117.
654 M. Krakowiak, *Rozprawa elektroniczna...*, pp. 222–223.
655 Journal of Laws 2010, No. 34, item 185.
656 Journal of Laws 2022, item 1648 (consolidated text).

The position that the above-mentioned act applies to remote hearings conducted under Article 15zzs[1](1) of the COVID-19 Special Act cannot be accepted. First of all, it should be emphasised that the statutory authorisation contained in Article 235 § 3 of the CCP empowers the Minister of Justice to determine the types of devices and technical means enabling the remote taking of evidence. Thus, the provision refers only to the taking of evidence and not to the court session. The provisions of Article 15zzs[1] of the COVID-19 Special Act are *lex specialis* in relation to the provisions of the Code of Civil Procedure and do not contain a similar authorisation. Moreover, the Ordinance of the Minister of Justice of 24 February 2010 was issued before the introduction of the special regulation on remote hearings, so it cannot be assumed that it can be applied to the later statutory regulation. Consequently, it must be assumed that there are no implementing rules that could be applied to remote hearings. The lack of detailed requirements on how remote hearings should be conducted leads to the conclusion that the catalogue of permissible technical solutions is broad, which may have provided the courts with a quick basis for videoconferencing, especially in the early stages of the pandemic[657], but also raises many practical doubts.

The lack of detailed technical provisions on how to conduct remote hearings means that parties' rights are not adequately protected in the event of videoconferencing equipment malfunction[658]. Practice in the application of the provision of Article 15zzs[1](1) of the COVID-19 Special Act shows that technical problems very often arise in the case of remote hearings This was particularly acute in the early stages of the provision's application, when courts were not sufficiently equipped to conduct hearings by videoconference. In a survey conducted in April 2021, more than half of the judges indicated that they had occasionally cancelled a hearing due to technical problems, and 14.91 % of the respondents indicated that this happened regularly[659]. In 2022, problems with participants' connection were a regular feature of remote hearings[660]. The prevalence of technical difficulties and the consequent need to postpone hearings, rather than the claimed speeding up of proceedings, may have the opposite effect.

When the technical problems lie with the participants, the legislation does not regulate the rules of conduct. In particular, the law has not determined whether the parties (or other participants in the hearing, e.g. witnesses) have an obligation to ensure the quality of the connection and what the consequences are if they fail to do so. The legislation is silent on how active the role of the court should be in

---

657 K. Klimas, [in:] *Postępowanie cywilne...*, pp. 115–116.

658 A. Machnikowska, *Zasada jawności...*, p. 115.

659 A. Begier, A. Wypych-Knieć, Ł. Małecki-Tepicht, Report of the Association of Polish Judges 'Iustitia', *Sądownictwo w czasie COVID-19 – raport z badania oceny wpływu pandemii COVID-19 na wymiar sprawiedliwości w* Polsce, Warsaw 2021, p. 37.

660 B. Plitowski, R. Sitniewska, P. Solowij, *Obywatelski Monitoring Sądów 2022,* Report of the Court Watch Polska Foundation, Toruń 2022, p. 38.

ensuring that all participants in the hearing have adequate remote access. Some courts have developed the practice of contacting participants in the hearing by phone to clarify any technical problems that may arise[661]. It should be stressed, however, that such an obligation on the part of the court is not explicitly laid down in the legislation. Moreover, in many cases the court will not have the contact details of the parties. Indeed, while Article 15zzs^{9}(1) of the COVID-19 Special Act provides for the obligation of the professional representative to provide contact details (e-mail, telephone number for contacting the court) in the first pleading, there is no such provision in relation to the parties to the proceedings.

Doubts may arise in a situation where the court has information that the participant in the hearing is trying to connect to the court, but for technical reasons this is difficult, or the quality of the connection does not allow stable video and audio transmission. It is also common for the court to be unaware that a participant is attempting to connect to the court and to proceed with the hearing (while displaying a message to the participant that the hearing is pending) – the court in this situation has no tools to determine whether a party or other participant in the hearing is voluntarily abandoning the hearing or whether there have been technical problems. Importantly, there are currently no tools to determine the reasons why a person has not connected to attend the hearing. The above issues are of great practical importance. Failure to adjourn a hearing that a party wished to attend but was unable to do so may result in a violation of that party's procedural rights. On the other hand, the adjournment of a hearing in any situation where there is no effective communication with all participants creates room for abuse by parties who may have an interest in prolonging the proceedings. The adjournment of a hearing in such a situation will result in an increase in the length of the proceedings due to the need to wait for the next hearing date.

The high level of generality in the regulation of remote hearings and the lack of guidelines on how to conduct these hearings leads to a wide variety of technical solutions being used by the courts. The recommended software for videoconferencing by general courts is JITSI[662], but software such as MS Teams, Scopia or Zoom were also used in practice. The lack of uniform software means that not all courts are integrated with the ReCourt system for recording proceedings by means of an audio and video recording device (Article 157 § 1 of the CCP). The minutes prepared in this way should include the image and sound received by the remote participants. Otherwise, it may be necessary to repeat the taking of evidence (Article 241 of the CCP). As stated by the Supreme Court in its decision of 23 March 2016[663], if the minutes prepared by means of a video and audio recording device do not enable the court to determine the content of the evidentiary proceedings, the court shall repeat taking of evidence to the appropriate extent. For

661 K. Klimas, [in:] *Postępowanie cywilne...*, p. 124.
662 K. Klimas, [in:] *Postępowanie cywilne...*, p. 126.
663 Resolution of the Supreme Court of 23 March 2016, III CZP 102/15.

example, if the audio and video of a participant in a remote hearing (e.g. a witness) is not properly recorded during the evidentiary process, the activity should be repeated. This risk arises in particular if the court uses software that is not properly integrated with the electronic minutes. It should also be noted that some of the tools used by the courts do not work with all operating systems (e.g. MacOS), which can disadvantage their users[664] and, in extreme cases, make it impossible to participate in a remote hearing. The use of different tools for remote hearings leads to a lack of uniform standards, especially as some of the systems are not adapted to the realities of justice[665].

Remote hearings may affect the application of the principle of directness in civil proceedings, according to which the court hearing the case should have personal contact with the evidence in order to be able to make the relevant observations which are primarily material to the assessment of the evidence[666]. The very form of conducting remote hearings by videoconference may limit the possibility of making a fair assessment of evidence from personal sources, due to the difficulty of perceiving reflexes and other physical reactions via video and audio transmission. There is no doubt that videoconferencing makes it easier for third parties to influence testimony[667]. In practice, there may also be problems in ensuring the independence of the witnesses' testimony, which may be difficult or even impossible to detect (e.g. reading testimony from pre-prepared materials or using third parties out of camera range). However, the software used does not provide an effective means of verifying that no unauthorised persons are present in the room where the witness is testifying, including witnesses who are to testify later. It should be noted that under the second sentence of Article 264 of the CCP, witnesses who have not yet testified may not be present during the examination of other witnesses. A. Michór points out that the presiding judge should always verify who is in the same room with the witness who is to testify before the court and carefully observe the dynamics of the questioning (e.g. to exclude a situation in which the witness deliberately breaks off the connection and fails to answer the question)[668].

Holding a remote hearing without the simultaneous presence of the participants in the courthouse can lead to problems with the circulation of documents and court correspondence, both during the preparation of the remote hearing and during the hearing itself. In order to hold a remote hearing, the participants must be provided with access data in advance, usually in the form of a videoconference address (link).

---

664 A. Begier, A. Wypych-Knieć, Ł. Małecki-Tepicht, *Sądownictwo w czasie COVID-19...*, p. 41.

665 K. Klimas, [in:] *Postępowanie cywilne...*, p. 126.

666 H. Dolecki, T. Radkiewicz, [in:] *Kodeks postępowania cywilnego...*, p. 1112.

667 K. Jasińska, *E-rozprawa w postępowaniu cywilnym a prawo do sądu i możliwość obrony swoich praw,* Studia Prawnicze. Rozprawy i Materiały 2021/2, p. 38.

668 A. Michór, *Postępowanie cywilne w okresie epidemii COVID-19,* Bussiness Law Journal 2021/9, p. 40.

In this respect, too, there seems to be a lack of rules governing the communication between the court and the participants[669]. Even if the applicable rules do not provide for such a requirement, it is desirable to offer the participants in the remote hearing instructions appropriate to the software used, as well as information on the manner of communication (including, for example, the order of connection in the event that a high number of witnesses are summoned to the hearing) and the possibility of making a test connection in order to check whether the participant's equipment meets the technical requirements for an adequate connection to the court[670].

Typically, summonses and notices of court appearances are sent to participants in paper form. This creates additional difficulties as the often-complicated videoconference address (link)[671] has to be manually transcribed into the browser window and is prone to errors. In this situation, in addition to sending a traditional notice or invitation to the remote hearing, it seems reasonable to send the link to the videoconference by electronic means, in particular by e-mail. The basis for such a measure could be Article 149^1 of the CCP, which provides for the possibility of addressing summonses to parties, witnesses, experts or other persons 'in the manner that the court deems most appropriate', without prejudice to the methods of service provided for in the provisions of the CCP. It should be stressed, however, that such a summons only has procedural effects if it has undoubtedly reached the addressee at least one week before the hearing, or three days in urgent cases (Article 149 § 2 of the CCP). However, it should be emphasised once again that the current legislation does not require the parties and other participants to inform the court of their contact details in the form of an e-mail address and telephone number (except for professional lawyers – Article 15zzs^9(1) of the COVID-19 Special Act). In many cases, therefore, the court will have no means of communicating with the participants in a remote hearing other than traditional correspondence.

Taking into account the practical doubts mentioned above, which may nevertheless have an impact on the correctness of the service of notices and summonses, it seems desirable to follow the practice that all information necessary to establish a connection with the court should be included in the court letter containing the notice and summons. The court will then have proof of service of the relevant notice or summons, leaving no doubt that the court letter reached the addressee in due time. In order to facilitate communication with the court and to avoid possible connection problems, it will be good practice to additionally send the address of the videoconference to the participants by e-mail, provided that the court has access to the addressee's e-mail. In the case of professional lawyers, the notice of the date of the hearing should normally be published on the Information Portal, which eliminates the need to additionally send the link to the remote hearing by e-mail. The issue of service of judicial documents via the Information Portal will be further discussed.

669 K. Klimas, [in:] *Postępowanie cywilne...*, p. 124.
670 K. Klimas, [in:] *Postępowanie cywilne...*, p. 124.
671 K. Klimas, [in:] *Postępowanie cywilne...*, p. 125.

The lack of clear implementing rules on important organisational issues means that courts have to develop their own methods of preparing and conducting remote hearings[672]. These standards vary from court to court, resulting in a lack of clearly defined obligations and procedural rights for parties and other participants in remote hearings.

If the meeting is held remotely, other problems relating to the circulation of documents may arise. These doubts are not resolved by the current provisions. In this respect, attention should first be paid to issues relating to the service of letters to be filed at the hearing, the proof of the representative's power of attorney or the filing of an annex to the minutes. In practice, a party may wish to submit a preparatory or evidentiary pleading during the hearing. The way in which the remote hearing is conducted prevents documents from being sent directly to the court. On the other hand, the current rules do not allow pleadings to be submitted to the court in electronic form. This is a significant limitation for the parties, which does not remain unaffected by the course of the proceedings, since it forces them to submit these pleadings sufficiently in advance so that the court can become acquainted with them at the latest during the hearing. Pursuant to § 99 of the Regulation on the Rules of Procedure of Common Courts, if the document to be served has been lodged at a time which makes it impossible to serve it before the date of the hearing, the document shall be served at the hearing by recording the fact of service in the minutes or in a note. However, this rule does not apply in the case of a remote hearing, which may result in the hearing having to be adjourned in order to enable a party to acquaint themselves with the opponent's statement, which has been lodged with the court without sufficient notice to enable it to be served by the court before the date of the hearing.

The formula of a remote meeting also calls into question the institution of an annex to the minutes, as referred to in Article 161 of the CCP. This provision states that 'during the hearing' requests, statements, additions and corrections to requests and statements may be included in an annex to the minutes. An annex to the minutes forms an integral part of the minutes and may be submitted at the latest immediately after the hearing, unless the presiding judge sets a different time limit for its submission at the request of a party[673]. Given the subsidiary nature of an annex to the minutes, its submission in advance of the hearing should be excluded, as it can only cover motions and statements already made at the hearing. An annex to the minutes should be limited to a recapitulation of the oral arguments presented at the hearing[674]. The conduct of the hearing in a remote session excludes, in principle, the possibility of submitting an annex to the minutes, since, as indicated above, the applicable rules do not provide for the submission of documents by electronic means. In view of the foregoing, the only possibility

672 K. Klimas, [in:] *Postępowanie cywilne...*, p. 124.
673 E. Stefańska, [in:] *Kodeks postępowania cywilnego...*, p. 563.
674 Judgment of the Supreme Court of 13 November 2003, I CK 229/02.

of submitting such a document is for the presiding judge to set an additional time limit for this purpose, which in turn may have a direct impact on the length of the proceedings in the case. It should also be noted that in a remote hearing at the end of which the case is closed, the submission of an annex to the minutes is not possible. This is because the closure of the hearing precludes the filing of further submissions containing the position of a party.

Other practical difficulties may arise in the course of a remote hearing, particularly in the evidentiary phase, in relation to the examination of witnesses or parties. In particular, doubts may arise as to whether the presiding judge should check the identity of the persons questioned. Pursuant to § 113 of the Regulation on the Rules of Procedure of Common Courts, the personal data of the person questioned shall be verified prior to the questioning on the basis of an identity card or other document confirming identity, and this shall be recorded in the minutes. In the absence of such a document, the presiding judge shall decide whether the activity is to be carried out with the participation of the person in question. The absence of an identity document shall be recorded in the minutes. If the hearing takes place in the premises of the court, the question of checking the identity of the person being heard shall not give rise to any doubt as to the violation of the right to privacy and protection of personal data. In such a case, the identity document is presented directly to the presiding judge and the other participants in the hearing do not have access to it. The situation is different in the case of a remote hearing, where, for lack of other solutions, the identification is based on the presentation of the document in front of the camera, without the possibility of presenting the document only to the presiding judge for inspection. Since the direct transmission of the image from the camera of the person being questioned is transmitted simultaneously to all participants and, moreover, should, as a rule, be recorded in the electronic protocol drawn up in accordance with Article 157 § 1 of the CCP, there is a risk that the sensitive data contained in the identity document will become known to other participants who may also record the transmitted image. Therefore, the risk of disclosure of the data contained in the identity document seems to be an argument in favour of refraining from verifying the identity of the witness by presenting the identity document in front of the camera, in particular if it does not give rise to reasonable doubts on the part of the presiding judge.

It should be noted that the provisions of the Code of Civil Procedure do not provide for an obligation to establish the identity of a witness and that this obligation arises from sub-statutory provisions. All the more, the protection of personal data should argue for a cautious approach to the question of the presentation of identity documents during a remote hearing. The Guidelines on Videoconferencing in Judicial Proceedings[675] prepared by the

675 Guidelines on videoconferencing in judicial proceedings, document adopted by the CEPEJ at its 36th plenary meeting in June 2021, https://rm.coe.int/cepej-2021-4-guidelines-videoconference-en/1680a2c2f4, access: 5 August 2024.

CEPEJ[676] emphasise that the court should verify the identity of all participants in the remote hearing, while the means of identification should remain within the limits of the applicable law and should not be unduly intrusive and burdensome. In addition, the court should protect the privacy of the participants in the hearing by taking appropriate measures to address potential privacy risks.

Another technical issue highlighted by the CEPEJ in the Guidelines is the question of displaying the documents in the case file to the participants in the hearing. In the course of a traditional hearing, the accepted practice is to show the witness the documents in the file, if the circumstances of the case so require. It is then accepted that both the person being heard and the lawyers will approach the judge's bench to observe which pages of the file the judge is showing to the witness. The technical solutions adopted by most courts basically prevent the presentation of the case file to the person being heard. Although most videoconferencing systems allow for sharing a judge's screen, this does not allow for a proper presentation of the documents in the file, given the lack of digitisation of the file in civil proceedings. In the above-mentioned guidelines, the CEPEJ states that the court should take steps to ensure that all participants can follow the evidence presented at the hearing online.

The lack of a detailed regulation of the issues related to the procedure for holding a remote hearing, the variety of solutions applied by the courts, as well as the significant differences in comparison with an in-person hearing, result in the fact that the solutions provided for in the provision of Article 15zzs^1 of the COVID-19 Special Act are of a provisional nature and do not constitute a comprehensive regulation of the matter in question. As a result, there is a risk that participation in a remote hearing may lead to a lowering of the level of procedural guarantees for the parties, and their obligations and rights during the hearing are not precisely defined.

6.4. 'Hybrid' hearings

The practice of holding so-called 'hybrid' hearings, i.e. in a mixed mode, where some of the participants in the hearing are connected to the court remotely, while the others are present in the courtroom where the hearing is held, has developed among courts. Such a mode of conducting hearings has become widespread in the practice of applying the provision of Article 15zzs^1(1) of the COVID-19 Special Act. One example is the District Court in Opoczno, where it was possible to appear in person in the courtroom if there is no technical possibility to participate in a remote session[677]. In such a case, it is up to the participant of the hearing to

676 European Commission on the Efficiency of Justice established on 18 September 2002 on the basis of Resolution Res(2002)12 of the Committee of Ministers of the Council of Europe.

677 https://opoczno.sr.gov.pl/wideokonferencje,m,mg,235, accessed 20 September 2022.

decide whether to participate via videoconference or to appear in person in the courtroom. In practice, it is common for a hearing to be initially scheduled as an in-person hearing, but at the request of the participant, a link to the remote connection is provided to allow the party to connect to the court. Equally common are situations where the hearing is scheduled as a remote hearing, but after the case has been called, the participant turns up unannounced in the courtroom and wishes to attend in person.

As already highlighted, the provision of Article 15zzs^{1}(1) of the COVID-19 Special Act (in particular in its version applicable after 3 July 2021) introduces the principle that all hearings shall be conducted remotely and that the holding of an in-person hearing requires the cumulative existence of two conditions: the need for an in-person hearing and the absence of undue risk to the health of the participants. The categorical wording of the provision in question seems to exclude a hybrid mode. On the other hand, however, Article 15zzs^{1}(1) of the COVID-19 Special Act states that persons participating in a remote session, including the members of the panel, 'need not' be present in the courthouse. Thus, the legislator did not explicitly state that the participants in the remote session 'must be outside the court building'. An attempt should therefore be made to answer the question whether the legislator allows the hybrid mode and, if so, in which situations.

It should be noted that pursuant to Article 15zzs^{1}(2) of the COVID-19 Special Act, if a party or a summoned person submits a request at least 5 days before the scheduled date of the remote hearing, the court shall provide them with the opportunity to participate in the videoconference in the courthouse, if the party or the summoned person states in the request that they do not have the technical equipment to participate in the videoconference outside the courthouse. The purpose of this provision is to ensure equality between the parties in a situation where one of them is at risk of being digitally excluded[678]. A. Machnikowska notes that the introduction of this provision further strengthens the position of the remote hearing, reducing the stationary form to the rank of an exception[679]. In turn, K. Klimas points out that this provision supports the admissibility of the hybrid mode, but, according to the author, it is not the only basis for holding a meeting with a mixed form of presence[680].

The position that Article 15zzs^{1}(2) of the COVID-19 Special Act is not a manifestation of the permissibility of hybrid hearings should be accepted. This provision allows participation in a remote hearing in the courthouse, as it provides for participants to participate in the session by providing them with the relevant ICT tools outside the courtroom where the hearing takes place. In other words, participants who declare that they do not have the technical facilities to participate in a remote hearing may participate in the hearing in the courthouse, but they

678 J. Gołaczyński, M. Dymitruk, *Rozprawa zdalna...*, p. 689.
679 A. Machnikowska, *Zasada jawności...*, p. 114.
680 K. Klimas, [in:] *Postępowanie cywilne...*, p. 121.

will still connect to the court remotely without being physically present in the courtroom. Thus, the introduction of Article 15zzs^1(2) of the COVID-19 Special Act shows that the legislator does not allow hearings to be held in a hybrid form, since it does not allow participation in the hearing in the courtroom even if the participant does not have the relevant technical means, but provides for such means to be made available to such a participant in the courthouse, but outside the courtroom.

It should be noted, however, that in operational practice the provision of Article 15zzs^1(2) of the COVID-19 Special Act has proved to be a dead letter. The main obstacle is organisational considerations, mainly related to the need to provide additional rooms for remote hearings and to ensure that they are serviced by secretarial staff. The demand for more separate rooms seems unrealistic in view of the accommodation conditions faced by many courts (lack of an adequate number of courtrooms)[681].

It was noted above that K. Klimas seems to allow for the possibility of holding the hearing in a hybrid form, pointing out that the provision of Article 15zzs^1(2) of the COVID-19 Special Act is rather a guarantee to ensure that both parties have remote access to the hearing, and not a requirement that all participants in the hearing participate in it in the same way. In the author's view, the presiding judge may in any event, taking into account the circumstances of the particular case, allow participants in the proceedings to be present in the courtroom, even for reasons unrelated to the lack of technical capacity[682]. However, such an approach seems to contradict both the literal wording of Article 15zzs^1 (1) and (2) of the COVID-19 Special Act and lacks a proper justification.

The reason for the introduction of remote hearings in the era of the coronavirus pandemic was to ensure the safety of participants and to speed up civil proceedings by preventing the paralysis of the judiciary in the event of disruption of the functioning of the courts due to an excessive number of infections. K. Jasińska observes that the hybrid procedure is questionable, first of all, from the point of view of the purpose of introducing the provision, which is to ensure the functioning of the courts with the lowest possible epidemic risk[683]. Contrary to the legislator's use of the unclear wording in the text of Article 15zzs^1(1) of the COVID-19 Special Act, 'the participants (...) need not be present in the court building', one should support the position according to which the legislator's intention was not to leave the decision on the manner of participation in the remote session to the discretion of the parties. In this context, it should be noted that the presence of some of the participants in the hearing in the courthouse is clearly contrary to the purpose intended by the legislator. At the same time, since the participant attends the hearing in the courthouse, there is an increased risk of COVID-19 being spread. It should

---

681 K. Jasińska, *E-rozprawa w postępowaniu cywilnym...*, p. 37.
682 K. Klimas, [in:] *Postępowanie cywilne...*, p. 121.
683 K. Jasińska, *E-rozprawa w postępowaniu cywilnym...*, pp. 35–36.

be recalled that although the legislator exempts the court from the obligation to hold a remote hearing in the event that the holding of a stationary session would not cause an excessive risk to the health of the participants, the above premise must occur in addition to the premise of 'necessity' discussed above. Therefore, the mere absence of an undue epidemic risk does not entitle the court to hold a hybrid hearing.

The wording of Article 15zzs[1](1) point 1 of the COVID-19 Special Act must therefore be read in conjunction with point 2, which expressly states that the holding of a remote meeting may be dispensed with 'only in the event (...)' of the need for a stationary hearing and the absence of an unreasonable epidemic risk. In an earlier section it was indicated what considerations might support the need for an in-person hearing. This is primarily related to the need to preserve the principle of directness. In the light of the above, it would seem that a hybrid hearing would have to be allowed in those cases where the court would be entitled to hold an in-person hearing. Participation in the hearing in the courtroom would then only be possible for the participant whose direct presence in the courthouse is necessary. The other participants who, in a given situation, are not affected by the conditions for waiving the remote hearing would then be able to connect to the court by means of videoconferencing. Such an interpretation of the provision in question allows for a flexible approach to the issue of remote hearings, allowing for the choice of an appropriate form of participation in the hearing, tailored to the needs of a particular participant, and relieves the presiding judge of the obligation to make an outright decision as to whether the hearing should be held remotely or in person. Similarly, K. Jasińska expresses her opinion, which allows to order holding a hearing in hybrid mode if the necessity of holding a hearing in person concerns only one party and at the same time the negative condition of excessive health risk is not met[684]. There is no reason to apply a broad interpretation of the provisions in question and to allow the participants to the hearing to choose freely how to participate in the court session. Any decision to hold a hybrid hearing should be subject to the presiding judge's assessment. Only such an understanding makes it possible to respect the legislator's aim in introducing Article 15zzs[1] of the COVID-19 Special Act, which, notwithstanding possible criticism of this solution, was to implement the principle that court hearings should be held remotely.

Irrespective of the model adopted, there is no doubt that the authorisation of hybrid hearings in any case requires that all participants – both those in the courtroom and those connected by videoconference – be given an equal opportunity to participate actively in the court session. Each participant in the hybrid hearing must be allowed to speak equally (in particular the parties). All participants must also have an equal opportunity to observe the proceedings, which can be challenging

684 K. Jasińska, *E-rozprawa w postępowaniu cywilnym...*, p. 38.

given the technical problems that often arise. Not all courts have the technical solutions in place to allow such participation in a hybrid session that provides video and audio to those in the courtroom as well as to those connecting remotely (in this regard, a frequently reported problem was the inaudibility of participants in the courtroom who were at a distance from the presiding judge's computer). Frequent problems with audibility in hybrid hearings were highlighted in the 2022 report of the Court Watch Poland Foundation. It was noted that participants attending the hearing via videoconference had problems with proper audio transmission from the courtroom[685].

6.5. Public participation in a remote hearing

Pursuant to Article 148 § 1 of the Code of Civil Procedure, court hearings are open to the public, unless a specific provision provides otherwise, and the court hears the case at a trial. It follows from the above that, as a general rule, a court hearing may be attended by the parties and other persons summoned, as well as by the public.

In view of the need to adapt the functioning of the courts to the threat of an epidemic spreading throughout the country, in May 2020 the Ministry of Justice issued recommendations to the presidents of the courts on procedures to ensure the health safety of court staff during the pandemic. The recommendations included a ban on the entry of persons other than those summoned to court and restrictions on public access to courtrooms[686]. Of the 392 courts operating in the country[687], in 345 courts (88 %), the president of the court issued an order restricting or even banning public access to the court[688]. Between 4 September 2021 and 30 April 2022, the ban was still in force in at least 25 courts in Poland. In contrast, restrictions on public access occurred in 60 courts[689]. For example, access to the Regional Court in Krakow was not restored until May 2022[690].

The introduction of restrictions on access to the courthouse by internal orders had the result of effectively excluding the public from attending court sessions. While the openness of the proceedings was not formally excluded, in practice

---

685 B. Plitowski, R. Sitniewska, P. Solowij, *Obywatelski Monitoring...*, p. 62.

686 A. Kościółek, *Jawność posiedzeń sądowych w postępowaniu cywilnym w dobie pandemii COVID-19*, Przegląd Sądowy 2021/5, p. 23.

687 As of June 2020.

688 B. Pilitowski, B. Kociołowicz-Wiśniewska, *Raport z przestrzegania w Polsce zasady jawnego procesu i publicznego ogłoszenia wyroku w czerwcu 2020 roku*, Toruń 2020, p. 3, https://courtwatch.pl/wp-content/uploads/2020/06/FCWP-Monitoring-jawności-2020-06-25.pdf, accessed 20 September 2022.

689 P. Sołowij, [in:] *Obywatelski Monitoring Sądów 2022*, Report of the Court Watch Polska Foundation, Toruń 2022, p. 123.

690 Order No. 28 of the President and Director of the District Court of Kraków dated 23.05.2022, Adm.SO.-0212–28/22.

a member of the public interested in attending the session was prevented from entering the court building[691].

As the complete opening of the courts to the public in the era of the COVID-19 pandemic may pose a threat to the health of citizens, the openness of court hearings should be ensured through the use of modern technical solutions[692], i.e. remote hearings. In practice, however, this potential has not been used by the courts. Article 15zzs[1] of the COVID-19 Special Act does not contain any specific rules regarding the participation of the public in a remote hearings, which should therefore lead to the assumption that the same rules apply in this respect as for in-person hearings[693]. Remote access to the court session should therefore be available not only to the parties and other persons connected with the proceedings in question (witnesses, experts, lawyers), but also to members of the public. In fact, there is no legal basis for limiting the openness of the hearing in relation to the public. On the contrary, as A. Kościółek observes, the legislator, by using the term 'trial and public hearing', automatically prejudges the scope of openness and access to it for third parties[694]. The author has already pointed out, on the basis of the provision contained in Article 151 § 2 of the Code of Civil Procedure, that the holding of a remote hearing must not adversely affect the possibility of its observation by its participants, but also by the public[695]. At the same time, it should not be overlooked that the specific nature of the remote hearings gives rise to a number of organisational and technical problems which may affect the implementation of the public's access to the court's proceedings[696].

First of all, it should be noted that the absence of technical provisions on the procedure for holding a remote hearing in principle excludes the real possibility for the public to participate in remote hearings. These regulations do not provide for the obligation to publish information on the possibility of remote connection to the court, with the consequence that a member of the public interested in attending the hearing is not able to obtain information on the date of the hearing and the address of the videoconference in sufficient time (in particular in the case of lack of access to the court building). The courts have adopted different practices in this respect. For example, the District Court for Łódź-Śródmieście in Łódź has introduced so-called electronic admission cards, which are made available upon request by a person interested in participating in a remote court session[697]. Some

691 J. Płaziuk, *Konieczność odstąpienia od przeprowadzania posiedzenia zdalnego w przypadku wyznaczenia rozprawy i posiedzenia jawnego w czasach COVID-19*, Polski Proces Cywilny 2022/1, p. 257.
692 A. Kościółek, *Jawność posiedzeń…*, p. 32.
693 K. Klimas, [in:] *Postępowanie cywilne…*, p. 128.
694 A. Kościółek, *Jawność posiedzeń…*, pp. 32–33.
695 A. Kościółek, *Elektroniczne czynności procesowe w świetle nowelizacji z 10.7.2015 r.*, Prawo Mediów Elektronicznych 2017/1, p. 8.
696 K. Klimas, [in:] *Postępowanie cywilne…*, p. 128.
697 K. Klimas, [in:] *Postępowanie cywilne…*, p. 128.

courts allow members of the public to attend the remote hearing by requesting the videoconference address[698]. On the other hand, in many cases public participation is not regulated at all or is even explicitly excluded. The Court Watch Polska Foundation, which monitors the courts, has also drawn attention to the informational chaos caused by the lack of labelling of remote hearings on videoconferencing and the unclear procedure for requesting access to the videoconference link and participating in the remote session itself. In the event of technical problems with the connection, the spectators are deprived of any possibility of communicating with the presiding judge or a court official in order to determine the reasons for the problems[699].

However, the participation of the public in remote court hearings via videoconferencing poses a number of risks or impediments to the proper conduct of the court's activities. Doubts about the participation of the public in remote hearings were raised by the Ombudsman, who sent a letter to the President of the District Court for Łódź-Śródmieście in Łódź (this court was the first to introduce electronic access cards for remote hearings), asking what technical and procedural solutions had been adopted to minimise threats to the privacy of participants in the proceedings. The Ombudsman drew attention to the possibility of third parties recording and transmitting the remote session[700]. This issue is of great importance in connection with the previously discussed procedure of verifying the identity of persons questioned by the court. One should agree with A. Kościółek, who notes that solutions enabling the public to have remote access to hearings must represent a compromise between the implementation of the principle of openness and the need to protect other values, in particular the privacy of participants[701]. However, the existing rules do not allow for a clear definition of this compromise.

Technical limitations to the participation of a large number of people in an online hearing, mainly due to network congestion, may also be a problem in practice[702]. Experience with remote hearings shows that significant problems arise mainly in cases with a large number of participants[703]. If the public attends a remote hearing, these problems may be amplified. A large number of participants

698 E.g. Warsaw District Court, Warsaw-Praga District Court in Warsaw, for example: https://bip.warszawa.so.gov.pl/artykul/1921/7376/rozprawy-zdalne, accessed 20 September 2022.

699 B. Plitowski, R. Sitniewska, P. Sołowij, *Obywatelski Monitoring...*, p. 38.

700 P. Rojek-Socha, *Jawność kontra prywatność – RPO krytykuje tryb „publiczności online", sąd go broni*, prawo.pl, 29 czerwca 2020 roku, 29 June 2020, https://www.prawo.pl/prawnicy-sady/e-rozprawy-publicznosc-online-naruszaja-konstytucje-opinie-rpo-i,501276.html, accessed 20 September 2022.

701 A. Kościółek, *Jawność posiedzeń...*, p. 34.

702 K. Klimas, [in:] *Postępowanie cywilne...*, p. 130.

703 A. Begier, A. Wypych-Knieć, Ł. Małecki-Tepicht, *Sądownictwo ...*, p. 39.

in a videoconference where a remote hearing is being broadcast can also make it difficult to control the conduct of the court session. However, it should be noted that possible technical barriers should not be a sufficient reason for refusing to allow the public to participate in a remote hearing. It is the responsibility of the court to organise the remote hearing in such a way that the person concerned is able to follow the proceedings. It should also be borne in mind that the presiding judge has a number of options for moderating the videoconference, including muting or even removing a participant from the meeting. In this respect, however, the court is bound by the general rules on the policing of meetings (Articles 48–49 of the Law on the Organisation of Common Courts). The videoconference should be treated as a virtual courtroom[704]. The presiding judge may therefore exclude the public from the videoconference if they behave inappropriately. It should therefore go without saying that the public and the participants in the remote hearing are subject to the same rigour as regards the need to maintain calm and order during the proceedings as in a traditional court session. In addition, all participants in a remote hearing must behave in a manner befitting the dignity of the court (Article 152 § 4 of the CCP).

Remote hearings, carried out by means of technical devices that allow the direct transmission of video and audio, open up completely new possibilities in terms of public access to court hearings. In theory, an unlimited number of people can attend the hearing, which would not be possible in the traditional way[705]. Quite the opposite has been the practice of the courts in the pandemic era. The lack of transparent procedures and implementing regulations providing for public participation in hearings in practice prevents or significantly hampers the implementation of the principle of external openness. When analysing the practical application of the regulation on remote hearings in the area of selected courts in Warsaw, Kraków, Wrocław and Poznań, K. Rogala pointed out a significant discrepancy in the internal rules on public participation in hearings[706]. The author notes that although general information with instructions on how to participate in a remote hearing was available on the websites of these courts, in most cases the courts did not provide specific information on the organisation of remote hearing or practical guidelines on how to gain access to a remote session in a specific case[707]. This means that there has to be an effective way for individuals to know when and how they can access the court hearing and thus exercise their right to take part in the hearing.

704 K. Klimas, [in:] *Postępowanie cywilne...*, pp. 130–131.

705 A. Kościółek, *Jawność posiedzeń...*, p. 33.

706 K. Rogala, [in:] *Postępowanie cywilne w czasie pandemii. E-doręczenia, rozprawa zdalna, posiedzenie niejawne, składnie pism procesowych*, J. Gołaczyński (ed.), Warsaw 2022, p. 151.

707 K. Rogala, [in:] *Postępowanie cywilne...*, p. 138.

6.6. Remote hearings and the right to a fair trial

One of the main objections to remote hearings concerns their impact on the implementation of the principle of openness of proceedings, in particular by preventing or significantly impeding public participation in court hearings. These restrictions do not derive from legal provisions, but are of a factual nature[708]. However, the legislator is fully aware of the deferential nature of the provision of Article 15zzs[1](1) of the COVID-19 Special Act with regard to the principle of openness. As indicated in the previous considerations, the explanatory memorandum to the Law of 28 May 2021 clearly emphasises that, given the clash of two values – the openness of the proceedings and their expediency – there is no doubt as to which of them should be given priority.

Allowing the public to attend the hearing does not simply mean allowing an interested person into the courtroom (or, in the case of remote hearings, allowing them to be connected by videoconference), but consists in providing effective notice of the time and place of the hearing well in advance, so that any member of the public can decide whether or not to attend[709]. In the case of remote hearings, this will consist of making publicly available information on the time of the hearing and the choice of ICT system to be used for the connection, as well as providing access details for the videoconference.

In connection with the introduction of remote hearings into the legal system pursuant to Article 15zzs[1] of the COVID-19 Special Act, it was also perceived that the standard of protection of the individual in the enforcement of his due rights was reduced. The right of a party to fully participate in a remote hearing with adequate video and audio quality was not ensured[710]. The absence of detailed implementing rules of a technical nature means that there is no guarantee for the individual that their participation in the remote hearing will be due and that the quality of the court proceedings will not be diminished by the need to hold the hearing remotely. Consequently, the regulation in question should be assessed not only in the context of the implementation of the principle of openness of proceedings, but also in relation to other components of the right to a fair trial, namely the right of access to court and the right to a fair procedure.

The first question, however, is whether a court session can be allowed at all without the direct participation of its participants, who are remotely connected to the court from any location outside the court building. This question has been answered by the European Court of Human Rights, inter alia, in the judgment *Bivolar v Romania*[711], which indicates that participation in a court session can

708 J. Płaziuk, *Konieczność odstąpienia...*, p. 252.
709 J. Roszkiewicz, *Jawność postępowania...*, p. 14.
710 A. Machnikowska, *Zasada jawności...*, p. 115.
711 Judgment of the European Court of Human Rights of 2 October 2018, Application No. 66580/12.

be ensured by means of videoconferencing. This is not in itself contrary to the standard of a fair trial, but it is necessary to ensure that the technical conditions allow for a connection of sufficient quality and security. The party participating in the hearing remotely should be guaranteed the opportunity to follow the proceedings and to participate actively in the hearing on the same basis as the other participants. In addition, the party should be able to communicate confidentially with their lawyer[712]. The court hearing, regardless of the format in which it is conducted (stationary or remote), must be accessible to the public, who must be given access either to the courtroom from which the panel of judges is connected or through a remote videoconference link.

In the light of the comments made in the earlier part, there should be no doubt that the provision of Article 15zzs¹(1) of the COVID-19 Special Act has affected the implementation of the principle of openness of proceedings. By failing to provide for arrangements to ensure the mandatory provision of an opportunity for the public to participate in a remote hearing, it has effectively excluded any participation by third parties in public hearings. Indeed, in the vast majority of cases, it is in practice impossible for a third party to find out the date of the remote court session and the address of the videoconference, as this information is not made available to the public. Some courts have adopted a practice whereby a person interested in attending a court hearing can request a link to the videoconference, but the question of how to obtain information on the date and procedure of a scheduled hearing remains unresolved, particularly in cases where the court does not have an e-docket service that allows the tracking of hearings held on a given day. These restrictions should be contrasted with the above-mentioned prohibition of access to the buildings of most courts, which was introduced by orders of the presidents of the courts. A. Kościółek correctly observes that the provision of Article 152 § 1 of the CCP, which provides for the possibility for all unarmed and adult persons to enter a court session, is violated not only when an outsider is not allowed to observe the proceedings, but also when the exercise of the right to enter the courtroom is connected with the necessity to perform additional acts not required by this provision. This may include the need to submit a request for permission to attend as a member of the public within a certain time limit, to provide additional information (case reference number) or to state the reasons why a person wishes to attend the hearing, and to limit the number of persons who may attend the hearing[713]. The above-mentioned restrictions must also be considered unacceptable in the case of remote hearings regulated by Article 15zzs¹ of the COVID-19 Special Act.

The right to a fair trial, including the constitutional principle of openness of proceedings, is not absolute. Exceptions to the full implementation of this principle are allowed. However, the restriction of the external openness of proceedings

---

712 *J. Roszkiewicz, Jawność postępowania...*, pp. 16–17.
713 A. Kościółek, *Zasada jawności...*, p. 29.

is possible only in compliance with the general requirements for the restriction of rights and freedoms resulting from Article 31(3) of the Constitution of the Republic of Poland. In particular, this means that the restriction of the external openness of proceedings may be imposed only on the basis of a statute[714]. For this reason alone, any existing restrictions on public participation in court hearings (including those held remotely) should be considered incompatible with the Constitution. The current statutory provisions do not provide for the possibility of limiting the external openness of proceedings (apart from the cases of ordering a hearing *in camera*, as provided for in Article 153 of the CCP), and the provisions of the COVID-19 Special Act have not introduced any solutions that would allow for an exception to this rule. As already mentioned, the limitations of the principle of external openness in the era of the pandemic (with regard to remote hearings) result from factual circumstances or internal orders of the presidents of the courts or other organisational rules. However, such internal acts cannot constitute grounds for refusing to allow the public to attend a court session.

It should be reiterated that in the current state of the law, there is no basis for denying members of the public access to the courts, and such decisions should be considered a violation of the constitutional right to court. However, it should not be overlooked that the full opening of courts to the public in the era of the COVID-19 pandemic would pose a threat to the health of citizens[715]. The question is whether a restriction on the external openness of proceedings would be permissible on the grounds of the need to protect public health if the legislature decided to adopt such a provision by statute. The answer to that question must be in the negative. While there is no doubt that the restriction of access to in-person hearings is objectively justified by the need to protect the health of the participants[716], the other elements of the 'proportionality test' are questionable. In accordance with the principle of the least restrictive measure, which derives from the principle of proportionality laid down in Article 31(3) of the Constitution, the legislator is obliged to choose the least burdensome of a number of available solutions leading to the restriction of a given right or freedom. Since, as a rule, in the event of a state of epidemic or epidemic threat (and for a year after the last state has been cancelled), court hearings are to be held remotely, unless there is a need for an in-person hearing, and there is no excessive threat of an epidemic, there is no reason to exclude the public from attending these hearings. The legislator, choosing the most lenient measure from the point of view of the right to be restricted, should therefore not opt for the complete exclusion of external public participation in court hearings, but instead allow the public to participate remotely under the same conditions as other participants. This is, in fact, a choice of a more lenient measure that allows for the protection of health as well as the exclusion of the public.

714 A. Kościółek, *Zasada jawności...*, p. 28.
715 A. Kościółek, *Zasada jawności...*, pp. 31–32.
716 A. Machnikowska, *Zasada jawności...*, p. 101.

On the other hand, if there is no epidemic risk and the hearing takes place in the courthouse, the public should not be restricted from attending at all, as this is not justified by health protection objectives in such a case. In this situation, members of the public should have the right to attend the hearing in the courthouse on the same terms as the parties. At the same time, it should be emphasised that, as the legislator has not provided for any specific rules guaranteeing the participation of the public in the hearing, the burden of ensuring the external publicity lies with the courts, to which, at the stage of the application of the law, the prohibition of restricting the right to a trial in a manner contrary to Article 31(3) of the Constitution is also addressed.

The way in which remote hearings are regulated in the COVID-19 Special Act also raises reasonable doubts as to their compliance with the principles of procedural fairness, which consists, inter alia, of the right to predictability of the course of proceedings[717]. The procedure for conducting a remote hearing has not been defined at all by the legislator, which results in the adoption of different procedural models in different courts, which sometimes even differ between judges who sit in the same court division. The vagueness of the discussed provision of Article 15zzs[1] of the COVID-19 Special Act leads to the conclusion that the rights of the parties to properly participate in the remote session have not been adequately protected.

Indeed, the provisions do not regulate who is responsible for ensuring adequate access to the hearing (i.e. the proper functioning of video and audio transmission) and what the consequences are of a party's failure to provide adequate technical means to ensure a stable connection to the court. The question arises as to whether technical problems on the part of the participant in the hearing should then be treated as an unjustified failure to appear at the hearing, assuming that through no fault of the participant proper equipment or an internet connection of adequate quality was not provided, or whether the court should adjourn the hearing in order to allow the participant to connect to the court at a later date. It is also impossible to assess unequivocally whether repeated technical problems at successive hearing sessions should then be assessed as an attempt to obstruct the proceedings (in a situation where the hearing cannot take place again through the fault of the participant) or whether the absence should be interpreted as depriving the participant of the opportunity to participate in the hearing. Undoubtedly, adjournment of a hearing in such a situation may give rise to considerable abuse by those who may have an interest in prolonging the proceedings.

The obligation to hold remote hearings, which is set out in very general terms in the provisions of the COVID-19 Special Act, also does not allow for a clear answer to the question of how active the role of the court should be in determining whether the participant intends to attend the remote hearing or whether their absence is due to connection problems (the practice of some courts, which is not supported by the current legislation, is to telephone absent participants).

717 E. Tkaczyk, *Konstytucyjne prawo do sądu...*, p. 41.

As a result, the participant is unable to assess in advance the consequences of their absence due to technical difficulties on the course of the proceedings. Indeed, it is fairly easy to imagine a situation in which the court issues a default judgment against a defendant who has failed to connect to a remote session, or in which the court imposes a fine on an absent witness. On the other hand, the court must be able to prevent the proceedings from being obstructed if a participant in a remote hearing deliberately fails to use the relevant technical facilities and merely pretends that they cannot connect[718]. The above-mentioned issues should be dealt with by the legislator in such a way that the conduct of the remote hearing is predictable for the participant.

The imposition of an obligation on the court to hold hearings remotely may also have a significant impact on the realisation of the right of access to court. Access to justice, i.e. the right of an individual to present their case before a court, must be real and effective. The mere formal granting of this right, while at the same time introducing such restrictions as to render it illusory, leads to a violation of the individual's right to a fair trial.

On the one hand, one cannot but agree with J. Gołaczyński and M. Dymitruk, who point out that the possibility of a remote connection with the court may contribute to the inclusion in the judicial process of those persons who, due to the necessity of a physical appearance before the court, have hitherto refrained to pursue their claims before the court or have not actively participated in the proceedings. This may include persons who have been excluded because of their state of health, disability or age, or persons who have been unable to attend because of geographical barriers[719]. On the other hand, the obligation to participate in a remote hearing may prove to be an obstacle for people facing digital exclusion due to a lack of skills or technical capacity to use the tools necessary to connect to the court[720]. To impose an obligation on such persons to participate in the court session remotely would be to deprive them of the possibility of realising their right to a fair trial. Therefore, the condition for holding a remote hearing should be, firstly, that the participant has access to the relevant equipment and, secondly, that they are able to use such equipment to the extent that they are able to actively participate in the remote hearing[721].

The principle of equality requires the creation of an adequate infrastructure to ensure the equality of the parties and the realisation of the procedural rights of the participants. In this context, A. Zalesińska draws attention to two problems: the equality of parties in the context of IT exclusion and the need to ensure uniform rights regardless of whether the proceedings are conducted traditionally or by means of electronic communication. The author argues that the legislator should

---

718 J Litowski, *Ograniczenie jawności...*, p. 73.
719 J. Gołaczyński, M. Dymitruk, *Rozprawa zdalna...*, p. 686.
720 K. Klimas, [in:] *Postępowanie cywilne...*, p. 120.
721 K. Jasińska, *E-rozprawa w postępowaniu cywilnym...*, pp. 32–33.

allow for hybrid proceedings. On the other hand, the author aptly observes that it is unacceptable to differentiate the procedural situation of the parties, let alone treat them differently, depending on their choice of means of communication with the court[722].

In this respect, the provision of Article 15zzs[1](2) of the COVID-19 Special Act, which stipulates that a party or other summoned person shall be guaranteed participation in a remote hearing in the court building, should be assessed positively. This is undoubtedly an instrument that removes barriers to access to justice[723] and promotes the implementation of the principle of equality. Similarly, reference should be made to the possibility, provided for in Article 15zzs[1](1) point 2 of the COVID-19 Special Act, to refrain from holding a remote hearing if it is necessary to hold a hearing in person. This condition should be considered to be met in cases where the holding of a teleconference constitutes a restriction of access to court for its participant.

Hybrid hearings and their possible implications for the maintenance of the principle of equality of arms should be given their own place. This principle implies the need for a 'fair balance', i.e. the possibility to present one's case to the court under conditions which do not put one in a worse position than the other party[724]. There is no doubt that the presence of both parties in the courtroom, or their simultaneous connection via videoconferencing, in principle gives them the same opportunity to actively participate in the hearing, to speak, to react to the current situation or to assess the credibility of the evidence presented, which often requires going beyond the purely verbal[725]. In a hybrid hearing, the party present in the courtroom hears the statements of the opposing party remotely from the loudspeakers. On the other hand, the party connecting by videoconference will see those present in the courtroom from some distance, depending on the positioning of the cameras in the courtroom, and the image will usually be less clear[726]. Since attending a remote hearing and following the proceedings from a computer screen in the courtroom can never be the same as attending an in-person hearing, one of the parties (the remote party) may be in a worse position to participate actively in the hearing, especially if there are problems with the video and audio transmission. The inferior position of the remotely connected party may result not only from the difficulty of following the proceedings, but also from the difficulty of speaking actively (the person in the courtroom has an easier opportunity to address the bench directly) or of reacting dynamically to the proceedings and

722 A. Zalesińska, *Wpływ informatyzacji na założenia konstrukcyjne procesu cywilnego*, Warsaw 2016, pp. 82–83.
723 J. Litowski, *Rozprawa zdalna...*, p. 689.
724 Guidelines on the application of Article 6 issued by the European Court of Human Rights, available at www.echr.coe.int, p. 52.
725 K. Jasińska, *E-rozprawa w postępowaniu cywilnym...*, p. 38.
726 A. Michór, *Postępowanie cywilne...*, p. 39.

perceived shortcomings. In practice, the opposite situation can also occur, where the person who is remotely connected has no problems in properly receiving the content transmitted in the courtroom, while the opponent, who is in the courthouse, has difficulties in receiving communications due to the distance from the presiding judge's computer through which the image and sound are received.

In this respect, it should go without saying that the minimum standard for hybrid hearings should be to ensure that all participants in the hearing can see and hear each other. In practice, there are often situations where only the judges can see all the participants in the hearing (those present in the courtroom – directly, while those connecting remotely – on the presiding judge's computer screen). The parties, both those present in the courtroom and those connecting remotely, should have the same opportunity to observe the persons being heard, whether they are connecting remotely or in the courtroom. Failure to comply with the above principles may result in an unequal exercise of the procedural rights of the parties, which in extreme cases may amount to a violation of the principle of equality of arms and, consequently, a deprivation of the right to a fair trial. However, the mere fact of holding a hybrid hearing cannot automatically lead to the conclusion that there has been a violation of the principle of equality of arms. The role of the presiding judge is to ensure that each party has an equal opportunity to present and defend its procedural position throughout the hearing.

6.7. Remote hearings after 14 March 2024

Despite the lifting of the state of epidemic threat on 1 July 2023, the legal status of remote hearings did not change. Article $15zzs^1(1)$ of the COVID-19 Special Act remained the basis for their use. For more than three years of the regulation, remote hearings have taken a permanent place in the courts' practice. Therefore, by the Act of 7 July 2023[727], remote hearings were permanently introduced into the Code of Civil Procedure. This provision entered into force on 14 March 2024. Pursuant to Article 151 § 2 of the CCP, the presiding judge may order a public hearing to be held using technical means enabling it to be conducted at a distance (remote hearing), if this is not prevented by the nature of the acts to be performed at the hearing and the conduct of the remote hearing guarantees full protection of the procedural rights of the parties and the proper course of the proceedings. In such a case, the judges and the court reporter shall be present in the courtroom and the other persons participating in the hearing need not be present in the courthouse where the hearing is held. The video and audio recording of the proceedings in the courtroom shall be transmitted to the location of the participants in the hearing who have declared their intention to participate in the hearing remotely,

727 Act of 7 July 2023 amending the Act - Code of Civil Procedure, the Act - Law on the System of Common Courts, the Act - Code of Criminal Procedure and certain other acts, Journal of Laws of 2023, item 1860.

and from the location of the participants in the hearing to the building of the court conducting the hearing.

The presiding judge may order a remote hearing *ex officio* or at the request of the participant (Article 151 § 3 of the CCP). The new regulation thus breaks with the approach of the COVID-19 Special Act, according to which remote hearings were (at least formally) mandatory. A remote hearing may be held only on the basis of a decision of the presiding judge and only if the judge considers that this is not precluded by the nature of the matters to be dealt with at the hearing and that the holding of a remote hearing will ensure full protection of the procedural rights of the parties and the proper conduct of the proceedings. A request for a remote hearing may be made no later than 7 days after the remote hearing and shall not be binding on the court.

The introduction of a time limit for filing a request for a remote hearing is intended to ensure the efficiency of the proceedings and to eliminate last-minute requests filed before the date of the court session. In order to speed up the circulation of court correspondence, the legislator has introduced a requirement for a party to provide an e-mail address in the request. In addition, the participants may be informed of their consent or refusal to the holding of a remote hearing, as well as of instructions for the proper organisation of the remote session, in the manner provided for in Article 149[1] of the CCP, i.e. by any means that the court deems most appropriate (e.g. by e-mail or telephone).

When a remote hearing is scheduled, the participants shall be informed of the possibility of appearing in the courtroom or of declaring their intention to participate in the hearing remotely. It shall also be pointed out that the participant in the remote hearing must declare his intention to participate in the remote hearing at least 3 working days before the date of the hearing (Article 151 § 5 of the CCP) and may do so by any means of remote communication, provided that such means allow the identification of the sender. In the failure to declare the intention to participate in a remote hearing, the participant is obliged to appear at the courthouse. The above rule should be viewed positively, as it allows the presiding judge to determine which parties will appear at the remote hearing. In the event of any technical problems, the court will be able to take appropriate measures to remedy the situation. This is a valuable tool to discipline the parties and to organise the remote session properly.

It is important to note that in Article 151 § 7 of the CCP, the legislator has expressly stated that procedural acts performed by the parties and other participants during a remote hearing outside the courtroom where the proceedings are conducted shall be effective, unless the law requires them to be performed in writing. Therefore, the legislator has not decided to solve the previously described problem of the circulation of documents during a public hearing and has not stipulated that the acts for which the Code of Civil Procedure reserves the written form must continue to be performed in this form.

It is also necessary to note the provision of Article 235 § 2 of the CCP, according to which, if the nature of the evidence does not oppose it, the court may decide that it shall be taken in a remote hearing. In the application for the taking of evidence (Article 235[1] of the CCP), a party may request that evidence be taken in a remote hearing. Article 263[1] of the CCP also introduces an important change. A party may object to the examination of a witness outside the courtroom in the course of a remote hearing, but no later than 7 days from the date on which it was informed of the intention to take evidence in this way. If the objection is successful, the court will summon the witness to appear in the courtroom in person.

Such a solution seems incomprehensible. It should be left solely to the court to decide whether it is possible to take evidence from witnesses in a remote hearing. A party's objection is binding on the court, which could lead to potential abuse where a party objects to a witness being heard remotely simply in order to postpone the hearing. This is because in many cases it will be necessary to summon the witness back to the courthouse, which may not be possible on the original date due to procedural deadlines.

6.8. Assessment and further legislative proposals for remote hearings

J. Płaziuk, reflecting on the advantages of remote hearings, pointed out that essentially the only objection to this tool is that it limits the external openness of the proceedings[728]. However, such a conclusion cannot be accepted. It has been shown above that remote hearings, as provided for in Article 15zzs[1] of the COVID-19 Special Act, entail risks not only for the openness of the proceedings, but also for access to justice and the equality of the parties. On the other hand, there should be no doubt that the introduction of remote hearings was a necessity at a time of the COVID-19 pandemic, which saved the judiciary from paralysis. The solution adopted should also be assessed in terms of the range of advantages and benefits it undoubtedly brings.

Remote hearings can improve the efficiency and reduce the costs of proceedings. For example, the necessary costs of a trial include, inter alia, the costs of the personal appearance of a party ordered by the court (Article 98 § 2 and 3 of the CCP). By conducting a remote hearing, it is possible to limit or even eliminate the need to incur such costs. The remote hearing reduces the need to postpone hearings due to conflict of dates and other unforeseen reasons. It allows lawyers to attend several hearings on the same day in different courts throughout the country[729].

Remote hearings also help to overcome geographical barriers by enabling persons who cannot attend a court session in person because they reside at a considerable distance from the court. This can be particularly important in cases with a

728 J. Płaziuk, *Konieczność odstąpienia...*, p. 253.

729 M. Uliasz, [in:] *Postępowanie cywilne w czasie pandemii. E-doręczenia, rozprawa zdalna, posiedzenie niejawne, składnie pism procesowych*, J. Gołaczyński (ed.), Warsaw 2022, p. 93.

foreign component, e.g. where a Polish citizen permanently residing outside the country needs to be heard. A remote hearing in such situations not only makes it possible to speed up the proceedings (by avoiding the need to use lengthy international instruments relating to the taking of evidence abroad), but also significantly reduces the costs of the proceedings. It also undoubtedly has a positive impact on the implementation of the principle of directness, since the person to be heard is not present in the court building, but the video and audio transmission allows contact in real time, which, compared to hearing such a person, for example, in writing through a consul, undoubtedly brings this solution closer to the personal appearance before the court.

At this point, it is important to mention a problem that has arisen in the application of the rules on remote sitting in cases with a cross-border component. According to Article 20 of the EU Regulation 2020/1783[730], the use of videoconferencing in another Member State of the European Union requires a request for the taking of evidence by a national court, with the court of the Member State concerned having to consider, in the light of the circumstances of the case, whether the use of such technology is appropriate. Furthermore, the direct taking of evidence in such a situation may only be carried out voluntarily and without the use of coercive measures (Article 19). On the basis of the provisions of Article 15zzs^{1}(1) of the COVID-19 Special Act, the Opole District Court referred a preliminary question to the CJEU to determine whether the relevant provisions of the EU Regulation 1206/2001[731] must be interpreted as meaning that a court which intends to hear a witness residing in another Member State must always, in the context of such a hearing, use the methods provided for by the EU Regulation 1206/2001, or whether it is entitled to use a method provided for by its national procedural law, such as hearing a witness in writing or by videoconference, without the assistance of the receiving agency and thus without obtaining the authorisation of the central body or competent authority of the requested Member State. In response to the question raised by the Polish court, the CJEU, in its judgment of 8 September 2022[732], held that the purpose of the Regulation is to ensure the simple, efficient and quick taking of evidence in cross-border cases. The taking of evidence in another Member State should not have the effect of prolonging of the proceedings before the national court. Therefore, the taking of evidence without the application of the Regulation may prove to be simpler, more efficient and quicker, and it should

730 Regulation 2020/1783 of the European Parliament and of the Council of the EU of 25 November 2020 on cooperation between the courts of the Member States in the taking of evidence in civil or commercial matters, OJ EU. L 405, 2.12.2020.

731 Council Regulation (EC) No 1206/2001 of 28 May 2001 on cooperation between the courts of the Member States in the taking of evidence in civil or commercial matters, OJ EU. L 174, 27.06.2001, which was replaced by Regulation 2020/1783.

732 Decision of the CJEU of 8 September 2022, C-188/22, LEX No. 3403185.

therefore be possible to take evidence by videoconference without first obtaining the authorisation of another Member State.

Remote hearings also make it possible to avoid the time-consuming procedures of obtaining evidence through legal aid from another Polish court and, at least in some cases, hearing a witness or party at home. In civil cases, remote hearings can also be used to reduce the costs of escorting witnesses or parties from penitentiary institutions to the courthouse.

In view of the above, it should be stated that the institution of remote hearings should find much wider application, even after the lifting of the state of epidemic and the epidemic threat. Its undoubted advantages, which make it possible to speed up proceedings and reduce their costs and the degree of complexity of the proceedings, argue in favour of introducing the institution of remote hearings into the Code of Civil Procedure on a permanent basis, after it has been adapted to the requirements of a fair trial.

At the same time, it should be borne in mind that since September 2016, the Code of Civil Procedure has included a provision that allows a public hearing to be held using technical means that allow it to be held remotely. However, it cannot be said with conviction that this facility has passed the test. It has not been properly used in the practice of the courts' work, so its importance is marginal. Conducting a hearing under Article 151 § 2 of the CCP required the presence of the participants of the hearing in the building of another court, which basically nullified most of the benefits that the potential of remote hearings from Article 15zzs[1] of the COVID-19 Special Act brought. The application of the provision under Article 151 § 2 of the CCP required a number of preparatory steps related to the setting of a date for the hearing, the need to allocate a courtroom in the summoned court, as well as the involvement of additional court staff to handle the videoconference. In addition, participation in the hearing required the presence of the participant at the courthouse.

It is therefore to be welcomed that the Code of Civil Procedure now provides for remote hearings and that Article 151 § 2 of the CCP has been amended to allow the presiding judge to order the holding of a hearing by means of technical equipment enabling the hearing to take place remotely without the need for the participants to be present in the courthouse.The provision removes the requirement for participants to be in the building of another court, thus eliminating a number of organisational obstacles related to the need for an additional room in the summoned court and its service by court staff. On the other hand, the provision differs from the rule provided for in Article 15zzs[1](1) points 1 and 2 of the COVID-19 Special Act in that it abandons the previous mandatory nature of the remote hearing and instead introduces the alternative of the presiding judge assuming a leading role in the organisation and conduct of the court hearing.

The choice of the form in which a hearing is to be held is left to the discretion of the presiding judge, who should decide whether considerations of procedural economy favour a remote hearing or whether the principle of directness or other compelling reasons require a hearing to be held in the courthouse. Priority should be given to traditional hearings, in particular with a view to preserving the due formality of procedural acts and the prestige of the administration of justice. The possibility of ordering a remote hearing should be determined by whether it will contribute to a more efficient examination of the case. A. Kościółek and A. Arkuszewska also postulated a reflection of the current model of remote hearings in Article 151 § 2 of the CCP, pointing out that remote hearings should remain an alternative and not replace traditional hearings[733].

The universal coverage of the grounds for holding a remote hearing will also allow this instrument to be used when external circumstances make it impossible to hold a hearing in a court building. This provision can be successfully applied in exceptional circumstances, such as the COVID-19 pandemic, so that it can be used flexibly when the epidemic situation requires it.

However, the introduction of remote hearings into the Code of Civil Procedure requires that the fairness of the proceedings, the security of the data transmission, an appropriate level of privacy for the participants in the proceedings and the due formalism and seriousness of the court's actions are guaranteed. It is also necessary to ensure adequate procedural rights in the event of technical problems. In particular, a party should be guaranteed that an innocent failure to connect will be treated in a similar way to an excused failure to appear at a court session and will result in a postponement and not in the continuation of the proceedings in the absence of a party or other participant at the session. To this end, it is necessary to adopt implementing provisions that will comprehensively standardise technical and organisational issues. Unfortunately, despite the amendment, the legislator has still not addressed these issues and has limited itself to authorising the Minister of Justice to issue a notice on the technical conditions to be met for a remote hearing (Article 151 § 9 of the CCP).

However, the provision of equal access to the court for the participants of the hearing is to be assessed positively. In particular, in the event that it is not possible to use technical means for remote connection to the court – due to the lack of such means or for other reasons, e.g. due to the inability to use them – the participant has the possibility to participate in the hearing in the courthouse. According to the new wording of Article 151 of the CCP, participation in a remote hearing is a right and not an obligation of a party. At the same time, the legislator has explicitly allowed so-called hybrid sessions, where only some of the participants, according to their choice, connect remotely or stay in the courtroom.

The large-scale introduction of remote hearings in civil cases requires that courts be equipped with the necessary technical infrastructure to handle both remote and hybrid hearings. In order to harmonise the standards for the conduct of these hearings, the courts should use software that takes into account the specificities of the court session. The videoconferencing system should be linked to a system that allows the recording of the hearing and the taking of electronic

733 A. Kościółek, A. Arkuszewska, *Zdalne posiedzenia sądowe…*, p. 63.

minutes in such a way that the proceedings of the remote hearing can be replayed afterwards. Unfortunately, this is still not guaranteed in every court in the country, despite the fact that several years have passed since the introduction of videoconferencing into the legal system.

As indicated in the previous considerations, the fact that a hearing is held remotely does not remove the obligation to ensure that the public can follow the proceedings. From the point of view of fair trial standards, ensuring public access to open court hearings is of paramount importance. It is therefore necessary to support the need to regulate this issue explicitly in the provisions of the Code of Civil Procedure. It should therefore be proposed that a provision be added to the effect that, in the case of a remote hearing, access to the hearing shall be provided by means of technical devices allowing direct transmission of images and sound to all persons of age, with the exception of persons who are in a condition incompatible with the dignity of the court.

Allowing the public to participate in a court session is not only about allowing them to enter the courtroom (or to be connected remotely), but also about allowing them to be informed in advance about the time and place (form) of the session. For this reason, a solution should be proposed to make it compulsory to publish the data allowing access to the remote session on the court's website as part of the e-docket. However, it should be borne in mind that the protection of other values, such as the privacy and security of the personal data of the participants in the remote hearing, should be guaranteed. For this reason, it should be postulated to introduce an application-free procedure for verifying the identity of a person attending the hearing as a member of the public, primarily with regard to the requirement of being of full age, by introducing the necessity to make relevant declarations or enter data (e.g. personal identification number – PESEL) immediately prior to joining the remote hearing of the court. It is also not difficult to imagine the possibility of making the proceedings of the court available live by means of livestreaming technology, especially as the proceedings of the court are already recorded by means of video and audio recording devices[734].

The progressive computerisation of the judiciary with regard to remote hearings has great potential for speeding up proceedings, but also for opening them up to the public interested in following the proceedings. In doing so, the legislator must bear in mind the obligation to maintain a minimum standard of a fair trial in terms of external openness of proceedings, equality of parties and access to justice.

A. Jarocha rightly observes that the computerisation of civil proceedings, in order to guarantee the equality of the parties, first of all requires an internally and externally coherent model for the implementation of changes, which should be evolutionary rather than revolutionary. The adoption of such solutions requires constant monitoring of the functioning and periodic modification of the model and the way in which each element of the procedure operates (on the basis of the

734 A. Kościółek, A. Arkuszewska, *Zdalne posiedzenia sądowe...*, p. 37.

shortcomings identified in practice and the theoretical achievements of jurisprudence and doctrine). Secondly, the proper functioning of the computerised civil procedure requires the safeguarding of the procedural guarantees of the parties. Finally, it is necessary to carry out consistent education and popularisation activities (both among the public and among legal practitioners) in order to minimise the natural fear of using the new forms of electronic civil procedure[735].

The introduction of remote hearings in civil proceedings under the formula set out in Article 15zzs[1] of COVID-19 Special Act was sudden and abrupt. The courts to which the obligation to hold remote hearings was imposed were not prepared from an organisational point of view. The lack of detailed guidelines led to many practical uncertainties. To some extent, this can be justified by the dynamic nature of the COVID-19 epidemic in 2020. However, despite the fact that four years have passed since the introduction of remote hearings, the legislature has not taken any significant steps to improve them and bring them into line with fair trial standards.

735 A. Jarocha, *Zasada równości stron w kontekście elektronizacji postępowania cywilnego,* [in:] *E-wymiar sprawiedliwości w aspekcie europejskim,* B. Śliwczyński, L. Łuczak-Noworolnik (eds), Poznań 2016, pp. 25–28.

7. Hearing of the case in a closed session

7.1. Article 15zzs[1] of the COVID-19 Special Act – legal status before 3 July 2021

The COVID-19 Special Act extended the possibility for the court to rule in a closed session. Previously, the catalogue of cases in which the court was not obliged to rule in a public hearing was limited and included, inter alia, situations specified in Article 148[1] of the CCP (when a hearing is not necessary and a party has not requested a public hearing in the first pleading), Article 148 § 3 of the CCP (in relation to court orders), Article 339 of the CCP (in relation to a default judgment), Article 514 of the CCP (in non-contentious proceedings, when a hearing is not required by law). The COVID-19 Special Act, in the wording valid until 2 July 2021, allowed a significant expansion of the catalogue of cases that could be referred for a closed session, and actually abolished it, allowing any case to be heard without a hearing, if the conditions set out in Article 15zzs[1](2) were met. In the explanatory memorandum to the government bill on amendments to certain acts in the field of protective measures in connection with the spread of the SARS-CoV-2 virus, no space was devoted to the reasons and purposes for the introduction of the provision of Article 15zzs[1] of the COVID-19 Special Act[736].

According to the cited provision, during the period of the state of epidemic threat or the state of epidemic declared on the basis of COVID-19, and within one year of the lifting of the latter, the presiding judge could order the holding of a closed hearing in cases heard in accordance with the provisions of the Code of Civil Procedure, if (1) it was considered necessary to hear the case; (2) the holding of a trial or public hearing would cause undue health risks; (3) a remote hearing cannot be held; (4) none of the parties objected to the holding of a closed hearing within 7 days of service of the notice of referral to a closed session. It follows from the above provision that the closed hearing was subsidiary to the remote hearing. Only if it was not possible to conduct the hearing by means of direct video and audio transmission was it permissible to schedule a closed hearing, but only after the presiding judge had considered that a public hearing (in the traditional format) would pose an undue risk to the health of the participants. However, the parties could object to the case being heard in a closed session within the said time limit. The first of these conditions, according to which the presiding judge's referral of a case to be heard *in camera* requires that the hearing of the case be considered

736 Explanatory Memorandum to the Government Bill on amending certain laws with respect to protective measures against the spread of the SARS-CoV-2 virus, Parliamentary paper No. 334 available at www.sejm.gov.pl/ sejm9.nsf/print.xsp?nr= 344.

'necessary', is questionable. Indeed, the question arises as to the situations in which the judge could consider it unnecessary to hear the case. If the legislator has provided for a civil procedure for a particular case and a party has initiated proceedings, consideration of the individual's right of access to a court dictates that his case should be heard. Moreover, the case should be heard without undue delay. There is no provision for the possibility to 'refrain' from hearing a case altogether. Thus, the hearing of a case by the court is always 'necessary' and there is no possibility to deviate from it. In order to give a reasonable meaning to the wording of the provision of Article 15zzs[1](2) of the COVID-19 Special Act, it would have to be assumed that the wording used by the legislator is to be understood in such a way that the presiding judge may consider that the examination of the case is not necessary at a certain stage and that it is reasonable to temporarily withhold the examination of the case, for example, until it is possible to hold a public hearing (remote or stationary). The need for such an interpretation of the condition in question is also pointed out by A. Machnikowska, who indicates that it should be interpreted as a case or action of high urgency[737]. A different assumption would lead to the conclusion that the premise of 'considering the case necessary' is of an empty nature and in fact does not affect in any way the possibility of referring the case to a closed hearing, since it is not possible to waive the recognition of the case. On the other hand, the recognition of the necessity to hear the case (in the sense that it is not possible to wait for a change in the situation which makes it impossible to hold a public hearing) would only allow the case to be referred to a closed hearing.

7.2. Legal status as of 3 July 2021

With effect from 3 July 2021, the provision of Article 15zzs[1] of the COVID-19 Special Act has been amended and the conditions for referring a case to a closed hearing have been changed. As the law stands after 3 July 2021, Article 15zzs[1](1) point 3 of the COVID-19 Special Act allows the presiding judge to order a closed hearing if a remote hearing cannot be held and a trial or public hearing is not necessary. As in the original wording, the provision is intended to apply during the period of either an epidemic threat or a state of epidemic declared on the basis of COVID-19 and within one year of the revocation of the latter.

Referral of a case to be heard in a closed session is permitted only if a remote hearing is not possible. The provision assumes as a rule that the case will be heard in public in a remote format. However, it is to be assumed that the referral of a case to a closed session will not only be admissible if a remote session is not possible, but only if the reasons for dispensing with a remote session in favour of a closed session as set out in Article 15zzs[1](1) point 2 of the COVID-19 Special Act do not exist. This refers to the lack of an objective possibility. In principle, however, this

737 A. Machnikowska, *Zasada jawności...*, p. 111.

does not apply to issues relating to the parties' access to the necessary technical facilities, since Article 15zzs^1(1) point 2 of the COVID-19 Special Act requires that a party or other person summoned to a hearing be given access to the remote hearing in the courthouse but outside the courtroom[738]. The range of situations in which it is objectively impossible to hold a public hearing (either remotely or in person) appears to be relatively narrow. In particular, it may cover situations where the court does not have the technical facilities to conduct a remote hearing. However, since it is the will of the legislator that the remote hearing should be the primary forum for the hearing of cases, such a situation should not arise at all – especially in view of the fact that more than two years have passed since the introduction of remote hearings into the legal order in May 2020, during which it was certainly possible to create adequate organisational conditions for holding remote hearings in the courts. There may also be situations in which it is not possible to hold a remote hearing due to the inability of a party or digital exclusion. In such a case, it will not be possible to hold a traditional hearing unless the epidemic premise is met, i.e. if holding the hearing in the court building would pose an undue risk to the health of the participants. Only then is it possible to refer the case for a hearing in closed session pursuant to Article 15zzs^1(1) point 3 of the COVID-19 Special Act. The need to refrain from holding a remote session may also be related to the inability to establish communication with the party for other reasons, such as disability, old age, which may result in limited possibilities to appear in person at the court building. Even in this case, even if the reasons for the epidemic would allow it, it seems acceptable to refer the case to be heard in closed session.

The Katowice Regional Court, among others, has commented on the consequences of hearing a case *in camera* despite the fact that the prerequisites have not been met. In its judgment of 9 June 2022[739], the court held that the referral of a case to be heard in closed session by the court of first instance without proving that it was not possible to hold a remote session in the given situation constituted a violation of Article 15zzs^1(1) point 3 of the COVID-19 Special Act and resulted in the deprivation of a party's ability to defend its rights and, consequently, the invalidity of the proceedings. In the grounds of the judgment, the Regional Court pointed out that the rule in civil proceedings is that the case is to be heard at a public hearing, and that any deviation is justified only by exceptions of statutory rank.

Another justification for organising a closed session instead of a public hearing is the 'lack of necessity' for the latter. Only superficially does it resemble the premise of 'necessity to hear the case' from Article 15zzs^1(2) of the COVID 19 Special Act, which was in force until 3 July 2021. Despite their similar wording, the two premises are fundamentally different[740]. Whereas the 'necessity to hear the case'

738 J. Litowski, *Zakres zmian...*, p. 73.
739 Judgment of the Regional Court in Katowice of 9 June 2022, IV Ca 167/22, not published.
740 A. Machnikowska, *Zasada jawności...*, p. 115.

refers to the urgency of the case, the 'necessity to hold a hearing' refers to the advisability of holding a public hearing. The necessity to hold a hearing should not be understood as a legal obligation (since, apart from the exceptions mentioned above, the hearing of a case is normally an obligation under both Article 42 § 2 and 3 of the Law on the Organisation of Common Courts and Article 148 § 1 of the Code of Civil Procedure), but as the need (necessity) to hold a hearing in order to determine the facts in dispute. In this sense, the premise of 'necessity' should be understood in the same way as in Article 148^1 of the Code of Civil Procedure[741]. Thus, it will only be possible to consider that there is no need for the case to be heard at a public hearing if the waiver of the hearing does not result in a violation of the party's right to participate in the proceedings. The minimum guarantee is that the parties are able to familiarise themselves with all the procedural material gathered in the case[742]. In view of the above, if the facts of the case require the direct taking of evidence before the court, the hearing of the case in closed session pursuant to Article $15zzs^1(1)$ point 3 of the COVID-19 Special Act shall be inadmissible.

The question therefore arises as to the relationship between the provision of Article $15zzs^1(1)$ point 3 of the COVID-19 Special Act and Article 148^1 of the Code of Civil Procedure, in particular whether the former has the character of a *lex specialis* excluding the application of Article 148^1 of the CCP, or whether the scope of these provisions does not overlap. In the judgment of the Court of Appeal in Białystok[743], it was accepted that the provision of Article $15zzs^1$ of the COVID-19 Special Act has the character of a special provision in relation to Article 148^1 of the CCP, and failure to comply with the procedure provided for therein leads to deprivation of the opportunity to defend the rights of a party, including the right to acquaint oneself with the documents and evidence collected in the case, and thus to the invalidity of the proceedings on the ground referred to in Article 379 § 5 of the CCP. In this decision, which was based on the law in force before 3 July 2021, the Court of Appeal criticised the Regional Court for having used the procedure provided for in Article 148^1 of the CCP and for having delivered a judgment *in camera*. According to the Court of Appeal, although the court is in principle entitled to refer the case to a closed session pursuant to Article 148^1 of the CCP, the Regional Court should take into account the special regulation introduced by the COVID-19 Special Act and, before issuing the judgment, notify the parties of the referral to a closed session and give them the opportunity to express any objections. The Court of Appeal therefore held that the COVID-19 Special Act was *lex specialis* and excluded the application of Article 148^1 of the CCP.

---

741 J. Litowski, *Zakres zmian...*, p. 73.

742 E. Stefańska, [in:] *Kodeks postępowania cywilnego...*, p. 526.

743 Judgment of the Court of Appeal in Białystok of 29 October 2020, III AUa 506/20, LEX No. 3089291.

A. Michór takes a different view, and one that should be accepted, pointing out that the conditions for the application of the two provisions are different and should be applied simultaneously[744]. Assuming that the provision of the COVID-19 Special Act excludes the application of Article 148[1] of the CCP would mean that in every case an attempt should first be made to refer the case to a remote hearing and only then, if this proves impossible, would it be permissible to refer the case to a closed session. Such a situation would apply to all cases, including those which could have been heard *in camera* under Article 148[1] of the CCP before the special provisions on closed sessions entered into force. This interpretation would lead to an unjustified prolongation of the proceedings in cases in which the conditions for a hearing *in camera* under Article 148[1] of the CCP are met.

The provision of Article 15zzs[1](1) point 3 of the COVID-19 Special Act does not exclude the application not only of Article 148[1] of the CCP, but also of other provisions allowing the case to be heard in closed session (e.g. Article 191[1], Article 374 of the CCP). This means that it is applicable only when the holding of a hearing is obligatory and allows, if the above conditions are met, to waive the hearing and refer the case to a closed session. The provision in question will also be applicable in non-contentious proceedings, but only in cases where a hearing is mandatory by law (e.g. in proceedings for the declaration of the acquisition of an inheritance – Article 669 of the CCP).

It is important to note the differences between the requirements for referring a case to a closed hearing under Article 15zzs[1](2) in the version in force before 3 July 2021 and Article 15zzs[1](1) point 3 of the COVID-19 Special Act in its later version. In the previous wording of the law, the legislator made the possibility of holding a closed session dependent on the occurrence of two obstacles: the impossibility of holding a remote hearing and the excessive health risk of holding a stationary hearing. In addition, there had to be a further positive condition in the form of 'necessity to hear the case'. After 3 July 2021, a finding that it is not possible to hold a remote hearing and that a public hearing is 'not necessary' will be sufficient to hold a closed session. The legislator has also removed the possibility for parties to object to the referral of a case to a closed session.

A. Machnikowska notes that this shows a tendency to reduce traditional public hearings in favour of the possibility of convening closed sessions[745]. There are arguments against this position. On the one hand, it is obvious that the abolition of the requirement to obtain the consent of a party to the designation of a hearing *in camera* will facilitate the court's decision in a closed session (speed up the examination of the case), since in such a situation the organisation of a closed session depends solely on the decision of the presiding judge. This significantly expands the catalogue of cases in which an *in camera* hearing will be possible. On the other hand, one should not lose sight of the fact that the current premise of

744 A. Michór, *Postępowanie cywilne...*, p. 42.
745 A. Machnikowska, *Zasada jawności...*, pp. 113–114.

'no necessity to hold a public hearing' differs from the premise stated in Article 15zzs¹ of the COVID-19 Special Act in its previous wording. The current wording of the 'requirement of necessity' should be interpreted more restrictively than in the previous state of the law. As previously indicated, the 'lack of necessity for a public hearing' (the current condition) will be fulfilled if the waiver of the hearing does not violate a party's right to participate in the proceedings. This will only be the case if the omission of a hearing does not affect the possibility of clarifying the circumstances relevant to the resolution of the case, i.e. primarily where the facts of the case are undisputed or the disputed circumstances can be established on the basis of documentary evidence and without requiring personal evidence[746]. In cases with complex facts, where it is necessary to take evidence from witnesses or parties, it will not be possible to dispense with a hearing and consequently to refer the case to a closed session. The scope of application of this provision corresponds to the scope of application of the provision of Article 148¹ of the CCP and is significantly narrower than the provision of Article 15zzs¹(2) of the COVID-19 Special Act as it applied prior to 3 July 2021. At that time, the nature of the case and the extent of the evidence to be taken did not limit the possibility of referring the case to an *in camera* hearing, as this depended on the 'necessity of hearing the case', i.e. the desirability of issuing a decision despite the impossibility of scheduling a hearing at a given stage, which was related to the issue of urgency of settling the case. Consequently, under the previous state of the law, any case could be heard *in camera*, regardless of the nature of the claims made by the parties and the evidence supporting them, if only the urgency of the case required it. Of course, this possibility was limited by granting the parties the right to object. However, Ł. Goździaszek notes that the current wording of Article 15zzs¹(1) point 3 of the COVID-19 Special Act is inconsistent. This is because if it is concluded that it is not possible to hold a remote hearing, this simultaneously means that it was necessary to hold this hearing, and therefore the premise of the lack of necessity to hold a hearing[747] is not realised.

Since, as stated above, the prerequisite for convening a closed session in a case under Article 15zzs¹(1) point 3 of the COVID-19 Special Act is to be interpreted similarly to the prerequisite for convening a closed session under Article 148¹ of the CCP (no necessity for a hearing), the question arises as to whether it is reasonable to introduce a special provision into the COVID-19 Special Act that allows for the referral to a closed session of those cases in respect of which Article 148¹ of the CCP could also be applied. Assuming that both provisions have the same scope of application, the introduction of the special provision would have to be assessed as a legal redundancy. However, despite a similar understanding of one of the

746 J. Litowski, *Zakres zmian…*, p. 73.

747 Ł. Goździaszek, [in:] *Postępowanie cywilne w czasie pandemii. E-doręczenia, rozprawa zdalna, posiedzenia niejawne, składanie pism procesowych,* J. Gołaczyński (ed.), Warsaw 2022, p. 183.

premises, the provisions in question are not identical and their scope overlaps. The fundamental difference between the two provisions is that, in the case of Article 148^1 of the CCP, the court is generally bound by the request for a hearing made by the party in the first pleading. On the other hand, in the case of Article $15zzs^1(1)$ point 3 the COVID-19 Special Act, the presiding judge is bound neither by the parties' request for a hearing nor by any objection.

J. Litowski considers this amendment to be positive, pointing out that the current wording of the provision makes it possible to prevent an undue prolongation of the conclusion of a case by a party interested in proceeding as long as possible in a situation of excessive risk of epidemics and inability to hold a remote hearing. Moreover, making the holding of a closed session subject to the absence of objections by the parties would bring this provision into line with Article 148^1 of the CCP[748]. A. Machnikowska, on the other hand, seems to be critical of the solutions adopted by the legislator, pointing out that it is a change in the standard of access to the principle of openness, in which the protection of a party in the exercise of its due rights has been reduced[749]. J. Płaziuk also gives a clearly negative assessment of the provision of Article $15zzs^1(1)$ point 3 of the COVID-19 Special Act, arguing that the hearing of a case in an *in camera* session should be an exception to the public hearing of the case, reserved only for those cases in which there is no doubt that holding a hearing is not necessary. There can be no such situation where a party has objected to the waiver of a hearing[750]. However, the author fails to mention that the inadmissibility of a party's objection does not automatically mean that every case can be heard in a closed session. This is because the court is constrained by two conditions – the impossibility of scheduling a public hearing and the impossibility of holding a remote hearing. Both conditions have to be met cumulatively, and it seems that these situations will not be frequent, as the possibility to decide a case in closed session appears to be very limited at present. It is also impossible to agree with the statement that wherever a party requests a hearing, there can be no doubt as to the need for a public hearing. The view expressed by J. Litowski that a party may not be interested in a prompt conclusion of the proceedings and, to that end, may file an objection requesting a hearing should be followed. As already indicated, the lack of need for a hearing should depend on the nature of the circumstances relevant to the determination of the case and not on the party's desire to be heard. While it may be the case that a party requests a hearing in order to present its position directly to the court, there may be situations where the circumstances raised by a party are not relevant to the outcome of the case. In the first case, it will be appropriate to refer the case for trial, as there will be no 'lack of necessity' for a trial. In the second case, on the other hand, if a party does not raise relevant circumstances from the point of view

748 J. Litowski, *Zakres zmian...*, p. 73.
749 A. Machnikowska, *Zasada jawności...*, p. 115.
750 J. Płaziuk, *Konieczność odstąpienia...*, pp. 256–257.

of the factual and legal basis of the dispute, it will be possible to make a decision in a closed session. The legislator has rightly left the assessment of what has occurred in a given case to the presiding judge in his powers relating to the organisation of the proceedings and to the court, which decides on the legitimacy of the evidentiary submissions made by the parties.

Another difference in the scope of application of the provisions of Article 148^1 of the CCP and Article $15zzs^1(1)$ point 3 of the COVID-19 Special Act is that the former applies only in trial (contradictory proceedings), while the latter applies to all proceedings conducted in accordance with the provisions of the Code of Civil Procedure. This means that the waiver of a hearing in favour of a closed session will also be possible in non-contentious proceedings (where a hearing is required by law) and in other proceedings, e.g. in enforcement proceedings (in these proceedings a hearing is held, for example, in cases where an enforcement title is reissued in place of a lost one – Article 794 of the CCP).

7.3. Closed sessions pursuant to Article $15zzs^2$ of the COVID-19 Special Act

Article $15zzs^2$ of the COVID-19 Special Act introduced an additional procedure for hearing a case in closed session. According to this provision, in a case heard in accordance with the provisions of the Code of Civil Procedure, if the evidentiary proceedings have been concluded in full, the court may close the trial and issue a decision in closed session after receiving the written positions of the parties or participants in the proceedings. This provision was introduced into the law on 16 May 2020 and has been repealed on 28 September 2023.

Unlike Article $15zzs^1$ of the COVID-19 Special Act, the provision of Article $15zzs^2$ does not specify its application period. For this reason, the solution adopted in the first of the above-mentioned provisions, according to which it is to be in force during the period of the state of epidemic or epidemic threat declared on the basis of COVID-19 and within one year of the lifting of the latter, has not been opted for. In view of this, it must be assumed that the provision is binding until it is expressly repealed by the legislator, which may be the case even after the state of epidemic or epidemic threat has ceased[751].

The application of the provision of Article $15zzs^2$ of the COVID-19 Special Act is subject to the existence of only one condition, namely the completion of the evidentiary phase of the proceedings. This is because the provision applies only to the stage of resolution of the case, i.e. the issuance of a final decision in the instance (by a judgment or decision on the merits)[752]. Therefore, the analysis of the issue should begin with the clarification of the notion of 'taking evidence in

751 J. Litowski, *Ograniczenie jawności...*, p. 70.
752 J. Litowski, *Ograniczenie jawności...*, p. 74.

full'. It should be assumed that it takes place when the court decides positively or negatively on all the evidentiary requests submitted by the parties[753] and then the admitted evidence is conducted in a manner appropriate to the nature of the evidence, i.e. it is introduced into the trial so that the parties and the court become familiar with its content.

It follows from the above that the admissibility of hearing a case in a closed session pursuant to Article 15zzs² of the COVID-19 Special Act will not depend on the nature of the case, as in the case of Article 15zzs¹, but on the stage of the proceedings. It is therefore necessary to ask in which cases it will be possible to make use of this institution, i.e. at what earliest stage it will be allowed. In particular, it has to be answered whether the provision requires a prior referral to a hearing or whether it is possible to conclude the taking of evidence in a closed session after the parties have completed the exchange of preparatory pleadings (e.g. in cases where the parties have only submitted documentary evidence). It should be recalled that, according to Article 243² of the CCP, documents included in or attached to the case file constitute evidence without a separate order.

To answer the above questions, it should first be noted that under Article 210 §§ 1 and 3 of the CCP, a hearing begins with the presiding judge announcing the case, i.e. that the court will hear said case. The presiding judge then gives the parties the opportunity to present their claims and requests orally and to present the arguments and evidence in support of them. The trial also includes the taking of evidence and the consideration of its results[754]. The taking of evidence is therefore an integral part of the trial and normally takes place before the court (Article 235 § 1 of the CCP)[755]. In this regard, the position of the Supreme Court should be noted, which, in the grounds of the judgment of 20 August 2001[756], stated that the trial includes the taking of evidence and consideration of its results, including documentary evidence. If no evidence is taken at the trial, it cannot be used to establish the facts on which the decision is based. The reference in the grounds of the judgment to documentary evidence which has not been taken constitutes, in turn, a breach of the general principles governing the taking of evidence, in particular the principles of directness, openness, equality of the parties and the adversarial system. Documentary evidence should therefore be taken at the trial, even if no separate evidentiary order was required (pursuant to Article 243² of the CCP). The taking of evidence from a document consists in its disclosure. This is because the parties must be able to know what documents are in the case file and to be able to respond to them.

From the above it can be concluded that the referral of a case to be decided in a closed session pursuant to Article 15zzs² of the COVID-19 Special Act requires a

---

753 A. Michór, *Postępowanie cywilne...*, p. 42.
754 E. Stefańska, [in:] *Kodeks postępowania cywilnego...*, pp. 822, 825.
755 H. Dolecki, T. Radkiewicz, [in:] *Kodeks postępowania cywilnego...*, p. 1113.
756 Judgment of the Supreme Court of 20 August 2001, I PKN 571/00, LEX No. 78998.

prior public hearing. Only at a hearing is it possible to take evidence, even if it is only documentary evidence. Notwithstanding the above argumentation, it should also be noted that the provision of Article 15zzs[2] allows the trial to be closed in a closed session. The trial is closed after the evidence has been taken and the parties have been heard (Article 224 § 1 of the CCP). It appears logical to assume that the closure of a trial presupposes that it has first been opened and conducted. Therefore, unlike in the case of a closed hearing pursuant to Article 15zzs[1] the COVID-19 Special Act, it is necessary to refer the case to a public hearing. Only in such a procedural setting will it be possible to conduct the evidence in full. It should also be noted that to allow the case to be referred to a closed hearing immediately after the parties have completed their exchange of preparatory pleadings would lead to the conclusion that the provision contained in Article 15zzs[1](1) point 3 of the COVID-19 Special Act is superfluous, since any case in which no evidence from personal sources is required – regardless of its nature – could be referred to a closed hearing under Article 15zzs[2] of the COVID-19 Special Act after the final written positions of the parties have been taken. This would blur the distinction between the two modes of hearing the case in a closed session[757].

J. Litowski points out that when applying the provision of Article 15zzs[2] of the COVID-19 Special Act, two different sequences of procedural actions are possible. According to the first position, the court in open session may close the trial after it has taken place, then collect the written positions of the parties and pronounce the judgment in a closed session. According to the second, the chronology of events should include the collection of written positions outside the hearing, then the closing of the trial and the delivery of the judgment, both of which should take place in a closed session. The author points out that the second approach seems to be more correct. This view should be shared, but with the proviso that the first suggested approach is not so much 'less correct' as it is incorrect. The taking of final written positions is the equivalent of the parties' closing speeches before the close of the trial. A closing statement after the trial is closed, on the other hand, is ineffective[758]. This is because the court takes into account the state of matters at the time of the closure of the trial (Article 316 § 1 of the CCP). It should also be borne in mind that, as a general rule, it is only at the end of the trial that a party may submit claims and evidence in support of its own claims or in rebuttal to the claims and evidence of the other party (Article 205[12] of the CCP). Therefore, it cannot be excluded that a party raises new circumstances or requests evidence only at the stage of the final written statement, if no preparatory hearing has taken place or an exchange of preparatory pleadings has been ordered, on pain of disregarding later claims and evidence. This chronology of procedural steps is indicated by the very literal wording of the provision of Article 15zzs[2] of the COVID-19 Special Act, according to which 'the court may close the trial and give its decision in a

757 J. Litowski, *Ograniczenie jawności...*, p. 75.
758 A. Michór, *Postępowanie cywilne...*, p. 42.

closed session after having received the final written statements of the parties or participants in the proceedings'. The closing of the trial must therefore be preceded by the collection of written submissions, and no reversal of this order is permissible. As the Court of Appeal in Warsaw has aptly pointed out[759], given that the provision of Article 15zzs^2 is an exception to the general rules governing the hearing of cases in court, its application must be strict and it is not permissible to deviate from the procedure laid down in this provision. Any deviation on the part of the court which limits the procedural guarantees of the parties provided for in this provision will result in a flagrant violation of Article 15zzs^2 the COVID-19 Special Act and therefore an expansive interpretation of this provision should be excluded.

The application of the procedure provided for in Article 15zzs^2 of the COVID-19 Special Act therefore requires that the case be referred to a public trial and that the evidence be taken in full. J. Litowski points out that the court should then adjourn the hearing without setting a date for the next hearing and then grant the parties a period for submitting written statements. However, it seems that the court's adjournment of the hearing in such a situation indicates that an additional date for the public hearing set for the trial is planned. Indeed, the adjournment of the case implies 'the postponement of the performance of all acts which could or should have been performed at that stage of the case'[760]. Meanwhile, the decision to refer the case to a closed session means that these actions – apart from the closing statements – have already been carried out. Therefore, there is no need to postpone the hearing to the next date, since no new actions will be taken in the public hearing set for the trial. On the other hand, however, the closure of the trial and the consideration of the principle of continuity of the hearing require some form of decision to give procedural expression to the stage of the case. The trial cannot be 'suspended in a vacuum'. In the light of the foregoing, it may be argued that the court wishing to decide the case under Article 15zzs^2 of the COVID-19 Special Act should make an order referring the case to a closed hearing for the purpose of taking final statements, closing the trial and making a ruling. The presiding judge should then (and given the principle of concentration of procedural material, it is reasonable to do this during the same hearing) set a deadline for the parties to submit final statements. This position will take the form of a written pleading which, pursuant to Article 125 § 1 of the CCP, will include requests and statements made outside the hearing[761]. The exchange of written pleadings is precisely ordered by the presiding judge in their organisational role.

A final assessment of whether the evidentiary procedure has been completed can be made once the parties have submitted their final written statements and the

---

759 Judgment of the Court of Appeal in Warsaw of 27 July 2021, VII AGa 658/20, LEX No. 3318281.

760 T. Żyznowski, [in:] *Kodeks postępowania cywilnego...*, p. 1039.

761 J. Litowski, *Ograniczenie jawności...*, p. 75.

court has taken cognisance of them (or after the expiry of the time limit, since it is the right and not the obligation of a party to submit a written statement). It should be recalled that, as a general rule, a party may present claims and evidence in support of them until the trial is closed. It is only when the evidence is deemed to be complete that the trial can be closed. However, the question arises as to the form in which the trial should be closed. Traditionally, the trial is closed by the presiding judge (Article 224 § 1 of the CCP). However, the provision of Article 15zzs^2 of the COVID-19 Special Act uses the phrase 'the court may close the trial. The form of the court's procedural decision, if it is not a judgment, is always an order (Article 354 of the CCP)[762]. This means that, since the legislator has given the court (and not the presiding judge) the power to close a case in a special provision, such a decision should take the form of a non-appealable order which must be served on the parties *ex officio* (Article 359 § 2 of the CCP). At the same time, there is nothing to prevent this decision from being served on the parties at the same time as the judgment, and it is even advisable for reasons of procedural economy. It is important that the decision to close the trial is precisely formulated in the form of an order of the court by means of a separate operative part. It is not permissible to close a trial implicitly, although it does not appear that this omission could have a significant impact on the outcome of the case. It is conceivable, however, that the order concluding the proceedings should be included in the judgment (as the first of its points). However, the solemn form of the judgment argues for the operative part of the order to be set out on a separate form.

As mentioned above, a party's final written statement constitutes a pleading. There should therefore be no doubt that it must be served on the other party to the proceedings in accordance with the general rules. In the light of the foregoing, the important question arises whether the copy of the final statement may be served together with the copy of the final judgment (and the copy of the order closing the trial). Certainly, the provision of Article 15zzs^2 of the COVID-19 Special Act does not expressly provide for the service of such a document before the conclusion of the trial. This position is also expressed in the doctrine[763]. It assumes that there is no need to serve the final position beforehand, since, as in the case of closing speech in open court, there is no provision for the parties to enter into polemics or to take an *ad vocem* position. However, this view cannot be accepted for the following reasons.

The difference between the closing argument at the hearing and the written statement is that the other party is present at the oral closing argument. The opponent therefore has the opportunity to respond to the arguments and claims made in that speech. In the case of a written closing statement, assuming it is served on the opponent together with the final judgment, the party has no opportunity

762 A. Jakubecki, [in:] *Kodeks postępowania cywilnego. Komentarz. Tom I*, T. Wisniewski (ed.), Warsaw 2021, pp. 1482–1483.

763 J. Litowski, *Ograniczenie jawności...*, p. 75.

to become acquainted with it before the judgment is rendered. Furthermore, the written statement or the closing speech is not a mere formality, but the last stage of the trial before the judgment is given, which allows the perceived deficiencies to be remedied, the requests of the parties to be taken into account[764] and, in extreme cases, even the submission of new evidence, which, in some procedural rules, a party may do until the end of the trial (Article 205^{12} § 2 of the CCP). This is because the closing statements are still part of the trial. At the same time, one cannot agree with the argument that, in the course of a public hearing, it is not acceptable to enter into a polemic with an opponent of the procedure during the closing statements. In practice, *ad vocem* speeches are common and the presiding judge may consider it necessary to give an additional response[765]. Failure to allow a party to be heard may deprive it of the opportunity to defend its rights and, consequently, may invalidate the proceedings[766]. Therefore, failure to serve the parties with the written closing statements before the trial is closed may, in some situations, be premature. In addition, a party is obliged to make a statement on the factual allegations of the other party (Article 210 § 2 of the CCP). However, this will not be possible in a situation where the party does not have the opportunity to become acquainted with the opponent's position before the trial is closed. Consequently, it would be necessary to adopt the position that, before the trial is closed and the final judgment in the case is delivered, the pleading containing the final statement should be served on the other party in order to enable it to become acquainted with the opponent's position and to allow for a possible response.

The provision in question may also raise questions in the context of the principle of the continuity of the panel, as expressed in Article 323 of the CCP. According to that provision, a judgment may only be rendered by the judges before whom the hearing directly preceding the rendering of the judgment was held. The question is whether Article 323 of the CCP precludes the case from being referred to a closed hearing pursuant to Article 15zzs^2 of the COVID-19 Special Act by a different panel of judges from those who participated in the public hearing immediately preceding the closing of the trial (in the event that it is necessary to change the composition of the panel after that hearing has taken place).

The provision of Article 323 of the CCP defines the limits of the principle of directness, which consists in the fact that the court that renders a decision in a case should be directly acquainted with the claims of the parties, the statements of the participants and the evidence. It gives effect to the constitutional right to a fair trial by ensuring that the judge issuing the judgment attends at least the hearing prior to the judgment. The provision of Article 323 of the CCP must be strictly observed; it is not merely indicative, and its violation leads to the invalidity of the proceedings on the grounds that the composition of the court is contrary to the

764 T. Żyznowski, [in:] *Kodeks postępowania cywilnego...*, p. 1060.
765 A. Stefaniak, *Wygłaszanie mowy w procesie cywilnym,* Palestra 1974/7, p. 24.
766 A. Stefaniak, *Wygłaszanie...*, p. 25.

law (Article 379 § 4 of the CCP). The principle of directness expressed in Article 323 of the CCP requires that the judgment be given by the judge before whom the hearing immediately preceding the judgment was held, the hearing in the sense of a single session designated for its conduct before the conclusion of the trial, and not in the sense of a sequence of acts of the parties and the court carried out in one or more public hearings[767]. As a general rule, in the light of Article 323 of the CCP, it would be inadmissible for the final judgment to be delivered in closed session by a different panel than that before which the hearing took place. However, it has to be examined whether the provision of Article 15zzs² of the COVID-19 Special Act as *lex specialis* excludes the application of Article 323 of the CCP.

On the basis of Article 15zzs¹ of the COVID-19 Special Act, the Court of Appeal in Kraków[768] answered in the negative, emphasising that the existence of a state of epidemic and the introduction of detailed legal provisions enabling the delivery of a judgment in a closed session do not change the basic premises which should guide the court when deciding to deliver a judgment without a public hearing. The Court of Appeal pointed out that the continuity of the court's composition is crucial for the implementation of the postulate of the efficiency of the proceedings, the pursuit of an accurate decision in the proceedings and, above all, from the point of view of guaranteeing the fairness of the proceedings. According to the Court of Appeal, the fact that there was no hearing in the case does not mean that Article 323 of the CCP is not applicable. The provisions of the COVID-19 Special Act provide the court with grounds for issuing a decision in a closed session, but this does not alter the assessment that the actions leading to the issuance of the decision should be subject to proceedings in the proper composition, in accordance with the views presented above.

It seems that a similar argument can be made with regard to the issuance of a judgment in a closed session pursuant to Article 15zzs². At this point, it should be recalled that an expansive interpretation of the normative level of Article 15zzs² of the COVID-19 Special Act is excluded[769]. Since this provision does not separately regulate the issue of the continuity of the composition of the panel, it must be assumed that the general principle expressed in Article 323 of the CCP remains applicable. Thus, the provision of Article 15zzs² of the COVID-19 Special Act does not constitute a *lex specialis* with respect to Article 323 of the CCP, but with respect to the provisions relating to the court's ruling in trial (Articles 148, 149, 316, 326 of the CCP). Moreover, the exclusion of one of the fundamental guarantees of the fairness of the proceedings, namely the principle of directness, the implementation

---

767 K. Weitz, *W kwestii składu wydającego wyrok (art. 323 k.p.c.),* Palestra 2008/3–4, p. 218–220.

768 Judgment of the Court of Appeal in Krakow of 2 July 2021, I ACa 174/21, LEX No. 322772.

769 Judgment of the Court of Appeal in Warsaw of 27 July 2021, VII AGa 658/20, LEX No. 3318281.

of which is the principle of the continuity of the composition of the panel, would require an express provision of statutory rank, and such a provision cannot be inferred from the content of Article 15zzs² of the COVID-19 Special Act. In view of the foregoing, it must be assumed that the provision of Article 15zzs² is to be interpreted in such a way that the decision concluding the proceedings may be issued only by the same composition of the court before which the hearing preceding the closed session took place.

The next question to be raised is that of the *ratio legis* of the regulation contained in Article 15zzs² of the COVID-19 Special Act. This provision was introduced into the legal system by the Act of 14 May 2020 amending the COVID-19 Special Act. As in the case of Article 15zzs¹, the explanatory memorandum to the government bill[770] does not indicate the reasons for which it was decided to introduce Article 15zzs². However, it can be inferred that it was intended as a response to the epidemic situation in the country and as a way of allowing the judiciary to function properly. Thus, the purpose of the amendment was to protect public health (preventing the spread of the SARS-CoV-2 virus and the need for the smooth functioning of the judiciary during the pandemic). In this context, the question arises as to whether the instrument provided for in Article 15zzs² of the COVID-19 Special Act is an effective measure to achieve this objective, i.e. whether it actually contributes to improving epidemic security and speeding up the adjudication of cases. The answer to this question is not clear.

It is rightly pointed out that the provision in question in fact introduces a quasi-publication of the judgment. It constitutes an alternative to its announcement in open court. On the one hand, the court assumes that there is no further date for a public hearing and, on the other hand, does not close the trial by referring the case to a closed session[771]. The first doubt is therefore whether the court that intends to conclude the evidentiary phase at the same public hearing scheduled for the trial – which is, after all, a condition for the application of Article 15zzs² of the COVID-19 Special Act – should not proceed to take the closing arguments and close the trial, instead of setting a deadline for the parties to submit their written statements. The first solution seems to be more in line with the principle of procedural efficiency, as it allows the trial to be closed in the same session without having to wait for the final statements to be received, which often involves additional time for the circulation of correspondence. If the publication of the judgment is postponed, as permitted by Article 326 § 1 of the CCP, the law provides for a specific fixed period after the closure of the hearing within which the judgment may be published (two weeks or, exceptionally, one month). If the case is referred to a closed hearing, the legislator has not specified the time limit within which the judgment must be delivered. In this case, therefore, there is no explicit procedural guarantee to ensure the party's right to have the case heard without undue delay. It should be

770 Parliamentary paper No. 334.
771 J. Litowski, *Ograniczenie jawności...*, p. 76.

recalled that once the decision to refer a case to a closed session has been made, the taking of evidence has already been completed – there is therefore no reason why the judgment in the case cannot be delivered immediately.

On the other hand, it should not be forgotten that the publication of the judgment takes place in a public hearing (Article 326 § 2 of the CCP) in which both the parties and members of the public can take part. Therefore, there should be no doubt that referring the case to a closed session and not holding the hearing in the courthouse significantly reduces the risk of spreading the coronavirus. In this respect, therefore, the provision of Article 15zzs[2] of the COVID-19 Special Act fulfils its function. However, it should be noted that the same health protection objective could be achieved by announcing the decision in a remote (public) hearing. It should also be noted that the admissibility of a judgment in a closed session under Article 15zzs[2] of the COVID-19 Special Act does not depend on the impossibility of holding a remote session, and therefore the provision can be applied in any case in which the evidentiary proceedings have been conducted in full. Consequently, it must be considered that the provision in question, although it has a positive effect on reducing the risk of spreading the coronavirus, may nevertheless lead to a prolongation of the duration of the proceedings.

7.4. Judgments in a closed session and the right to a fair trial

There should be no doubt that the provisions of Article 15zzs[1](1) point 3 and Article 15zzs[2] of the COVID-19 Special Act, adopted in connection with the pandemic, have had a significant impact on the realisation of the right to a fair trial and, in particular, on the right to a public hearing. These provisions have broadened the grounds for the holding of closed sessions, which has resulted in a greater frequency of their use instead of a public hearing[772]. By its very nature, where the legislature allows the court to rule in a closed session, the right to a public hearing is limited. At this stage of the analysis, it seems a truism to say that the right to a fair trial is not absolute and may be subject to certain limitations. An attempt should therefore be made to answer the question of how these provisions restrict the right to a fair trial and whether these restrictions are in line with the constitutional and European standards which the previous chapters have attempted to characterise.

K. Gajda-Roszczynialska points out that the openness of hearings and the public nature of judgments have been virtually eliminated by special regulations adopted during the pandemic[773]. There can be no agreement with this view of the matter. Once again, it should be pointed out that the right to a public hearing includes, in

772 A. Machnikowska, *Zasada jawności...*, p. 101.
773 K. Gajda-Roszczynialska, *Przebudowa wymiaru sprawiedliwości...*, p. 26.

addition to the right to attend the court hearing, the openness of the proceedings and the publicity of the decision. Openness can be considered in its external and internal aspects.

With regard to the hearing of the case in a closed session pursuant to Article 15zzs[1](1) point 3 of the COVID-19 Special Act, it should be recalled that the case is not referred to a hearing at all and that the exchange of pleadings by the parties is followed by a final ruling. In this case, the first aspect of the principle of openness, i.e. the right of the parties and the public to attend the hearing, is excluded. This is because only summoned persons have access to a closed hearing (Article 152 § 2 of the CCP) and the provision in question does not provide for the summoning of parties or other persons to the hearing at which the judgment is to be delivered. This provision does not, however, affect the second aspect of the principle of openness, namely the right of openness of proceedings, which amounts to the possibility of inquiring about the proceedings. In this respect, the provisions of Article 15zzs[1] and Article 15zzs[2] of the COVID-19 Special Act do not change the existing rules in any way. However, these provisions undoubtedly have an impact on the right to public announcement of the judgment. While the right of the parties to be informed of the judgment is not restricted in terms of internal publicity, since a judgment (or an order on the merits) delivered *in camera* is served *ex officio* on all parties (Article 327 § 3 of the CCP), which is tantamount to its publication, in this form a party does not have the opportunity to be informed of the essential reasons for the judgment, which is an element of oral pronouncement of the judgment. Of course, a party is not deprived of the right to request a written statement of the reasons for the judgment (Article 328 §§ 1 and 2 of the CCP). On the other hand, in terms of external openness, the right to be informed of the court's decision is considerably restricted, as there is no public announcement of the decision at the hearing to which the public would have access.

In the case of application of the procedure under Article 15zzs[2] of the COVID-19 Special Act, the difference amounts to the fact that it is necessary to convene a public hearing for the purpose of conducting the hearing, to which both the parties and the public have access (with the proviso that, in the case of a remote hearing, the public may effectively be excluded from the hearing). The main part of the hearing, including the positions of the parties and, in particular, the entire evidentiary hearing, is not subject to the restrictions of the principle of publicity.

Consequently, it should be considered that the provisions of the COVID-19 Special Act which allow cases to be heard in a closed session do not completely eliminate the right to a public hearing, but limit this right in certain aspects. The next step is therefore to consider whether the restrictions described above are acceptable under the standards of the right to a fair trial and, if not, on what grounds.

The assessment should begin by recalling that it is clear from the ECHR case-law discussed earlier that a public hearing is not absolutely necessary in certain types of cases and that considerations of procedural economy and the obligation to hear the case within a reasonable time may justify dispensing with a hearing. This applies in particular to cases where there is no dispute as to the facts or the credibility of the evidence and where the facts of the case can be established solely on the basis of documentary evidence or the statements of the parties themselves. The ECHR has also pointed out that the right to a public hearing does not mean that all stages of the procedure must be oral. On the contrary, it is permissible for some of them to be written.

In the light of the foregoing, there should be no undue doubt that, although the provisions in question exclude (Article 15zzs^{1}(1)) or partially restrict (Article 15zzs^{2}) the right to attend a court hearing, these restrictions fall within the above-mentioned standard resulting from the Strasbourg case-law. With regard to the mode of Article 15zzs^{1}(1) point 3 of the COVID-19 Special Act, the legislator has limited the possibility of referring a case to a closed hearing only to those cases in which 'the holding of a hearing or a public hearing is not necessary'. As indicated above, these are primarily cases where it is not necessary to conduct an evidentiary hearing based on the testimony of witnesses or parties, and cases where the facts are either undisputed or can be established on the basis of documentary evidence. In this respect, the legislator has duly adapted the regulation to the requirements of Article 6(1) of the ECHR by limiting the catalogue of cases in which a final decision may be taken *in camera*. Under the law in force prior to 3 July 2021, the issue of waiving a hearing in favour of a closed session raised even fewer concerns in the context of the implementation of the right to a fair trial. The prerequisite for the application of the then applicable provision of Article 15zzs^{1}(2) was the absence of an objection by a party to the hearing of the case *in camera*. A party not represented by a professional representative was informed of the right to object. The case law of the ECHR expresses the view that a party may itself waive the right to a public hearing[774]. Therefore, if a party, duly informed of its right, has not objected by not requesting a hearing, there can be no violation of the right to a fair trial. This does not mean, however, that a party's objection in the present state of the case will always constitute a violation of its right to a fair trial. The decision as to whether a hearing is necessary is left to the discretion of the court, which should, however, take into account the (non-binding) positions of the parties on this issue.

On the other hand, in the case of the procedure under Article 15zzs^{2} of the COVID-19 Special Act, the examination of the case normally takes place in open court, and only the final phase after the conclusion of the evidence, including the closing statements, the closure of the trial and the delivery of the judgment takes place in closed session. As noted above, the ECHR standard allows for written proceedings at certain stages of the procedure. This provision should therefore not raise any major objections.

The question of another aspect of the principle of openness of proceedings, namely the right to publicity of a decision, will be different. Under the European

774 Judgment of the European Court of Human Rights of 26 July 2011, Application No. 58222/09, LEX No. 863837.

Convention on Human Rights, it is accepted that the public announcement of a decision should be treated with a certain degree of flexibility and need not always take the form of its being pronounced in a hearing open to the general public[775]. There is also no doubt in constitutional law that, where it is permissible to take a decision *in camera*, the public announcement of the decision may take a different form from its proclamation in public. This is particularly true in civil cases, where the standard is lower than in criminal cases. It should be noted, however, that the fact that the final judgment need not be announced in open court does not mean that no other form of publication is required. While the provisions of the Code of Civil Procedure provide for the service of judgments rendered in closed session on the parties, there is no equivalent to the public announcement of the judgment on members of the public.

The provision contained in Article 15zzs^2 of the COVID-19 Special Act may also raise legitimate questions in relation to another element of the right to a fair trial, namely the adversarial principle and the right to be heard. According to the case law of the ECHR, the adversarial nature of the proceedings means that each party should be guaranteed the opportunity to be fully aware of the opponent's position and to respond to it. The right to be heard allows for the presentation of a party's position on the circumstances relevant to the outcome of the case. As already mentioned, the provision of Article 15zzs^2 of the COVID-19 Special Act does not provide for the service of final statements on the opponent before the closing of the trial. Even if such positions are served directly on each other by the parties' attorneys pursuant to Article 132 § 1 of the CCP, there is, in principle, no provision for a response to the contentions raised therein. This may make the right to a final statement illusory, since the party does not have the opportunity to read the opponent's submissions before the judgment, let alone to respond to them. If the pleading containing the final statements is served on the party after the judgment has been delivered, the position it contains loses the importance it had during the proceedings (addressing the opponent's position and convincing the court of its reasoning) and is essentially reduced to a formality. It should be noted, however, that the adversarial principle in the case-law of the ECHR is not absolute and cannot lead to the parties being arbitrarily allowed to submit further written submissions. However, if a party's final statement contains new submissions or evidence or arguments not previously raised at the hearing, the adversarial principle requires that the other party be given an opportunity to respond.

Related to the above is also another component of the right to a fair trial, which is weakened in the case of the regulation of Article 15zzs^2 of the COVID-19 Special Act, i.e. the right to be heard. Constitutional law studies assume that this right includes, first of all, the right to present arguments and claims, the right to be acquainted with the opponent's position and the right of the court to take into

775 Judgment of the European Court of Human Rights of 21 September 2006, Application No. 12643/02, LEX No. 192766.

account the party's position. Closing the trial immediately after receiving the parties' final written statements may lead to a denial of a party's right to be heard. In particular, the provision increases the risk of arbitrariness of the decision of the court, whose action is limited to the closure of the trial and the subsequent service on the parties of the final statement of the opposing party. The absence of the need to serve the parties with each other's statements before the decision is given weakens the parties' guarantee that the court will get to know them and take into account the arguments put forward in the statement.

It must be agreed that the legal solutions introduced with a view to extending the possibility for the court to rule *in camera* represent a certain breach of the principle of openness, which entails the risk of violating the right to a fair trial. It is therefore necessary to define precisely the limits of application of the provisions in question[776]. Both Article $15zzs^1$ and Article $15zzs^2$ of the COVID-19 Special Act introduce premises that allow for the possibility of referring only a certain category of cases to a closed session. The first of these provisions should be applied strictly, allowing referral to a closed session only a fragment of cases, i.e. those in which a hearing is not necessary. Meanwhile, there is a practice of frequent use of the instruments provided for by the COVID-19 Special Act by the courts and a liberal interpretation of the conditions of admissibility of the referral of a case to a closed session, which is becoming the standard. In civil cases, 71.90 % of judges stated that they had increased the number of cases heard *in camera* during the COVID-19 pandemic[777]. The trend towards more frequent use of closed sessions is observed regardless of the current spread of the pandemic or the restrictions in place[778]. The courts' practice should be assessed negatively. The provisions of the COVID-19 Special Act introduced special rules for closed sessions, which were intended to prevent the paralysis of the judiciary. However, the principle that cases should be heard in public should remain. As it was not possible to give a strict forecast of when the pandemic would end, it was expected that the provisions of the special law would remain in force, if not permanently, at least for several years[779]. Therefore, during periods of reduced epidemic risk, characterised by a low number of cases and a lower risk of coronavirus spread, it should be advocated that courts should use the tools provided by the COVID-19 Special Act with caution and only when necessary to ensure the orderly conduct of proceedings. Wherever possible, the general provisions of the Code of Civil Procedure should be applied. On the

776 J. Litowski, *Zakres zmian...*, p. 72.
777 A. Begier, A. Wypych-Knieć, Ł. Małecki-Tepicht, *Sądownictwo w czasie COVID-19...*, p. 75.
778 A. Partyk, P. Rojek-Socha, *COVID odchodzi w niepamięć, a w sądach nadal jednoosobowe składy i posiedzenia niejawne*, https://www.prawo.pl/prawnicy-sady/jednoosobowe-sklady-i-posiedzenia-niejawne-pomimo-konca-epidemii,515549.html, accessed 28 July 2022.
779 J. Litowski, *Zakres zmian...*, p. 72.

other hand, the provisions in question, which are of an exceptional nature, should certainly not be applied on the basis of an extended interpretation, according to the principle *exceptiones non sunt extendendae.*

7.5. Closed hearings after 1 July 2023

Article 15zzs[2] of the COVID-19 Special Act was repealed with effect from 28 September 2023, while Article 15zzs[1] was repealed with effect from 14 March 2024. However, the legal status of closed hearings in the Code of Civil Procedure had already changed earlier, as of 1 July 2023, due to the amendment of Article 148[1] of the CCP and Article 224 of the CCP.

According to the current wording of Article 148[1] of the CCP, the court may hear the case in closed session if the defendant has admitted the claim or if, after the parties have filed their pleadings and documents, including an objection to an order for payment or an objection to a default judgment, the court, having regard to all the submissions and requests for evidence, considers that it is not necessary to hold a hearing (§ 1). The wording of § 1 has thus remained unchanged compared to the previous legal state. However, the legislator has amended § 2 of this Article. According to this regulation, the provision of § 1 does not apply if a party has requested in the first pleading to be heard or if a special provision provides for such an obligation, unless the defendant has admitted the claim. The change is therefore that, previously, the court could not give judgment *in camera* if a party had requested a hearing in its first pleading. Now a party must request to be 'heard at a hearing', so a mere request to hold a hearing will not be sufficient. The explanatory memorandum to the bill states that the amendment is intended to 'remove the obstacles arising from the possibility of judgment in closed session'[780]. In doing so, the legislator has once again extended the possibility of ruling in a closed session, further weakening the principle of openness. As the law currently stands, the legislator has decided that a hearing must be held if a party actually wishes to be heard at the hearing. However, it should be noted that the need to obtain a party's consent to waive the right to a public hearing is not an element of the right to a fair trial in civil cases within the meaning of Article 6(1) of the ECHR and Article 45(1) of the Constitution. Therefore, a provision under which the decision to waive a hearing is left exclusively to the court does not constitute a violation of the right to a fair trial. Consequently, the direction of the changes should be assessed positively.

Article 505[1a] of the CCP, concerning simplified proceedings, further states that the provision of Article 148[1] § 3 of the CCP does not apply in cases where the value of the subject matter of the dispute does not exceed PLN 4,000. Therefore, in such

780 Explanatory Memorandum to the Government's Bill on Amendments to the Civil Procedure Code and Certain Other Acts, Parliamentary paper No. 2650 (9th Sejm), p. 15.

cases, the court may issue a judgment in a closed session, regardless of the party's request for a hearing. The legislator thus assumed that cases in this category are of a trivial nature and that the postulate of prompt consideration of cases should take precedence.

By the Act of 9 March 2023 amending the Code of Civil Procedure and certain other acts (in force since 1 July 2023), an institution, the prototype of which was Article 15zzs^{2} of the COVID-19 Special Act, was permanently introduced into the Code. Pursuant to Article 224 § 3 of the CCP, the court may close a trial in a closed session if this contributes to a more efficient consideration of the case and the appointment of further hearings is unnecessary. The parties shall be notified of the possibility of closing the trial and shall be given the opportunity to submit a written statement within a period of at least seven days. The court shall close the trial within one month of the expiry of the period for the parties to make submissions. The judgment may be delivered only by the judges before whom the last public hearing immediately preceding the closure of the trial was held.

The legislator has therefore essentially proposed to transfer the provisions of Article 15zzs^{2} of the COVID-19 Special Act to the Code of Civil Procedure, while at the same time specifying in what form and within what timeframe the trial is to be closed. In the light of the foregoing considerations, the proposed provision should be noted with approval. The current wording of Article 224 § 3 of the CCP contains several important changes in comparison with the provision in Article 15zzs^{2} of the COVID-19 Special Act. Firstly, the time limit for submitting a closing statement cannot be shorter than 7 days – Article 15zzs^{2} of the COVID-19 Special Act did not contain such a provision. Secondly, it should be noted that the legislator introduced a time limit of one month for the closing of the trial. The time limit is merely indicative and there are no procedural consequences for exceeding it by the court. Nevertheless, this solution should be assessed positively, as it undoubtedly affects the implementation of the postulate of the efficiency of proceedings. Until now, the court has not been bound by the time limit for issuing a judgment after receiving the parties' final written statements. Finally, the legislator has decided to remove doubts as to the composition of the court that may close the hearing and issue the judgment, by explicitly stating that the hearing may be closed only by the court in the composition before which the last public hearing was held.

7.6. Assessment and further legislative proposals for judgments in closed sessions

In the foregoing considerations, it has been pointed out that the right to a fair trial in civil matters, as laid down in Article 6(1) of the ECHR and Article 45(1) of the Constitution, does not preclude the hearing of certain categories of cases in closed sessions, in particular where this is required by the principle of efficiency of proceedings. It has also been established that the provisions of Article 15zzs^{1}(1) point 3 and Article 15zzs^{2} of the COVID-19 Special Act do not fully comply with the standards established by the case-law of the ECHR and the Polish Constitutional Tribunal. The measures introduced also do not fully comply with the principle of proportionality expressed in Article 31(3) of the Constitution.

First of all, it should be noted that the method of drafting legal norms of considerable importance for the individual's right to a fair trial among provisions regulating much less important issues has been criticised in legal studies[781]. Attention has been drawn to the incoherence, *ad hoc* nature, causality and questionable quality of legislative changes[782]. The current rigid and casuistic procedures should be replaced by abstract and modern pandemic-proof procedures[783]. It was also pointed out that, although the temporary solutions provided for in the COVID-19 Special Act deserve approval, the legislator should be required to ensure that the institutions introduced do not jeopardise the fundamental principles of the civil procedure[784]. The above-mentioned voices in the discourse on the design of the rules of civil procedure in the era of the COVID-19 pandemic should be acknowledged. Therefore, the introduction of the provisions of Article 148^1 of the CCP and Article 224 § 3 of the CCP should be accepted with approval, which will allow for the safe and efficient examination of cases not only during the pandemic, but also in other crisis situations that may arise in the future. It is important, however, that the proposed rules respect the principle of legal certainty and predictability and are sufficiently general to avoid the need for constant amendments. The rules should also serve to improve the efficiency of civil proceedings, but with the absolute priority of maintaining the full standard of a fair trial.

As already mentioned, the legislator has taken a step in this direction. However, in the light of the above, it would be appropriate to propose the addition of a proviso to Article 224 § 3 of the CCP, according to which the closing of the trial and the pronouncement of a judgment shall be inadmissible if a party, in the final written statement, raises new claims or evidence admissible under Article 205^{12} § 2 of the CCP. In addition, the rules should provide that a judgment delivered in a closed session shall be made available on the court's website after it has been anonymised. This will eliminate possible allegations of a breach of the principle of openness of proceedings in relation to the lack of public announcement of the judgment.

The purpose of the amendments to the Code of Civil Procedure is to expedite proceedings in cases in which a hearing is not necessary in view of the claims and evidence submitted by the parties (Article 148^1 of the CCP) and in cases in which the evidentiary proceedings have been fully conducted in a hearing, but the decision closing the proceedings in the case cannot be taken at the same hearing, e.g. because of the need to give the parties an additional opportunity to comment

781 A. Machnikowska, *Zasada jawności...*, p. 114.
782 K. Gajda-Roszczynialska, *Przebudowa wymiaru sprawiedliwości...*, p. 19.
783 K. Gajda-Roszczynialska, *Przebudowa wymiaru sprawiedliwości..*, p. 12.
784 T. Zembrzuski, *Ograniczenia jawności postępowania...*, pp. 15–16.

on the evidence submitted in writing (Article 224 § 3 of the CCP). These provisions constitute a significant departure from the principle of external openness of proceedings, which is, however, permissible in the light of Article 6(1) of the ECHR and Article 45(1) of the Constitution, in order to realise another protected value, namely the right to have a case heard without undue delay. The hearing of a case *in camera* is optional and the court may decide not to hold a hearing and to announce the judgment in public only if precisely defined conditions are met. These include, first and foremost, cases which are factually undisputed or uncontested and so-called 'trivial' cases or cases in which a possible dispute over the facts has been previously clarified in the course of the taking of evidence (Article 224 § 3 of the CCP).

The new provision of Article 148^1 § 1 of the CCP can be applied mainly to repetitive cases (e.g. consumer cases, insurance cases) in which the dispute mainly concerns a legal assessment. In such cases, in the current state of the law, the hearing is very often limited to confirming the previous written position and is a formality that does not bring any new significant circumstances for the resolution of the case. The length of the waiting period for the hearing is very often a decisive factor for the duration of the proceedings. For example, there are so-called mass action plaintiffs who purchase consumer claims in order to enforce them in court, e.g. against insurance companies. In these cases, which do not concern individuals, the right to be heard can be successfully exercised in writing without the need for an oral hearing (a large proportion of such cases, which nevertheless make up a significant proportion of the cases before the district courts, take place in an empty courtroom). The possibility of hearing such cases in a closed session will not only reduce the duration of these proceedings, but also improve the currently limited availability of public hearing dates, where cases requiring direct contact between the court and the parties and evidence should be heard in the first place. It should be left to the discretion of the court to decide which cases require a public hearing and which can be heard *in camera* without compromising the fairness of the proceedings. This will avoid situations where a party requests a hearing for the sole purpose of prolonging the proceedings. It is therefore right that the legislator now requires a motion to be heard, rather than just a request for a hearing.

However, the legislator should opt for a more far-reaching solution. The wish of a party to be heard should not be the sole factor determining the need for a hearing. A party should be heard in a public hearing if the court, after analysing all the factual and legal circumstances of the case, considers that such a hearing is necessary. In doing so, the court should not be bound by the position of the parties to the proceedings. The subjective belief in the need to be heard may not be reflected in the actual state of the case. For example, a party may make such a request only for reasons of procedural prudence or in order to prolong the proceedings.

With regard to the rule contained in Article 224 § 3 of the CCP, it should be noted that the need to preserve the adversarial procedure and the party's right to be heard requires that the parties be given the opportunity to familiarise themselves with the opponent's final written statement before the closure of the trial in a closed session. In cases where new claims and evidence may be presented up to the end of the trial (i.e., where there has been no preparatory hearing or the presiding judge has not ordered the exchange of preparatory written submissions), it may be that a party raises new facts or evidence only in its final written statement. In these cases, it should not be permissible to close the trial and the court should first take steps to rule on the evidence presented or to allow the other party to comment on the new submissions.

At the same time, the provisions in question, both Article 148^1 and Article 224 § 3 of the CCP, do not lead to a limitation of the principle of openness of the proceedings in the internal aspect, since the right of a party to participate in the proceedings is not infringed in any way. However, there is undoubtedly a significant limitation of the principle of external openness as regards the right to participate in the hearing. However, the exclusion of the public from the hearing is justified by the need to protect other values, in particular the right of the party to have the case heard within a reasonable time. External publicity should be ensured by the proposed obligation to publish judgments on the court's website. Such a form of publication of judgments is accepted both in constitutional studies and in the case-law of the ECHR. The regulation also does not affect the right of third parties to obtain information on pending cases, as provided for in separate regulations.

8. Court composition in civil proceedings in the era of the COVID-19 pandemic

8.1. The provisions of the Code of Civil Procedure relating to the composition of the court (until 3 July 2021)

Until July 2021, Article 47 § 1 of the Code of Civil Procedure provided that cases in the court of first instance were heard by a single judge. However, special provisions allowed for exceptions to this rule. The first of these was contained in Article 47 § 2 of the CCP, which regulated the composition of the bench in certain labour and family cases listed in that provision. In addition, some exceptions to the principle of collegiality in the first instance are provided for: Article 509 of the CCP (adoption cases are decided by the court composed of one professional judge and two lay judges), Article 544 of the CCP (guardianship cases are decided by the court composed of one judge and two lay judges), Article 18 of the CCP (decision of a district court to refuse to hear a case referred to it by a district court on the grounds of a question of law raising serious doubts). In addition, special provisions on exceptions to the single-member composition of courts may result from provisions outside the Code of Civil Procedure itself. Article 3(2) of the Act of 17 December 2009 on the Enforcement of Claims in Group Proceedings may serve as an example[785].

Article 47 § 4 of the CCP provides for a special power of the president of the court of first instance to order that a case be heard by three judges if he considers it advisable on account of the particular complexity of the case or its precedential character. Such an order may not be of a general nature and applicable to all cases of a given category, but may be made only in respect of a specific case which, in the opinion of the president of the court, satisfies the conditions of particular complexity or precedential character of the case[786]. Due to the location of the provision among the provisions of the CCP on first instance proceedings, it should be assumed that it does not apply to appellate courts, even in cases where a decision by a single judge is provided for. The above provision raises systemic and constitutional objections and may be considered as a means of inadmissible, quasi-administrative interference in the sphere of judicial independence, since this power is exercised by the president of the court, i.e. the administrative supervisory body, by means of a non-appealable measure. Potentially, the use of this instrument may lead to the manipulation of the composition of the panel[787]. However,

785 Journal of Laws 2020, item 446 (consolidated text).
786 T. Żyznowski, [in:] *Kodeks postępowania cywilnego...*, p. 277.
787 A. Olaś, *Kolegialność a jednoosobowość...*, pp. 522–523.

the doctrine also argues that the real significance of the institution is marginal because it is extremely rarely used on the president's own initiative[788].

There were different rules on the composition of the court in appeal proceedings, where the court normally sat with three judges. In closed session, the court ruled as a single judge, but this did not apply to the delivery of the judgment (Article 367 § 3 of the CCP). Thus, the rule was a collegial composition of three professional judges, and this applied to the delivery of a judgment both at the trial and in closed session. An exception to the collegial composition in appeal proceedings is provided for in Article 505^{10} § 1 of the CCP, according to which, in simplified proceedings, the court shall hear the appeal by a single judge.

In complaint proceedings, too, the court ruled in a panel of three judges (Article 397 § 1 of the CCP). This applied both to the complaint to the court of second instance (Article 394 of the CCP) and to the so-called horizontal complaints, for which a different composition of the court of first instance (Article 394^{1a} of the CCP) or of the court of second instance (Article 394^{2} of the CCP) is competent. A three-member panel of the court had jurisdiction to hear an appeal against a decision of that court in enforcement proceedings (Article 767^{4} § 1^{1} of the CCP) and in security and injunction proceedings (Article 741 § 2 of the CCP). However, the situation is different when considering an appeal against a decision issued in electronic payment order proceedings and an appeal against a decision on granting an enforcement clause to an enforceable title issued in such proceedings. In these cases, the appeal is heard by a single judge, as provided for in Article 505^{38} of the CCP.

As a rule, therefore, the appellate court heard cases in a panel of three judges. However, in addition to the exceptions to this rule mentioned above, it should also be noted that the court of second instance hears an appeal against a decision of a judicial clerk with a single judge (Article 398^{23} § 3 of the CCP). This also applies to the case of recognition of an appeal against a decision of a judicial clerk in enforcement proceedings (Article 767^{3a} § 3 of the CCP).

It should be noted that Article 47b § 1 of the Law on the Organisation of Common Courts establishes the principle of the continuity of the composition of the court. Pursuant to this provision, the composition of the court may be changed only in the event of an impossibility or long-term obstacle to the hearing of the case by the existing panel. The principle of continuity of the composition is not expressly provided for in the provisions of the CCP (although its manifestations are visible in Article 323 of the CCP). However, it has a general nature, i.e. it takes precedence over the provisions of the Code of Civil Procedure, since it is a manifestation of the constitutional principle of the right to a court and is therefore applicable in the field of civil procedure[789]. It is emphasised, however, that in civil proceedings the principle of the continuity of the composition of the panel is not absolute and that

788 A. Olaś, *Kolegialność a jednoosobowość...*, p. 522.
789 Resolution of the Supreme Court of 5 December 2019, III UZP 10/19, LEX No. 2746933.

a condition for the correct delivery of a judgment is that it must be delivered by the judges before whom the last hearing was held[790].

It should be noted that, according to Article 379 § 4 of the CCP, proceedings are null and void if the composition of the court is contrary to the provisions of the law. It is often pointed out, following the Supreme Court, that 'there is no better or worse composition of the court – there is only a composition in accordance with or contrary to the provisions of the law'[791]. The invalidity of the proceedings also arises in the event of a breach of the principle of the unity of the composition, laid down in Article 47b § 1 of the Law on the Organisation of the Common Courts, notwithstanding the fact that this provision is not strictly procedural[792].

8.2. Composition of the court in the COVID-19 Special Act

With effect from 3 July 2021, the Act of 28 May 2021[793] has introduced far-reaching changes to the rules governing the composition of panels of judges. In Article 15zzs^1(1) point 4 of the COVID-19 Special Act, the legislator determined that during the period of a state of epidemic threat or a state of epidemic declared on the basis of COVID-19, and within one year of the revocation of the latter, the court shall hear cases in the first and second instance with a single judge in cases heard in accordance with the provisions of the Code of Civil Procedure. The president of the court may order that a case be heard by three judges if it is deemed advisable on account of the particular complexity or precedential nature of the case.

On the one hand, the temporal scope of the invoked provision was determined by the legislator's indication of the end date of the cited regulation (one year after the end of the state of epidemic or the state of epidemic threat). On the other hand, in Article 6(2) of the Act of 28 May 2021, the legislator determined that the provision of Article 15zzs^1(1) point 4 of the COVID-19 Special Act applies to all cases, including pending ones. The temporal scope of application of the provision was thus not limited only to cases initiated after 3 July 2021, i.e. after the entry into force of the provision. Cases heard in collegial panels after the entry into force of the amending Act should continue to be heard by the single judge to whom the case had been assigned as a reporting judge. The Act therefore changed the composition of all pending cases which had previously been heard in collegial panels. The existing composition of the court was dissolved and a new composition of the court, consisting only of the reporting judge, was created in its place without the need for any order or decree[794]. The members of the panel, excluding the reporting judge, therefore ceased to be authorised to sit on the panel.

790 Resolution of the Supreme Court of 26 May 2022, III CZP 86/22, LEX No. 3347779.
791 Resolution of the Supreme Court of 18 December 1968, III CZP 119/68, LEX No. 4655.
792 Resolution of the Supreme Court of 5 December 2019, III UZP 10/19, LEX No. 2746933.
793 Act of 28 May 2021 amending the Act – Code of Civil Procedure and certain other acts, Journal of Laws 2021, item 1090.
794 Resolution of the Supreme Court of 26 May 2022, III CZP 86/22, LEX No. 3347779.

The provision of Article 15zzs[1](1) point 4 of the COVID-19 Special Act refers in its wording to the above-mentioned Article 47 § 4 of the Code of Civil Procedure, which is its prototype[795] and provides for the same conditions for ordering the examination of a case in an extended three-member panel, i.e. the particular complexity or the precedential character of the case. It therefore appears that the two provisions should be interpreted by analogy. The 'particular complexity' of a case should be understood as the degree of complexity of the case which, for the average judge, exceeds the complexity of general cases[796]. First and foremost, this will apply to legal complexity, but complexity arising from the particularly complicated facts of the case cannot be excluded in advance. A precedent case, on the other hand, need not be complicated, but requires particularly careful and mature assessment because of the emergence of new, previously unknown, and important legal issues[797].

On the basis of Article 47 § 4 of the CCP, it has been pointed out that the order of the president of the court of first instance is of an institutional nature, since it allows to depart from the provisions of the law. At the same time, the procedural nature of such an order, which determines a matter as important as the composition of the court, cannot be overlooked. The issuance of such an order falls within the discretionary power of the president of the court, who independently assesses whether there are grounds for a change in the composition of the court[798]. The president of the court cannot delegate this power to the president of a court division or other judge. Nor does the court hearing the case have the power to apply Article 47 § 4 of the CCP by itself[799]. Reference should also be made to Article 15zzs[1](1) point 4 of the COVID-19 Special Act.

It should be considered at what stage of the proceedings an order to change (extend) the composition of the court is possible. In particular, doubts may arise as to whether such a decision may be taken only before the case is assigned, i.e. at the stage of determining the composition of the court, or whether it may be taken at any stage of the proceedings. The answer to this question was given by the Supreme Court[800] on the basis of the provisions of Article 47 § 4 of the CCP, which states that the president of the court may order that a case be heard at first instance by a panel of three judges at any stage of the proceedings, if it becomes apparent during the course of the proceedings that the case is particularly complex or has a precedential character. This position must be accepted. While in principle

795 III CZP 86/22.

796 I. Kunicki, [in:] *Kodeks postępowania cywilnego. Tom I A*, A. Góra-Błaszczykowska (ed.), Warsaw 2020, Article 47, Nb 32, Legalis.

797 J. Gudowski, [in:] *Kodeks postępowania cywilnego. Komentarz. Tom I. Postępowanie rozpoznawcze,* T. Ereciński (ed.), Warsaw 2016, p. 344.

798 Resolution of the Supreme Court of 18 December 2014, III SZP 3/14, LEX No. 1554560.

799 I. Kunicki, [in:] *Kodeks postępowania cywilnego...*, Article 47, Nb 32, Legalis.

800 Resolution of the Supreme Court of 18 December 2014, III SZP 3/14, LEX No. 1554560.

it is desirable that the composition of the panel should not change during the proceedings, in accordance with the principle of continuity, which may undoubtedly also affect the application of the principle of directness, it is easy to imagine a situation in which the precedential character of a case is determined by factual or legal circumstances which come to light or become apparent at a later stage of the proceedings. Restricting the possibility of extending the composition of the panel to cases that have not been assigned would unduly limit the scope of the provision of Article 15zzs^1(1) point 4 of the COVID-19 Special Act in a way that is not apparent from its wording. Moreover, it would contradict the wording of the transitional provision of Article 6(2) of the Law of 28 May 2021, which states that it also applies to cases in which a panel was appointed before 3 July 2021.

In the same ruling, the Supreme Court stated that the opposite situation is also possible, whereby an initially complicated or precedent-setting case loses this character due to changed circumstances. This may occur as a result of a change in the subject of the case, a partial withdrawal of the action, a reversal of the judgment by the court of second instance and its referral back to the court of first instance for reconsideration (since the court of first instance will then be bound by the instructions of the appellate court as to further proceedings in the case and will be bound by the legal assessment expressed by the court of second instance), or, finally, as a result of a change in the law or the adoption of a decision by the enlarged composition of the Supreme Court, the issuance of a judgment by the Constitutional Tribunal or the Court of Justice of the EU. In such a situation, if the circumstances change in the course of the case, the president of the court may, on the basis of Article 359 § 1 of the CCP in conjunction with Article 362 of the CCP, revoke the previous decision, which will lead to a return to the examination of the case by the panel directly specified by the law[801]. The same view has also been expressed in the doctrine[802].

However, it is not possible to agree with the above position on the basis of Article 15zzs^1(1) point 4 of the COVID-19 Special Act. As the Supreme Court rightly stated in its decision of 26 May 2022, this provision is an exception to the principle of the continuity of the composition of the panel and results from an express choice of the legislator dictated by special circumstances related to the pandemic[803]. As a special provision, it should therefore be interpreted restrictively, and any departure from the general rules on composition of the panel requires an express statutory basis. The power of the president of the court to decide on the composition of the court should therefore be limited to situations arising directly from a provision of statutory rank. While the legislature has expressly provided for the president's power to enlarge the composition, there is no legal basis for reducing it. Since the decision to enlarge the composition of the court is intended

801 III SZP 3/14.
802 I. Kunicki, [in:] *Kodeks postępowania cywilnego...*, Article 47, Nb 32, Legalis.
803 Resolution of the Supreme Court of 26 May 2022, III CZP 86/22, LEX No. 3347779.

to ensure greater professionalism and a higher level of procedural guarantees for the parties[804], the annulment of such a decision may have the opposite effect and disrupt the transparency of the rules governing the allocation of cases. Situations in which an administrative factor (the president of the court) has an indirect influence on the standard of legal protection[805] should not occur, or at least be limited to the necessary minimum, and only in cases expressly provided for in the law. This is because the possibility to revoke an order issued under Article 15zzs^1(1) point 4 of the COVID-19 Special Act provides room for manipulation of the composition of the court as a result of a non-appealable decision of the president of the court. Furthermore, there is no basis for assuming that such a decision is rationally justified. Even if, in the course of the proceedings, it should transpire that the case has lost its complex or precedential character, there are no considerations which preclude further proceedings in an enlarged composition. In particular, consideration of the efficiency of the proceedings cannot be regarded as a sufficient basis for such a decision. Finally, it should be noted that, as stated above, the order of the president of the court is of an institutional nature and, although it undoubtedly has procedural effects, this decision does not have the character of an order referred to in Article 47 § 3^1 of the CCP. It therefore seems questionable to apply to such a procedural decision the provision of Article 359 § 1 of the CCP, in conjunction with Article 362 of the CCP, which concerns orders of the presiding judge. In view of the foregoing, the position that the president of the court may not revoke an order issued pursuant to Article 15zzs^1(1) point 4 of the COVID-19 Special Act and thus lead to a renewed change of the panel to a single judge should be supported.

In practice, a situation may arise where a panel originally composed of three judges has been reduced to a single judge by the amendment of 28 May 2021 and the president of the court has subsequently ordered that the case be heard by an expanded panel. The question then arises as to the composition of such a panel of the court, namely whether, in addition to the judge who continued to hear the case, that panel should include the other two judges who had been appointed to hear the case before 3 July 2021 (i.e. whether it should be the same panel as before the Act of 28 May 2021 entered into force), or whether the composition of the court in terms of those two judges should be redetermined after the president of the court has made an order to that effect. The above issue was considered by the Supreme Court in response to a legal question submitted by the Court of Appeal in Gdańsk[806]. The Supreme Court indicated that such a case should be heard by a panel of the court composed of the previous reporting judge, while the remaining judges should be

804 K. Markiewicz, *Wpływ regulacji „covidowych" na zasadę niezmienności (stabilności) oraz kolegialność składów sądów odwoławczych*, Polski Proces Cywilny 2022/1, p. 47.

805 T. Zembrzuski, *Przeciwdziałanie i zwalczanie epidemii COVID-19 w postępowaniu cywilnym, czyli pożegnanie z kolegialnością orzekania*, Polski Proces Cywilny 2022/1, p. 67.

806 Resolution of the Supreme Court of 26 May 2022, III CZP 86/22, LEX No. 3347779.

reassigned (by drawing) according to Article 47a of the Law on Organisation of Common Courts, even if a three-judge panel had previously been appointed to hear the case. In the grounds of the decision, it was emphasised that there was no reason to assume that the moment the president of the court issued an order to hear the case in a three-judge composition, the previous composition competent to hear the case before 3 July 2021 would be reinstated. This is because the previous composition of the court has been dissolved and the legislator did not endow the president of the court with the power to 'undo the effects of the amendment'. If this had been the legislator's intention, an express provision would have had to authorise the president of the court to hear the case in the existing composition. In contrast, the provision of Article $15zzs^1(1)$ point 4 of the COVID-19 Special Act provides only for the power to change the composition of the court. Moreover, the assumption that it is permissible to reinstate the composition by order of the president of the court would in fact lead to the recognition that he is entitled to decide not only on the type of composition of the court in question, but also on its specific personal composition. The Supreme Court also emphasised, although this was not explicitly addressed in the legal question posed by the Court of Appeal, that the newly created composition of three judges should include the existing reporting judge, although this is not explicitly implied in the provision of Article $15zzs^1(1)$ point 4 of the COVID-19 Special Act. This solution is supported by the fact that the order of the president of the court must, by its very nature, entail a change in the composition of the court, but this should be as minimal as possible, i.e. involving only the other two members of the panel.

The abolition of collegiate panels by virtue of Article 6(2) of the Law of 28 May 2021, *lege non distinguente*, also applied to panels with lay judges. This means that the institution of the jury has been temporarily abolished in civil proceedings[807]. T. Zembrzuski argues that, in this respect, the provision of Article $15zzs^1(1)$ point 4 of the COVID-19 Special Act is directly contrary to the norm contained in Article 182 of the Constitution, which provides for the participation of citizens in the administration of justice[808]. K. Markiewicz points out that this solution has led to the temporary suspension of the application of a provision of constitutional rank, by virtue of a statue[809]. The same doubts were raised by the District Court of Katowice-Zachód in Katowice, which, on the basis of a claim for damages for breach of the principles of equal treatment in employment (which, on the basis of Artictle 47 § 2(1b) of the CCP should be heard by the panel of one judge and two lay judges), submitted a legal question to the Constitutional Tribunal to examine whether Article $15zzs^1(1)$ point 4 of the COVID-19 Special Act is compatible with Articles 182, 31(3) and 45(1) of the Constitution of the Republic of Poland[810].

807 T. Zembrzuski, *Przeciwdziałanie i zwalczanie...*, p. 67.
808 T. Zembrzuski, *Przeciwdziałanie i zwalczanie...*, p. 67.
809 K. Markiewicz, *Wpływ regulacji...*, p. 49.
810 https://trybunal.gov.pl/s/p-13-21.

In support of the legal question, the District Court pointed out that the reasoning in the explanatory memorandum to the draft law of 28 May 2021 was contradictory. It is based on the assumption that the adjudication of cases in multi-member panels poses an epidemic risk to members of the judiciary and court staff. Furthermore, there is no objective and verifiable data to suggest that a judgment delivered by a single judge would be less fair than one delivered by an enlarged panel. Meanwhile, according to the District Court, the one-judge rule was introduced at a time when the epidemic situation in the country had improved to the extent that cultural facilities were opened and made available, gastronomy and the use of tourist facilities were allowed without significant restrictions, and the national vaccination programme was launched. The reduction of the citizen factor in the administration of justice was therefore mainly due to the desire to speed up proceedings rather than to the epidemic. In addition, the law introduced the principle of conducting court hearings remotely, on the understanding that members of the panel need not be present in the courthouse, so there was no need to introduce further restrictions by eliminating lay judges from the panels altogether. On 17 May 2023, the Constitutional Tribunal discontinued the proceedings and did not answer the legal question (reference P 13/21).

Sharing the constitutional doubts expressed above, it should be noted that the provision of Article 15zzs^1(1) point 4 of the COVID-19 Special Act leads to the abolition of lay judge formations in all cases, while at the same time giving the president of the court the power to order that a case be heard by a collegial composition in particularly complex or precedent-setting cases. The question therefore arises as to whether the second sentence of the above provision is to be interpreted as meaning that the president of the court may order a case to be heard by one judge and two lay judges in cases where this was originally provided for in Article 47 § 2 of the CCP, or whether the hearing of a case by 'three judges' means only professional judges.

It is emphasised that the participation of lay judges in the administration of justice makes it possible to bring to the bench their knowledge of social realities and to confront the professional judge's assessment of the facts of the case, particularly in terms of the consequences for the individual concerned. A mixed composition of professional judges and lay judges offers a greater guarantee of arriving at the truth because of their life experience, sensitivity and familiarity with the environment[811]. It therefore appears that the participation of jurors in certain particularly complex or precedent-setting cases can add value and contribute to a fuller clarification of the case and a more accurate decision, notwithstanding the fact that jurors do not have the professional training and knowledge to resolve advanced legal issues.

---

811 A. Kwaśniak, *Praktyczne implikacje zasady udziału obywateli w sprawowaniu wymiaru sprawiedliwości, wynikającej z art. 182 Konstytucji RP, w kontekście najnowszych regulacji,* Monitor Prawniczy 2022/8, pp. 430–431.

On the basis of an identical provision contained in Article 47 § 4 of the CCP, the view was expressed that the president of the court can extend the panel only to three professional judges. This is because whenever the provisions of the Code of Civil Procedure mention 'judges', they always refer to professional judges. On the other hand, a non-professional judge is always referred to as a 'lay judge'[812]. It should therefore be agreed that the wording of the provision of Article 15zzs[1](1) point 4 of the COVID-19 Special Act leaves no doubt that it refers to the possibility of expanding the panel to include only two additional professional judges. Otherwise, the legislator would have expressly indicated that the president of the court may order that the case be heard by three judges or by one judge and two lay judges. Irrespective of the negative assessment of the current regulation, it should be pointed out that, as the law stood, the rules of civil procedure did not provide for any situation in which the participation of lay judges in the composition of the panel of common courts would be permissible. The above position was confirmed by the Supreme Court in its decision of 14 December 2023, which stated that if such a case is heard by one judge and two lay judges, the proceedings are invalid[813].

It has already been pointed out above that the second sentence of Article 15zzs[1](1) point 4 of the COVID-19 Special Act is a repetition of the provision contained in Article 47 § 4 of the CCP. It is therefore necessary to ask whether the introduction of the former provision was necessary or whether it constitutes a statutory *superfluum*, and to what type of cases it can be applied. There is no doubt that the provision in question of the COVID-19 Special Act is *lex specialis* in relation to Article 47 of the CCP, including § 4 thereof. Consequently, the lack of repetition in Article 15zzs[1] of the COVID-19 Special Act the provision allowing the president of the court to order the extension of the composition would lead to the conclusion that the issuance of such a decision is not allowed, in accordance with the principle *lex specialis derogat legi generali.* If the second sentence of Article 15zzs[1](1) point 4 of the COVID-19 Special Act is omitted, the interpretation of this provision would lead to the assumption that the legislator allows only single-member compositions, without providing for exceptions to the rule thus defined. The repetition of the wording of Article 47 § 4 of the CCP in the wording of Article 15zzs[1](1) point 4 of the COVID-19 Special Act was therefore a deliberate and necessary effort on the part of the legislator, who thus wished to clearly emphasise that the president of the court is granted an additional power to change the composition of the court.

Notwithstanding the foregoing, it should be noted that, despite the identical wording of the two provisions, their scope of application is different. It has been pointed out in previous remarks that Article 47 § 4 of the CCP applies only to proceedings before the court of first instance. This is due, on the one hand, to the fact that it is one of the provisions governing the composition of the court of first

812 I. Kunicki, [in:] *Kodeks postępowania cywilnego...*, Article 47, Nb 31, Nb 38, Legalis.
813 Resolution of the Supreme Court of 14 December 2023, III CZP 32/23, LEX No. 3644665.

instance and, on the other hand, to the fact that the legislator has, as a rule, provided for three-member compositions in appeal proceedings, so that there is no need for a similar provision in these cases. On the other hand, with regard to the provision of Article 15zzs^{1}(1) point 4, second sentence, of the COVID-19 Special Act, it should be pointed out that it refers to the cases mentioned in the first sentence of this provision, i.e. those heard 'in the first and second instance'. In fact, the legislator did not limit in any way the power of the president of the court to order a change of composition, nor did he restrict it to a specific category of cases. It must therefore be assumed that this provision applied to all cases heard by civil courts. Thus, the possibility of extending the composition of the panel applied primarily to cases that have been heard (before 3 July 2021) by three-judge formations (appeals and complaints), but also to all other cases heard by the court of first instance (both by a single judge and by a panel). It should therefore be noted that there is a partial overlap in the scope of application of the provision of Article 47 § 4 of the CCP and Article 15zzs^{1}(1) point 4, second sentence, of the COVID-19 Special Act. The latter provision applied to all cases falling within the scope of application of Article 47 § 4 of the CCP and, in addition, to cases previously heard by three judges which were later heard by a single judge pursuant to the provision of the COVID-19 Special Act.

8.3. Composition of the court after 28 September 2023

With the Act of 7 July 2023[814], the legislator decided to reorganise the composition of the court panels in the Code of Civil Procedure, while repealing Article 15zzs^{1} of the COVID-19 Special Act. The most significant change concerns the appeal proceedings. Pursuant to the new Article 367^{1} § 1 of the CCP, the court shall hear an appeal before a single judge. However, the provision introduces a number of exceptions. Cases will be heard by three judges in: 1) cases concerning property rights, where the value of the claim in at least one of the appeals lodged exceeds one million PLN; 2) cases heard in the first instance as a regional court, taking into account point 1; 3) cases heard in the first instance by a panel of three judges pursuant to Article 47 § 4 of the CCP. In addition, the president of the court may order that the appeal be heard by a panel of three judges if he deems it advisable because of the particular complexity or precedential nature of the case (Article 367^{1} § 3 of the CCP).

The above provision broke with the principle of collegiality of appeal panels in a significant proportion of cases, including the majority of cases heard by the regional court as a court of second instance. Significantly, this provision was not

814 Act of 7 July 2023 amending the Act - Code of Civil Procedure, the Act - Law on the Organisation of Common Courts, the Act - Code of Criminal Procedure and certain other acts (Journal of Laws of 2023, item 1860).

included in the original bill[815], but was added by way of amendments after the first reading at the Sejm session on 15 June 2023. There is therefore no justification in the government draft for the changes made.

The Amending Act also changed the composition of the panel of judges in complaint proceedings. A complaint to the court of second instance (Article 394 of the CCP) is now heard by a single judge in accordance with Article 397 § 1 of the CCP. On the other hand, the so-called horizontal complaints, i.e. complaints to another panel of the court of first (Article 394^{1a} of the CCP) and second (Article 394^{2} of the CCP) instance, are heard by a panel of three judges, according to Article 394^{1a} § 1^{2} of the CCP and Article 394^{2} § 1^{3} of the CCP.

It should be recalled that previously, i.e. before the introduction of the provisions discussed in this section, the court in appeal proceedings was generally composed of three judges. An exception to the collective decision in appeal proceedings was provided for in Article 505^{10} § 1 of the CCP, according to which in simplified proceedings the court heard the appeal with a single judge. In complaint proceedings, the court also ruled in a panel of three judges (Article 397 § 1 of the CCP). This applied both to complaints to the court of second instance (Article 394 of the CCP) and to horizontal complaints, for which a different composition of the court of first instance (Article 394^{1a} of the CCP) or of second instance (Article 394^{2} of the CCP) is competent. At the same time, the rule has been maintained that a three-member panel of the court has jurisdiction to hear an appeal against a decision of that court in enforcement proceedings (Article 767^{4} § 1^{1} of the CCP). However, the situation is different with regard to the examination of a complaint against a decision issued in electronic payment order proceedings and a complaint against a decision on the granting of an enforcement clause to an enforceable title issued in such proceedings. In these cases, the complaint is heard by a single judge, as provided for in Article 505^{38} of the CCP.

Pursuant to Article 40 of the Amending Act of 7 July 2023, the provisions relating to the formation of court enter into force 14 days after the publication of the Act in the Journal of Laws and are therefore effective as of 28 September 2023. The transitional provision is contained in Article 32 of the Act. Pursuant to this provision, in proceedings commenced and not concluded before the date of entry into force of the Act, the court shall hear the case in accordance with the provisions as amended by the Act, with the proviso that in cases previously heard by a panel of three judges and now heard by a single judge, the continuation of the case shall be taken over by the reporting judge. In addition, if a trial has been

815 Government bill on amendments to the Act - Code of Civil Procedure, the Act - Law on the Organisation of Common Courts, the Act - Code of Criminal Procedure and some other acts, parliamentary print no. 3216, available on the website of the Sejm of the Republic of Poland:
https://www.sejm.gov.pl/sejm9.nsf/druk.xsp?nr=3216, accessed 4.12.2023.

closed before the date of entry into force of the amending Act, the court will continue to hear the case in its previous composition.

The new rules on composition of the court have given rise to a number of problems of interpretation. As an example, it is worth mentioning the legal questions that have been submitted to the Supreme Court, despite the short period of time that the new regulation has been in force. In particular, it is worth mentioning the legal question raised by the Regional Court in Wrocław as to whether the composition of the court hearing the appeal against the decision of the court of first instance on the confirmation of the acquisition of the inheritance determines the value of the subject of the appeal and, if so, whether its indication constitutes a formal requirement of the appeal[816]. On 12 April 2024, the Supreme Court answered the above question by stating that an appeal in a case of confirmation of the acquisition of an inheritance filed after 27 September 2023 will be heard by a court composed of a single judge.

It should be noted that the answer to the above question provided important interpretative guidance also with regard to a number of other cases heard in non-contentious proceedings. The Supreme Court's answer means that the majority of cases will be heard by a single judge in the regional courts, even though they are usually cassation cases (Article 519^1 § 1 of the CCP).

The relationship between the provisions of Article 367^1 § 1 points 1 and 2 of the CCP has also raised doubts in the courts. According to the second point of § 1 of the cited provision, cases heard by a regional court as a court of first instance shall be heard on appeal by a panel of three judges 'having regard to the provisions of the point 1'. In the light of this provision, the Warsaw Court of Appeal referred the following legal question to the Supreme Court: 'Is the composition of the court hearing an appeal in a case concerning the annulment of a decision of a homeowner association determined by the value of the appeal filed (Article 367^1 § 1 point 1 of the CCP) or by the fact that the case is heard in the first instance by a regional court as a court of first instance regardless of the value of the appeal (Article 367^1 § 1 point 2 of the CCP in conjunction with Article 17 § 4 point 2 of the CCP)?'[817]. This is because the wording of the cited provisions gives rise to reasonable doubt as to whether the appellate court shall hear appeals against judgments rendered by a three-judges panel regional court: 1) only if the value of the subject matter of the appeal exceeds one million PLN, 2) or always if the regional court has jurisdiction at first instance, even if the value of the subject matter of the appeal does not exceed one million PLN, 3) only if the regional court has jurisdiction at first instance, regardless of the value of the subject matter of the dispute, 3) or finally if the value of the subject matter of the dispute at first instance exceeds one million PLN and the value of the subject matter of the appeal does not exceed one million PLN. In its decision of 9 April 2024, the Supreme Court agreed with the

816 III CZP 55/23.
817 III CZP 59/23.

first of the above-mentioned positions, stating that the appellate court shall consider an appeal in a case concerning the annulment of a decision of a homeowner association by a single judge if the value of the subject of the appeal in any of the appeals filed does not exceed one million PLN[818].

Moreover, the provisions governing the complaint procedure gave rise to problems concerning the proper composition of the panel. Pursuant to Article 741 § 2 of the CCP, a decision of the court of second instance may be appealed to another panel of the court. On the basis of this provision, the Court of Appeal in Warsaw raised the question as to the composition of the court in proceedings based on a complaint against a decision of the court of second instance on the granting of injunction, i.e. whether such a complaint should be considered by a different composition of the court consisting of three judges (Article 394^2 § 1^3 of the CCP) or by a single judge (Article 397 § 3 of the CCP)[819]. In a decision of 30 April 2024, the Supreme Court stated that a complaint against the decision of a court of second instance to grant an injunction is subject to review by another panel of three judges of that court (Article 394^2 § 1^3 of the CCP *per analogiam*).

8.4. The court composed of a single judge and right to a fair trial

The assessment of the provision of Article $15zzs^1(1)$ point 4 of COVID-19 Special Act in terms of its compliance with the standard of the right to a fair trial should begin with the statement that the appointment of a panel of judges from among the duly authorised judges is one of the basic guarantees of a fair trial. Only a court sitting in the composition prescribed by law for a particular case fulfils the condition of a competent court referred to in Article 45(1) of the Constitution[820]. The need to standardise the composition of the court (including its number and degree of professionalism) in provisions of at least statutory rank is therefore a constitutional requirement[821]. It should be recalled that the European Court of Human Rights has also emphasised in its case law that the concept of a 'court established by law' implies, inter alia, that there must be rules determining the jurisdiction of the court (including its composition), which should be applied in a rational and uniform manner. These rules should be defined in advance by provisions of statutory rank[822].

However, it must be emphasised that the concept of the right to a fair trial, which is derived both from Article 45(1) of the Constitution and from Article 6(1) of the ECHR, does not include the right to a collegial court. In accordance with the

818 Resolution of the Supreme Court of 9 April 2024, III CZP 59/23.
819 III CZP 60/23.
820 A. Łazarska, *Rzetelny proces...*, p. 192.
821 A. Olaś, *Kolegialność a jednoosobowość...*, p. 500.
822 A. Łazarska, *Rzetelny proces...*, p. 188.

principle of procedural autonomy, the decision on the formation of a panel belongs to the national legislator, who is entitled to adopt a certain procedural model. The choice between single-member and collegiate composition is an expression of the legislator's current preference for certain values or even the current possibilities of the judiciary[823]. In its judgment of 3 May 2011, the European Court of Human Rights accepted that it was not its task to assess the legitimacy of the national authorities' decision to assign a case to a particular judge or court, but that the Court had to examine whether such a decision complied with the requirements of Article 6(1) of the ECHR concerning the independence and impartiality of the court[824]. Therefore, it cannot be accepted *a priori* that the introduction of a statutory rule that all types of civil cases are decided by a single judge violates the right to a fair trial. The above view also applies to appellate review, which, it should be noted, is not at all recognised by the case law of the ECHR as an element of the right to a fair trial (however, where the legislator has decided to introduce an appellate review, fair trial standards must be respected). The Constitution of Poland regulates the issue differently, providing in Article 78 for the right to appeal against judgments and decisions of the first instance, and in Article 176 for the right to at least a two-instance court procedure. However, it is not possible to derive from these provisions an obligation on the part of the legislator to provide for collegial composition in appeal proceedings. There is therefore no obstacle to a single judge appeal. On the other hand, however, W. Sanetra emphasises that the general framework for legislation established by the provisions of the Constitution does not mean that the ordinary legislator may completely arbitrarily form the legal rules determining the composition of the courts in which certain types of cases are to be decided[825].

The introduction of the provision of Article 15zzs[1](1) point 4 of the COVID-19 Special Act into the legal system has launched a broad discussion in both the jurisprudence and the doctrine on the constitutionality of the adopted solution, both in the context of lowering the standard of legal protection of an individual and in the aspect of violating the principle of the continuity of the panel. A manifestation of the doubts expressed was a legal question submitted to the Supreme Court by the Regional Court in Katowice, based on a case concerning the division of joint property of spouses[826], as to whether the provision of Article 15zzs[1](1) point 4 of the COVID-19 Special Act applies to cases initiated prior to the entry into force of this Act and in respect of which a three-judge panel had already been appointed.

---

823 A. Olaś, *Kolegialność a jednoosobowość...*, pp. 502–503.

824 Judgment of the European Court of Human Rights of 3 May 2011, Application No. 30024/02, LEX No. 787369.

825 W. Sanetra, *Sąd właściwy w rozumieniu Konstytucji RP*, Przegląd Sądowy 2011/9, p. 22.

826 Decision of the Regional Court in Katowice of 21 October 2021, IV Ca 311/21, LEX No. 3247618.

The Regional Court took the view that, although the clear wording of the provision of Article 6(2) of the Amending Act of 28 May 2021 leads to the conclusion that there will be a change from collegiate to single-judge formations as of 3 July 2021, the literal interpretation of this provision must be regarded as a completely inadequate interpretative guideline. The Regional Court held that the transitional provision was contrary to the principle of continuity of composition, which constitutes an important guarantee of the right to a competent court within the meaning of Article 45(1) of the Constitution. In addition, the Court found that the amendments resulted in a lowering of the standard of legal protection in the consideration of appeals, which is due to the undoubted advantages of collegial adjudication in appeal proceedings. This issue should be assessed in the context of the previous case law of the CJEU, according to which the right to an independent court also applies to the composition of the court hearing the case. While the national legislature has the right to reorganise the judiciary, including the composition of the court, this must not lead to a reduction in the protection of EU values and a weakening of the rule of law. According to the Regional Court, the contested amendment may be regarded as a means of controlling the content of judicial decisions, since it affects the scope of cases assigned to judges. In the absence of a clearly stated relationship worthy of legal protection, this regulation must be assessed as an instrumental measure interfering with the composition of the courts hearing the case. Consequently, the Regional Court doubted whether the primacy of the principle of the right to a competent court should not determine the application of the principle of continuity of composition to cases commenced before 3 July 2021 and for which a composition of three judges was designated during that period. On the other hand, the intertemporal rule laid down in Article 6(2) of the amending act is contrary to the principle referred to.

The Polish Ombudsman has taken a stand on this issue[827]. The Ombudsman pointed out that the legislator's freedom to regulate court proceedings does not mean that it is permissible to introduce arbitrary solutions that excessively restrict a party's procedural rights. There is a violation of the constitutional guarantees relating to the right to a court if the limitation of a party's procedural rights is unnecessary from the point of view of the objectives pursued by the legislator and, at the same time, violates the rules of procedural fairness and leads to the risk of an arbitrary resolution of the case. He also stated that the intertemporal solutions adopted in the Amending Act of 28 May 2021 raise serious doubts from the point of view of respecting the principle of legitimate expectations, expressed in Article 2 of the Constitution, which guarantees to subjects of law that the hitherto binding law, on the basis of which actions are taken, will not be arbitrarily changed in the course of proceedings. The Ombudsman also considered the regulation at issue to be inconsistent with Article 31(3) of the Constitution. This is because it cannot be

827 Ombudsman's pleading of 1 February 2022 in Case III CZP 73/21, https://bip.brpo.gov.pl/sites/default/files/2022-02/RPO_SN_sklady_1.02.2022.pdf, access: 7 August 2024.

assumed that the need to introduce single-member composition of court was motivated by considerations of health protection, when at the same time the epidemic restrictions on meetings or official and professional gatherings were lifted. The solutions introduced by the above-mentioned Act with regard to the composition of the court are disproportionate and violate the right to have a case heard by a competent, impartial and independent court, which in turn leads to a violation of Article 2, Article 31(3) and Article 45(1) of the Constitution.

In a decision of 29 April 2022, the Supreme Court refused to adopt a resolution answering the question[828]. In its reasoning, however, the Supreme Court referred to the arguments put forward by the Regional Court in Katowice, firstly stating that the literal meaning of the provision of Article 6(2) of the Act of 28 May 2021 was clear and that there was no sufficient reason to deviate from this interpretation, especially as this would mean its *de facto* derogation. However, the Supreme Court agreed with the Regional Court, pointing out that the collegiality of the panel, which is a well-established principle in appeal proceedings, undoubtedly ensures a higher standard of review, allowing decisions to be shaped by discourse and clashing perspectives. It also strengthens the impartiality, independence and autonomy of the judiciary and enhances the legitimacy of the court in the eyes of the public, and is also desirable from the point of view of adequate protection of the rights of the parties and participants in the proceedings. At the same time, the Supreme Court stated that the above does not mean that the deviation from the principle of collegiality is tantamount to a violation of Article 45(1) of the Constitution, and that the previous jurisprudence of the Supreme Court does not question the admissibility of deviation from the principle of collegiality, but points out that this should be done by means of a clear legal regulation. In particular, the mere encroachment upon the principle of the continuity of the composition of the panel does not constitute an impermissible violation of Article 45(1) of the Constitution, as this is only a principle of statutory rank, which, moreover, is of limited application in civil proceedings by virtue of the wording of Article 323 of the CCP. Moreover, the amendment does not completely break with this principle, as it provides for the case to be heard by the judge who previously was appointed reporting judge. The Supreme Court stated that the right to a court of competent jurisdiction implies the prohibition of determining the manner of composition of the court *ad hoc* and the order to determine it *ex ante*, in an abstract manner, for cases of a certain type.

It should be noted that, with regard to the Regional Court's reservations concerning the compliance of the contested provisions with EU law, the Supreme Court stated that only the Court of Justice of the European Union had jurisdiction to interpret EU law in order to assess the conflict with national law. It should also be noted that the Regional Court did not refer to any connection between the case under consideration and EU law when it posed the legal question. The

828 Decision of the Supreme Court of 29 April 2022, III CZP 77/22, LEX No. 3361825.

legal question was raised in the context of a case concerning the division of joint property, and it cannot therefore be assumed that the case is of an EU nature. Therefore, the question raised by the Regional Court should not be examined from the perspective of the EU legal order at all and, consequently, the Regional Court's reference to the case law of the CJEU should be regarded as incorrect, as it is inapplicable in the context of a case which does not have an EU connection.

With reference to the position expressed in the above-mentioned decision, it should be noted that the Supreme Court seems to share the view expressed at the outset, according to which the introduction by the legislator of exclusively single-member formations of the court, including the court of appeal, does not *per se* violate the right to a fair trial, provided that it is determined in compliance with the constitutional requirement of the right to a competent court, i.e. on the basis of clear and predetermined legal provisions. Similarly, the derogation from the principle of the continuity of the composition of the court by virtue of an intertemporal provision (Article 6(2) of the Amending Act) cannot constitute a violation of the right to a fair trial, since this principle is of a legal nature and stems from Article 47b § 1 of the Law on Organisation of Common Courts.

Doubts about the admissibility of the formation of a single-member court in appeal proceedings were also raised by the District Court of Katowice-Zachód in Katowice, which submitted a question of law to the Supreme Court[829] in order to clarify whether a single-member court resulting from the episodic provisions of Article $15zzs^1(1)$ point 4 of the COVID-19 Special Act is a 'court established by law' within the meaning of Article 6(1) of the ECHR and, if not, whether it is reasonable under Article 91(2) of the Constitution to disregard this provision and to determine the composition of the court in the appeal proceedings on the basis of the provisions of the Code of Civil Procedure.

On 26 April 2023, seven Justices of the Supreme Court adopted a resolution[830] according to which the hearing of a civil case by a court of second instance with a single judge formed on the basis of Article $15zzs^1(1)$ point 4 of the COVID-19 Special Act restricts the right to a fair trial (Article 45(1) of the Constitution), as it is not necessary for the protection of public health (Articles 2 and 31(3) of the Constitution) and leads to the invalidity of the proceedings (Article 379(4) of the CCP).The Supreme Court decided to give the resolution the force of a legal principle and stated that the interpretation of the law adopted in the resolution was valid from the date of its enactment, i.e. from the date of its adoption by the Supreme Court.

In the statement of reasons for the decision, the Supreme Court held that, although the national legislator's abandonment of a collegial composition in

829 Decision of the District Court Katowice-Zachód in Katowice of 5 July 2022, III Pz 5/22, not published.

830 Resolution of 7 Judges of the Supreme Court of 26 April 2023, III PZP 6/22, OSNP 2023/10/104.

favour of a single-member composition without presenting objective arguments demonstrating a threat to the independence and impartiality of the court did not constitute a violation of the Convention standard, the assessment of the provision of Article 15zzs[1](1) point 4 of the COVID-19 Special Act should also be assessed through the prism of the constitutional standard, with a detailed justification of why, in the opinion of the Supreme Court, the assessment of the constitutionality of a provision of statutory rank is not reserved to the exclusive competence of the Constitutional Tribunal.

The Supreme Court pointed out that the collegiality of appellate panels has a long tradition and is a well-established principle of civil procedure and is therefore part of the established standard of the right to a fair trial. For these reasons, restrictions on the principle of collegiality of appellate panels must be assessed from the perspective of upholding the standard of conduct inherent in the right to a fair trial. In this regard, changing this standard by abolishing, even temporarily, the principle of collegiality of the judiciary constitutes an interference with the current constitutional standard of the right to a fair trial.

The Supreme Court emphasised that the collegiality of panel influences the level of practical implementation of the requirement of a comprehensive and objective assessment of the circumstances of the case and contributes to the fairness of the judicial decision by ensuring that the court's decisions are not arbitrary.

The Supreme Court then assessed the disputed provision of the COVID-19 Special Act in the light of the principle of proportionality, as expressed in Article 31(3) of the Constitution, and found that the COVID-19 pandemic had become an opportunity for the authorities to abruptly and drastically restrict civil rights and freedoms, 'introduced chaotically, thoughtlessly and often unlawfully under the guise of health protection'. At the time the Amendment Act of 28 May 2021 was passed, the pandemic situation was stable, infection rates remained low, the COVID-19 vaccine was available and virtually all pandemic restrictions had been lifted. Therefore, the Supreme Court held that the answer to the question of the necessity of the restrictions on the grounds of health protection must be unequivocally negative.

The statement of reasons for the resolution also emphasises that the provision is systemically inconsistent, since the collegiality of the judiciary is maintained in criminal cases, in administrative proceedings and before the Supreme Court. The introduction of the provision was also not preceded by any empirical studies. Furthermore, the legislator extended the duration of this solution to one year after the end of the state of epidemic or the state of epidemic threat and, above all, ignored the possibility of achieving the same objective with less restrictive measures.

The position expressed in the above-mentioned resolution cannot be considered convincing. Although the Supreme Court is correct in stating that the regulation in question does not pass the proportionality test of Article 31(3) of the Constitution, it must be stated that the Supreme Court proceeded on the basis of an erroneous – and, moreover, insufficiently justified – assumption that the collegiality of the appellate panels is part of the constitutional standard of the right to a fair trial. The mere fact that the appellate panels were collegial when the Polish Constitution entered into force does not permit the simple conclusion that the constitutional standard of the right to a fair trial includes the right to a collegial court. There is no sufficient argument for assuming that the constitutional standard is broader than the Strasbourg one. On the contrary, there is reason to believe that the formation of a panel of judges in a particular way is not covered by the content of the right to a fair trial. The constitutional guarantee of a competent court means that the legislator is obliged *ex ante* and in the abstract to determine the jurisdiction of the court, so that the individual has the possibility of determining in advance which court has jurisdiction to hear his case. The main purpose of this is to ensure the predictability of the courts' jurisdiction and to exclude any manipulation of jurisdiction in relation to a particular case. The jurisdiction of the court should be determined in advance in as stable and predictable a manner as possible, without the possibility of discretionary interference by the public authorities as to which court will hear a particular case[831].

The principle that courts of first and second instance hear cases on a single-judge basis was introduced by a provision of statutory rank. The provision of Article 15zzs^1(1) point 4 of the COVID-19 Special Act clearly determined the composition of the panels of judges. Therefore, there is no reason to believe that the amendment deprived the individual of the right to a competent court, since the contested regulation does not allow for arbitrary determination of the composition of the court, but on the contrary provides for the same composition of the court for all types of cases, thus regulating the matter in the abstract. On the basis of the provision relied on, the individual was able to determine *ex ante* how the composition of the court would be shaped in his case. Therefore, the arguments set out above concerning the incompatibility of the regulation in question with the right to a fair trial as enshrined in Article 45(1) of the Constitution must be regarded as unfounded. Another issue, which does not affect the above assessment, is the purpose of the adopted regulation and its impact on the standard of appellate review.

At this point, it is necessary to return to the issue raised earlier concerning the lowering of the standard of legal protection afforded to an individual in connection with the transformation of the appellate courts into exclusively single-member panels. This will allow for further consideration of the assessment of the provision contained in Article 15zzs^1(1) point 4 of the COVID-19 Special Act in relation to the other allegations raised in the public discourse, in particular the presented issue of contradiction with the principles of procedural justice and violation of Article 31(3) of the Constitution.

A. Olaś points out that both single-member and collegiate courts have certain advantages and disadvantages. Judgments rendered in multi-judge panels are the result of discussions, conflicting opinions and different views on a given issue,

831 P. Grzegorczyk, K. Weitz, [in:] *Konstytucja...*, p. 1121.

which in turn reduces the risk of factual and legal errors. Collegial judgments therefore ensure a fuller and more thorough decision-making process, which increases the chances of arriving at the truth. Collegial courts also increase the guarantee of the judge's independence, as it makes it clear that the entire panel is responsible for the decision taken. On the other hand, a judge acting alone is more vulnerable to possible pressure. Decisions taken collectively also tend to have greater authority[832].

On the other hand, considerations of the social and financial costs of the judiciary and the efficiency of the procedure argue in favour of single-judge formations. A single judge appears to be more accessible to the parties, which enhances the effectiveness of a judge as a dispute resolution professional. At the same time, it is argued that a single judge does not necessarily have a negative impact on the quality of the judgment, since the judge, acting independently, takes responsibility for the correctness of the decision, so that there is no 'dilution of responsibility'[833]. T. Zembrzuski, on the other hand, points out directly that the collegial composition of the court ensures higher standards and thus the realisation of the right to a higher level of justice. At the same time, the author notes that it is impossible to determine the extent to which a single-member composition contributes to the acceleration of proceedings[834]. A more far-reaching position is expressed by K. Markiewicz, who points out that it is obvious that a collegial composition of the court ensures a higher level of professionalism, a greater standard of adjudication and a higher level of guarantee of the right to a fair trial[835].

It should be noted that a collegial court, particularly in appeal proceedings, contributes to a more comprehensive consideration of the relevant circumstances of the case and allows for a more thorough analysis of the issues before the appellate court. There is therefore no doubt that a multi-member panel increases the likelihood of a correct ruling. However, a degree of caution should be applied to those who claim that the collegial composition of the court gives the parties the right to a higher standard of justice. While, for the reasons stated above, it should be agreed that the collegial composition of the appeal court constitutes an additional procedural guarantee for the parties, it cannot be simply concluded from such a statement that there is a violation of the right to a fair trial when the court of second instance is composed of a single judge. It should be stressed again that the collegiality of the composition of the court is not an element of the right to a court as such. Thus, the collegiality of the panel may contribute to strengthening the guarantees of the independence of a judge, but this does not automatically mean that a judge sitting alone is deprived of such guarantees and thus cannot exercise an independent judicial review.

---

832 A. Olaś, *Kolegialność a jednoosobowość...*, pp. 503–504.
833 A. Olaś, *Kolegialność a jednoosobowość...*, pp. 504–505.
834 T. Zembrzuski, *Przeciwdziałanie i zwalczanie...*, p. 68.
835 K. Markiewicz, *Wpływ regulacji...*, pp. 47–48.

Thus, even assuming that the limitation of the composition of the court of appeal to one judge constitutes a certain lowering of the standard, there is no convincing reason to claim that it falls below the constitutional and Convention minimum. If the legislator had made the preservation of the right to a fair trial dependent on the collegiality of the panel, it would have included such a reservation directly in the text of the Constitution. In the meantime, this issue has been left to the ordinary legislature (Article 176(2) of the Constitution). It should also be borne in mind that the legislator has left open the possibility of extending the single-member composition in cases involving highly complex or precedential issues. Thus, the collegiality of the appellate judiciary has not been completely abolished.

As indicated in the previous considerations, the aim of the legislator in introducing single-person formations in all types of cases heard at first and second instance was to limit the epidemiological threat posed by three persons sitting together in a panel[836]. K. Markiewicz pointed out that this was only a declared objective and not a real one, which was due to the fact that the legislator had simultaneously abandoned provisions imposing other restrictions. The author's doubts were also raised by the duration of the regulation, which provided for it to remain in force for one year after the end of the state of epidemic or epidemic threat, which has no medical or organisational justification. Therefore, in terms of expediency, the provision does not meet the standards of an episodic regulation[837]. The Supreme Court took a different view in its above-mentioned decision of 29 April 2022[838], pointing out that the collegiality of the panel clearly increases the epidemiological risk and thus the risk to the health of the members of the panel and to the efficiency of the proceedings, since the illness of one member of the panel could lead to the illness and quarantine of the other members and to a delay in the conduct of the proceedings. There can therefore be no question of a complete disconnect between the legislator's intentions and the stated purpose of the amendment.

Another issue, apart from the rationality of the introduced regulation, is its compliance with the principle of the most lenient measure (principle of utility) arising from Article 31(3) of the Constitution, according to which the least burdensome measure available should be chosen. It should be noted that the amendment of 28 May 2021, in addition to the single-member court formations, also introduced the principle that a remote hearing may be held without the simultaneous presence in the court building not only of the participants but also of the members of the panel (Article 15zzs^{1}(1) point 1 of the COVID-19 Special Act). In this way, the law provides another instrument that can be equally successful in preventing the

---

836 Explanatory Memorandum to the Government's Bill on Amendments to the Act - Code of Civil Procedure and Certain Other Acts, Parliamentary Paper No. 899.

837 K. Markiewicz, *Wpływ regulacji...*, pp. 45–46.

838 Decision of the Supreme Court of 29 April 2022, III CZP 77/22, LEX No. 3361825.

exposure of panel members to mutual contagion. At the same time, it should be regarded as a less severe restriction than a change in the composition of the court.

Regardless of the above considerations concerning the proportionality of the introduced regulations, it should be noted that it does not appear necessary to examine them from the point of view of their compliance with Article 31(3) of the Constitution. As it has been shown above, the provision of Article 15zzs^{1}(1) point 4 of the COVID-19 Special Act does not constitute a restriction on the exercise of constitutional rights and freedoms due to the fact that Article 45(1) of the Constitution does not grant an individual the right to a court with a specific composition of panel (number of judges).

The criticisms levelled against the amendment as being contrary to the principle of procedural fairness are also unfounded. The principle means that proceedings before a court should be predictable and certain for an individual. As A. Łazarska points out, the concept of procedural justice includes its certainty, openness and comprehensibility[839]. Although the principle of procedural fairness includes the prohibition of taking an individual by surprise and of making arbitrary changes with consequences that are difficult to foresee for the individual, it is not possible to derive automatically from this principle a prohibition of changing procedural rules in the course of the proceedings. Moreover, it is not possible to speak of a violation of the principle of procedural fairness in the case of a change in rules that does not directly affect the rights and obligations of a party to the proceedings. While it may be debatable whether a single-judge appellate review reduces the standard of legal protection afforded to an individual, it is not possible to conclude from this that the amendment in question exposes an individual to certain legal consequences which could not have been foreseen in advance. Indeed, a change in the composition of the court in the course of proceedings does not directly affect the procedural situation of the parties. Nor can it be assumed that an individual takes a decision to challenge a decision on the basis of the way in which the legislature has decided to regulate the question of the composition of the court. Furthermore, it cannot be said that the provisions adopted in the Amending Act constitute an arbitrary decision and come as a surprise to the citizen. Indeed, the Amending Act of 28 May 2021 was adopted after the legislative process and the amendment in question entered into force after the period of *vacatio legis* (Article 7). Moreover, it should be stressed that it is difficult to claim arbitrariness in determining the composition of the court, since uniform rules have been adopted for all types of cases.

Contrary to the views of the doctrine presented above, the position should be supported that the introduced change concerning the hearing of cases in civil proceedings in single-member formations does not violate the right to a fair trial, in particular in the aspect of the constitutional right to a competent court. However, fundamental doubts in this respect may be raised by the power granted to the

---

839 A. Łazarska, *Rzetelny proces...*, pp. 327–328.

president of the court in Article 15zzs^1(1) point 4 of the COVID-19 Special Act to order the hearing of a case in a three-member panel. As stated above, such a decision may be taken by the president at his own discretion and is not subject to appeal. As T. Zembrzuski points out, such a legislative solution has the effect of making the composition of the court, and thus the standard of legal protection provided, dependent on an arbitrary administrative factor[840]. K. Markiewicz also notes that granting such a power to an administrative supervisory body creates the possibility of excessive influence on the constitutional and European standard, which is the recognition of a case by a court established by law[841]. Similar doubts were expressed by A. Olaś on the basis of Article 47 § 4 of the CCP, pointing out that such a power of the president of the court may be perceived as a means of unacceptable interference in the jurisdiction of the judge. The author suggests that the presiding judge and the parties should have the right to request that the case be heard by a panel of three judges, or even that this power should be vested directly in the deciding court[842].

In the light of the above, it should be recalled that the president of the court is the internal administrative supervisory body responsible for ensuring the proper functioning of the court's internal administration (Article 8(2) and Article 9a(1) of the Law on Organisation of Common Courts). The president of the court directs the administrative activities of the court and in this respect is subordinate to the Minister of Justice (Article 22). The composition of the court can certainly not be considered as an activity that ensures the internal functioning of the court, especially when it depends on the fulfilment of substantive requirements (the particular complexity or precedential character of the case), the implementation of which requires prior analysis and assessment. Once again, it should be emphasised that the right to a 'competent' court, provided for in Article 45(1) of the Constitution, requires the legislator to adopt a legal regulation that excludes the *ad hoc* and arbitrary determination of the panel of judges. Giving the president of the court, rather than the court itself, the power to determine the composition of the court on the basis of an unappealable decision does not meet these requirements.

However, it should be noted that the legislator has given the president of the court the power to extend the composition of the court and not to change it at will (in particular, to reduce it). Such a decision by the president may, in principle, have a positive impact on the level of legal protection provided, which is emphasised by the authors, who see in the president's decision a threat to the independence of the judiciary. It should not be forgotten that the president of the court does not have the power to personally designate certain members of the bench who will be randomly assigned to hear the case (Article 47a(1) of the Law on Organisation of Common Courts). In the end, therefore, the position should be supported that the

840 T. Zembrzuski, *Przeciwdziałanie i zwalczanie...*, pp. 66–67.
841 K. Markiewicz, *Wpływ regulacji...*, p. 49.
842 A. Olaś, *Kolegialność a jednoosobowość...*, pp. 522–523.

threat to the standard of the right to a competent court in the case of the regulation contained in Article 15zzs¹(1) point 4 of the COVID-19 Special Act is only potential, which does not mean, however, that changes to the institution in question should not be postulated.

8.5. Conclusions and further legislative proposals concerning the composition of the court in civil proceedings

The assessment made in the previous section leads to the conclusion that not all the allegations made in the doctrine concerning the violation of the fair trial standard by the provision contained in Article 15zzs¹(1) point 4 of the COVID-19 Special Act can be considered valid. However, this does not mean that the provision in question has no impact on the achievement of the objectives of civil proceedings and the proper functioning of the judicial system. In the light of the foregoing, the assertions made in the explanatory memorandum of the Amending Act, which was finally enacted on 28 May 2021, are laconic and not supported by sufficient argumentation[843].

In particular, it cannot be considered sufficient to point out that the members of the collegiate panels pose an epidemiological risk to each other in a situation where, firstly, no other measures have been taken to isolate the court staff (judges, but also secretarial and administrative staff) from each other, who are still forced to remain in the court buildings, often in offices shared by several people[844]. Secondly, it should be noted that the adoption of the provision in question has made it possible for members of the bench to take part in remote hearings outside the court building. The latter solution seems sufficient to minimise the risk of transmission of coronavirus between the members of the panel. It is also impossible, for obvious reasons, to share the legislator's view that 'it does not matter whether one or three judges decide the case'[845]. At this stage, it can be stated with conviction that a collegiate court, particularly at the appeal stage, has undoubted advantages, in particular in terms of encouraging a full consideration of all the circumstances of the case and increasing the likelihood of a correct decision.

The explanatory memorandum to the draft amendment also states that the purpose of hearing cases in single-member formations is to prevent judicial paralysis. At the same time, there is no convincing evidence that the introduction of single-judge courts in civil proceedings would have such an impact on the speed with which the courts examine cases as to justify abandoning the advantages of

843 T. Zembrzuski, *Przeciwdziałanie i zwalczanie...*, p. 65.
844 K. Markiewicz, *Wpływ regulacji...*, p. 46.
845 Explanatory Memorandum to the Government's Bill on Amendments to the Act - Code of Civil Procedure and Certain Other Acts, Parliamentary Paper No. 899.

collegiate formations. Although the requirement of efficiency of proceedings is justified by Article 45(1) of the Constitution, other values, which are also protected by law, cannot be abandoned for the sake of its implementation. The changes in the composition of the court, which came into force on 28 September 2023, should be assessed in a similar manner.

However, the abolition of the collegiality of the judiciary did not only apply to appeal proceedings, but also to the composition of the bench of the court of first instance. Thus, the principle of citizen participation in the administration of justice (Article 182 of the Constitution) is the constitutional value that the legislator has almost completely eliminated from civil proceedings. It is emphasised that such a judicial procedure, which would remove the jury from the court proceedings, would be contrary to the Constitution[846]. Juries are not the only (albeit fundamental) manifestation of citizen participation in the administration of justice, as other forms of implementation of Article 182 of the Constitution include public scrutiny of courts, exercised under the principle of openness of proceedings. It should be noted, however, that even in the era of the COVID-19 pandemic, the external openness of proceedings was significantly reduced. For this reason, the return to trials involving lay judges should be viewed with approval. As of 15 April 2023, the legislator withdrew from this solution by amending the provision of Article $15zzs^1(1)$ point 4 of the COVID-19 Special Act, expressly stating that the court of first and second instance shall hear cases with a single judge, with the exception of cases heard by a judge and two lay judges.

In the light of the above, a return to the general rules on the composition of the court in civil proceedings in force before 3 July 2021 should be proposed. In fact, the arguments presented lead to the conclusion that both the provisions of the COVID-19 Special Act and the current rules in the CCP should be considered harmful and unnecessary. It is difficult to find a convincing justification for them and, moreover, there is insufficient evidence that they contribute to the improvement of proceedings before the appellate courts. It should be noted that the principle of a three-member bench of the court of appeal has a particularly long tradition in civil cases. At the same time, the potential advantages of a single-judge courts cannot be regarded as sufficient to justify abandoning the collegiality of the judiciary, especially as it is impossible to determine with certainty the reasons for the introduction of single-member courts. In particular, there is no convincing justification for setting the criterion of the value of the appeal at the level of one million PLN. It cannot be automatically assumed that a case exceeding this threshold will be more complex and require more in-depth analysis than a case where the value of the appeal does not reach this limit. It is also difficult to find a justification for the current model, whereby complaints to the so-called horizontal instance (i.e. concerning decisions on usually minor issues that do not require review by a

846 K. Knoppek, *Udział obywateli w sprawowaniu wymiaru sprawiedliwości w postępowaniu cywilnym,* Ius Novum 2014/1, p. 26.

higher court) are heard by a panel of three judges, and complaints to the court of second instance (which usually concern decisions that are most important for the course of the proceedings) are heard by one judge.

It has also been pointed out in the previous considerations that the provision of Article 15zzs[1](1) point 4, second sentence, of the COVID-19 Special Act does not fully comply with the fair trial standard, in particular with regard to the right to a court of 'competent jurisdiction'. It has also been noted that, on the basis of the identical Article 47 § 4 of the CCP, proposals have been made in the doctrine to give the court, instead of an administrative body such as the president of the court, the power to order the hearing of a case in a wider composition. These proposals should be supported, with the proposed amendments not only to the provision contained in the COVID-19 Special Act, but also to Article 47 § 4 of the CCP, which should read as follows '§ 4. The court of first instance may decide to hear a case in a panel of three judges if it considers this advisable on account of the particular complexity or precedential nature of the case'.

The proposed amendment will first of all eliminate arbitrariness in the decision of the president of the court on the composition of the panel and prevent any possible attempts to manipulate the composition of the court. It will be left to the court itself, i.e. an impartial and independent body, to decide on this issue. There is also no doubt that there are obvious advantages in the fact that the examination as to whether the conditions for the application of the provision are met will be carried out by a court which is better acquainted with the case than the president of the court, thus allowing a more complete substantive assessment of the nature of the case.

9. Service of judicial documents via the Information Portal of the Common Courts

9.1. Introductory remarks

The Information Portal of the Common Courts (the Information Portal) is a tool that has been implemented nationwide since 2014[847]. It is an electronic system that allows parties and attorneys to access information about a case, including the status of the case, actions taken by the court, dates of hearings, documents generated by the court, information on incoming correspondence, minutes of hearings in electronic version with the possibility of playing the video and audio recording[848]. The Portal was intended to have a purely informative function, with the aim of speeding up court proceedings and reducing the workload of court staff by giving users direct access to information on the status of a case without having to obtain it from the court secretariat[849]. The legal basis for the operation of the Portal is § 132 of the Regulation on the Rules of Procedure of Common Courts, which provides in section 1 that the president of the court may order that data on the case, the content of the minutes and court and trial correspondence be made available to the parties or participants in non-contentious proceedings and their representatives, attorneys and defenders through accounts in the ICT system.

As of 3 July 2021[850], the role of the Information Portal has been substantially expanded. In addition to its informational function, the Portal has become a tool for the delivery of court documents to certain attorneys, after a provision was added to the COVID-19 Special Act introducing the obligation to deliver court documents via an 'ICT system for the delivery of such documents'. According to the content of Article 15zzs[9] of the COVID-19 Special Act, 'during the state of epidemic threat or the state of epidemic declared on the basis of COVID-19 and within one year from the repealing of the last of them, in the absence of the possibility to use the ICT system for serving court documents, the court shall serve court documents to an attorney, legal counsel, patent attorney or the General Prosecutor's Office of the Republic of Poland by placing their content in the ICT system for providing access to such documents (information portal). This does not apply to documents that

847 N. Wójcik-Krokowska, *Informatyzacja sądownictwa oraz postępowania cywilnego - postulaty de lege lata i de lege ferenda*, Monitor Prawniczy 2021/3, p. 136.

848 J. Korolczuk, *Informatyzacja postępowania sądowego. Szanse i zagrożenia*, Młody Jurysta 2018/4, p. 47.

849 N. Wójcik-Krokowska, *Informatyzacja...*, p. 136.

850 Pursuant to the Act of 28 May 2021 amending the Act - Code of Civil Procedure and certain other acts, Journal of Laws 2021, item 1090.

must be served together with copies of the parties' pleadings or other documents that do not originate from the court'. The explanatory memorandum[851] to the government bill introducing electronic service through the Portal states that the aim of the regulation is to speed up proceedings in urgent cases and reduce the need to leave one's home, e.g. to the post office. Irrespective of the motives stated by the author of the draft amendment, it should be noted that the delivery of court documents via the Information Portal makes it possible to significantly speed up the circulation of documents between the parties and the court, to reduce the costs associated with traditional postal delivery and, in times of increased spread of the coronavirus, also to reduce the risk of infection (e.g. due to the need to visit a post office or the postman).

Significantly, the provision of the Information Portal with additional functionalities related to the court service was planned even before the outbreak of the COVID-19 pandemic, but in the end the proposed provision of Article 131[2] of the CCP was deleted from the draft law at the inter-ministerial agreement stage[852], which was subsequently adopted as the Act of 4 July 2019 amending the Code of Civil Procedure[853]. The paralysis of the judiciary in the course of the coronavirus outbreak led to the idea of setting up an electronic service through the Information Portal, which already had most of the mechanisms for adding this functionality without incurring excessive costs[854].

Pursuant to the provision of Article 125 § 2[1] of the CCP, in force since 8 September 2016, a party may choose to file pleadings via the 'information and communication system for court proceedings'. In practice, however, this possibility is purely hypothetical, as the applicability of this provision is suspended due to the lack of technical infrastructure[855]. According to the provisions of Article 53 § 1a of the Law on Organisation of Common Courts, an ICT system serving court proceedings is used for the creation and processing of case files. This system is also referred to by the legislator in the second sentence of Article 9 § 1 of the CCP, according to which 'the content of minutes and court documents may also be made

---

851 Explanatory Memorandum to the Government Bill on amending certain laws with respect to protective measures against the spread of the SARS-CoV-2 virus, Parliamentary paper No. 334 available at www.sejm.gov.pl/ sejm9.nsf/print.xsp?nr=344.

852 J. Gołaczyński, A. Zalesińska, *Kierunki informatyzacji postępowania cywilnego po nowelizacji Kodeksu postępowania cywilnego z 4.7.2019 r.*, Monitor Prawniczy 2020/7, pp. 351–352.

853 Journal of Laws 2019, item 1469.

854 J. Gołaczyński, A. Zalesińska, *Nowe technologie w sądach na przykładzie wideokonferencji i składania pism procesowych i doręczeń elektronicznych w dobie pandemii COVID-19*, Monitor Prawniczy 2020/12, p. 641.

855 Ł. Goździaszek, *Normy informatyczne w prawie postępowania cywilnego*, Przegląd Sądowy 2017/2, p. 58.

available in electronic form through an ICT system serving court proceedings (ICT system) or another ICT system serving the purpose of making such minutes or court documents available'. As this system has not been implemented, it is not possible to use it. Therefore, according to Article 15zzs^9(2) of the COVID-19 Special Act, the first of the prerequisites for using the Information Portal as a platform for providing services is updated. In the light of the above provision, the Information Portal may be used for the purpose specified therein only if it is not possible to use the ICT system serving court proceedings.

9.2. Scope of application of Article 15zzs^9 of the COVID-19 Special Act.

The provision of Article 15zzs^9(2) of the COVID-19 Special Act introduces the obligation to serve court documents during the state of an epidemic threat or a state of epidemic declared on the basis of COVID-19 and within one year after the last one has been revoked, by publishing them on the Information Portal. The analysis of the issue should begin with an attempt to define the term 'court document'. The Code of Civil Procedure uses this term repeatedly in the chapter on service (e.g. Article 131 § 2, Article 133 § 3, Article 135 § 2, Article 136 § 2, Article 138 § 1, Article 141 § 2), as well as in other parts of the Code (e.g. Article 626^{12} § 3 of the CCP in the chapter on land and mortgage register proceedings). Court letters are also referred to in the aforementioned § 132 of the Regulation on the Rules of Procedure of Common Courts, which forms the basis for the operation of the Portal. However, neither of these provisions contains a legal definition of a court document.

Of the above-mentioned provisions, it is worth noting the first, i.e. Article 131 § 2 of the CCP, which contains a statutory authorisation for the Minister of Justice to determine, by means of an ordinance, the detailed procedure and manner of service of court documents. On this basis, the Ordinance of the Minister of Justice of 6 May 2020 on the Detailed Procedure and Manner of Service of Court Documents in Civil Proceedings was issued[856]. The purpose of the regulation (Article 1) is to 'determine the detailed procedure and manner of service of court documents intended for the parties, lawyers and witnesses, experts and other persons involved in civil proceedings'. On the basis of this regulation, an attempt can be made to construct a definition of a 'court document', the meaning of which will include all documents originating from the court (issued by the court) and intended for and subject to service on the parties to the proceedings. In civil procedure theory, it is pointed out that court documents can be divided into 1) judgments, 2) orders, 3) minutes, 4) notices and notes, 5) other court documents[857].

856 Journal of Laws 2020, item 819.
857 B. Bladowski, *Pisma sądowe w sprawach cywilnych*, Warsaw 2012, p. 21.

Another question to be considered is whether all court documents, regardless of their type, are subject to service by posting their content on the Portal. On the basis of Article 140 of the Code of Civil Procedure and § 21(4) of the Secretarial Manual in the initial period of Article 15zzs[9] of the COVID-19 Special Act, doubts have arisen as to whether court rulings were subject to service through the Information Portal. According to Article 140 § 1 of the CCP, pleadings and judgments shall be served in certified copies. In turn, § 2 provides that instead of a certified copy, a document obtained from an ICT system may be served, provided that it has features enabling the existence and content of a document or a judgment in that system to be verified. A copy of a decision is to be understood as a document which faithfully reproduces the content of the original decision or a copy thereof, without the need for the document to be authenticated[858]. Paragraph 31(1) of the Secratial Manual sets out the characteristics that a certified copy of a document from a court file must contain a round official seal and the signature of the certifying person, together with their particulars, including name, official position or function held, and the date on which the copy was signed. An electronic copy shall be made by making an electronic copy of the document and affixing the electronic signature of the authenticator (section 1a).

The aforementioned § 21(4) of the Secretarial Manual provides that court documents listed in Appendix No. 3, which are posted in the court information and communication system and recorded as issued therein, may be sent without a signature. The appendix lists the following court documents that do not require a signature: summonses, notifications, orders for the return of a pleading, payment orders, non-appealable orders, cover letters in which copies of letters served by the court are sent, instructions. It should be noted that the Appendix does not include court orders (with the exception of non-appealable orders) among the copies of court documents that do not require a signature. In the view of the above, doubts have arisen as to whether it is permissible to serve a court order by posting its content on the Information Portal. According to § 31 of the Secretarial Manual, the service of a court document containing a copy of a court decision requires that the document is stamped with the official seal of the court. On the other hand, the document the content of which is accessible to the user of the Portal is not a true copy of the original decision with the signature and the official seal, but an electronic document reproducing the content of the decision in the case file without additional elements indicating its authenticity.

One of the views expressed on this issue was that since, according to Article 140 § 1 of the CCP, judgments are served in certified copies, and a copy of a judgment requires the signature of the person making it and the official seal, it is not possible to effectively serve a judgment by posting its content on the Portal. This measure also does not comply with the requirements for electronic copies (Article 140 § 2 of the CCP). The electronic service mentioned in Article 131[1] of the CCP

858 Order of the Supreme Court of 27 January 2006, III CK 369/05, LEX No. 178249.

refers to the service by means of the ICT system supporting court proceedings, which has not been implemented. The document uploaded to the Information Portal does not have any features allowing the existence and content of the court document to be verified in the ICT system, which is a requirement under Article 140 § 2 of the CCP. As a result, it was considered that service through the Information Portal could only concern those judicial documents listed in Appendix No. 3 to the Secretarial Manual, for which it was determined that they did not require a signature[859].

The opposing concept assumed that all court documents, regardless of their nature, including court orders and judgments, are subject to electronic service via the Portal. This is because the provision of Article 15zzs^{9}(2) of the COVID-19 Special Act does not refer to 'electronic service of a copy of a court document', but to 'placing its content in the ICT system'. Service via the Information Portal does not consist of placing the court document there in the traditional sense (as a reproduction of the document in the file), but of allowing the attorney to view its content. The term 'content of the document' is more comprehensive and refers to the content of the document and not to the form in which it is recorded[860]. In view of this, § 21(4) of the Secretarial Manual, which expressly refers to 'documents sent by the court'[861], does not apply to service pursuant to Article 15zzs^{9}(2) of the COVID-19 Special Act. Notwithstanding the foregoing, it should be noted that the provision of Article 15zzs^{9}(2) undoubtedly constitutes a *lex specialis* in relation to the provisions of the Code of Civil Procedure governing the service of judicial documents[862]. Consequently, the application of the provision of Article 140 § 1 of the CCP, which provides for service of court documents in certified copies, is not applicable. There is also no reason to assume that the provisions of the Ordinance of the Minister of Justice exclude or limit the scope of application of a provision of statutory rank, such as Article 15zzs^{9}(2) of the COVID-19 Special Act. Therefore, the position that the court documents to be served by the Information Portal include all court documents, regardless of their type, should be accepted.

9.3. The waiver of the service via the Information Portal

The method of service specified in Article 15zzs^{9}(2) of the COVID-19 Special Act does not apply to court documents that must be served together with copies of the parties' pleadings or other documents that do not originate from the court. The rule contained in the second sentence of the provision concerns situations in

859 J. Gołaczyński, M. Dymitruk, *Rozprawa zdalna...*, p. 694.

860 G. Karaś, A. Zalesińska, [in:] *Postępowanie cywilne w czasie pandemii. E-doręczenia, rozprawa zdalna, posiedzenia niejawne, składanie pism procesowych*, J. Gołaczyński (ed.), Warsaw 2022, pp. 52–53.

861 G. Karaś, A. Zalesińska, [in:] *Postępowanie...*, p. 55.

862 J. Gołaczyński, M. Dymitruk, *Rozprawa zdalna...*, p. 695.

which the court serves, in addition to a court document, another document not subject to service through the Information Portal. The principles of procedural economy argue in favour of the service of the court documents by means of the same delivery which also contains a document of a different nature. This will most often be the case where a party not represented by a professional lawyer files a pleading with the court together with a copy to be served on the other party represented by a lawyer, who will be served with the court documents through the Portal. Second, an exception to the rule of service of court documents in the above-mentioned manner occurs when documents other than court documents are served at the same time, and this refers mainly to the service of expert opinions filed with the court together with copies for the parties. There is no doubt that, in such a situation, it would be pointless to serve the expert opinion on the party's lawyer by traditional mail and a separate electronic service of the court document in which the court obliges the lawyer to respond to its contents.

As a rule, Article 15zzs^9 of the COVID-19 Special Act does not leave any doubt that the service of court documents through the Portal is mandatory with respect to the persons mentioned in this provision (as evidenced by the wording 'the court shall serve'). However, the basis for waiving service of a judicial document via the Portal is Article 15zzs^9(5) of the COVID-19 Special Act, according to which the presiding judge orders waiver of such service if it is impossible due to the nature of the document. At this point, it is necessary to consider which judicial documents are not subject to service via the Portal and what 'nature' of these documents supports the necessity of waiving the procedure provided for in Article 15zzs^9(2) of the COVID-19 Special Act. In principle, it is possible to distinguish only two cases in which the provision applies.

This applies in particular to situations where it is necessary to serve a certified copy of a court document on a lawyer in a traditional form for official use. The lack of possibility to serve a court document via the Portal arises when it is necessary to serve a copy of a decision constituting a security title or an enforcement title containing an enforceability clause[863]. With regard to these writs, it would not be sufficient to obtain a computer printout from the Portal. This is because such a document is not a copy and cannot be used in the same way as a certified copy of a decision with a round seal and relevant annotations.

The second example of a court document for which it is necessary to consider whether it can be served via the Information Portal is a decision on the security injunction issued in the course of pre-trial proceedings. Pursuant to Article 740 § 1 of the CCP, a decision taken in closed session to refuse to grant security injunction, as well as a decision to grant security enforceable by a competent authority, must be served only on the party entitled to it, unless a specific provision provides otherwise. Such an order is not served on the obligor, which is dictated by the need to fulfil the function of the security procedure (premature knowledge of such an

863 G. Karaś, A. Zalesińska, [in:] *Postępowanie...*, p. 53.

order by the obligor could lead to the weakening of the effectiveness of the security). In the previous considerations, it has been pointed out that the provision of Article 740 of the CCP is a manifestation of a limitation of the principle of openness of proceedings, albeit justified by its objectives.

To illustrate where the problem lies in serving an order through the Information Portal, it is first necessary to indicate how such service occurs. First of all, it must be stressed that the Information Portal is linked to the court system (SAWA, Sędzia 2), which means that the publication of a document on the Portal requires that it has been approved for publication in this system. Between 3 July and 28 November 2021, as soon as a judicial document was published in the court system, it was automatically placed on the Information Portal under the 'Documents' tab. All documents, both those addressed to the parties and other documents drawn up by the court secretariat, appeared in this tab. As a result, doubts arose as to which court document was subject to service and which was placed on the Portal for information purposes only. From 29 November 2021, the Portal has been equipped with a new functionality by adding a tab called 'My Service', where only those court documents addressed to a specific recipient are published. The service of a judicial document on a lawyer now requires the drafting of the relevant correspondence in the court system and its publication. The mere publication of a document constituting a judicial document in this system does not automatically result in its being sent for service, but it will still appear in the 'Documents' tab, which has only an informative function. It is also important to note that the creation of correspondence for a lawyer to be placed in the Portal, for example containing a court decision, requires the prior publication of that decision in the court system, which means that it is not possible to serve the letter without also placing its content in that part of the Portal which is available to all users with access to the case. Although this measure does not constitute service within the meaning of Article 15zzs^{9}(2) of the COVID-19 Special Act, it does allow the content of the decision to be seen even by the party to whom service is not directly addressed.

In the case of an order granting or refusing security injunction, this leads to the conclusion that an attempt to serve it on the authorised representative through the Information Portal may imply the simultaneous notification of the mere fact of its issuance and of the content of the order to other parties, including the obligor or his representative. If the obligor becomes aware of the order before it is served by the enforcement authority, this may in turn deprive such an order of its actual effectiveness, depending of course on the circumstances of the specific case. Therefore, it must be assumed that the nature of the order granting or refusing security injunction renders its service under Article 15zzs^{9}(2) of the COVID-19 Special Act impossible and that it is necessary to refrain from service under section 5 of the said provision. This is because the functionality of the Information Portal does not allow the order to be served in such a way that other parties do not have the opportunity to become acquainted with its contents.

The discussed Article 15zzs^{9}(5) of the COVID-19 Special Act provides a basis for waiving service of a judicial document through the Portal if 'service is impossible due to the nature of the document'. The above ground should be understood to mean that a court document cannot be served if it is technically impossible to serve it, and this should be due to reasons related to the nature of the document to be served and not to external circumstances (such as technical failure, lack of access to the Portal by a lawyer). It is therefore necessary to refrain from serving a judicial document via the Information Portal if there are circumstances that make it impossible to use the functionality of the Portal[864]. However, the practice of the courts in applying this provision is different and covers all cases in which service via the Portal is not so much impossible as impractical. By way of example, it should be noted that service via the Portal may be dispensed with in the following cases 1) if the lawyer does not have an account in the Portal, 2) if the first document in the case is to be served, 3) if the case number has changed or the proceedings have been resumed after a long period of suspension, 4) if there is doubt whether the lawyer will read the court letter to be served. It is necessary to take the position that the above cases do not justify dispensing with service through the Information Portal, which is now the rule under current regulations[865]. However, due to the laconic nature of the provision and the lack of technical rules specifying the procedure for service, as well as the strict definition of the conditions for waiving service via the Information Portal, it was necessary to adapt the practice followed by the courts to the realities of serving judicial documents, especially in the initial phase of applying the provision.

Irrespective of the accepted understanding of the premise set out in Article 15zzs^{9}(5) of the COVID-19 Special Act, it should be noted that the waiver of service of a court document via the Information Portal requires a corresponding procedural decision in each case. This is expressly stated in the wording of the cited provision, according to which 'the presiding judge orders the waiver (....)'. The waiver of service of a judicial document through the Portal and its general service should take the form of an order of the presiding judge. In the absence of such an order, the court correspondence addressed to the professional lawyer should be served in accordance with Article 15zzs^{9} of the COVID-19 Special Act, as this is currently the default form of service.

The question of a waiver was particularly important during the first period of the regulation (until 28 November 2021), when all documents published on the Portal were displayed in a single tab ('Documents'), regardless of whether they were subject to service. The absence of an order waiving electronic service, while there was no other mention of the manner in which the document was published, may have given rise to confusion, particularly among lawyers, as to how to calculate the time limits which start to run from the service of a judicial document. The need for the presiding judge to issue an order is indicated by § 18a(3) of the Secretarial Manual, which orders that the content of the decision be made available

864 J. Gołaczyński, M. Dymitruk, *Rozprawa zdalna...*, p. 694.
865 Decision of the Supreme Court of 25 January 2022, III CZ 58/22, LEX No. 3303514.

together with the court document to be served in the form of an integrated file. The waiver of service of a judicial decision via the Information Portal therefore requires the inclusion of the content of the presiding judge's order indicating that the published decision is not subject to service pursuant to Article 15zzs^{9}(2) of the COVID-19 Special Act.

9.4. Personal scope of service via the Information Portal

As can be seen from the wording of Article 15zzs^{9}(2) of the COVID-19 Special Act, the method of electronic service applies only to court documents addressed to an advocate (attorney), legal counsel[866], patent attorney or the Solicitor General's Office of the Republic of Poland. The ambiguous wording of this provision ('the court shall serve the document on an attorney, legal counsel or patent attorney') gives rise to interpretative doubts as to whether it applies only in cases where members of the aforementioned professions act as legal representatives of a party (participant in the proceedings) or also in other procedural situations – for example, where the attorney (legal counsel) acts as a curator for a person whose place of residence is unknown or where the attorney (legal counsel) themself is a party to the proceedings. In this respect, as in the case of a similar interpretation of Article 132 of the CCP, two different views can be adopted. On the one hand, it is pointed out that the cited provisions do not contain the reservation that they apply only between the persons mentioned therein when they act as legal representatives. Consequently, the application of the provision should apply to all lawyers, irrespective of their role in the case[867]. The opposing position assumes that the *ratio legis* of the provision of Article 15zzs^{9}(2) of the COVID-19 Special Act dictates that the personal scope of its application should be limited only to cases where an attorney, legal counsel or patent attorney acts as a legal representative in a case. This is also supported by a systemic interpretation. Whenever the Code of Civil Procedure refers to attorneys or legal counsels (e.g. Article 89 § 1, Article 94 § 2), it refers to their role in the proceedings as legal representatives. An attorney, legal counsel or patent attorney is singled out as a person with special characteristics by virtue of the fact that they are lawyers. In fact, a party or other person (such as a guardian *ad litem*) is not required to indicate that they act as a professional lawyer[868]. For these reasons, the answer should be in favour of the second view. In addition, it should be noted that the provision of Article 15zzs^{9}(2) of the

866 It should be emphasised that in Poland both an attorney (adwokat) and a legal counsellor (radca prawny) have identical procedural rights in civil proceedings. The National Chamber of Legal Counsels calls for the use of the English term 'attorney-at-law' to refer to legal counsels.

867 Judgment of the Regional Court in Szczecin of 20 September 2016, II Ca 278/16, LEX No. 2370345.

868 G. Karaś, A. Zalesińska, [in:] *Postępowanie...*, pp. 44–45.

COVID-19 Special Act, as *lex specialis* in relation to the provisions of the Code of Civil Procedure governing service of court documents, should not be interpreted in a broad manner. In conclusion, it should be assumed that the service of a court document through the Information Portal to an attorney, legal counsel or patent attorney is possible only if such person is acting as a legal representative in the case. This position was also taken by the Supreme Court, which pointed out that the provision of Article 15zzs^9 of the COVID-19 Special Act provides for obligatory service on professional lawyers[869].

This issue is regulated differently in relation to the Solicitor General's Office of the Republic of Poland. In this case, the legislator does not use the concept of delivery to individual solicitor, but to the Office as an institution. For the Solicitor General's Office of the Republic of Poland, a so-called public institution account is created. In addition, sub-accounts will be created for users, which can be used by individual solicitors[870]. However, the service will be effective only in relation to the Solicitor General's Office as an institution, and not in relation to a particular solicitor[871].

As a result of the application of the regulation under Article 15zzs^9(2)-(4) of the COVID-19 Special Act, an important question has arisen as to whether a professional lawyer is obliged to have an account on the Information Portal through which electronic service is provided. Prior to the entry into force of this provision, the Portal had a purely informational function, and it was not mandatory to have a user account. With the introduction of Article 15zzs^9 of the COVID-19 Special Act, the situation has not changed, and no provision has been adopted requiring a professional lawyer to have such an account. However, for technical reasons, the service of a court document through the Portal requires the registration of an account and access to a specific case. The question therefore arises as to whether a professional lawyer is obliged to have an account on the Information Portal, despite the absence of a relevant provision expressly requiring this. If the answer is in the affirmative, another doubt is what are the consequences of not fulfilling the condition of having an account on the Information Portal and whether it is possible to assume the effect of service in relation to a lawyer who does not have such an account.

The first of the positions, represented by I. Wolwiak, assumes that the lawyer is not obliged to have an account in the Information Portal and that the obligation to receive a correspondence placed by the court in the Portal only materialises

869 Decision of the Supreme Court of 25 January 2022, III CZ 58/22, LEX no. 3303514 and decision of the Supreme Court of 27 January 2022, III CZ 70/22, LEX no. 3329661.

870 Order of the President of the Court of Appeal in Krakow No. 20/21/Adm - Regulations of the Information Portal of Common Courts from the area of the Krakow Appeal (accessed 22 October 2022), https://www.krakow.sa.gov.pl/portal-informacyjny,m,mg,235,284.

871 G. Karaś, A. Zalesińska, [in:] *Postępowanie...*, p. 45.

if the lawyer has created an account which allows them to access the content of the court document. Therefore, the effect of service of a court document cannot be assumed with respect to a lawyer who has not applied for an account in the Information Portal[872]. The author points out that the Code of Civil Procedure links a specific method of service with the appropriate place of its performance – the action of service is performed only in a specific place (where the recipient resides), therefore they should be aware that the court's action of service against them will be performed in this place. Since the execution of the action is linked to the designated place, it is also necessary in the case of electronic service that the court places the document at the location where the document is received, provided that the recipient has the appropriate access point to such a network[873]. In addition, Article 15zzs[9] of the COVID-19 Special Act does not contain an explicit provision that would construe an order for the recipient of a correspondence to act in such a way as to obtain access to the Information Portal by creating an account. Such a norm cannot be derived from the provisions of Article 15zzs[9](2) and (3) of the COVID-19 Special Act on the basis of linguistic interpretation, and further interpretive procedures in the area of systemic or functional interpretation are not necessary, since there is no reason to deviate from the linguistic directive, let alone from the interpretation *sensu largo*[874].

The view that the effect of service cannot be assumed with respect to a lawyer who does not have an account on the Information Portal or access to the case has also been expressed in the practice of the common courts. In one of the rulings, the Regional Court in Krakow[875] accepted that since access to the case in the Information Portal is provided upon request, after the case reference number has been determined, the fact of obtaining such access is not entirely dependent on the lawyer. In turn, the COVID-19 Special Act cannot impose obligations that are impossible to fulfil or provide for the effect of service in a situation where the lawyer did not actually have access to the case in the Information Portal because they did not receive it or received it late. The Regional Court considered that the imposition of an obligation with the risk of sanctions in the event of non-compliance must take the form of a positive provision and cannot be implied. It does not appear from any provision that professional lawyers are obliged to have an account on the Information Portal.

The opposite view is also presented, according to which a professional lawyer is obliged to have an account in the Information Portal, and failure to do so will result in the delivery of correspondence after 14 days, despite the lack

872 I. Wolwiak, *Czy można przyjąć skutek doręczenia względem pełnomocnika, który nie złożył wniosku o założenie konta w portalu informacyjnym dla zapoznania się z treścią pisma sądowego?*, Polski Proces Cywilny 2022/1, p. 244.

873 I. Wolwiak, *Czy można...*, pp. 236–238.

874 I. Wolwiak, *Czy można...*, p. 244.

875 Order of the Regional Court in Krakow of 27 July 2022, II Cz 353/22, not published.

of actual knowledge of the court document[876]. J. Gołaczyński and M. Dymitruk draw attention to the fact that, unlike Article 131^1 § 1 of the CCP, the provision of Article $15zzs^9$ of the COVID-19 Special Act does not contain a prerequisite in the form of submitting a pleading or choosing to submit pleadings via the ICT system. The authors conclude from this that service via the Information Portal has a much wider scope and does not depend on the prior will or choice of the professional representative. Therefore, the court may effectively serve court documents via the Information Portal even without the knowledge and will of the legal representative, and Article $15zzs^9$(2)-(4) of the COVID-19 Special Act is a *lex specialis* in relation to the provisions of the Code of Civil Procedure, but with temporary effects[877].

This view has also been expressed in the case law of the Supreme Court. In its decision of 25 January 2022[878], the Supreme Court pointed out that, although the legislation does not explicitly provide for the obligation of the attorneys to have an account on the Information Portal, this obligation can be derived from the content of Article $15zzs^9$ of the COVID-19 Special Act. Since the service of a court document through the Information Portal is mandatory and its effectiveness does not depend on the existence of an account or access to the case, it follows that the effect of service may arise if the document was not retrieved by the lawyer due to the lack of an account on the Portal. The Supreme Court stated that, just as there is no obligation to examine the case file in order to determine whether a procedural measure requiring a response from the legal representative has been taken, there is no obligation to create an account on the Information Portal and review all the documents made available there. However, this does not mean that if the professional representative does not act in this respect, the effect of service will not occur. The Supreme Court made a similar statement in its decision of 27 January 2022[879], in which it noted that Article $15zzs^9$(3) of the COVID-19 Special Act imposes a kind of new procedural burden on professional lawyers and even an obligation to verify the information published on the Information Portal. In any case, the consequences of the lawyer's negligence in this respect are borne by the party. The Supreme Court pointed out that the conclusions resulting from the linguistic interpretation clearly indicate that the condition which constitutes the basis for considering a court document as served is its placement on the Information Portal and not the possibility for the recipient to become acquainted with it.

In line with the reasoning of the Supreme Court, the second point of view should be followed. The arguments put forward by I. Wolwiak cannot be considered

876 J. Gołaczyński, M. Dymitruk, *Rozprawa zdalna...*, p. 696.
877 J. Gołaczyński, M. Dymitruk, *Rozprawa zdalna...*, p. 695.
878 Order of the Supreme Court of 25 January 2022, III CZ 58/22, LEX No. 3303514.
879 Order of the Supreme Court of 27 January 2022, III CZ 70/22, LEX No. 3329661.

convincing. Although it is undoubtedly true that electronic service is linked to the placement of the document by the court at a specific 'receiving point', this action is in no way linked to the lawyer's access to this point, especially since, as the author himself points out, access to this point depends on the will of the professional lawyer, who must make a request to this effect. The law links the effect of service to the placement of the court document in the Information Portal, and this action is possible regardless of whether the individual has created the required access account. The fact that the lawyer does not have access to the case in the Information Portal does not in any way alter the fact that the document has been published there. The 'access point' therefore exists, it is only the lawyer who does not have the relevant account who has not 'joined' it, as a result of their own decision not to apply for access to the case. Nor can it be said that, in view of the clear wording of the provision, there is no need to go beyond linguistic interpretation to a process of functional or systemic interpretation.

The view taken by the Regional Court in Krakow, quoted above, does not deserve to prevail either. The Court does not seem to distinguish between a situation in which the lawyer did not make a proper request for access to the case on the Information Portal (or did not open an account there at all) and a situation in which the lawyer made such a request but was not granted access or was granted access with a delay. The situations described are fundamentally different. In the first case, the professional representative fails to access the case, either by omission or intentionally (which may be a procedural tactic to delay the case). In the second scenario, the lawyer expresses his willingness to have access to the case, but such access is not granted – the lawyer therefore has no real opportunity to acquaint themself with the content of the court document to be served. Nor is it possible to agree with the Regional Court that there is no positive provision which imposes a sanction on a lawyer who fails to familiarise themself with a court document which is addressed to them. Such a provision is contained in Article 15zzs^{9}(3), second sentence, of the COVID-19 Special Act, according to which, in the case of failure to familiarise oneself with the correspondence, the document is deemed to have been served after the expiry of 14 days from the date of its publication on the Information Portal. The Act does not make the effect of service dependent on access to the Information Portal. The conditions for the document to be considered served are: placement of the court document on the Portal, failure of the recipient to become acquainted with the document (the reasons for which are not specified in the Act) and the expiry of 14 days. Assuming that the effect referred to in the second sentence of Article 15zzs^{9}(3) of the COVID-19 Special Act can only occur if the lawyer has applied for access to the Information Portal, this would mean that the effectiveness of the service depends on the will of the lawyer and not on the actions of the court. Consequently, it should be considered that the service of a court document pursuant to Article 15zzs^{9}(2)-(4) of the COVID-19 Special Act is possible regardless of whether the recipient, who is a professional lawyer, has access to the case on the Information Portal.

9.5. The effect of service of a judicial document

Pursuant to Article 15zzs^{9}(3) of the COVID-19 Special Act, the date of service of a judicial document is the date on which the recipient became aware of the document posted on the Information Portal. On the other hand, if the recipient does not get acquainted with the document, the document is deemed to have been served 14 days after its publication on the Information Portal.

As previously indicated, the Information Portal was not adapted to support the additional function of service of judicial documents during the period from 3 July to 28 November 2021. Service was made by placing a file containing the content of a court document in the 'Documents' tab. The date on which the content of the court document became delivered within the meaning of Article 15zzs^{9}(3) of the COVID-19 Special Act was the date on which the file was downloaded, which was recorded in the Portal. At that moment, the lawyer had the opportunity to actually read the correspondence[880]. All other court documents, including those that were not subject to service, were also published on this tab.

On the other hand, the module to support e-services, in the form of the 'My Service' tab, has only been added to the Portal on 29 November 2021[881]. Previously, placing a court document on the Information Portal required only the publication of an approved draft in the court system[882], but after the introduction of the 'My Service' functionality on the Portal, it is necessary to create a so-called e-document, which, once published, can be downloaded by the recipient in this tab. Files containing court judgments or other documents to be served can be attached to the electronic document. However, their attachment requires prior publication in the court system. Consequently, such a file containing the content of a court correspondence will first appear (as before the introduction of the new Portal functionality in November 2021) in the 'Documents' tab, and only after the e-document has been created – in the 'My Service' tab, where the document can be read by a professional lawyer, resulting in the generation of a proof of service of that document. The 'My Service' tab is not available for other account types, so a party who has not been represented by a professional lawyer cannot receive a court document through this module.

At this point, it is necessary to consider when the effect of service occurs, which the legislator associates with 'becoming acquainted' with the content of the document. As already indicated, the professional lawyer can become acquainted with the judicial document to be served in the 'Documents' tab even before they are served with the e-document via 'My Service'. It is also necessary to consider when the effect of service occurs if the lawyer does not read the court document addressed to him. The answer should be given separately for service between 3 July

880 J. Gołaczyński, M. Dymitruk, *Rozprawa zdalna...*, p. 694.
881 Order of the Supreme Court of 25 January 2022, III CZ 58/22, LEX No. 3303514.
882 Notes on the example of the SAWA programme (Currenda).

and 28 November 2021 and after 29 November 2021. The effect of service made during this first period may still be relevant to pending cases, despite the change in the way the Portal operates.

The above issue was dealt with by the Supreme Court in the aforementioned decision of 25 January 2022. As noted above, prior to 29 November 2021, the practice of courts with regard to the labelling of court document posted on the Information Portal for the purpose of service was not uniform. Some courts labelled such letters as 'e-service of a document', while others used a title referring to the content of the letter (e.g. an order for payment). The lack of a specific tab for service prior to 29 November 2021 made it impossible to easily determine which of the correspondence placed in the 'Documents' tab constituted an electronic document to be served and which were placed there for information purposes only. Thus, there was no basis for automatically assuming that every single letter placed on the Information Portal constituted service pursuant to Article $15zzs^9(2)$ of the COVID-19 Special Act. The Supreme Court pointed out that a lawyer could not be required to guess or seek information as to which letter had been posted on the Portal for the purpose of service and which letter had been posted there for information purposes only, as this would lead to an obligation for lawyers to immediately familiarise themselves with all documents posted on the Portal. However, the legislator did not provide for such an obligation. Consequently, the Supreme Court concluded that elementary procedural loyalty to the parties requires that the possibility of accepting the effect of service under Article $15zzs^9(3)$ of the COVID-19 Special Act should be made dependent on whether the court letter was accompanied by clear information on the consequences of not opening the correspondence. This does not refer to the information contained in the content of the document itself, but to the information available to the lawyer immediately after logging into the Portal and before deciding to download the document. However, if the attorney has become aware of the content of the document within 14 days of its publication on the Portal, the effect of service may be assumed even if the above condition is not met, provided that the content of the court letter itself contains the information that it is a service pursuant to Article $15zzs^9(2)$ of the COVID-19 Special Act. A similar position was taken by the Supreme Court in its decision of 23 February 2022[883].

Thus, accepting the view of the Supreme Court expressed above, during the period from 3 July 2021 to 28 November 2021, the effect of service of a court document occurred when the lawyer became aware of its content, i.e. when the lawyer downloaded the file using the appropriate button (which was recorded in the Portal by a corresponding note of the date and time of reading the document, but no electronic receipt was generated[884]), whereby familiarisation with the court document to be served could take place within 14 days of its content being posted on the Portal. However, the correct effect of service only occurred if, after logging in to

883 Decision of the Supreme Court of 23 February 2022, III CZ 31/22, LEX No. 3403021.
884 G. Karaś, A. Zalesińska, [in:] *Postępowanie...*, p. 60.

the Portal, the lawyer was able to determine that the document in question was subject to service under Article 15zzs^9(2) of the COVID-19 Special Act or, in the absence of such information, a relevant reference to service under this procedure was included in the content of the document. On the other hand, if the content of the court letter was not read by the lawyer – regardless of whether they had access to the case on the Information Portal – the effect of service occurred 14 days after the content of the letter was posted on the Portal, only if the title of the document clearly indicated that it was an e-service.

However, the position of the Supreme Court must be considered as too far-reaching. Therefore, it can only be partially accepted. It is necessary to agree with the Supreme Court that the lack of information in the content of the court document that it has been placed on the Information Portal for the purpose of service pursuant to Article 15zzs^9 of the COVID-19 Special Act nullifies the effect of service both in the case where the lawyer has become aware of the content of the document within 14 days and in the case where he has not done so (due to lack of access to the Portal or for other reasons). In such a case, until 28 November 2021, in the absence of the relevant information, it was not possible to determine unequivocally whether the letter posted on the Portal was subject to service or whether this action was merely informative. This, in turn, made it impossible to determine whether or not the procedural time-limits for service of the letter have started to run. Indeed, a lawyer did not know whether a court letter published on the Portal would be served in the traditional way or whether the court would not take any further action in relation to service.

On the other hand, it is impossible to agree with the Supreme Court that the condition for effective service is the information already available after logging in to the Portal as to whether the court document has been published by way of electronic service. In the first place, such a condition does not follow from the provisions governing service through the Information Portal, which, moreover, do not specify the detailed procedure for electronic service. The condition imposed by the Supreme Court must be regarded as overly formalistic. Secondly, there is no reason to assume that the failure to include the title of the served document with the appropriate reference to electronic service constitutes a manifestation of the court's disloyalty towards parties. As a rule, and as the Supreme Court has rightly pointed out, files containing court documents uploaded to the Portal are provided with a title referring to their content (e.g. an order), the date on which they were drawn up and the date on which they were published on the Portal. The type of document is also indicated (e.g. order, decision, minutes, correspondence). It would seem that the very act of titling a document in this way allows the professional to decide whether they wish to read the content of the document. The expectation that the professional lawyer will keep up to date with the documents published on the Portal does not seem too rigorous, particularly in view of the limited number of documents that are usually published in each case on a given day. Moreover, even the addition to the name of the document of an indication that it is an electronic delivery, as adopted by the Supreme Court, would not be sufficient to clearly identify to whom it is addressed. In the previous version of the Information Portal, all documents were published in the 'Documents' tab and any user with access to a given case could access them, regardless of whether they were addressed to them. Only the inclusion of a relevant annotation in the content of the court document itself allowed the lawyers to make an assessment on this issue. Therefore, it is to be assumed that for the proper service of a court document pursuant to Article 15zzs^2(2) of the COVID-19 Special Act, it is sufficient to clearly indicate in the body of the letter itself that it is subject to service on this basis. Such a practice sufficiently safeguards the procedural rights of the parties by making it clear which document is subject to electronic service.

As from 29 November 2021, any document that can be served through the Information Portal is placed on the 'My Service' tab, which provides clear and unambiguous information on the manner of service of a judicial document and the consequences of failing to familiarise oneself with it within 14 days of its placement on the Portal. The act of familiarising with a court document should be understood as the act of downloading it and not the act of actually reading it, which is irrelevant to the effect of service of the correspondence[885]. At present, the served document is only available to the recipient in the 'My Service' tab, which removes most of the doubts that may have existed previously regarding the obligation to read the document. It should be noted, however, that the Information Portal continues to be used for information purposes, which means that regardless of the placement of the court letter in the 'My service' tab, it will also be published in the 'Documents'. In many courts, it is common practice for the staff of the registry to prepare correspondence for e-service with a delay in relation to the publication of the document in the court system (it is often normal practice for the accepted draft of the document to be published by the judge and for the subsequent execution of the e-service order to be carried out by the registry staff, even with a delay of several days). The publication of a given judicial document in the Information Portal will then take place in the 'Documents' tab before the identical document appears in the 'My service' tab. The professional lawyer thus has the opportunity to read the court document without having to generate a proof of delivery. It is therefore uncertain whether the prior reading of the court letter via the 'Documents' tab can be equated with the effect of service within the meaning of Article 15zzs^9(3) of the COVID-19 Special Act.

This question must be answered in the negative. The effect of service, although it does not follow from the cited provision in any way, can take place only upon receipt of the court letter in the module adapted for that purpose ('My Service'). A contrary interpretation would basically mean a return to the previous situation, which would undoubtedly lead to the same doubts and inconveniences related to the lack of individualisation of the service[886]. The current solution, which is partly

885 Decision of the Supreme Court of 25 January 2022, III CZ 58/22, LEX No. 3303514.
886 G. Karaś, A. Zalesińska, [in:] *Civil proceedings...*, pp. 59–60.

due to the laconic regulation of Article 15zzs[9] of the COVID-19 Special Act, and partly due to technical limitations caused by the use of an ICT system for e-service that was intended to perform completely different functions, should be critically assessed. Electronic communication between the court and lawyers should streamline and speed up proceedings, as it is in principle much more efficient than communication on paper[887]. However, the current solutions leave considerable room for potential abuse, which could lead to a prolongation of the procedure by the party concerned. For example, a lawyer can read the content of a court letter in the 'Documents' tab, but not receive it via 'My Service'. In this way, they gain an extra 14 days, delaying the effect of the service. At the same time as the deadline for reading the document is running, the lawyer already knows its content. This can lead, for example, in the case of service of a copy of the judgment, to an effective extension of the time for preparing the appeal to 28 days instead of the statutory two weeks. Obviously, such a practice can be compared to a traditional postal service, which is notified twice and received on the last day of the deadline. In such a situation, the lawyer could also download the content of the judgment from the Information Portal. The difference, however, is that in the case of traditional service by post, it was common practice for the courts to withhold the content of the statement of reasons for the judgment until the parcel was actually received. At present, however, this is technically impossible, since the service of a judicial document via the 'My Service' tab requires that it be published on the Information Portal under the 'Documents' tab in advance.

Notwithstanding the foregoing, it must be assumed that, in the present state of affairs, the publication of a court document solely in the 'Documents' tab does not constitute proper service within the meaning of Article 15zzs[9] of the COVID-19 Special Act. This has far-reaching consequences. First of all, the publication of a judicial decision in this way does not trigger the 14-day period for serving the decision. Similarly, the downloading of the judicial document from the 'Documents' tab does not start the other time limits arising from the content of the correspondence. Furthermore, a party who has not requested a statement of reasons for a judgment (Article 331 § 1 of the CCP), but has obtained its content by downloading it from the Information Portal, cannot effectively challenge such a judgment (Article 369 § 1 of the CCP).

Since the time limit cannot start to run before knowledge of the document served has been obtained through the 'My Service' section of the Portal, it is necessary to consider whether a procedural act performed before the formal effect of service has been obtained can have certain effects or whether it should be declared ineffective as premature. This will be particularly important for the assessment of the admissibility of appeals. In resolving a similar issue in the context of enforcement clause proceedings, the Supreme Court held that an action brought before the commencement of the time limit for bringing an action cannot be dismissed[888]. The

887 J. Gołaczyński, M. Dymitruk, *Rozprawa zdalna...*, pp. 691–692.
888 Resolution of the Supreme Court of 2 December 2003, III CZP 2003, LEX No. 82113.

jurisprudence of the courts has adopted this position, noting that the Supreme Court, in the justification of the resolution, raised arguments concerning general appeals[889]. Firstly, it should be noted that the legislator has only provided for the consequences of failing to comply with the time limit. On the other hand, there is no provision specifying the consequences of lodging an appeal before the beginning of the time limit. The time limits for lodging an appeal are generally classified as maximum time limits, which means that a certain procedural act must be performed before the deadline expires.

The Supreme Court[890] shared the view expressed in the above-mentioned 2003 resolution and stated that it also applied to the legal situation created by the Act of 4 July 2009 amending the Code of Civil Procedure, which introduced the principle that the condition for the admissibility of filing a complaint or appeal is the prior submission of an effective request for the statement of reasons for the contested decision. The aim of this principle is to ensure that the applicant is aware of the reasons for the decision before it is challenged, which will enable the applicant to prepare their defence and improve the quality of the appeal. However, the Supreme Court noted that in a situation where the applicant does not wait for the reasons for the decision to be delivered but decides to challenge the decision without knowing the reasons for it, the applicant puts themself in a worse procedural position. The court of appeal, on the other hand, will be able to carry out a proper review since the decision will have been taken by the court of first instance as a result of a correct application by the party.

As regards the question of service through the Information Portal under consideration, it should also be noted that there is no risk that the applicant will not be aware of the reasons for the decision before challenging it. Indeed, the issue in question concerns a situation in which a party has become aware of the grounds of the decision, but before it has been duly served. In agreement with the position of the Supreme Court, it should be noted that rejecting the appeal on the grounds that it is untimely would be a manifestation of unjustified and disproportionate procedural rigour, calling into question the party's right of access to court. It is therefore necessary to support the position that a procedural act performed before the commencement of the time limit in connection with the service of a judicial decision through the Information Portal is effective.

9.6. Service of a court document under Article 15zzs⁹ of the COVID-19 Special Act and the right to a fair trial

The introduction of Article 15zzs⁹ of the COVID-19 Special Act triggered a broad discussion on the legitimacy of such a solution, and its undeveloped content led to

889 Decision of the Court of Appeal in Krakow of 24 June 2013, I Acz 1051/13, LEX No 1454488.

890 Resolution of the Supreme Court of 26 October 2021, III CZP 55/20, LEX No. 3246819.

many doubts about its interpretation[891]. The laconic nature of the provisions, the lack of implementing rules and the excessively short *vacatio legis* of only 14 days were pointed out, which, when set against the importance of the regulation, raised legitimate concerns about the emergence of practical difficulties in the implementation of e-service. The short period between the adoption of the regulation and its entry into force essentially prevented the creation of a technical tool that would allow secure and unambiguous delivery and the training of court staff[892]. The regulation of Article 15zzs[9] of the COVID-19 Special Act also raised concerns for the Ombudsman, who addressed a letter to the Minister of Justice in September 2021[893], pointing out that the provisions, due to their vagueness and fragmentary nature, cause problems in the practice of professional lawyers, as well as discrepancies in their application by the courts, which affects the implementation of the right to a fair trial. In particular, the Ombudsman pointed to doubts as to the interpretation of the lawyer's obligation to have an account on the Information Portal, which does not follow from the wording of the provisions, and the lack of a clearly defined catalogue of court documents that must be e-served. The Ombudsman also expressed reservations about the absence of a complaint procedure, which exists in the case of traditional service, and the insufficient preparation of the functionality of the Information Portal. According to the Ombudsman, the current regulation may contradict the principle of trust in the State and the laws enacted by it, which derives from Article 2 of the Constitution. This is because the law should be enacted and applied in such a way that a citizens can conduct their affairs with confidence that they will not be exposed to unfavourable legal consequences that could not be foreseen.

Objections have also been raised by the legal community. The National Chamber of Legal Counsels, in its opinion already submitted at the stage of the legislative process concerning the previous bill of April 2020[894] (which provided for analogous solutions), pointed out that the introduction of compulsory electronic service leads to a different situation for parties represented by lawyers and those who are not represented by professionals with regard to the fundamental procedural institution, which is the service of court documents. Doubts have been raised about the ambiguity of the regulation and the lack of explicit confirmation of service of a judicial document[895].

---

891 J. Gołaczyński, M. Dymitruk, *Rozprawa zdalna...*, pp. 691–692.

892 J. Gołaczyński, M. Dymitruk, *Rozprawa zdalna...*, p. 696.

893 https://bip.brpo.gov.pl/pl/content/rpo-watpliwosci-doreczenia-portal-informacyjny-sady.

894 Government bill on amending certain laws on protective measures in connection with the spread of the SARS-CoV-2 virus, Parliamentary paper No. 344.

895 Position of the Centre for Research, Studies and Legislation of the National Chamber of Legal Counsels to the Act of 20 April 2021 amending the Act - Code of Civil Procedure and certain other Acts with regard to certain amendments to the COVID Act (Senate paper No. 384), pp. 3, 8.

Also in the literature, based on the previous legal status, the question was raised as to whether the use of the Information Portal might violate the principle of equality of the parties, since it would enable one of the parties to the proceedings to obtain information on the proceedings more quickly. At that time, T. Januszkiewicz pointed out that there was no such risk, as the Portal was available to all authorised entities, which could create the necessary account free of charge. Moreover, the use of the Portal has so far only been an alternative to traditional communication with the court[896]. This question is relevant again in the context of providing the Portal with the functionality of service of court documents. The provision of Article 15zzs[9] of the COVID-19 Special Act applies only to lawyers. A party who is not represented by such a professional may not receive correspondence through the Portal. The account created by such a party has an informative function only.

In the light of the above observations, an attempt should be made to answer the question of whether the provisions of Article 15zzs[9] of COVID-19 Special Act under discussion meet the requirements of the right to a fair trial as set out in Article 6(1) of the ECHR and Article 45(1) of the Constitution. In connection with the voices raised concerning the unjustified differentiation of the situation of parties depending on whether they are represented by lawyers, the assessment of the implementation of the right to a fair trial should be carried out from the perspective of the principle of equality as well as the principle of procedural fairness. The considerations should begin with a reminder that, in the light of the case law of the Constitutional Tribunal, Article 45(1) of the Constitution imposes an obligation to organise judicial proceedings in such a way as to meet the requirements of fairness. It is incumbent upon the legislator to provide for a method of service, including from a technical point of view, which reduces the risk of the recipient's ignorance of the court correspondence[897]. The fairness of the court should consist in not taking advantage of the parties' disadvantage to bring the case to a formal conclusion[898]. Thus, the court may not use the effect of service in relation to the party's lack of knowledge of the letter as an instrument to expedite the proceedings.

However, it should be borne in mind that, in accordance with the principle of procedural autonomy, the legislator may regulate the judicial procedure (including the question of service) in any way it chooses, provided that it complies with the standard of a fair trial. With this in mind, it should be concluded that the legislator may, in principle, regulate the issue of service of process in such a way

896 T. Januszkiewicz, *Jawność...*, p. 208.
897 Judgment of the Constitutional Tribunal of 17 September 2002, SK 35/01, LEX No. 56620.
898 K. Flaga-Gieruszyńska, *E-wymiar sprawiedliwości w sprawach cywilnych jako przykład rozwoju nowych technologii w sferze publicznej*, Ekonomiczne Problemy Usług 2017/1, p. 341.

that it takes place by means of electronic communication. The standard derived from the case-law of the European Court of Human Rights and the Constitutional Tribunal does not require that all service take place in the form of traditional postal correspondence.

The principles of procedural justice dictate that the legislator should regulate the issue of electronic service in such a way that a party is not deprived of the opportunity to become acquainted with a court document addressed to them without undue difficulty and in a manner that does not raise doubts. When assessing the above issue through the prism of the regulation of Article 15zzs^{9} of the COVID-19 Special Act, attention should first be drawn to the lack of implementing provisions regulating the rules of electronic service through the Information Portal. In addition, the provisions of the Act do not specify in detail how service is to be effected, but merely state that the content of the court's decision should be published on the Portal and indicate the moment when the service becomes effective. In practice, therefore, the procedure for service through this ICT system has been left not to the legislator but to the administrator of the Information Portal. In principle, the provisions of the COVID-19 Special Act do not introduce any procedural guarantees for parties represented by lawyers, nor do they explicitly specify the obligations of lawyers in relation to electronic service.

Although the technical solutions adopted as of 29 November 2021 (the addition of the 'My Service' tab) have the effect of eliminating most of the doubts that existed in the previous period as to which court documents are subject to service pursuant to Article 15zzs^{9} of the COVID-19 Special Act, this is not the result of clear statutory or regulatory provisions, but of the arbitrary technical solutions currently adopted. However, the procedure for service through the Portal, as well as the scope of powers and obligations of the parties to which electronic service is made, is still not clearly defined. Taking into account the different practices of the courts in the scope of application of the provisions under discussion, the lack of clear implementing rules leads to doubts of interpretation, as indicated in the previous considerations, regarding the conditions necessary for the effect of service of a judicial document or the obligation for a professional representative to have an account on the Information Portal. Consequently, it should be considered that the provisions of Article 15zzs^{9}(2)-(5) of the COVID-19 Special Act do not meet the requirements of the right to a fair trial in terms of the principles of procedural justice, which require the adoption of such solutions in the field of service of court documents that allow for the proper performance of the function of service and duly guarantee the procedural rights of the parties. In accordance with the principle of procedural fairness, the procedural rules should be predictable and transparent so that the parties can clearly determine the extent of their obligations and privileges.

Next, it should be considered whether the introduction of compulsory service only in relation to lawyers constitutes an unjustified departure from the principle of equal rights of the parties and whether it is a manifestation of excessive formalism limiting the right to justice in relation to lawyers. At this point, it should be recalled that the Constitutional Tribunal accepts, as a matter of principle, the differentiation of procedural strictness in relation to parties represented by a professional lawyer as compared to parties acting on their own. Indeed, the professional nature of the activity of lawyers justifies the expectation of greater diligence on their part[899]. Therefore, in the case of lawyers, as a rule, there will be no restriction of the right to court on the grounds of excessive procedural strictness. As mentioned in the previous section, the Constitutional Tribunal has emphasised in its jurisprudence that the equality of the subjects involved in a civil dispute requires that the procedure be designed in such a way that the rights of the parties are balanced[900]. This does not mean that all parties to proceedings should have the same rights and obligations. Indeed, some differentiation of the procedural situation of the parties is permissible, but it must be justified and based on clearly defined criteria.

With regard to electronic service via the Information Portal, the legislator distinguishes between the status of the parties to the proceedings. An important criterion is that the parties are represented by a professional lawyer. Considering, first of all, the professional nature of the activity of a lawyer, it should be assumed that the provision of Article 15zzs[9] of the COVID-19 Special Act does not violate the principle of equality in this respect, and the imposition of additional obligations on lawyers should be assessed as a differentiation of their procedural status, which, however, finds sufficient justification. The requirements imposed on professional lawyers in relation to electronic service cannot be considered excessive, since they essentially amount to the need to exercise elementary diligence, knowledge of the law and the registration of an account in the Information Portal. In this respect, it must be concluded that the provisions in question do not violate the right to a fair trial within the meaning of the principle of equality.

However, it seems that a violation of the principle of equality can be found in the opposite situation, i.e. the lack of availability of the possibility to receive court documents sent via the Information Portal by parties who are not represented by professional lawyers. Electronic service is more accessible, faster and more convenient. At the same time, there are no justifiable reasons why the possibility of using electronic service has been denied to only some parties. Although it could be an excessive burden to impose a general obligation on a party directly to receive correspondence via the Information Portal, there is nothing to prevent such a possibility being offered to parties interested in this form of service, which would allow them to dispense with the need to receive traditional correspondence.

Finally, attention should be drawn to the positive impact of the introduced regulation on the principle of efficiency of proceedings, which is an element of the party's right to have a case heard without undue delay. The solutions adopted

899 Judgment of the Constitutional Tribunal of 20 December 2007, P 39/06, LEX No. 322831.

900 Judgment of the Constitutional Tribunal of 28 July 2004, P 2/04, LEX No. 121582.

certainly constitute a means of speeding up proceedings, since electronic communication is usually much more efficient than traditional correspondence. The use of electronic means of communication in the courts naturally has an impact on the rationalisation of the costs of proceedings (primarily in terms of minimising the costs of service), as well as on the reduction of their duration. In the case of the COVID-19 pandemic, it also makes it possible to reduce to a certain extent the risk of epidemics associated with the necessity to collect correspondence from the postman or at the post office[901].

9.7. Conclusions and further proposals for electronic service

One of the main objections to Article 15zzs[9] of the COVID-19 Special Act is the use of the Information Portal for electronic services, which was not sufficiently adapted for this purpose, as it was intended to have a purely informational function. As of 29 November 2021, the functionality of the Portal has been extended by a module intended for service, but this still does not solve all potential problems that may arise in the practice of using the Portal (e.g. publication of court documents in the 'Documents' tab before their publication in 'My service').

At the same time, as early as 8 September 2016, a provision allowing electronic communication with the courts was introduced into the CCP[902]. The Amending Act introduced, among other things, the possibility of filing pleadings via an ICT system supporting court proceedings (Article 125 § 2[1] of the CCP) and electronic service (Article 131[1] of the CCP). At the same time, Article 20 of the Act of 10 July 2015 stipulates that, for a period of three years from the entry into force of the Act, the option of filing pleadings via the ICT system supporting court proceedings and the further filing of these pleadings shall be allowed if it is possible for technical reasons on the part of the court. This provision has been introduced to allow for the establishment of an appropriate ICT system, commonly referred to as the Electronic Filing Office, and the implementation of a pilot programme in selected courts[903]. However, this project has not been implemented and the provisions of Article 20 of the Law of 10 July 2015 have been repealed with effect from 21 August 2020[904]. Although the ICT system for court proceedings is not yet in place, the

901 J. Gołaczyński, M. Dymitruk, *Rozprawa zdalna...*, pp. 691–692.

902 Act of 10 July 2015 amending the Civil Code Act, the Civil Procedure Code Act and certain other acts, Journal of Laws 2015, item 1311.

903 J. Gołaczyński, S. Kotecka-Kral, *Elektronizacja pism procesowych, doręczeń i posiedzeń jawnych w postępowaniu cywilnym w okresie pandemii COVID-19,* Polski Proces Cywilny 2020/4, *p.* 643.

904 *Ibid*, p. 654.

necessary implementing provisions for its introduction have been introduced, regulating issues such as electronic service[905].

It was pointed out that there was nothing to prevent the Information Portal from becoming the ICT system serving court proceedings. It would only be necessary for the Ministry of Justice to expressly designate it as the ICT system serving court proceedings and to update the implementing rules accordingly[906].

In light of the above, it should be noted that the problem is not the need for electronic service provisions, as these are in place, but the lack of implementation of an appropriate ICT system. It is emphasised that the current provision on electronic service, contained in Article 15zzs[9] of the COVID-19 Special Act, is limited in time precisely because of the planned future introduction of the Electronic Filing Office[907]. However, the challenges of the coronavirus pandemic have forced the legislator to urgently introduce an interim solution, and this is how the adaptation of the Information Portal to the new function should be defined.

It is clear, however, that the implementation of a single ICT system serving court proceedings is a costly and time-consuming challenge. Instead, the legislator is opting for fragmented and selective solutions. The various ICT tools for improving the administration of justice, including e-service, are unconnected and address only selected areas of the justice system. K. Flaga-Gieruszyńska calls such a form of computerisation 'insular', indicating that it is less effective due to the lack of cohesion between individual solutions[908]. Although the amendment of 10 July 2015 should have given the process of computerisation a comprehensive character, without the implementation of the adopted legislative solutions, the changes introduced have only a theoretical dimension and are in no way reflected in the actual course of civil proceedings. Instead of a comprehensive process, the legislator decided to introduce individual services[909] and to return to 'insular' informatisation. This is particularly evident in the era of COVID-19, in the example of remote hearings and service through the Information Portal. Given that the launch of the Electronic Filing Office is not imminent, it is appropriate to call for the necessary amendments to the rules on electronic service via the Information Portal in order to remove the threat to the due process standard assessed earlier in this section of the deliberations.

---

905 Ordinance of the Minister of Justice of 20 October 2015 on the mode and manner of electronic service, Journal of Laws 2015, item 1776.

906 J. Gołaczyński, A. Zalesińska, *Nowe technologie...*, p. 641.

907 J. Gołaczyński, M. Dymitruk, *Rozprawa zdalna...*, p. 695.

908 K. Flaga-Gieruszyńska, *E-wymiar sprawiedliwości...*, pp. 347–348.

909 A. Zalesińska, *Doręczenia elektroniczne w postępowaniu cywilnym*, [in:] *Prawo Nowych Technologii. Księga jubileuszowa z okazji jubileuszu 20-lecia działalności Centrum Badań Problemów Prawnych i Ekonomicznych Komunikacji Elektronicznej i Studenckiego Koła Naukowego – Blok Prawa Komputerowego*, J. Gołaczyński (ed.), Warsaw 2022, pp. 140–141.

As of 14 March 2024, electronic service via the Information Portal has been incorporated into the Code of Civil Procedure. Article 131^{1a} § 1 of the Code of Civil Procedure, it was amended to read: 'If service by means of an ICT system serving court proceedings is not possible, the court shall serve court documents on an attorney, legal counsel, patent attorney, public prosecutor, pension authority designated by the Minister of Internal Affairs and the Solicitor General's Office of the Republic of Poland exclusively by posting their content on the Information Portal in such a way that the recipient can obtain a document confirming service. This does not apply to court documents that must be served together with copies of the parties' pleadings or other documents that do not originate from the court, unless the court has recorded a copy of them in electronic form'. However, the legislator has not in any way adapted electronic service to the problems identified in the previous chapters. Nor has the functionality of the Information Portal been changed.

The doubts raised in relation to the scope of duties of professional lawyers require the addition of the following provision to Article 131^{1a} of the CCP: 'An attorney, legal counsel, patent attorney or counsel of the Solicitor General's Office of the Republic of Poland shall be obliged to register an account in the Information Portal and submit an application for access to the case. Failure to submit such a request shall not prevent the court document from being deemed served in accordance with the procedure set forth in § 1'. The proposed provision will allow the effect of service to be presumed in situations where the professional representative does not take any action to access the case through the Portal. At present, such a conclusion follows from the case law of the Supreme Court, but it seems advisable to explicitly introduce an obligation to access the case.

In view of the benefits associated with the use of electronic means in civil proceedings, in particular the acceleration of the circulation of correspondence, which has a direct impact on the efficiency of the proceedings, the optional use of electronic service should be considered for parties who are not professional lawyers. There is no reason why the rigours of service via the Information Portal could not also be applied to parties who voluntarily agree to it. This would not only help to streamline the circulation of correspondence and reduce costs, but would also have undoubted public health benefits at a time of increased risk of coronavirus spread. It should be noted that the current Article 131^{1} of the Civil Procedure Code, which provides for electronic service, does not limit the scope of application to professional lawyers, but makes it conditional on the correspondence being sent by means of an ICT system or on the choice of such. The addressee may refuse electronic service (§ 2^{1}).

The introduction of compulsory electronic service on each party to the proceedings does not seem feasible at this stage. In the opinion of A. Kościółek, it would be unacceptable to replace traditional service exclusively with electronic service. Obliging a certain group of recipients to submit to electronic delivery raises legitimate doubts in the context of the right to justice, as it imposes the necessity to use electronic means of communication (and consequently to have access to appropriate tools), whereas no social or professional group is fully computerised[910]. A. Zalesińska also believes that electronic service should not be mandatory in all types and cases and for all addressees, as the digitally excluded should be taken into account. However, according to the author, it is possible to distinguish certain groups (entrepreneurs, lawyers or public entities) to which such obligations may be imposed by the legislator[911]. A. Kościółek proposes the introduction of optional electronic service if the party has consented to it or has requested such service from the court. It is also necessary to introduce an appropriate regulation setting out detailed organisational and technical conditions[912]. For the reasons set out above, the introduction of the obligation to use electronic service by professional lawyers cannot be considered as a violation of the right to a fair trial. However, the idea of introducing optional electronic service for all parties interested in this form of communication with the court should be accepted with approval.

Irrespective of the proposed legislative changes, it is necessary to reiterate the need to introduce technical regulations (with the status of a sub-statutory act) that regulate in detail the procedure for electronic delivery through the Information Portal. This is because these issues require the existence of clear and predetermined implementing provisions in order to eliminate the existing difficulties and practical discrepancies related to service. Certainly, the procedure of service should not depend on the current functionalities of the Portal, which can be freely modified by its creators. However, the Ordinance of the Minister of Justice of 12 March 2024 on the service of court documents through the Information Portal in civil proceedings is worth mentioning. Unfortunately, the ordinance does not provide a detailed procedure for service, other than to indicate that the letter is served through the Information Portal by posting the content of the correspondence in the 'My Service' module.

The computerisation of civil proceedings makes it possible to rationalise and reduce the costs of court administration. In the area of information, it will make it possible to make the best use of the Internet as a means of communication, thereby increasing public confidence in the courts by opening them up to the public seeking information on the progress of proceedings[913]. For these reasons, the introduction of the electronic service should in principle be assessed positively. However, as the current model of using the Information Portal for this purpose does not fully comply with the standard of the right to a fair trial, it is essential to introduce the necessary changes discussed above.

910 A. Kościółek, *Elektroniczne czynności procesowe w sądowym...*, p. 280.
911 A. Zalesińska, *Doręczenia...*, p. 146.
912 A. Kościółek, *Elektroniczne czynności procesowe w sądowym...*, p. 281.
913 K. Flaga-Gieruszyńska, *E-wymiar sprawiedliwości...*, p. 340.

Notwithstanding the above, it should be noted that, according to K. Flaga-Gieruszyńska, the first obstacle to the computerisation of courts is still the mentality and level of digital literacy of court employees and citizens seeking court protection[914]. In addition to the development of optimal technical solutions and the adoption of appropriate legislation, it is necessary to undertake activities in the field of education of society and persons involved in civil proceedings in order to popularise new forms of electronic access to justice.

914 K. Flaga-Gieruszyńska, *Influence...*, p. 123.

10. Suspension of procedural time limits in the era of the COVID-19 pandemic

10.1. Period of validity of Article 15zzs of the COVID-19 Special Act

The coronavirus pandemic, especially in its early stages, undoubtedly had a significant impact on the functioning of the judiciary. In view of the increasing scale of the disease in the country from March 2020 and the threat of paralysis of the functioning of public institutions, including the courts, the legislator took measures to limit the negative effects of the epidemic situation, including the suspension of time limits. This solution was intended to allow the rights of parties and litigants affected by the increasing incidence of the coronavirus to be properly defended, so that communication with the court was impossible or severely hampered. With effect from 31 March 2020, Article 15zzs of the COVID-19 Special Act on this matter entered into force. According to the first section of this Article, during the period of the state of epidemic threat or the state of epidemic declared in accordance with COVID, the running of procedural and court time limits in court proceedings, including judicial and administrative proceedings, shall not commence, and those that have commenced shall be suspended for this period. However, the legislator stipulated in Article 15zzs(2) that the suspension of the commencement and the suspension of the running of time shall not apply to the time limits in cases before the courts referred to in Article 14a(4) and (5) of the COVID-19 Special Act. This provision contained a catalogue of urgent cases excluded from the scope of Article 15zzs(1) of the COVID-19 Special Act.

Due to the fact that the state of epidemic emergency was in force in Poland from 14 March 2020, while the state of epidemic was declared on 20 March 2020 (i.e. before the entry into force of Article 15zzs of the COVID-19 Special Act), doubts have arisen as to when the suspension of procedural and court time limits in civil proceedings began. The first position was that, since the legislator linked the beginning of the suspension of time limits to the declaration of the state of epidemic threat or the state of epidemic, which took place on 14 March 2020, the effect provided for in Article 15zzs(1) of the COVID-19 Special Act entered into force as of that date[915]. This provision would therefore have retroactive effect. M. Łochowski expressed a similar opinion, pointing out that the retroactivity follows both from the purpose of the Act and from the clear wording of the provision. Since, according

915 A. Dauter-Kozłowska, B. Dauter, *Bieg terminów procesowych w postępowaniu sądowoadministracyjnym w związku z ogłoszonym stanem zagrożenia epidemicznego, a następnie stanem epidemii z powodu COVID-19*, LEX.

to Article 15zzs(1) of the COVID-19 Special Act, time limits do not start to run 'during' the state of epidemic or epidemic threat, court and procedural time limits, the commencement of which was determined by events occurring after 14 March 2020, did not start to run or were suspended[916].

According to the second view, since the provision of Article 15zzs of the COVID-19 Special Act entered into force on 31 March 2020, the time limits laid down therein were suspended only from that date[917]. The second view presented should be accepted. As P. Sławicki points out[918], this conclusion follows from the wording of the intertemporal provisions[919], according to which the provision of Article 15zzs of the COVID-19 Special Act enters into force on the day of publication, without providing for an exception in favour of retroactivity. According to the author, such a conclusion is also confirmed by § 51 of the Principles of Legislative Techniques, according to which the retroactive effect of a provision requires that it be drafted in such a way as to indicate unambiguously the events or situations to which the commencement of the provision applies. In view of this, the intertemporal provisions should explicitly state that Article 15zzs of the COVID-19 Special Act applies retroactively from the date of the introduction of a state of epidemic emergency. However, the provision of Article 101 of the Act of 31 March 2020 amending the COVID-19 Special Act does not contain such a provision in relation to Article 15zzs. Significantly, the legislator in Article 101(2) gave retroactive effect to some of the provisions of the amending Act, but did not mention the Article 15zzs in question in this catalogue. It is therefore unreasonable to assume that provisions not mentioned in section 2 have also been given retroactive effect without explicit statutory provision[920].

According to the legislator's intention, the suspension of time limits should be in force for the entire period of the state of epidemic or the state epidemic threat. It should be recalled that the state of epidemic threat was in force from 14 to 20 March 2020, followed by the state of epidemic from 20 March 2020 to 16 May

916 M. Łochowski, [in:] *Zmiany w KPC wynikające z regulacji COVID-19. Komentarz*, T. Szanciło (ed.), Warsaw 2020, p. 9.

917 P. Wisniewski, *Wpływ ogłoszenia stanu zagrożenia epidemicznego lub stanu epidemii z powodu COVID-19 na bieg biegu terminów procesowych w postępowaniach cywilnych*, LEX.

918 P. Slawicki, *Wpływ ustawy o przeciwdziałaniu COVID-19 na terminy w prawie cywilnym*, Monitor Prawniczy 2020/12, p. 619.

919 Article 101 of the Act of 31 March 2020 amending the Act on special solutions related to the prevention, prevention and combating of COVID-19, other infectious diseases and emergencies caused by them and some other acts, Journal of Laws of 2020, item 568.

920 E. Gapska, *Bieg postępowania w sprawach cywilnych w czasie epidemii. Cz. II – wstrzymanie rozpoczęcia i zawieszenie biegu terminów procesowych*, Monitor Prawniczy 2020/18, p. 953.

2022, and the state of epidemic threat was declared again on 16 May 2022[921]. The state of epidemic threat was not lifted until 1 July 2023. Therefore, from 31 March 2020 until 1 July 2023, the condition for the suspension of the time limits provided for in the original Article 15zzs(1) of the COVID-19 Special Act was met. The legislator repealed the provision of Article 15zzs by virtue of Article 46(20) of the Act of 14 May 2020 amending certain laws with regard to protective measures in connection with the spread of the SARS-CoV-2[922]. Pursuant to Article 76 of the Act of 14 May 2020, the amendment entered into force on 16 May 2020. At the same time, Article 68(6) and (7) of this Act stipulates that the time limits in the proceedings referred to in Article 15zzs of the COVID-19 Special Act, respectively: 1) the proceedings of which have not yet commenced – shall commence after the expiration of 7 days from the entry into force of the amending Act; 2) the proceedings of which have been suspended – shall continue to run after the expiration of 7 days from the entry into force of the amending Act.

As a result, the time limits previously suspended pursuant to Article 15zzs of the COVID-19 Special Act began or resumed on 23 May 2020 (i.e., after the expiration of 7 days from 16 May 2020, when the Act entered into force). As this day fell on a Saturday, the regulation of Article 165 § 1 of the Code of Civil Procedure in conjunction with Article 115 of the Civil Code should be taken into account when assessing the end of the 'unfrozen' time limits. This provision was relevant to the time limits calculated in weeks, the beginning of which was 23 May 2020. According to the cited provision, if the end of the time limit for the performance of an act falls on a holiday or Saturday, the time limit expires on the next day that is not a holiday or Saturday. All time limits counted in weeks beginning on 23 May 2020 have therefore been extended to the next day that is not a holiday.

10.2. Material scope of application of Article 15zzs of the COVID-19 Special Act

In the context of civil proceedings, a 'procedural time limit' is a time limit set by the Code of Civil Procedure for procedural actions to be taken by the parties to the proceedings, as well as for certain actions of the judicial authorities. However, this concept does not include cases in which the time limit for action is determined by reference to other procedural acts or stages of the proceedings (e.g. the time limit for primary intervention laid down in Article 75 of the CCP – 'until the closing of the trial at first instance'). In fact, procedural time limits in the above sense are always expressed in terms of days, weeks, months or years[923]. Civil procedure law

921 Ordinance of the Minister of Health of 12 May 2022 on the cancellation of an epidemic state in the territory of the Republic of Poland, Journal of Laws 2022, item 1027.

922 Journal of Laws 2020, item 875.

923 T. Żyznowski, [in:] *Kodeks postępowania cywilnego...*, pp. 719–720.

distinguishes between statutory, court and contractual time limits. Statutory time limits are laid down directly in the Code of Civil Procedure for certain procedural acts (e.g. time limits for lodging appeals), and their length and commencement do not depend on decisions of judicial bodies or parties. Nor can they be extended or shortened[924]. The definition of a 'court time limit' is contained in Article 164 of the CCP, according to which it is a time limit set by the court or the presiding judge. An example of a judicial time limit is the time limit for filing a statement of defence (Article 205^1 § 1 of the CCP). These time limits may be extended depending on the circumstances (Article 166 of the CCP). Contractual time limits are determined by the parties (the only contractual time limit in the CCP is the time limit for the suspension of proceedings at the joint request of the parties – Article 178 of the CCP and Article 181 §§ 1 and 2 of the CCP).

Already the above brief analysis makes it possible to see that the legislator in Article 15zzs of the COVID-19 Special Act has used the imprecise concept of 'procedural and court time limits', implying that they are unrelated concepts. Such an approach was reasonably considered to be methodologically flawed, as court time limits are a category of procedural time limits. Consequently, it must be assumed that Article 15zzs of the COVID-19 Special Act applies to all procedural time limits[925], and that the separate distinction of court time limits in the provision in question was at least unnecessary. On the other hand, the provision of Article 15zzs of the COVID-19 Special Act does not affect the running of substantive time limits, such as limitation or prescription periods. Nor does it apply to substantive time limits laid down in the Code of Civil Procedure (e.g. Article 841 § 3 of the CCP, which contains a time limit for bringing an adverse action)[926].

The provision of Article 15zzs of the COVID-19 Special Act does not affect the time limits for service applicable to substitute service under Article 139 § 1 of the CCP. This provision sets a time limit of seven days for the receipt of mail deposited with a postal service after the notice has been posted on the door of an apartment or in a letter box. However, it is not a procedural time limit, but is independent of civil proceedings since it is addressed to the postal carrier. Article 15zzs therefore does not affect the suspension or withholding of time limits for service of judicial documents[927]. On the other hand, M. Łochowski takes a different view, arguing that failure to comply with the time limit for receipt of a notice has significant procedural consequences, i.e. it means the effectiveness of service, which in turn often means the commencement of the time limit for taking procedural action. In view of this, even in the case of failure to collect a court letter, it is not possible to assume the effect of service and it will be necessary to repeat the service[928].

---

924 T. Żyznowski, [in:] *Kodeks postępowania cywilnego...*, p. 720.
925 E. Gapska, *Bieg postępowania w sprawach cywilnych w czasie epidemii. Cz. II...*, p. 951.
926 R. Kulski, *Wpływ stanu zagrożenia epidemicznego lub stanu epidemii ogłoszonego z powodu COVID-19 na postępowanie cywilne*, Monitor Prawniczy 2020/9, p. 445.
927 P. Sławicki, *Wpływ ustawy...*, p. 622.
928 M. Łochowski, [in:] *Zmiany w KPC...*, p. 3.

An important point is also highlighted by R. Kulski, who points out that Article 15zzs of the COVID-19 Special Act will not apply to cases in which the proceedings were suspended before 31 March 2020 – until the proceedings are resumed. This is because in such cases Article 179 § 2 of the CCP will apply, according to which no time limits run during the suspension of the proceedings. On the other hand, if the proceedings are resumed during the state of epidemic threat or the state of epidemic, it should be assumed that the time limits do not start running anew from the moment the proceedings are resumed, but that Article 15zzs of the COVID-19 Special Act should apply from that moment. It seems that after the repeal of Article 15zzs of the COVID-19 Special Act as of 16 May 2020, in the case of proceedings commenced before that date, all procedural time limits should start running anew in accordance with the provision of Article 179 § 2 of the CCP, regardless of what part of the time limit has elapsed before the proceedings were suspended. In fact, the running of the time limits was interrupted by the suspension of the proceedings[929], and not suspended pursuant to Article 15zzs of the COVID-19 Special Act. However, it should be noted that the intertemporal provisions of the Act of 14 May 2020, which repealed the provision of Article 15zzs, indicated that the resumption of the running of procedural time limits would not take place until seven days after the entry into force of the Act. It is Article 68(6) of the Amending Act, which provides for the resumption of the running of procedural time limits, and not Article 68(7), which provides that time limits the running of which has been suspended shall continue to run. Thus, if the suspended proceedings were resumed before the repeal of the provision of Article 15zzs, all procedural time limits will start to run anew on 23 May 2020.

However, the situation is different where the proceedings have been suspended at the joint motion of the parties. In this case, pursuant to Article 179 § 1 of the CCP, only the court time limits do not continue running until the proceedings are reopened. Taking into account the provisions of Article 15zzs of the COVID-19 Special Act, it must be concluded that the court time limits were suspended by virtue of Article 179 § 1 of the CCP and should continue to run from 23 May 2020 after the resumption of the proceedings and the repeal of Article 15zzs – thus, contrary to the situation described above, Article 68(7) of the Amending Act should apply. In the case of all other time limits that have not been suspended pursuant to Article 179 § 1 of the CCP (statutory and contractual time limits), it should be assumed that they have been suspended pursuant to Article 15zzs. This is of great importance for the calculation of the time limit for requesting the resumption of proceedings suspended at the joint motion of the parties. The time limit must be calculated according to when the proceedings were suspended pursuant to Article 178 of the CCP. If the proceedings were suspended before 31 March 2020, the time limit for filing a request to resume the proceedings (of at least three months, unless the parties set a longer time limit – Article 181 § 1 point 2 of the CCP) started to run when the proceedings

929 R. Kulski, *Wpływ stanu zagrożenia...*, p. 446.

were suspended, but was suspended on 31 March 2020 due to the entry into force of Article 15zzs. As the time limit has already started to run, Article 68(7) of the Amendment Act will apply, and the period should continue to run from 23 May 2020 and not start again. The situation will be different if the suspension of proceedings took place between 31 March and 16 May 2020. In that case, the time limit for filing a request to reopen proceedings has not started at all, which means that it should only be counted from 23 May 2020 pursuant to Article 68(6) of the Amendment Act.

The provision of Article 15zzs of the COVID-19 Special Act leads to a suspension of the procedural time limits, but does not imply a suspension of the proceedings themselves. In this respect, in the period from 31 March 2020 to 15 May 2020, the case could be continued if its current state allowed it (for example, it was possible to serve a pleading on a party). However, the provision of Article 15zzs of the COVID-19 Special Act contained certain limitations which excluded some procedural acts. Article 15zzs(6) provided that no public hearings were to be held during the state of epidemic or epidemic threat. It was therefore permissible for the court to take other measures, including the setting of court time limits, provided that they did not commence during the period of Article 15zzs(1). The legislator did not completely exclude the possibility for the courts to act, but with the proviso that such action could not have the effect of starting the expiry of procedural time limits[930]. This is indicated by the wording of the provision of Article 15zzs(7) of the COVID-19 Special Act, according to which actions taken during state of epidemics or state of epidemic threat are effective. The opposite view was expressed by R. Kulski, who pointed out that the restrictions on actions refer to those actions, the performance of which is connected with the necessity of observing the prescribed procedural time limits. Since the procedural time limits have been suspended, the actions for which the time limits have been prescribed may be performed as soon as the state of epidemic or epidemic threat is lifted[931].

However, this view cannot be accepted. The fact that a procedural time limit has not yet started to run does not mean that an action taken by a party can be considered ineffective. The majority of procedural time limits are of a maximum nature, which means that negative consequences are linked to the exceeding of the time limit and not to the taking of an action before the time limit. Declaring a party's action ineffective if it is taken before the time limit has expired should be assessed in terms of excessive formalism. It should be emphasised once again that there was no suspension of the proceedings under Article 15zzs(1) of the COVID-19 Special Act, and therefore there is no reason to apply a construction similar to that provided for in Article 179 § 3 of the CCP, which makes the effectiveness of the parties' actions dependent on the commencement of the proceedings. If the legislator had wished to achieve the effect of a general 'freezing' of all proceedings by preventing the parties from taking those procedural actions whose effectiveness

---

930 E. Gapska, *Bieg postępowania w sprawach cywilnych w czasie epidemii. Cz. II...*, p. 955.
931 R. Kulski, *Wpływ stanu zagrożenia...*, p. 447.

depends on the observance of a procedural time limit, this should have resulted directly from the provision. Article 15zzs(7) of the COVID-19 Special Act, on the other hand, leads to a directly opposite conclusion, since it provides that such measures are effective. The same position is also taken by E. Gapska, who, using the example of an application for service of a statement of reasons for the judgment, points out that there are no sufficient grounds to deny the effectiveness of an action taken in the state of epidemic or epidemic threat. The same can be said of a party's appeal, especially since no provision of the Code of Civil Procedure allows for its rejection in such a case[932].

As already indicated, in accordance with Article 15zzs(2) of the COVID-19 Special Act, the suspension of time limits did not apply to cases heard by the courts, as indicated in Article 14a (4) and (5), which defines the catalogue of urgent cases. The said section 4 contains a detailed enumeration covering 23 types of cases (this catalogue has been extended twice, on 18 April 2020 and 16 May 2020[933]), the vast majority of which concern criminal cases. As far as civil cases are concerned, these are mainly family and guardianship cases, as well as cases in which a person is heard by the court for the purpose of preserving evidence or where it is feared that they will not be able to be heard at the hearing (point 16), cases concerning reorganisation proceedings (point 17), cases in which bankruptcy is declared and which are conducted after the declaration of bankruptcy (point 17a), cases in accordance with Article 11a of the Act of 29 July 2005 on combating domestic violence (point 18), for consent to the performance of medical acts (point 19) and for the determination of disability (point 20). On the other hand, according to the wording of Article 14a(5), urgent cases are those for which the law sets a time limit for their consideration by the court and cases of applications to suspend the execution of an act or measure. Thus, the legislator has determined that the nature of an urgent case includes all cases for which a time limit is fixed in advance for their consideration by the court. By way of example, the following cases may be mentioned: security and injunction proceedings (Article 737 of the CCP), an application for the granting of an enforcement clause (Article 781^1 of the CCP), a complaint against the actions of a bailiff (Article 767^2 of the CCP). In the above-mentioned cases of urgency, there was no suspension of the time limits for the proceedings, and it was possible to hold public hearings and trials (whereas the above-mentioned cases are not usually heard in public hearings).

Pursuant to Article 14a(9) of the COVID-19 Special Act, the president of the competent court could order the hearing of any case as urgent if its suspension could cause danger to human or animal life or health, serious harm to the public interest or due to the threat of irreparable material damage, and if the interests of justice so require. On the other hand, the provision of Article 15zzs(2) of the

---

932 E. Gapska, *Bieg postępowania w sprawach cywilnych w czasie epidemii. Cz. II...*, p. 955.

933 E. Gapska, *Bieg postępowania w sprawach cywilnych w czasie epidemii. Cz. I – sprawy pilne*, Monitor Prawniczy 2020/17, pp. 895–896.

COVID-19 Special Act excluded from the scope of section 1, by virtue of which the suspension of procedural time limits occurred, 'the cases referred to in Article 14a(4) and (5)'. The question therefore arises as to whether the suspension of time limits also applied to the cases referred to in Article 14a(9), in respect of which the president of the court had ordered that the case be heard as a matter of urgency, since the provision of Article 15zzs(2) of the COVID-19 Special Act does not expressly refer to this provision.

P. Slawicki answers in the affirmative[934], and this position should be supported. Although Article 15zzs(2) of the COVID-19 Special Act does not expressly refer to Article 14a(9), this cannot be regarded as a deliberate act of the legislator, but rather as an oversight. If Article 15zzs(2) were not to apply to cases which, by decision of the president of the court, have acquired the character of an urgent case, this would mean that the procedural time limits in these cases would be suspended. This, in turn, would lead to the conclusion that the parties could not be bound by obligations which depended on a court time limit, or even that time limits for appeals would not run. Such an approach would be incompatible with the urgency of the case, which by definition must be heard as soon as possible. A suspension of time limits in such cases would directly undermine the objective pursued. It must therefore be assumed that the suspension of procedural time limits occurred not only in the cases expressly referred to in Article 14a(4) and (5) of the COVID-19 Special Act, but also in the cases which acquired the status of an urgent case by order of the president of the court. Separately, it should be noted that the granting of such a power to the president of the court has been criticised in doctrine due to the possibility of a discretionary interpretation of the conditions set out in Article 14a(9) of the COVID-19 Special Act[935].

According to Article 15zzt of the COVID-19 Special Act, the provision of Article 15zzs(1) does not apply to 'time limits related to the prevention, combating and countering of COVID-19 and the emergencies caused by them'. The wording used by the legislator may raise doubts as to its scope. R. Kulski notes that it refers to the situation in which the performance of a certain act of the proceedings within a certain procedural time limit is connected with a crisis situation caused by combating (preventing, countering) COVID-19, which does not exclude the significance of this regulation for security or enforcement proceedings[936]. It should be noted, however, that by virtue of Article 15zzs(2) in conjunction with Article 14a(5) of the COVID-19 Special Act, cases concerning injunction applications are excluded from the scope of the provision of Article 15zzs(1) of the COVID-19 Special Act. However, despite the use of imprecise wording by the legislator, it appears that the purpose of the provision of Article 15zzt was to exclude the application of Article 15zzs(1) in relation to all cases involving the prevention, suppression and combating of COVID-19.

---

934 P. Sławicki, *Wpływ ustawy...*, p. 623.
935 E. Gapska, *Bieg postępowania w sprawach cywilnych w czasie epidemii. Cz. I...*, p. 895.
936 R. Kulski, *Wpływ stanu zagrożenia...*, p. 445.

10.3. Suspension of procedural time limits and the right to a fair trial

In order to assess the compliance of the provision of Article 15zzs of the COVID-19 Special Act with the standard of the right to a fair trial, it is first necessary to answer the question of the purpose of the introduction of this provision. In the explanatory memorandum to the government bill, in the section on changes to the time limits provided for in civil and administrative law, no space was devoted to the purpose of the regulation[937]. In general terms, the whole bill referred to 'the need to introduce specific solutions to counteract the negative economic effects of the epidemic situation'[938]. However, according to E. Gapska, the purpose of the introduction of the regulation in question must be considered to be connected with the need to ensure the proper exercise of the right to justice in conditions of threat to health and life. The suspension of procedural time limits should be linked to the lack of need for the parties to undertake the defence of their rights by means of actions requiring an appearance at a post office or the consultation of a lawyer, in a situation in which the party's ability to act is limited or even deprived[939]. In the context of the above-mentioned objectives of the Act, the introduced regulation should be assessed in relation to two aspects of the right to a fair trial, i.e. access to court and the right to a hearing without undue delay. In particular, an attempt should be made to answer the question of whether the provision of Article 15zzs of the COVID-19 Special Act has actually contributed to the protection of the right to court as intended by the legislator.

Firstly, it should be noted that after the regulation had been in force for a few weeks, legal circles argued that the suspension of time limits meant a restriction of the right to court and called for the repeal of the provision of Article 15zzs[940]. The above views are fully shared. It should be noted that the suspension of all procedural time limits and the introduction of a ban on holding public hearings, including trials, meant in practice that the operation of the courts, which did not carry out most of their activities, was frozen, and in many cases even the sending of court correspondence was ceased. The suspension of procedural time limits, although not a suspension of proceedings, had the *de facto* effect of depriving the parties of access to court. Although the individual had a formal right of access to the court, as they had the opportunity to bring a civil claim before the court, in practice they could not obtain a final decision because, during the period of

937 Explanatory Memorandum to the Government's Draft Law on Amendments to the Law on special solutions relating to the prevention and Control of COVID-19, other communicable diseases and crisis situations caused by them and certain other laws, Parliamentary Paper No. 299, p. 55.

938 *Ibid*, p. 1.

939 E. Gapska, *Bieg postępowania w sprawach cywilnych w czasie epidemii. Cz. I...*, p. 952.

940 E. Gapska, *Bieg postępowania w sprawach cywilnych w czasie epidemii. Cz. I...*, p. 952.

application of Article 15zzs of the COVID-19 Special Act, it was only possible to give the case a limited course of action. In particular, the court did not have the possibility to hold a hearing, and the suspension of time limits meant that it was not possible to enforce the procedural obligations of the parties, the effectiveness of which depended on compliance with the deadline (e.g. the time limit for filing a statement of defence did not start to run, and consequently the defendant was not obliged to enter an appearance on the merits). The provision also excluded the real possibility of appealing against the court's decision, which made it impossible to obtain a final decision. Thus, access to justice existed because a party had the possibility of formally initiating proceedings, but this was only theoretical and the possibility of having the case heard by the court was excluded.

The above question can therefore only be answered in the negative. The provision of Article 15zzs of the COVID-19 Special Act has not only failed to achieve the objective set by the legislature, but has actually had the opposite effect in the form of a *de facto* paralysis of the judicial system, which for an individual means the exclusion of the right of access to court. Similarly, the provision in question must be assessed in the light of the right to a trial without undue delay. It is pointed out that the obvious effect of the solution adopted was to lengthen the duration of proceedings[941]. At the same time, it should be noted that the suspension of procedural time limits was provided for the entire duration of the state of epidemic or epidemic threat. Therefore, when the provision of Article 15zzs entered into force, it was impossible to assess how long this situation would last. This potentially meant that proceedings were suspended indefinitely, regardless of how the epidemic situation actually developed.

It should be recalled that the right to court, pursuant to the content of Article 233(1) of the Constitution, may not be restricted during martial law and state of emergency. It seems all the more incomprehensible that such a far-reaching limitation of the right of access to court during a state of epidemics or epidemic threat, which are not anchored in the provisions of the Constitution.

Another aspect of the denial of access to court should be mentioned here. According to the wording of Article 15zzs(11) of the COVID-19 Special Act, the court's suspension of proceedings during the state of epidemic threat or the state of epidemic cannot be the basis for a complaint of inaction, delay or violation of a party's right to have a case heard without undue delay. Therefore, the legislator has excluded the possibility for a party to file a complaint for protraction of civil proceedings. It should be noted that this exclusion did not apply only to cases in which procedural time limits were suspended, but was of a general nature. The inadmissibility of a complaint of delay based on the Law of 17 June 2004[942], *lege non distinguente*, also applied to those cases which were of an urgent nature on the

941 E. Gapska, *Bieg postępowania w sprawach cywilnych w czasie epidemii. Cz. II...*, p. 952.
942 Act of 17 June 2004 on a complaint for violation of a party's right to hear a case in pre-trial proceedings conducted or supervised by a prosecutor and court proceedings without undue delay, consolidated text Dz.U. of 2018, item 75.

basis of Article 14a (4) and (5), of the COVID-19 Special Act or on the basis of an order of the president of the court, i.e. even to those cases in which the time limits were not suspended and which should have been examined without undue delay in the course of the proceedings. The above solution must be regarded as a disproportionate deprivation of a party's access to court, in so far as the party was previously able to request an assessment of whether their case was being conducted in a prolonged manner. This provision also constituted a significant limitation of the guarantee of a trial within a reasonable time.

It is worth noting the reservations expressed on the basis of Article 14a of the COVID-19 Special Act regarding the compatibility of the regulation of urgent cases with the principle of equality, given that some of these categories of cases were privileged. While the legitimacy of the above objection cannot be shared with regard to the catalogue of cases specified in Article 14a(4) and (5) of the COVID-19 Special Act, serious doubts may be raised with regard to the power of the president of the court, provided for in Article 14a(9), to order the hearing of any case as urgent. The practice of the application of this provision shows that it has been used in a highly discretionary manner, especially in the interpretation of the last condition of the provision, which is the interest of justice (for example, if both parties agreed to participate in the videoconference, the case was considered urgent so that it could proceed)[943]. Under the above provision, the president of the competent court could decide, by means of a non-appealable order, that any case is considered urgent. In this respect, it is questionable whether the authority exercising administrative supervision over the court has the power to influence the course of the proceedings. On the basis of the discussed Article 15zzs of the COVID-19 Special Act, this led to a situation where the resumption of procedural deadlines in a given case was decided by the president of the court, i.e. a non-judicial body, on a one-person basis. It seems that such a power should be vested in the court, which enjoys guarantees of impartiality and independence.

The solutions introduced in Article 15zzs of the COVID-19 Special Act cannot be considered to be in accordance with the principle of proportionality as expressed in Article 31(3) of the Constitution. As stated above, they do not fulfil the purpose for which they were introduced. In fact, the regulation does not protect the right to court granted to individuals, which has a positive effect on the procedural guarantees of the parties, but in practice excludes access to court and has a negative effect on the right to have a case heard without undue delay. The above provision should be assessed as an *ad hoc* and unjustified amendment in view of its effects[944]. It is also questionable whether the suspension of procedural time limits was a necessary solution at all. First of all, it should be noted that access to court was not excluded or restricted as a result of the epidemic in such a way that the parties

943 E. Gapska, *Bieg postępowania w sprawach cywilnych w czasie epidemii. Cz. I…*, p. 895.
944 E. Gapska, *Bieg postępowania w sprawach cywilnych w czasie epidemii. Cz. II…*, p. 955.

were completely deprived of the possibility to act[945]. The reason for implementing the provision of Article 15zzs of the COVID-19 Special Act was not the actual course of the pandemic in Poland (the scale of infections, which was low in March and April 2020). The suspension of the time limits was linked to the declaration of the state of epidemic or epidemic threat in the country. The regulation in question was therefore applied irrespective of the actual number of infections and, consequently, irrespective of the actual deprivation of the parties of the possibility of taking action to defend their rights or the actual suspension of the operation of the courts.

Notwithstanding the foregoing, attention should be drawn to the possibility of using other, pre-existing instruments which would allow the above objectives to be achieved and which, at the same time, would not have such far-reaching consequences for the parties in terms of limiting the right of access to court. Firstly, there is the provision in Article 173 of the CCP that provides for the automatic suspension of the proceedings if the court is prevented from acting by reason of *force majeure*. There should be no doubt that the state of epidemics can be qualified as *force majeure*[946]. The application of the provision in question would achieve the objective behind Article 15zzs of the COVID-19 Special Act in cases where it is absolutely necessary, i.e. where the court has ceased to function because of the spread of the coronavirus. On the other hand, where the courts were able to operate normally, there was no need to suspend all procedural time limits. It should be recalled that the provisions of the Code of Civil Procedure allow the negative consequences of the expiry of a time limit to be remedied, primarily by reinstating the time limit (Article 168 of the CCP). Therefore, the provisions of the Code of Civil Procedure alone may be considered sufficient to ensure the proper conduct of proceedings in the event of a pandemic. It should also be borne in mind that the COVID-19 Special Act provides for a number of other solutions to ensure proper implementation of access to justice, such as remote hearings or the possibility of hearing a case in closed session. In view of the above, it must be concluded that the provision of Article 15zzs of the COVID-19 Special Act does not meet the conditions of proportionality provided for in Article 31(3) of the Constitution. The legislator, having at its disposal less burdensome means of achieving the desired objective, has applied a solution which not only cannot be considered the least burdensome, but, above all, has chosen a measure which does not allow for the actual achievement of the objective which is supposed to justify the introduced solution. It should be recalled, however, that similar solutions have been adopted in many countries of the European Union, including Spain, Cyprus, Italy, Belgium, Bulgaria, Romania and Slovenia. The Polish approach was therefore not isolated from other European countries.

---

945 E. Gapska, *Bieg postępowania w sprawach cywilnych w czasie epidemii. Cz. II...*, p. 952.
946 E. Gapska, *Bieg postępowania w sprawach cywilnych w czasie epidemii. Cz. I...*, p. 893.

As it appears, it was the inadequacy of the regulation contained in Article 15zzs of the COVID-19 Special Act and its negative impact on the right to a fair trial that led to the repeal of this provision. At this point, however, it is necessary to point out the far-reaching effects of this provision, even after its repeal on 16 May 2020. The resumption of procedural time limits has been accompanied by a massive increase in the sending of court correspondence and, as a result, a significant accumulation of tasks, mainly for professional lawyers[947]. The simultaneous commencement of the procedural time limits as of 23 May 2020 in all cases in which the time limits had previously been suspended pursuant to the provisions of Article 15zzs of the COVID-19 Special Act also had a similar effect.

947 E. Gapska, *Bieg postępowania w sprawach cywilnych w czasie epidemii. Cz. II...*, p. 952.

11. Impact of the COVID-19 pandemic on the course of enforcement proceedings

11.1. Suspension of judicial auctions of housing properties

As of 30 May 2020, Article 952[1] has been added to the Code of Civil Procedure pursuant to Article 2 of the Act of 14 May 2020 amending certain laws with regard to protective measures in connection with the spread of the SARS-CoV-2 virus[948]. According to the wording of § 5, the auction of a dwelling or land with a residential building that serves to satisfy the debtor's housing needs shall not be held during the state of epidemic threat or the state of epidemic and for 90 days after its termination.

In the explanatory memorandum of the government bill[949], the author of the bill did not pay attention to the above-mentioned solution, as the original bill did not include the provision contained in § 5, which was introduced only at the stage of the first reading in the Parliament. P. Kamiński points out that, nevertheless, the purpose of this provision is clear and consists in strengthening the protection of the debtor from being deprived of the possibility of satisfying housing needs in a situation in which, due to the state of the COVID-19 epidemic, it may not be possible to find an alternative[950]. It should be noted, however, that the provision of Article 952[1] § 5 of the CCP, although episodic in nature, applies not only to a COVID-19 epidemic, but to any other infectious disease (i.e. a disease caused by a biological agent[951]). This seems to be the reason why it was included in the CCP and not in the COVID-19 Special Act, although the *ratio legis* of its introduction was undoubtedly linked to the coronavirus pandemic.

Pursuant to the transitional provision contained in Article 64 of the Act of 14 May 2020, the provision of Article 952[1] § 5 of the CCP shall apply to proceedings initiated and not concluded before the entry into force of the Act, if the creditor has not submitted a request for the setting of a date for the first auction of the property before that date. It should be noted that the above provision is poorly

---

948 Journal of Laws 2020, item 875.

949 Parliamentary paper No. 334.

950 P. Kamiński, *Licytacja lokalu mieszkalnego lub nieruchomości gruntowej zabudowanej budynkiem mieszkalnym służącym zaspokojeniu potrzeb mieszkaniowych dłużnika*, Przegląd Prawa Egzekucyjnego 2021/4, section 4, Legalis.

951 Article 2(3) of the Epidemic Control Act.

drafted and cannot be applied according to its literal wording[952]. Prior to the entry into force of article 952^1 of the CCP, the first auction of real estate was ordered by the bailiff *ex officio*, even if it concerned real estate used to satisfy the debtor's housing needs[953]. Although it was possible for a creditor to submit such a request to the bailiff prior to 30 May 2020, it was not of a constitutive nature and, in practice, it was not usually submitted. In view of the foregoing, it must be assumed that the provision of Article 64 of the Amending Act of 14 May 2020 is to be understood in such a way that the application of the provision of Article 952^1 § 5 of the CCP is determined not only by the absence of a request by a creditor to set a date for the first auction before 30 May 2020, but also by the failure of the bailiff to set this date *ex officio*. Only such an interpretation makes it possible to give a reasonable meaning to the transitional provision[954]. On the other hand, the rulings of the courts have expressed a different view, in which it has been accepted that the norm expressed in Article 64 of the Amending Act does not in any way affect the prohibition existing as of 30 May 2020 to set a date for the judicial auction of a dwelling under the conditions indicated in Article 952^1 § 5 of the CCP, and that the provision of Article 64 allows to derogate from the strictness provided for in Article 952^1 of the CCP, but only in relation to its §§ 2 and 3[955]. However, the position taken by the District Court has not been convincingly justified and, moreover, is in full contradiction with the wording of the cited Article 64 of the Amending Act, which refers not only to §§ 2 and 3, but to the entire Article 952^1 of the CCP. For these reasons, it cannot be accepted.

The provision of Article 952^1 § 5 of the CCP provides for the prohibition of setting the first judicial auction date for a property that 'serves to satisfy the debtor's housing needs'. The object of enforcement fulfils the above condition if it has at least a predominant residential function, i.e. the debtor's centre of life is concentrated there. It should be noted that this does not have to be the debtor's permanent residence, but there should be a certain stability or frequency of residence there. In fact, one's housing needs may be met periodically in different places[956]. Although such a position can be found in the jurisprudence of the Supreme Court[957], it should be noted that it was expressed on the basis of the Income Tax Act and concerned the tax deduction of expenses for one's own housing needs. However, since the

---

952 I. Kunicki, *Ograniczenie wyznaczenia i przeprowadzenia licytacji nieruchomości z mocy art. 952[1] k.p.c.*, Przegląd Prawa Egzekucyjnego 2020/12, section 1, Legalis.

953 A. Adamczuk, [in:] *Kodeks postępowania cywilnego. Komentarz. Tom II*, M. Manowska (ed.), Warsaw 2021, p. 2904.

954 I. Kunicki, *Ograniczenie wyznaczenia...*, section 1, Legalis.

955 Decision of the District Court Poznań - Nowe Miasto and Wilda in Poznań of 22 December 2021, II Cz 120/21, LEX No. 3339644.

956 T. Demendecki, *Ograniczenia egzekucji z nieruchomości służącej zaspokojeniu potrzeb mieszkaniowych dłużnika w świetle nowelizacji Kodeksu postępowania cywilnego z dnia 14 maja 2020 r.*, Nieruchomości 2020/4, pp. 45–46.

957 Judgment of the Supreme Court of 12 July 2000, III RN 207/99, LEX No. 45255.

purpose of article 952[1] § 5 of the CCP is to protect one of the basic necessities of life, namely housing[958], the position according to which a debtor may have several places of residence where he satisfies their housing needs would constitute an unjustified extension of the scope of the provision, which, given its exceptional nature, must be interpreted strictly. Indeed, the protection of the debtor against the loss of his habitual residence is already sufficiently guaranteed by the presumption that the housing needs are satisfied in a single property which constitutes the debtor's permanent residence. Indeed, the very concept of the centre of one's life implies that one's entire life is centred on a given property, i.e. that all one's personal and property affairs are concentrated there[959]. Consequently, it must be assumed that the protection of the debtor against the judicial auction of the property used to satisfy housing needs, as provided for in Article 952[1] § 5 of the CCP, can only extend to a property in which the debtor's entire life activities are concentrated. This applies only to the debtor's housing needs and not to those of other persons to whom he has given the property for use[960]. As a result, even if the object of enforcement is a dwelling or a land with a residential building, but the debtor does not live in it, such property cannot be considered to serve the debtor's housing needs[961].

The question arises as to whether the provision of Article 952[1] § 5 of the CCP is also applicable in cases where the debtor actually occupies the property, but it is not of a residential nature (e.g. where the debtor has occupied a commercial property to satisfy residential needs). Two different views can be expressed on this ground. According to the first, the character of the property as residential is determined by its actual use[962]. According to the second, the provision of Article 952[1] § 5 of the CCP applies only to real estate in which there are premises intended for the permanent residence of persons or which enable such residence[963]. The latter view should be accepted for the following reasons. While it is true that there is no legal definition of 'dwelling or land with a residential building', this does not mean that any property which is actually used by the debtor for the purpose of living therein can be considered as property of a residential nature. In this respect, the actual purpose (and not the use) of the property should be decisive. Otherwise, this could lead to a situation where the debtor could arbitrarily change the purpose of the premises, thereby hindering the enforcement of the property. An interpretation

958 T. Demendecki, *Ograniczenia egzekucji...*, p. 41.
959 Judgment of the Supreme Court of 12 September 2001, V CKN 1827/00, LEX No. 52401.
960 A. Sikorska-Lewandowska, *Zmiana regulacji prawnych w zakresie egzekucji z nieruchomości wprowadzona w związku ze stanem epidemii*, Nieruchomości 2021/2, p. 6.
961 P. Kamiński, *Licytacja lokalu mieszkalnego...*, section 3, Legalis.
962 T. Demendecki, *Ograniczenia egzekucji...*, p. 41.
963 P. Kamiński, *Licytacja lokalu mieszkalnego...*, section 3, Legalis.

according to which premises or real estate with a residential building could be any real estate, regardless of its intended use, would lead to an interpretation contrary to the purpose of the law, which in principle would include all real estate within the scope of this provision, as long as the debtor resides therein.

If a request is made to set a date for the first judicial auction, the bailiff should assess whether the conditions set out in Article 952[1] § 5 of the CCP are met and, if the bailiff decides that the property serves to satisfy the debtor's housing needs (and this circumstance should be apparent from the description and evaluation – Article 947 § 6 of the CCP), the bailiff should reject the request. This decision is subject to a complaint against the bailiff's actions to the court supervising the execution of real estate[964]. On the other hand, a complaint may be lodged against the court's decision rejecting the creditor's application (Article 952[1] § 5 of the CCP). It should be noted that the right to lodge a complaint against the court's decision is granted only to the creditor whose application has been rejected. If the date of the first judicial auction is set by the court, the debtor does not have the right to appeal.

The provision of Article 952[1] § 5 of the CCP was repealed by Article 2 of the Law of 8 April 2022 Amending the Law on Assistance to Citizens of Ukraine in Connection with the Armed Conflict on the Territory of Ukraine and Certain Other Laws[965]. Pursuant to Article 33 of the Amending Law, the provision was repealed with retroactive effect from 24 February 2022. The explanatory memorandum to the Law does not specify the reasons for which the provision was repealed[966].

11.2. Suspension of enforcement orders to vacate residential premises

Article 15zzu(1) of the COVID-19 Special Act provided another solution concerning the course of enforcement proceedings. According to the wording of this provision, enforcement orders ordering the eviction of residential premises shall not be enforced during the state of epidemic threat or state of epidemic declared on the basis of COVID-19. The provision was originally added to the COVID-19 Special Act on 31 March 2020[967]. At the same time, it should be noted that it was repealed as of 15 April 2022 by the Law of 8 April 2022 amending the Law on

964 A. Szymańska-Grodzka, [in:] *Zmiany w KPC wynikające z regulacji COVID-19. Komentarz,* T. Szanciło (ed.), Warsaw 2020, p. 35.

965 Journal of Laws 2022, item 830.

966 Explanatory Memorandum to the Government's Draft Law on Amendments to the Law on Assistance to Citizens of Ukraine in Connection with the Armed Conflict on the Territory of Ukraine and Certain Other Laws, Parliamentary Paper No. 2147.

967 Act of 31 March 2020 amending the Act on special solutions related to the prevention and control of COVID-19, other infectious diseases and emergencies caused by them, and some other acts, Journal of Laws of 2020, item 568.

Assistance to Citizens of Ukraine in Connection with the Armed Conflict on the Territory of Ukraine and Certain Other Laws.

Pursuant to the provision of Article 15zzu(1) of the COVID-19 Special Act, during the state of epidemic or epidemic threat, the measures necessary to enable the creditor to obtain possession pursuant to Article 1046 of the CCP shall not be taken. This provision does not mean, however, that the mere granting of an enforcement clause to a writ of execution ordering the vacating of a dwelling is inadmissible, and it is addressed to the bailiff who executes such a writ.

According to A. Sikorska-Lewandowska, the provision is worded too broadly, and its scope covers all cases of eviction from residential premises, even if in the eviction judgment the court has established the right to conclude a lease agreement for social premises with the relevant municipality. In cases where the debtor has been offered such a lease, there is no reason to refuse to vacate the previous premises, as the debtor has the possibility to move to the premises of the municipality. It should also be borne in mind that Article 1046 § 4 of the CCP does not provide for eviction 'on the street', but only to social premises, other lodging or premises to which the debtor has a legal title, and, as a last resort, to temporary premises[968]. It should also be noted that when deciding on the right to conclude a lease agreement for social premises in an eviction judgment, the court takes into account the particular material and family situation (Article 14(3) of the Act on the Protection of Tenants' Rights[969]), and in particular whether the evicted person has a legal title to other premises or is able to satisfy their housing needs.

From the above it can be concluded that in many cases an evicted person who is not entitled to a social tenancy agreement will be able to solve his housing situation independently. For this reason, the solution used in Article 15zzu(1) of the COVID-19 Special Act should be considered too broad. A more appropriate solution, which would make it possible to limit the suspension of the execution of the eviction to specific cases where it is indeed necessary, would be to introduce the possibility for the debtor to apply for a suspension of the execution on the grounds of the lack of premises to which the eviction could take place. On the other hand, suspending the enforcement of all enforcement titles ordering the vacating of residential premises should be considered as the inappropriate solution. Similar measures, which exclude the automatic granting of protection to debtors, have been adopted, for example, in Austria and Spain.

It should only be mentioned in passing that the provision of Article 15zzu of the COVID-19 Special Act has been amended on two occasions. As of 18 April 2020, a second paragraph was introduced, according to which the suspension of the execution of an eviction does not apply to decisions issued on the basis of Article 11a

---

968 A. Sikorska-Lewandowska, *Zmiana regulacji...*, p. 5.

969 Act of 21 June 2001 on the protection of tenants' rights, the housing stock of the municipality and the amendment of the Civil Code, Journal of Laws 2022, item 172 (consolidated text).

of the Act of 29 July 2005 on the prevention of domestic violence. In turn, as of 21 January 2021, the catalogue of exceptions was extended to include decisions on a number of construction investments related to the construction of the Central Communication Port.

11.3. Suspension of judicial auctions and eviction orders concerning residential premises and the right to a fair trial

The above-mentioned regulations raised constitutional concerns in the public discourse, mainly due to the fact that the prohibitions were maintained for an indefinite period of time and that the obligations of the state to prevent homelessness were shifted to citizens (property owners). Such a position was expressed, inter alia, by the Ombudsman[970]. However, doubts have been expressed mainly with regard to the protection of the right to property provided for in the Constitution (Article 64). At this point, an attempt should be made to answer the question whether the provisions of Article 952[1] § 5 of the CCP and Article 15zzu of the COVID-19 Special Act affect the realisation of the right to a fair trial.

The assessment should begin by recalling that the first chapters emphasised that both Article 6(1) of the ECHR and Article 45(1) of the Constitution consider enforcement proceedings to be an extension of the trial. Therefore, the same guarantees of the right to a fair trial apply at the enforcement stage as at the trial stage. A different assumption would lead to the conclusion that the right to a fair trial is only illusory, since it guarantees obtaining a binding court decision, but not its actual enforcement. In practical terms, this means, inter alia, that enforcement proceedings should be conducted without undue delay. The need to ensure an effective enforcement procedure for the creditor has been highlighted by the European Court of Human Rights[971].

Real estate enforcement is used only when the debtor's other assets are insufficient to satisfy the creditor. As a general rule, the creditor is entitled to request the judicial auction of real estate used to satisfy the debtor's housing needs if the amount of the enforced claim is at least one-twentieth of the value of the real estate (Article 952[1] § 2 of the CCP). The auction of real estate is the *ultima ratio* and will not be carried out if the debtor's other assets are sufficient to cover the enforced claim. It follows from the above that, in the vast majority of cases, the refusal to auction off real estate will mean the actual impossibility of enforcing a

970 The Ombudsman's speech to the Prime Minister of 3 October 2021, https://bip.brpo.gov.pl/sites/default/files/2021-10/Do_premiera_zakaz_eksmisja_3.10.2021.pdf, accessed 29 August 2022.

971 Judgment of the European Court of Human Rights of 25 April 2017, Application no. 31371/12, LEX No. 2274956.

final judgment. This is because if enforcement proceedings against real estate have already been initiated, it is highly likely that the debtor does not have any other assets to satisfy the creditor.

The suspension of the judicial auction of the real estate intended for the debtor's housing needs, which is the next stage after the stage of seizure of the real estate and its description and evaluation, results in a *de facto* suspension of the enforcement proceedings, in which Article 952^1 § 5 of the CCP was applied. Therefore, there is no satisfaction of the creditor – since the judicial auction of the property will not take place, it is obvious that the purchase of the property and the payment of the price by the auction purchaser will not take place.

Similarly, the suspension of the enforcement of orders to vacate residential premises, provided for in the repealed Article 15zzu of the COVID-19 Special Act, should be assessed. During the period in which this provision was in force, the enforcement of all evictions from residential premises was excluded *a limine*, so that the creditor had no real possibility of enforcing a final judgment ordering the debtor to vacate the premises. Moreover, the creditor could not foresee how long this limitation would last.

Therefore, there should be no doubt that the provisions of Article 952^1 § 5 of the CCP and Article 15zzu of the COVID-19 Special Act constitute a clear example of restriction of the right to court in the course of enforcement proceedings due to the fact that they make the execution of the enforcement title impossible in practice. However, the question arises whether this restriction can be considered justified, i.e. whether these provisions constitute a proportionate interference with the right to court (Article 31(3) of the Constitution, Article 18 of the ECHR). The purpose of introducing the two provisions in question, although there is no such declaration in the explanatory memorandum, was to protect the debtor from being deprived of his place of residence in the era of the coronavirus pandemic, during which it is assumed that it may be considerably more difficult for the debtor to find other premises and it is necessary to maintain social distance. As stated by the Constitutional Tribunal, street eviction is considered inhumane and contrary to human dignity[972]. In the light of the foregoing, it is reasonable to assume that there is a clash of values in the matter in question: the right to justice in terms of the right to effective enforcement of the judgment by the creditor and the right to property, on the one hand, and the personal dignity and health of the debtor, on the other. In this context, it seems reasonable to conclude that the legislator was right to give priority to the second group. The right to court, as has been pointed out on many occasions, is not absolute and may be subject to restrictions in conflict with other fundamental values. Human dignity can certainly be included in the catalogue of values that can justify certain restrictions on the right to a fair trial.

However, the above statement does not automatically mean that the solutions adopted are in accordance with the principle of the least restrictive measure,

---

972 Judgment of the Constitutional Tribunal of 4 March 2008, S 2/08, LEX No. 392307.

according to which the legislator is obliged to apply the measures that are least burdensome for the persons whose rights or freedoms are restricted[973]. With regard to both the provisions of Article 952[1] § 5 of the CCP and Article 15zzu of the COVID-19 Special Act, it should be noted that the legislator has decided to significantly privilege the situation of debtors, without taking into account the interests of creditors in the same way[974].

The introduction of a prohibition on the judicial auction of any property intended for the debtor's residence seems to be a solution that would go too far. This is because it does not take into account the debtor's real property and living situation, in particular whether he has the possibility of resolving their housing situation in another way, for example by living in other premises owned by them or their family or, finally, by renting the premises themself. It should be recalled that the prohibition of judicial auctions provided for in Article 952[1] § 5 of the CCP was binding irrespective of the number of properties owned by the debtor. The general prohibition of auctions also applied in isolation from the current epidemic situation in the country, and thus regardless of whether the debtor was actually exposed to the negative consequences associated with the increased risk of contracting the coronavirus. The above solution must therefore be considered disproportionate and leading to unnecessary interference with the creditor's right to enforce the court's judgment and thus the right to a fair trial.

Real estate enforcement is a complex and time-consuming process. At the end of the judicial auction, the court issues an order awarding the property to the highest bidder (Article 987 of the CCP). Once this decision has become final and the auction purchaser has fulfilled the conditions of the auction, the ownership of the property is transferred to the bidder (Article 998 of the CCP). Only then will the purchaser take possession (Article 999 of the CCP). Meanwhile, the provision of Article 952[1] § 5 of the CCP shifts the protection granted to the debtor to an earlier stage of the enforcement procedure, i.e. the auction stage, which has no convincing justification. The legislator's decision to link the prohibition of eviction of the debtor to the stage of the judicial auction of the property must therefore be considered inappropriate and even unnecessary. At the same time, two solutions affecting the course of enforcement proceedings have been introduced – the suspension of the judicial auctions of residential property and the suspension of enforcement orders for eviction from residential premises. However, the objective, which is identical for both solutions, could only be achieved by the provision of Article 15zzu of the COVID-19 Special Act, without the need to duplicate it in Article 952[1] § 5 of the CCP. It should be noted that a final order on the transfer of ownership is an enforceable title to put the purchaser in possession of the property (Article 999 § 1 of the CCP). Therefore, the provision of Article 952[1] § 5 of the CCP introduces an unnecessary suspension of the real estate enforcement, which prevents the

---

973 Judgment of the Constitutional Tribunal of 11 May 1999, K 13/98, LEX No. 37319.
974 A. Sikorska-Lewandowska, *Zmiana regulacji...*, p. 7.

creditor from effectively executing the claims specified in the enforcement title. A sufficient solution, from the point of view of the debtor's protection, would be to suspend the execution of the decision on the transfer of ownership to the extent that the auction purchaser takes possession. The debtor would then remain under the protection of Article 15zzu of the COVID-19 Special Act, but without the need for undue interference in the preceding stages of real estate enforcement. While the adoption of such a solution would shift the burden of preventing the debtor's eviction to the auction purchaser, it should be noted that the purchaser would have the opportunity to assess whether they agree to the restrictions under Article 15zzu of the COVID-19 Special Act. In this respect, it would undoubtedly be a less severe restriction of the right to enforce the enforcement title than that provided for in Article 952^1 § 5 of the CCP.

The solution adopted in Article 15zzu of the COVID-19 Special Act must also be regarded as a disproportionate restriction of the right to a fair trial in relation to the right to effective enforcement of the judgment. With respect to this provision, the comments made above regarding the lack of consideration of the debtor's actual situation remain valid. At this point, it should be recalled that the introduced prohibition of eviction from residential premises applied to all enforcement titles, regardless of whether the debtor was granted the right to enter into a social tenancy agreement with the municipality in the judgment ordering eviction. The suspension of the eviction also did not depend on the debtor's housing situation, and it was irrelevant whether the debtor had other premises or had the possibility of satisfying their own housing situation in another way. The provision of Article 15zzu of the COVID-19 Special Act thus provided for complete automaticity, excluding any examination of the debtor's situation. Such a provision unjustifiably deprived creditors of protection and therefore constituted an excessive restriction of the right to court, contrary to the principle of proportionality.

In conclusion, both with regard to Article 15zzu of the COVID-19 Special Act and with regard to Article 952^1 § 5 of the CCP, it should be noted that although the restriction of the right to court is in principle permissible in order to protect the values for which the provisions under consideration were introduced, the condition of proportionality has not been met, i.e. the effects of the regulation are not in an appropriate relationship to the burden imposed on creditors[975]. The legislator's interference must therefore be considered excessive.

975 Judgment of the Constitutional Tribunal of 23 November 2009, P 61/08, LEX No. 528409.

Conclusions

The analysis carried out in the study allowed for a partial confirmation of the research thesis posed at the beginning. The solutions adopted in the COVID-19 Special Act, which are the subject of the study, do not comply with the minimum standard of the right to a fair trial set out in Article 45(1) of the Constitution of the Republic of Poland, Article 6(1) of the ECHR and Article 47 of the CFR. However, the above conclusion does not apply to the provision contained in Article 15zzs1(1) point 4 of the COVID-19 Special Act, which refers to the formation of the court in civil proceedings. The study proves that this provision does not violate the guarantee of the right to court. In this respect, therefore, the research thesis has proved to be false.

The considerations presented in Chapters VI – IX have also made it possible to confirm the research hypothesis put forward, according to which the instruments relating to remote hearings, closed sessions and electronic service of judicial documents contained in the COVID-19 Special Act contribute significantly to increasing the efficiency of civil proceedings and, taking into account the need to adapt these institutions to the fair trial standard described in the study, can successfully become permanent elements of the civil proceedings model.

The considerations carried out in this study have also led to specific conclusions that justify the above statements:

1. The right to a fair trial, also referred to as the right to court or the right to effective judicial protection, is regulated by Article 45(1) of the Constitution, Article 6(1) of the ECHR and Article 47 of the CFR. These provisions do not prescribe specific solutions, but require the achievement of a certain result (minimum standard) in terms of a fair trial. The right to a fair trial consists of a set of procedural guarantees, primarily relating to the right of access to court, the fairness of the proceedings based on the principles of equality and openness, the right to obtain a binding decision within a reasonable time and to receive the reasons for the decision, but also institutional guarantees of the formation of the court as an impartial and independent body with appropriate organisational features. An element of the right to a fair trial is also the right to have the decision enforced by the state. The right to a fair trial, whether regulated by the Polish Constitution or by the ECHR, does not in itself include the right to appeal the judgment.
2. In principle, the constitutional right to court provides the same guarantees as Article 6(1) of the ECHR. Moreover, the EU standard under the CFR corresponds to the level of protection provided by the Convention. At the same time, the standard of the right to a fair trial set by the Charter of Fundamental Rights cannot be lower than that set by the Convention, which follows directly from the provision of Article 52(3) of the CFR. The Convention right to a fair

trial, derived from Article 6(1) of the ECHR, applies only to actual and serious disputes, the outcome of which affects the rights and obligations of individuals of a civil law nature. Article 45(1) of the Constitution does not provide for such a condition, and therefore it should be considered that in this respect the constitutional standard of the right to a fair trial has a wider scope of application than that set out in Article 6(1) of the ECHR. An individual will not be able to claim a violation of the right to a fair trial under the Convention if it is of a minimal nature. However, there is no such limitation in either the Polish Constitution or the CFR. On the other hand, the right to a fair trial under the Charter of Fundamental Rights can only be invoked by an individual in EU cases, i.e. where the facts on which a party bases its claim fall within the scope of EU law. Where EU law does not apply, the right to a fair trial is not supported by Article 47 of the CFR. However, this does not mean that in such cases the individual is not protected by the ECHR and the Constitution.

3. The right to court under the Constitution, the ECHR and the CFR, is not absolute and may be subject to limitations which, however, must remain proportionate to the purpose they are intended to secure and must not violate the very essence of the right to a fair trial. Limitations to the right to a fair trial may arise from the need to ensure the proper functioning of the justice system, including the guarantee of a reasonable duration of proceedings, other important values such as the protection of individual privacy or, as in the case of the COVID-19 pandemic, the protection of citizens' health.
4. On 14 March 2020, the state of epidemic threat was declared in Poland, which was subsequently lifted on 20 March 2020 and replaced by the state of epidemic. The state of epidemic was then lifted on 16 May 2022 and the state of epidemic threat was declared again. The state of epidemic threat remained in force until 1 July 2023. Thus, a special legal regime was in place for more than three years, which updated the conditions for the application of a number of provisions of the COVID-19 Special Act. The significant decrease in the number of COVID-19 cases observed since March 2022 did not entail a change in the special regime during the pandemic period. The legislator also did not provide for a clear end date for the epidemic states declared on the basis of the COVID-19, nor an obligation to review the legitimacy of their maintenance.
5. The solution adopted in the COVID-19 Special Act, according to which the duration of the majority of restrictions in civil procedural relations was set for the state of epidemic, the state of epidemic threat and one year after the lifting of the latter, should be considered as a solution that disproportionately restricts the right to court. The legislator, bound by the prohibition of excessive interference with constitutional rights and freedoms, should constantly monitor whether all the restrictions of the COVID-19 Special Act are necessary to protect the health of citizens. Such steps have not been taken, and most of the provisions resulting in restrictions of the right to court have been in force continuously since March 2020, even after the state of epidemic threat was lifted and despite a significant decrease in the danger to public health in the country.

6. The provisions of the COVID-19 Special Act, which are the subject of this study, are to a large extent the consequence of the application of an incorrect legislative technique, characterised by chaotic and vague provisions. The legislator uses general clauses, as well as imprecise and unclear concepts that require interpretation through a process of in-depth and multiple clarifications. The intertemporal provisions adopted are often unclear or even flawed. The poor quality of the provisions results in a lower standard of legal certainty.
7. A characteristic feature of the provisions contained in the COVID-19 Special Act is that, in addition to the stated aim of protecting the health of citizens, they almost always aim to expedite civil proceedings. The tendency of the legislator to shorten court proceedings is a visible motive for the changes in the civil procedure in recent years. In order to permanently change the civil procedure model, the legislator should not use the solutions adopted in the Special Act, which by definition should be temporary.
8. The introduction of remote hearings under Article 15zzs[1] of the COVID-19 Special Act was dictated by health protection objectives in view of the need to reduce face-to-face social contact while allowing the uninterrupted functioning of the courts. The existing provisions on remote hearings (Article 151 § 2 of the CCP) were not sufficient to ensure the proper functioning of the judiciary during the COVID-19 pandemic, as they required the presence of the participants of the hearing in the building of another court. However, the amendment to Article 15zzs[1] of the COVID-19 Special Act, which came into force on 3 July 2021 and tightened the conditions for waiving a remote hearing, was aimed not only at protecting health, as stated in the draft, but also at meeting the demand for accelerating and computerising civil proceedings.
9. The holding of a remote hearing by videoconference does not in itself violate the right to a fair trial. The participation of a party in the proceedings may be ensured by means of videoconferencing, but it is necessary to ensure that appropriate technical conditions are in place to allow the party connecting remotely to participate actively in the hearing on the same basis as other participants.
10. The provision of Article 15zzs[1](1) of the COVID-19 Special Act concerning the organisation of remote hearings violates the right to a fair trial in terms of the external openness of the proceedings, as it does not ensure the participation of the public in court hearings. Restrictions on this right have not been introduced by a legal provision, but by internal rules and orders of the presidents of individual courts. While the abolition of the external openness of hearings, combined with the significant restriction of access to court buildings, was an expedient solution in view of the need to minimise the risk of the spread of the SARS-CoV-2 virus, it constituted a disproportionate means of restricting the right to court, as it should have been combined with the establishment of explicit guarantees of public participation in remote hearings.
11. The introduction of remote hearings also violated the right to a fair trial in terms of the principle of procedural fairness. The guarantees of the parties participating

in the remote hearing are not sufficiently guaranteed by the provisions of statutory rank, and the proceedings do not meet the requirement of predictability due to the lack of definition of the procedure for holding the remote hearing, including the technical conditions with which it should comply.

12. The way in which remote hearings are regulated in the COVID-19 Special Act has not had the effect of restricting access to the courts. Indeed, the legislator has provided for the possibility of waiving remote hearings and the obligation to provide access to the appropriate technical equipment necessary for connection in the courthouse to persons who declare that they do not have it. On the contrary, in some cases remote hearings make it possible to provide a person with broader access to the court by involving in the active participation in the proceedings persons who have not previously had the opportunity to appear in person in the courthouse.
13. The model of remote hearings, in which the participants can connect to each other from any place outside the court building, is an instrument that has a positive impact on the efficiency of the proceedings. The model of remote hearings introduced in the Code of Civil Procedure should therefore be welcomed. Remote hearings should not be mandatory and the choice of this form should be left to the discretion of the presiding judge. It should be noted that videoconference hearings were a popular tool in other European Union countries during the COVID-19 pandemic. However, in none of the Member States was the court obliged to hold all hearings remotely and it was left to the discretion of the court. The permanent introduction of remote hearings in civil proceedings should ensure an appropriate level of procedural guarantees for the parties, security of data transmission and an appropriate level of formality and proper conduct of the hearing. The organisation of a remote hearing in a given case should ensure an adequate opportunity for the public to have access to the hearing. It is necessary to adopt detailed implementing rules which will comprehensively regulate technical and organisational issues. Despite the amendments to the Code of Civil Procedure in 2024, these conditions have not been fully met.
14. In deciding to introduce the possibility of hearing a case in closed session (Article $15zzs^1(1)$ point 3 and Article $15zzs^2$ of the COVID-19 Special Act), the legislator was guided by the desire to expedite civil proceedings in the era of the COVID-19 pandemic, the need to prevent judicial paralysis and to reduce the number of situations in which a session of the court requiring the presence of the parties is convened. The purpose of extending the possibility of adjudication in closed session was therefore to protect health and to meet the demand for the efficient functioning of the courts during the pandemic.
15. The departure from the principle of openness and orality in certain categories of cases in favour of their consideration in written procedure and in a closed session is not contrary to the right to a fair trial. Therefore, the provisions of Article $15zzs^1(1)$ point 3 and $15zzs^2$ of the COVID-19 Special Act do not constitute a violation of the right to a fair trial in respect to the parties to the proceedings.

16. However, the provision contained in Article 15zzs^{2} of the COVID-19 Special Act constitutes a limitation of the principle of external openness (in relation to persons outside the proceedings themselves). Instead of the public proclamation of the court's decision, this regulation provides for the decision to be issued in a closed session and delivered only to the parties. This provision was introduced to protect public health by eliminating the need to schedule another public hearing for the publication of the judgment. However, it does not meet the requirements of proportionality. A remote hearing for the publication of the judgment would have been a sufficient measure and would have achieved the same objective of health protection. In addition, the possibility provided for in Article 15zzs^{1}(1) point 3 of the COVID-19 Special Act to issue a decision in a closed session without a hearing significantly limits the external openness of the proceedings, as it does not provide for the publication of the judgment. In order to ensure that the provisions in question fully comply with the standard of the right to a fair trial court deriving from the Constitution and the ECHR, it is necessary to adopt a procedure for the publication of the decision in a form other than announcement in open court. It is possible to postulate an obligation to publish decisions terminating proceedings on the court's website.
17. The provision of Article 15zzs^{1}(1) point 3 of the COVID-19 Special Act has a positive effect on the demand for effectiveness in certain categories of proceedings by expanding the catalogue of cases in which it is permissible to dispense with a public hearing. On the other hand, the fact that the court is not bound by the time limit for issuing a decision pursuant to Article 15zzs^{2} of the COVID-19 Special Act weakens the guarantee for the parties to obtain a judgment without undue delay. Therefore, the decision of the legislator, who determined in Article 224 § 3 of the CCP that the conclusion of the trial in a closed session may take place at the latest within one month from the date on which the deadline for the parties to make their final statements expired, should be assessed positively.
18. The laconic provision contained in Article 15zzs^{2} of the COVID-19 Special Act raises questions with regard to compliance with the adversarial principle and the right to be heard. In order to uphold the standard of the right to a fair trial, it should be guaranteed that a party has the opportunity to review and comment on the final written position of the other party before a judgment is delivered. This guarantee has not been introduced in the amended Article 224 § 3 of the CCP.
19. The legislator's tendency to abandon the need to refer all cases for trial is to be assessed positively. At the same time, the current provision of Article 148^{1} of the CCP, which allows for the waiver of a trial, must be considered too restrictive and of little practical significance. For this reason, it should be proposed that the instruments provided for in this regard by the COVID-19 Special Act be incorporated into the Code of Civil Procedure, while at the same time ensuring that judgments in a given instance are published in such

a way as to enable the public to become acquainted with them. The possibility of delivering judgments in closed session should be limited to cases where there is no need for extensive evidentiary proceedings and where the facts are undisputed or can be established on the basis of documentary evidence. However, an open hearing should remain the rule and the exceptions to its holding should be clearly defined in the legislation.

20. The purpose of the regulation under Article 15zzs^{1}(1) point 4 of the COVID-19 Special Act on single-member formations of the court in civil proceedings, which was supposed to be the need for health protection in connection with the epidemic threat posed to each other by persons sitting in multi-member formations, must be assessed as ostensible from the explanatory memorandum to the bill. This is due to the fact that the same law of 28 May 2021 provided for the remote participation in the hearing by the members of the panel, which was previously not generally allowed. The disputed provision was introduced at a time when the epidemic situation in the country had significantly improved and a number of important restrictions on the economy had been lifted. The real intention of the legislator was to expedite civil proceedings by dispensing with the need for collegial panels.
21. The formation of a collegial court in proceedings before in the second instance leads to a higher standard of appellate review, strengthens the impartiality of the judiciary and is desirable from the point of view of the protection of individual rights. However, there is no reason to assume that the right of an individual to a fair trial has been violated as a result of the introduction of the provision of Article 15zzs^{1}(1) point 4 of the COVID-19 Special Act. Neither the standard of the right to a fair trial under Article 45(1) of the Constitution nor the ECHR require that the composition of the court be collegial. Therefore, the regulation fulfils the requirement of the right to a competent court, i.e. the obligation to establish clear and pre-established legal rules on how the composition of the court is to be formed in a given category of cases.
22. However, the power granted by Article 15zzs^{1}(1) point 4 sentence 2 of the COVID-19 Special Act to influence the composition of the court by means of a non-appealable decision of the president of the court should be assessed differently. The possibility for the president of the court to influence the composition of the court in an *ad hoc* and arbitrary manner can be considered a violation of the right to a competent court. In practice, however, the influence of the president of the court on the implementation of the individual right to a fair trial will be marginal, especially since the president's competence is limited to expanding the composition of the court with additional judges to be selected by drawing lots. It should not be forgotten that Article 6(1) of the ECHR protects the individual against serious and actual violations of the right to a fair trial, and the above failure does not pose such a threat.
23. In view of the long tradition of collegiality in the composition of appellate courts and its impact on the proper functioning of the judiciary, as well as the lack of objective reasons for maintaining the regulation referred to in Article

15zzs[1](1) point 4 of the COVID-19 Special Act, it should be advocated to return as soon as possible to the rules for determining the composition of the panel resulting from the provisions of the Code of Civil Procedure in force before the COVID-19 pandemic.

24. The stated aim of the introduction of electronic service through the Information Portal (Article 15zzs[9] (2)-(5) of the COVID-19 Special Act) was to expedite proceedings and to reduce the risk of the spread of a coronavirus in connection with the service of court correspondence in the traditional form. Despite the elimination of the risk associated with this form of service, it continues to be used as an element to significantly reduce the costs associated with service of process and to influence its acceleration.
25. The use of the Information Portal for e-service, which was intended to have a purely informational function, rather than a dedicated ICT system, raises many practical doubts. This solution should be evaluated critically. The vagueness and incomplete nature of the regulation, as well as the lack of implementing provisions on how the electronic service through the Information Portal is to be carried out, leads to the conclusion that the regulation of Article 15zzs[9] (2)-(5) of the COVID-19 Special Act contradicts the right to a fair trial in the sense of the principle of procedural fairness, which presupposes predictability of procedural rules. The regulation does not introduce any procedural guarantees for the parties, which would regulate the issue of electronic service in such a way that a party is not deprived of the opportunity to acquaint itself with the court documents addressed to him.
26. Depriving parties who are not represented by professional lawyers of the possibility to receive court correspondence via the Information Portal is not justified by objective reasons and may be considered as a violation of the principle of equality, which is an integral part of the right to a fair trial.
27. Notwithstanding the doubts expressed above, the postulate of introducing electronic service in civil proceedings should be accepted with approval. The positive impact of the regulation on increasing the efficiency of civil proceedings should not be overlooked. The solutions adopted make it possible to speed up communication between lawyers and the court and to reduce the costs of service. Therefore, it is necessary to postulate the implementation of the Electronic Filing Office, the basis for the operation of which has already been established in the relevant legislative and executive regulations. Until this service is operational, the legislator should take the necessary steps to adapt the provisions on e-servie to the requirements of a fair trial. In particular, the possibility of optional introduction of electronic service through the Information Portal in relation to other participants in civil proceedings should be considered.
28. The suspension of procedural time limits under Article 15zzs of the COVID-19 Special Act was intended by the legislator as a remedy to the threatened paralysis of the administration of justice and to limit the negative effects of this on the realisation of the individual's right to court. Time limits for civil proceedings have been suspended from 31 March to 22 May 2020.

29. The provision of Article 15zzs of the COVID-19 Special Act did not adequately achieve the objective intended by the legislator. The suspension of time limits resulted in a restriction of the right of access to court and did not guarantee its proper implementation. The solution must also be considered disproportionate. The provision, as originally intended, was to apply throughout the state of epidemic and the state of epidemic threat, regardless of the course of the COVID-19 pandemic, and thus in isolation from the actual need. The legislator, who had more lenient measures at his disposal, introduced a solution that severely restricted the right of access to justice. Irrespective of the fact that similar solutions have been adopted in a number of other Member States of the European Union, the regulation should be assessed as *ad hoc* and inappropriate.
30. The legislator's purpose in introducing the provisions of Article 15zzu of the COVID-19 Special Act and Article 952^1 § 5 of the CCP was to strengthen the protection of the debtor with regard to his housing needs, the fulfilment of which could prove difficult in the era of the COVID-19 pandemic. The protection afforded by these provisions was defined too broadly, in isolation from the debtor's actual housing and living situation. The indefinite maintenance of the orders led to their being disconnected from the real needs of the pandemic. Although similar solutions could be observed in other countries of the European Union, they were characterised by the fact that the protection granted was subject to an appropriate request by the debtor. Its consideration was preceded by an assessment of the real housing needs of the debtor. On the other hand, the instruments adopted in Poland were based on full automatism, which should be considered as an interference with the right to a fair trial, contrary to the principle of proportionality.

The guarantees of the right to a fair trial provided by the Constitution of the Republic of Poland, the European Convention on Human Rights and the Charter of Fundamental Rights of the European Union are of considerable importance in a democratic state. The comprehensive analysis carried out in this study has made it possible to identify the threats, but also the positive aspects of the solutions introduced in the era of the COVID-19 pandemic, which affect the status of the individual. This work has attempted to show how the instruments introduced into the legal system by the COVID-19 Special Act should be shaped in the future. It is to be hoped that in the further development of the civil procedure model, the legislator will choose a direction that is fully in line with the constitutional and international standard of the right to a fair trial, bearing in mind that it is necessary to guarantee the parties not only a prompt resolution of their case by the court, but also (and perhaps above all) a fair resolution.

Bibliography

Commentaries, monographs and Internet publications

Adamczuk A., [in:] *Kodeks postępowania cywilnego. Komentarz. Tom II,* Manowska M. (ed.), Warsaw 2021.

Alunaru C., Bojin L., *Coronavirus and the law in Romania,* [in:] *Coronavirus and the law in Europe,* Hondius E., Santos Silva M., Nicolussi A., Salvador Coderch P., Wendehorst C., Zoll F. (ed.), Cambridge 2021.

Barcz J., *Odniesienia do Karty Praw Podstawowych w toku procedury ratyfikacyjnej Traktatu z Lizbony w Polsce,* [in:] *60 lat Rady Europy. Tworzenie i stosowanie standardów prawnych,* Machińska H. (ed.), Warsaw 2009.

Begier A., Wypych-Knieć A., Małecki-Tepicht Ł., Report of the Association of Polish Judges 'Iustitia', *Sądownictwo w czasie COVID-19 – raport z badania oceny wpływu pandemii COVID-19 na wymiar sprawiedliwości w* Polsce, Warsaw 2021.

Białecki M., *Organizacja postępowania jako próba realizacji postulatu szybkości postępowania cywilnego a nadużycie prawa procesowego przez strony i uczestników* postępowania, [in:] *Nowelizacja postępowania cywilnego. Wpływ zmian na praktykę sądową,* Kotas-Turoboyska S., Manikowski F. (ed.), Warsaw 2021.

Biernat S., *Czy Karta Praw Podstawowych Unii Europejskiej obowiązuje w* Polsce, [in:] *Państwo prawa i prawo karne. Księga jubileuszowa profesora Andrzeja Zolla, t. I,* Kardas P., Sroka T., Wróbel W. (eds), Warsaw 2012.

Bladowski B., *Pisma sądowe w sprawach cywilnych,* Warsaw 2012.

Bodnar A., [in:] *Ochrona praw podstawowych w Unii Europejskiej,* Barcz J. (ed.), Warsaw 2008.

Boluk N., Karolczyk B., [in:] *Postępowanie cywilne po nowelizacji,* Karolczyk B. (ed.), Warsaw 2020.

Borys A., [in:] *Regulacje służące usprawnieniu cywilnego postępowania rozpoznawczego,* Gil I. (red.), Warsaw 2020.

Bosek L., *Stan epidemii. Konstrukcja prawna,* Warsaw 2022.

Bosek L., [in:] *Ustawa o zapobieganiu oraz zwalczaniu zakażeń i chorób zakaźnych u ludzi. Komentarz.,* Bosek L. (ed.), Warsaw 2020, Legalis.

Brodecki Z., Koncewicz T., *Karta Praw Podstawowych i zasady ogólne prawa wspólnotowego,* [in:] *Karta Praw Podstawowych w europejskim i krajowym porządku prawnym,* Wróbel A. (ed.), Warsaw 2009.

Dauter-Kozłowska A., Dauter B., *Bieg terminów procesowych w postępowaniu sądowoadministracyjnym w związku z ogłoszonym stanem zagrożenia epidemicznego, a następnie stanem epidemii z powodu COVID-19,* LEX.

De Gaetano V., *Reasonable time and hasty decisions – the article 6 and dilemma for domestic courts,* [in:] *Przewlekłość postępowania sądowego,* Piaskowska O., Piesiewicz P. (eds), Warsaw 2018.

Dolecki H., Radkiewicz T., [in:] *Kodeks postępowania cywilnego. Komentarz. Tom I,* Wiśniewski T. (ed.), Warsaw 2021.

Feliga P., [in:] *Kodeks postępowania cywilnego. Komentarz. Tom I,* Szanciło T. (ed.), Warszawa 2019.

Florczak-Wątor M., [in:] *Konstytucja Rzeczypospolitej Polskiej. Komentarz,* Tuleja P. (ed.), Warsaw 2019.

Gajda-Roszczynialska K., [in:] *Kodeks postępowania cywilnego. Koszty sądowe w sprawach cywilnych. Dochodzenie roszczeń w postępowaniu grupowym. Przepisy przejściowe. Komentarz do zmian,* Zembrzuski T. (ed.), Warsaw 2020.

Gapska E., *Przygotowanie rozprawy cywilnej – niewykorzystana szansa,* [in:] *Postępowanie cywilne w dobie przemian,* Warsaw 2017.

Gil P., [in:] *Regulacje służące usprawnieniu cywilnego postępowania rozpoznawczego,* Gil I. (ed.), Warsaw 2020.

Goździaszek Ł., [in:] *Postępowanie cywilne w czasie pandemii. E-doręczenia, rozprawa zdalna, posiedzenia niejawne, składanie pism procesowych,* Gołaczyński J. (ed.), Warsaw 2022.

Górski K., [in:] *Kodeks postępowania cywilnego. Komentarz. Tom I,* Szanciło T. (ed.), Warsaw 2019.

Gromska-Szuster I., [in:] *Kodeks postępowania cywilnego. Komentarz. Tom I,* Wiśniewski T. (ed.), Warsaw 2021.

Grzegorczyk P., Weitz K., [in:] *Konstytucja RP. Komentarz. Tom I,* M. Safjan, L. Bosek (eds), Warsaw 2016.

Grzeszczak R., *„Mapa" judykatury Trybunału Konstytucyjnego dotyczącej członkostwa Polski w Unii Europejskiej,* [in:] *Wokół kryzysu praworządności, demokracji i praw człowieka. Księga jubileuszowa Profesora Mirosława Wyrzykowskiego,* A. Bodnar, A Ploszka (eds), Warsaw 2020.

Gudowski J., [in:] *Kodeks postępowania cywilnego. Komentarz. Tom I. Postępowanie rozpoznawcze,* Ereciński T. (ed.), Warsaw 2016.

Hofmański P., Wróbel A., [in:] *Konwencja o Ochronie Praw Człowieka i Podstawowych Wolności. Komentarz do artykułów 1–18,* Garlicki L. (ed.), Warsaw 2010.

Izdebski H., [in:] *Pandemia COVID-19 a prawa i wolności obywatela,* Gardocka T., Jagiełło D. (eds), Warsaw 2020.

Jakubecki A., *Naczelne zasady postępowania cywilnego w świetle nowelizacji kodeksu postępowania cywilnego,* [in:] *Czterdziestolecie Kodeksu postępowania cywilnego. Zjazd katedr postępowania cywilnego w Zakopanem (7–9.10.2005 r.),* Kraków 2006.

Jakubecki A., [in:] *Kodeks postępowania cywilnego. Komentarz. Tom I*, Wiśniewski T. (ed.), Warsaw 2021.

Januszkiewicz T., [in:] *Jawność i jej ograniczenia. Tom VIII. Postępowania sądowe*, Gołaczyński J., Szpor G. (eds), Warsaw 2015.

Jarocha A., *Zasada równości stron w kontekście elektronizacji postępowania cywilnego*, [in:] *E-wymiar sprawiedliwości w aspekcie europejskim*, Śliwczyński B., Łuczak-Noworolnik L. (eds), Poznań 2016.

Jarzmus K., [in:] *Nowe technologie. nowa Sprawiedliwość. Nowe pytania. Wdrażanie nowych technologii w wymiarze sprawiedliwości*, Report of the Helsinki Foundation for Human Rights, Kładoczny P., Wiśniewska K. (eds), Warsaw 2021.

Jasiński F., *Karta Praw Podstawowych Unii Europejskiej*, Warsaw 2003.

Jurczyk T., *Zasady ogólne prawa Unii Europejskiej a Karta Praw Podstawowych*, [in:] *Rządy prawa i europejska kultura prawna*, Bator A., Helios J., Jedlecka W. (eds), Wrocław 2014.

Kamiński G., *Zakaz nadużycia praw procesowych*, Warsaw 2021.

Karaś G., Zalesińska A., [in:] *Postępowanie cywilne w czasie pandemii. E-doręczenia, rozprawa zdalna, posiedzenia niejawne, składanie pism procesowych*, Gołaczyński J. (ed.), Warsaw 2022.

Karlik P., Wiliński P., [in:] *Konstytucja RP. Tom II. Komentarz do art. 87–243*, Safjan M., Bosek L. (eds), Warsaw 2016, Legalis.

Klimas K., [in:] *Postępowanie cywilne w czasie pandemii. E-doręczenia, rozprawa zdalna, posiedzenie niejawne, składnie pism procesowych*, Gołaczyński J. (ed.), Warsaw 2022.

Kościółek A., *Elektroniczne czynności procesowe w sądowym postępowaniu cywilnym*, Warsaw 2012.

Kościółek A., *Zasada jawności w sądowym postępowaniu cywilnym*, Warsaw 2018.

Kościółek A., Arkuszewska A., *Zdalne posiedzenia sądowe – ewolucja czy rewolucja*, [in:] *Prawo Nowych Technologii. Księga jubileuszowa z okazji jubileuszu 20-lecia działalności Centrum Badań Problemów Prawnych i Ekonomicznych Komunikacji Elektronicznej i Studenckiego Koła Naukowego – Blok Prawa Komputerowego*, Gołaczyński J. (ed.), Warsaw 2022.

Kotas-Turoboyska S., *Pojęcie dobra wymiaru sprawiedliwości w rozumieniu art. 44[1] k.p.c.*, [in:] *Rozstrzyganie spraw cywilnych. Aktualne wyzwania i perspektywy*, Białecki M., Kotas-Turoboyska S., Manikowski F, Słyk J., Szczepanowska E. (eds), Warsaw 2022.

Kotecka S., [in:] *Jawność i jej ograniczenia. Tom VIII. Postępowania sądowe*, Gołaczyński J., Szpor G. (eds), Warsaw 2015.

Kotecka-Kral S., *Informatyzacja działalności korporacji prawniczych na przykładzie postępowania cywilnego*, [in:] *Prawo nowych technologii*, Flaga-Gieruszyńska K., Gołaczyński J. (eds), Warsaw 2021.

Kowalski P., [in:] *Pandemia COVID-19 a prawa i wolności obywatela,* Gardocka T., Jagiełło D. (eds), Warsaw 2020.

Krajewski M., [in:] *Podręcznik prawa Unii Europejskiej,* A. Zawidzka-Łojek, A. Łazowski (eds), Warsaw 2018.

Krakowiak M., *Rozprawa elektroniczna w polskim postępowaniu cywilnym,* [in:] *Rozstrzyganie spraw cywilnych,* Białecki M., Kotas-Turoboyska S., Manikowski F., Szczepanowska E. (eds), Warsaw 2022.

Kremer J., [in:] *Prawo o ustroju sądów powszechnych. Komentarz,* Górski A. (ed), Warsaw 2013.

Kunicki I., [in:] *Kodeks postępowania cywilnego. Tom I A,* Góra-Błaszczykowska A. (ed.), Warsaw 2020, Legalis.

Lichoń K., *Obowiązywanie zasady równości stron w postępowaniu przed sądem polubownym,* [in:] *Folia Iuridica Wratislaviensis,* L. Górnicki (ed.), Wrocław 2013.

Łazarska A., Rzetelny proces cywilny, Warsaw 2012.

Łazarska A., [in:] *Kodeks postępowania cywilnego. Komentarz. Tom I,* Szanciło T. (ed.), Warsaw 2019.

Łętowska E., *Prawo do sądu – różnice perspektywy,* [in:] *Aurea praxis Aurea theoria. Księga pamiątkowa ku czci Profesora Tadeusza Erecińskiego. Tom II,* Gudowski J., Weitz K. (eds), Warsaw 2011.

Łochowski M., [in:] *Zmiany w KPC wynikające z regulacji COVID-19. Komentarz,* Szanciło T. (ed.), Warsaw 2020.

Manowska M., [in:] *Kodeks postępowania cywilnego. Komentarz. Tom I,* Manowska M. (ed.), Warsaw 2021.

Marcisz P., [in:] *Podręcznik prawa Unii Europejskiej,* Zawidzka-Łojek A., Łazowski A. (ed.), Warsaw 2018.

May J., *Rozwiązania usprawniające proces cywilny (zagadnienia wybrane),* [in:] *Postępowanie cywilne w dobie przemian,* Gil I. (ed.), Warsaw 2017.

May J., *Usprawnienie i przyspieszenie procesu cywilnego: nowe rozwiązania prawne czy stare sprawdzone metody? – wybrane zagadnienia,* [in:] *Rozstrzyganie spraw cywilnych. Aktualne wyzwania i perspektywy,* Białecki M., Kotas-Turoboyska S., Manikowski F., Słyk J., Szczepanowska E. (eds), Warsaw 2022.

Mazur R., *Karta Praw Podstawowych,* [in:] *Ochrona Praw Podstawowych w Unii Europejskiej. Wybrane zagadnienia,* Florczak A. (ed.), Warsaw 2009.

Mik C., [in:] *Ochrona praw podstawowych w Unii Europejskiej,* Barcz J. (ed.), Warszawa 2008.

Mikèlenas V., *A Lithuanian Experience of Coronavirus and the Law,* [in:] *Coronavirus and the law in Europe,* Hondius E., Santos Silva M., Nicolussi A., Salvador Coderch P., Wendehorst C., Zoll F. (eds), Cambridge 2021.

Nowicki M. A., *Europejski Trybunał Praw Człowieka. Orzecznictwo. Tom 1 Prawo do rzetelnego procesu sądowego,* Kraków 2001.

Nowicki M. A., *Wokół Konwencji Europejskiej. Komentarz do Europejskiej Konwencji Praw Człowieka,* Warsaw 2013.

Nowicki M. A., *Wokół Konwencji Europejskiej. Komentarz do Europejskiej Konwencji Praw Człowieka,* Warsaw 2021.

Paszkowski J., [in:] *Kodeks postępowania cywilnego. Komentarz. Tom I,* Szanciło T. (ed.), Warsaw 2019.

Piaskowska O., Piesiewicz P., *Instytucja przewlekłości postępowania,* [in:] *Przewlekłość postępowania sądowego,* Piaskowska O., Piesiewicz P. (eds), Warsaw 2018.

Piaskowska O., Piesiewicz P., *Instytucja przewlekłości postępowania. Wprowadzenie do problematyki,* [in:] *Przewlekłość postępowania sądowego,* Piaskowska O., Piesiewicz P. (eds), Warsaw 2018.

Piesiewicz P., *Korzystanie z uprawnień procesowych przez stronę a przewlekłość postępowania sądowego,* [in:] *Przewlekłość postępowania sądowego,* Piaskowska O., Piesiewicz P. (eds), Warsaw 2018.

Pietrzkowski H., *Metodyka pracy sędziego w sprawach cywilnych,* Warsaw 2021.

Pilitowski B., Kociołowicz-Wiśniewska B., *Raport z przestrzegania w Polsce zasady jawnego procesu i publicznego ogłoszenia wyroku w czerwcu 2020 roku,* Court Watch Polska Foundation, Toruń 2020.

Plitowski B., Sitniewska R., Sołowij P., *Obywatelski Monitoring Sądów 2022,* Report of the Court Watch Polska Foundation, Toruń 2022.

Pogonowski P., *Realizacja prawa do sądu w postępowaniu cywilnym,* Warsaw 2005.

Pogonowski P., *Wpływ wejścia w życie Konstytucji RP z 1997 r. na sądowe postępowanie cywilne,* [in:] *Czterdziestolecie Kodeksu postępowania cywilnego. Zjazd katedr postępowania cywilnego w Zakopanem (7-9.10.2005 r.),* Kraków 2006.

Pogonowski P., [in:] *Kodeks postępowania cywilnego. Komentarz. Tom I,* Wiśniewski T. (ed.), Warsaw 2021.

Półtorak N., [in:] *Karta Praw Podstawowych Unii Europejskiej. Komentarz,* Wróbel A. (ed.), Warsaw 2020.

Radajewski M., [in:] *Pandemia COVID-19 a prawa i wolności obywatela,* Gardocka T., Jagiełło D. (ed.), Warsaw 2020.

Rogala K., [in:] *Postępowanie cywilne w czasie pandemii. E-doręczenia, rozprawa zdalna, posiedzenie niejawne, składnie pism procesowych,* J. Gołaczyński (ed.), Warsaw 2022.

Rożek S., *Sprawność postępowania cywilnego na tle rozstrzygania spraw spadkowych,* Warsaw 2022.

Sarnecki P., [in:] *Konstytucja Rzeczypospolitej Polskiej. Komentarz,* L. Garlicki, M. Zubik (eds), Warsaw 2016.

Sarżyński H., *Zmiany w art. 148[1] k.p.c. jako środek przyspieszający postępowanie, kosztem zasady jawności i kontradyktoryjności,* [in:] *Postępowanie cywilne w dobie przemian,* Gil I. (ed.), Warsaw 2017.

Stawicka A., Stawicki R., *Pandemia COVID-19. Sytuacja w wybranych krajach europejskich,* Report of the Office of Analysis, Documentation and Correspondence of the Senate Chancellery, Warsaw 2020.

Stefańska E., [in:] *Kodeks postępowania cywilnego. Komentarz. Tom I,* Manowska M. (ed.), Warsaw 2021.

Stefańska E., [w:] *Kodeks postępowania cywilnego. Komentarz aktualizowany,* Manowska M. (ed.), LEX 2022.

Szymańska-Grodzka A., [in:] *Zmiany w KPC wynikające z regulacji COVID-19. Komentarz,* Szanciło T. (ed.), Warsaw 2019.

Trociuk S., *Prawa i wolności w stanie epidemii,* Warsaw 2021.

Tuleja P., [in:] *Konstytucja Rzeczypospolitej Polskiej. Komentarz,* P. Tuleja (ed.), Warsaw 2019.

Uliasz M., [in:] *Postępowanie cywilne w czasie pandemii. E-doręczenia, rozprawa zdalna, posiedzenie niejawne, składnie pism procesowych,* Gołaczyński J. (ed.), Warsaw 2022.

Warso Z., [in:] *Podręcznik prawa Unii Europejskiej,* Zawidzka-Łojek A., Łazowski A. (eds), Warsaw 2018.

Wieruszewski R., [in:] *Ochrona praw podstawowych w Unii Europejskiej,* Barcz J. (ed.), Warsaw 2008.

Wiśniewski P., *Wpływ ogłoszenia stanu zagrożenia epidemicznego lub stanu epidemii z powodu COVID-19 na bieg terminów procesowych w postępowaniach cywilnych,* LEX.

Wróbel A., [in:] *Stosowanie prawa Unii Europejskiej przez sądy,* Wróbel A. (red.), Warsaw 2005.

Wróbel A., *O niektórych problemach sądowego stosowania Karty Praw Podstawowych,* [in:] *Karta Praw Podstawowych w europejskim i krajowym porządku prawnym,* Wróbel A. (ed.), Warsaw 2009.

Wróbel A., [in:] *Karta Praw Podstawowych Unii Europejskiej. Komentarz,* Wróbel A. (ed.) Warsaw 2020.

Wyrozumska A., [in:] *Ochrona praw podstawowych w Unii Europejskiej,* Barcz J. (ed.), Warsaw 2008.

Wyrzykowski M., [in:] *Ochrona praw podstawowych w Unii Europejskiej,* Barcz J. (ed.), Warsaw 2008.

Zalesińska A., *Wpływ informatyzacji na założenia konstrukcyjne procesu cywilnego*, Warsaw 2016.

Zalesińska A., *Doręczenia elektroniczne w postępowaniu cywilnym*, [in:] *Prawo Nowych Technologii. Księga jubileuszowa z okazji jubileuszu 20-lecia działalności Centrum Badań Problemów Prawnych i Ekonomicznych Komunikacji Elektronicznej i Studenckiego Koła Naukowego – Blok Prawa Komputerowego*, J. Gołaczyński (ed.), Warsaw 2022.

Zalizowski G., *Prawo do sądu na tle Konstytucji Rzeczypospolitej Polskiej w kontekście europejskiej Konwencji o ochronie praw człowieka i podstawowych wolności*, [in:] *Duch praw w krajach Europy Środkowo-Wschodniej*, Wrocław 2016.

Zawistowski D., [in:] *Kodeks Postępowania Cywilnego. Komentarz. Tom IV.*, Wiśniewski T. (ed.), Warsaw 2021.

Żyznowski T., [in:] *Kodeks postępowania cywilnego. Komentarz. Tom I*, Wiśniewski T. (ed.), Warsaw 2021.

Journals and periodicals

Balcerzak M., *The Doctrine of Precedent in the International Court of Justice and the European Court of Human Rights*, Polish Yearbook of International Law 2004–2005.

Barcik J., *Niezawisłość sędziowska jako wartość konstytucyjna Unii Europejskiej – glosa do wyroku Trybunału Sprawiedliwości z 27.02.2018 r., C-64/16, Associação Sindical dos Juízes Portugueses*, Europejski Przegląd Sądowy 2018, No. 5.

Bodio J., Graliński W., *Znaczenie zasady równouprawnienia strony w procesie cywilnym*, Studia Iuridica Lublinensia 2016, No.1.

Bodnar A., *Zmiana konstytucji jako konsekwencja wykonania wyroku ETPCz*, Europejski Przegląd Sądowy 2010, No.10.

Czarnow S., *Między stanem epidemii a stanem klęski żywiołowej – COVID-19 a niektóre prawa człowieka*, Radca Prawny. Zeszyty Naukowe 2021, No. 3.

Czeszejko-Sochacki Z., *Prawo do sądu w świetle Konstytucji Rzeczypospolitej Polskiej (Ogólna charakterystyka)*, Państwo i Prawo 1997, Nos 11–12.

Dąbrowski S., *Niezależność sędziowska a podział władz*, Kwartalnik Krajowej Rady Sądownictwa 2004, No. 1.

Demendecki T., *Ograniczenia egzekucji z nieruchomości służącej zaspokojeniu potrzeb mieszkaniowych dłużnika w świetle nowelizacji Kodeksu postępowania cywilnego z dnia 14 maja 2020 r.*, Nieruchomości 2020, No. 4.

Dziurda M., *Czy nadchodzi zmierzch zasady ustności w postępowaniu cywilnym?*, Polski Proces Cywilny 2022, No. 1.

Filipek P., *Rozproszona europejska kontrola przestrzegania prawa do rzetelnego procesu sądowego w świetle zasady wzajemnego zaufania i wyroku C-216/18 PPU, LM*, Europejski Przegląd Sądowy 2019, No. 2.

Flaga-Gieruszyńska K., *Problem sprawności i efektywności postępowania arbitrażowego*, Kwartalnik ADR 2011, No. 4.

Flaga-Gieruszyńska K., *E-wymiar sprawiedliwości w sprawach cywilnych jako przykład rozwoju nowych technologii w sferze publicznej*, Ekonomiczne Problemy Usług 2017, No. 1.

Flaga-Gieruszyńska K., *Szybkość, sprawność i efektywność postępowania cywilnego – zagadnienia podstawowe*, Zeszyty Naukowe KUL 2017, No. 3.

Flaga-Gieruszyńska K., *Influence of informatization on the effectiveness and reliability of civil proceedings on the example of Polish solutions*, Fiat Iustitia 2018, No. 1.

Florczak-Wątor M., *Prawo do sądu jako prawo jednostki i jako gwarancja horyzontalnego działania praw i wolności*, Przegląd Prawa Konstytucyjnego, 2016, No. 3.

Florczak-Wątor M., *Niekonstytucyjność ograniczeń praw i wolności jednostki wprowadzonych w związku z epidemią COVID-19 jako przesłanka odpowiedzialności odszkodowawczej państwa*, Państwo i Prawo 2020, No. 12.

Gajda-Roszczynialska K., *System koncentracji materiału procesowego po zmianach wprowadzonych na mocy ustawy z 4.07.2019 r. o zmianie ustawy – Kodeks postępowania cywilnego oraz niektórych innych ustaw w postępowaniu zwyczajnym*, Polski Proces Cywilny 2020, No. 1.

Gajda-Roszczynialska K., *Przebudowa wymiaru sprawiedliwości w czasach pandemii COVID-19 ze szczególnym uwzględnieniem postępowania cywilnego*, Polski Proces Cywilny 2022, No. 1.

Gapska E., *Bieg postępowania w sprawach cywilnych w czasie epidemii. Cz. I – sprawy pilne*, Monitor Prawniczy 2020, No.17.

Gapska E., *Bieg postępowania w sprawach cywilnych w czasie epidemii. Cz. II – wstrzymanie rozpoczęcia i zawieszenie biegu terminów procesowych*, Monitor Prawniczy 2020, No. 18.

Gołaczyński J., Kotecka-Kral S., *Elektronizacja pism procesowych, doręczeń i posiedzeń jawnych w postępowaniu cywilnym w okresie pandemii COVID-19*, Polski Proces Cywilny 2020, No. 4.

Gołaczyński J., Zalesińska A., *Kierunki informatyzacji postępowania cywilnego po nowelizacji Kodeksu postępowania cywilnego z 4.7.2019 r.*, Monitor Prawniczy 2020, No. 7.

Gołaczyński J., Zalesińska A., *Nowe technologie w sądach na przykładzie wideokonferencji i składania pism procesowych i doręczeń elektronicznych w dobie pandemii COVID-19*, Monitor Prawniczy 2020, No. 12.

Gołaczyński J., Dymitruk M., *Rozprawa zdalna i doręczenia elektroniczne w dobie pandemii COVID-19 po wejściu w życie nowelizacji z 28.5.2021 r.*, Monitor Prawniczy 2021, No. 13.

Goździaszek Ł., *Normy informatyczne w prawie postępowania cywilnego*, Przegląd Sądowy 2017, No. 2.

Górniak K, *Jawność posiedzeń sądowych w postępowaniu nieprocesowym*, Przegląd Sądowy 2017, Nos 11–12.

Górski M., *Prawo do skutecznego środka prawnego w art. 47 Karty Praw Podstawowych UE – znaczenie i deficyty*, Europejski Przegląd Sądowy 2016, No. 8.

Grzeszczak R., Krajewski M., *„Sąd" w świetle przepisów art. 47 KPP oraz art. 267 TFUE*, Europejski Przegląd Sądowy 2014, No. 6.

Jakubecki A., *Sankcje za nadużycie uprawnień procesowych w Kodeksie postępowania cywilnego*, Palestra 2019, Nos 11–12.

Jasińska K., *E-rozprawa w postępowaniu cywilnym a prawo do sądu i możliwość obrony swoich praw*, Studia Prawnicze. Rozprawy i Materiały 2021, No. 2.

Juchniewicz J., *O granicach swobody ustawodawcy w kształtowaniu standardów prawa do sądu*, Przegląd Prawa Konstytucyjnego 2016, No. 3.

Kamiński P., *Licytacja lokalu mieszkalnego lub nieruchomości gruntowej zabudowanej budynkiem mieszkalnym służącym zaspokojeniu potrzeb mieszkaniowych dłużnika*, Przegląd Prawa Egzekucyjnego 2021, No. 4, Legalis.

Knoppek K., Udział obywateli w sprawowaniu wymiaru sprawiedliwości w postępowaniu cywilnym, Ius Novum 2014, No. 1.

Kociubiński J., *Dostęp do niezawisłego i bezstronnego sądu jako element prawa do rzetelnego procesu karnego w orzecznictwie Europejskiego Trybunału Praw Człowieka*, Nowa Kodyfikacja Prawa Karnego. Volume XXVII.

Koncewicz T., *Prawo do egzekucji wyroku jako element prawa do rzetelnej procedury w prawie europejskim*, Palestra 2014, Nos 7–8.

Korolczuk J., *Informatyzacja postępowania sądowego. Szanse i zagrożenia*, Młody Jurysta 2018, No. 4.

Kościółek A., *Elektroniczne czynności procesowe w świetle nowelizacji z 10.7.2015 r.*, Prawo Mediów Elektronicznych 2017 No. 1.

Kościółek A., *Jawność posiedzeń sądowych w postępowaniu cywilnym w dobie pandemii COVID-19*, Przegląd Sądowy 2021, No. 5.

Kożuch M., *Karta Praw Podstawowych – samoistne źródło prawa czy zbiór zasad interpretacyjnych*, Europejski Przegląd Sądowy 2015, No. 10.

Kulski R., *Wpływ stanu zagrożenia epidemicznego lub stanu epidemii ogłoszonego z powodu COVID-19 na postępowanie cywilne*, Monitor Prawniczy 2020, No. 9.

Kunicki I., *Ograniczenie wyznaczenia i przeprowadzenia licytacji nieruchomości z mocy art. 952[1] k.p.c.*, Przegląd Prawa Egzekucyjnego 2020, No. 12, Legalis.

Kutwin M., *Prawo do sądu w orzecznictwie Trybunału Konstytucyjnego oraz Europejskiego Trybunału Praw Człowieka*, Studia Iuridica, Volume LXXVI.

Kwaśniak A., *Praktyczne implikacje zasady udziału obywateli w sprawowaniu wymiaru sprawiedliwości, wynikającej z art. 182 Konstytucji RP, w kontekście najnowszych regulacji*, Monitor Prawniczy 2022, No. 8.

Lach A., *Werdykt ławy przysięgłych w świetle prawa do rzetelnego procesu*, Palestra 2011, Nos 1–2.

Lenaers K., *Aby Karta Praw Podstawowych Unii Europejskiej była rzeczywistością dla wszystkich: 10 lat, odkąd Karta jest prawnie wiążąca*, Europejski Przegląd Sądowy 2020, No. 2.

Litowski J., *Ograniczenie jawności postępowania cywilnego z uwagi na stan epidemii wywołany wirusem COVID-19*, Monitor Prawniczy 2021, No. 2.

Litowski J., *Zakres zmian art. 15zzs[1] ustawy z 2.3.2020 r. – uwagi na tle stanu prawnego obowiązującego od 3.7.2021 r.*, Monitor Prawniczy 2022, No. 2.

Łętowska E., *Multicentryczność współczesnego systemu prawa i jej konsekwencje*, Państwo i Prawo 2005, No. 4.

Machnikowska A., Organizacja procesu cywilnego przed sądem pierwszej instancji z perspektywy posiedzenia przygotowawczego, Palestra 2019, No. 11–12.

Machnikowska A., *Zasada jawności w postępowaniu procesowym – modernizacja czy marginalizacja? Wybrane zagadnienia*, Polski Proces Cywilny 2022, No. 1.

Markiewicz K., *Wpływ regulacji „covidowych" na zasadę niezmienności (stabilności) oraz kolegialność składów sądów odwoławczych*, Polski Proces Cywilny 2022, No. 1.

Michór A., *Postępowanie cywilne w okresie epidemii COVID-19*, Bussiness Law Journal 2021, No. 9.

Misztal-Konecka J., *O obowiązywaniu zasady kontradyktoryjności w postępowaniu nieprocesowym: przyczynek do dyskusji*, Zeszyty Prawnicze 2016, No. 3.

Nowicki M. A., *Prawo do rzetelnego procesu sądowego: część „cywilna"*, Palestra 1996, Nos 7–8.

Nowicki M. A., *„Rzetelny proces w rozsądnym terminie" w orzecznictwie europejskim*, Studia Europejskie 1997, No. 2.

Nowicki M. A., *Europejski Trybunał Praw Człowieka – Przegląd orzecznictwa (styczeń-marzec 2021 r.)*, Palestra 2021, No. 4.

Olaś A., *Kolegialność a jednoosobowość – skład sądu I instancji w procesie cywilnym: doświadczenia i pespektywy*, Polski Proces Cywilny 2020, No. 3.

Pagiela A., *Zasada „fair trial" w orzecznictwie Europejskiego Trybunału Praw Człowieka,* Ruch Prawniczy, Ekonomiczny i Socjologiczny 2003, No. 2.

Piaskowska O., *Prawo do sądu a oddalenie oczywiście bezzasadnego powództwa w świetle projektu zmian z 27.11.2017 r. do Kodeksu postępowania cywilnego,* Studia Prawnicze 2018, No. 1.

Pietrzykowski T., Wojciechowski B., *Równość, prawda i sprawiedliwość w procesie cywilnym. Rozważania na tle nowelizacji k.p.c.,* Palestra 2004, Nos 9–10.

Płaziuk J., *Konieczność odstąpienia od przeprowadzania posiedzenia zdalnego w przypadku wyznaczenia rozprawy i posiedzenia jawnego w czasach COVID-19,* Polski Proces Cywilny 2022, No. 1.

Pogonowski P., *Efektywność filarem sprawiedliwego postępowania cywilnego,* Polski Proces Cywilny 2021, No. 3.

Półtorak N., *Przystąpienie Unii Europejskiej do Konwencji o Ochronie Praw Człowieka – projekt umowy akcesyjnej a prawo UE,* Europejski Przegląd Sądowy 2012, No. 9.

Półtorak N., *Zakres związania państw członkowskich Kartą Praw Podstawowych Unii Europejskiej,* Europejski Przegląd Sądowy 2014, No. 9.

Radajewski M., *Stan zagrożenia epidemicznego oraz stan epidemii jako formy prawne ochrony zdrowia publicznego,* Przegląd Legislacyjny 2021, No. 4.

Roszkiewicz J., *Jawność postępowania sądowego w świetle Europejskiej Konwencji Praw Człowieka,* Radca Prawny. Zeszyty Naukowe 2021, No. 2.

Roszkiewicz J., *Granice ograniczeń wolności gospodarczej wprowadzonych w celu przeciwdziałania epidemii (uwagi na tle orzecznictwa sądów administracyjnych),* Zeszyty Naukowe Sądownictwa Administracyjnego 2022, No. 2.

Rzucidło-Grochowska I., *Brak obowiązku uzasadnienia i uzasadnienie skrócone a prawo do sądu,* Studia Prawnicze 2014, No. 4.

Safjan M., *Prawo do skutecznego środka prawnego i bezstronnego sądu – art. 47 Karty Praw Podstawowych w relacjach horyzontalnych – kilka uwag w związku z wyrokiem TSUE w sprawach połączonych C-585/18; C-624/18, C-625/18,* Palestra nr 2020, No. 5.

Sanders A., *Video-Hearings in Europe Before, During and After the COVID-19 Pandemic,* International Journal for Court Administration 2020, No. 12.

Sanetra W., *Sąd właściwy w rozumieniu Konstytucji RP,* Przegląd Sądowy 2011, No. 9.

Sikora A., *Glosa do wyroku TSUE z 27.02.2018 r., C-64/16, Associação Sindical dos Juízes Portugueses (art. 19 TUE jako autonomiczny i samodzielny wzorzec kontroli legalności*), Państwo i Prawo 2018, No. 11.

Sikorska-Lewandowska A., *Zmiana regulacji prawnych w zakresie egzekucji z nieruchomości wprowadzona w związku ze stanem epidemii,* Nieruchomości 2021, No. 2.

Skorupka A., Realizacja zasady równości w aspekcie materialnym na przykładzie osób niewidomych, Polski Proces Cywilny 2018, No. 3.

Skowron A., *Rzetelny proces karny w ujęciu Karty Praw Podstawowych Unii Europejskiej oraz Europejskiej Konwencji o Ochronie Praw Człowieka i Podstawowych Wolności*, Prokuratura i Prawo 2017, No. 11.

Skrzydło J., *Karta Praw Podstawowych UE w praktyce brytyjskiej*, Europejski Przegląd Sądowy 2015, No. 10.

Sławicki P., *Wpływ ustawy o przeciwdziałaniu COVID-19 na terminy w prawie cywilnym*, Monitor Prawniczy 2020, No. 12.

Sobczak J., *Niezawisłość sędziowska i niezależność sądów. Problem ważny i ciągle aktualny*, Gdańskie Studia Prawnicze 2015, No. 4.

Stefaniak A., *Wygłaszanie mowy w procesie cywilnym*, Palestra 1974, No. 7.

Szczepankowska-Kozłowska K., *Prawo do skutecznego środka prawnego i bezstronnego sądu – art. 47 Karty Praw Podstawowych w relacjach horyzontalnych – kilka uwag w związku z wyrokiem TSUE w sprawach połączonych C-585/18, C-624/18, C-625/18*, Palestra 2020, No. 5.

Taborowski M., *Poziom ochrony praw podstawowych wynikający z Karty Praw Podstawowych UE jako przeszkoda dla przystąpienia Unii Europejskiej do Europejskiej Konwencji Praw Człowieka*, Europejski Przegląd Sądowy 2015, No. 12.

Tizzano A., *Stosowanie Karty Praw Podstawowych UE w państwach członkowskich (art. 51 ust. 1 Karty)*, Europejski Przegląd Sądowy 2014, No. 9.

Tkaczyk E., *Konstytucyjne prawo do sądu jako jedna z najważniejszych gwarancji praw człowieka w państwie demokratycznym. Aspekt teoretyczny*, Studia Prawnicze i Administracyjne 2017, No. 2.

Tuleja P., *Pandemia COVID-19 a konstytucyjne stany nadzwyczajne*, Palestra 2020, No. 9.

Weitz K., *W kwestii składu wydającego wyrok (art. 323 k.p.c.)*, Palestra 2008, Nos 3–4.

Weitz K., *Nadużycie „prawa" procesowego cywilnego*, Polski Proces Cywilny 2020, No. 1.

Wiśniewski A., *Europejski Trybunał Praw Człowieka trybunałem konstytucyjnym Europy?*, Prawo i Więź 2020, No. 4.

Wolwiak I., *Czy można przyjąć skutek doręczenia względem pełnomocnika, który nie złożył wniosku o założenie konta w portalu informacyjnym dla zapoznania się z treścią pisma sądowego?*, Polski Proces Cywilny 2022, No. 1.

Wójcik-Krokowska N., *Informatyzacja sądownictwa oraz postępowania cywilnego – postulaty de lege lata i de lege ferenda*, Monitor Prawniczy 2021, No. 3.

Wróbel A., *Autonomia proceduralna państw członkowskich. Zasada efektywności i zasada efektywnej ochrony sądowej w prawie Unii Europejskiej*, Ruch Prawniczy, Ekonomiczny i Socjologiczny 2005, No. 1.

Wróbel A., *Dekalog akcesyjny, czyli dziesięć argumentów Trybunału Sprawiedliwości przeciwko przystąpieniu Unii Europejskiej do Europejskiej Konwencji Praw Człowieka*, Europejski Przegląd Sądowy 2015, No. 12.

Wyrozumska A., *Znaczenie prawne zmiany statusu Karty Praw Podstawowych Unii Europejskiej w traktacie Lizbońskim oraz Protokołu polsko-brytyjskiego*, Przegląd Sejmowy 2008, No. 2.

Załucki M., *Nowe technologie a sprawność i przyszłość sądownictwa w Polsce*, Przegląd Sądowy 2021, Nos 11–12.

Zembrzuski T., *Ograniczenia jawności postępowania w sprawach cywilnych w dobie pandemii – potrzeba chwili czy trwałe rozwiązanie?*, Forum Prawnicze 2021, No. 3.

Zembrzuski T., *Przeciwdziałanie i zwalczanie epidemii COVID-19 w postępowaniu cywilnym, czyli pożegnanie z kolegialnością orzekania*, Polski Proces Cywilny 2022, No. 1.

Jurisprudence

Constitutional Tribunal of the Republic of Poland

Judgment of the Constitutional Tribunal of 26 April 1995, K 11/94.

Judgment of the Constitutional Tribunal of 9 June 1998, K 28/97.

Judgment of the Constitutional Tribunal of 11 May 1999, K 13/98.

Judgment of the Constitutional Tribunal of 10 May 2000, K 21/99.

Judgment of the Constitutional Tribunal of 13 May 2002, SK 32/01.

Judgment of the Constitutional Tribunal of 11 June 2002, SK 5/02.

Judgment of the Constitutional Tribunal of 9 July 2002, P 4/01.

Judgment of the Constitutional Tribunal of 24 February 2003, K 28/02.

Judgment of the Constitutional Tribunal of 2 July 2003, K 25/01.

Judgment of the Constitutional Tribunal of 17 September 2002, SK 35/01.

Judgment of the Constitutional Tribunal of 8 July 2003, P 10/02.

Judgment of the Constitutional Tribunal of 28 July 2004, P 2/04.

Judgment of the Constitutional Tribunal of 7 September 2004, P 4/04.

Judgment of the Constitutional Tribunal of 11 May 2005, K 18/04.

Judgment of the Constitutional Tribunal of 16 January 2006, SK 30/05.

Judgment of the Constitutional Tribunal of 12 September 2006, SK 21/05.

Judgment of the Constitutional Tribunal of 2 October 2006, SK 34/06.

Judgment of the Constitutional Tribunal of 24 October 2007, SK 7/06.

Judgment of the Constitutional Tribunal of 26 February 2008, SK 89/06.

Judgment of the Constitutional Tribunal of 4 March 2008, S 2/08.

Judgment of the Constitutional Tribunal of 27 May 2008, SK 57/06.

Judgment of the Constitutional Tribunal of 17 November 2008, SK 33/07.

Judgment of the Constitutional Tribunal of 15 January 2009, K 45/07.

Order of the Constitutional Tribunal of 17 December 2009, U 6/08.

Judgment of the Constitutional Tribunal of 23 November 2009, P 61/08.

Judgment of the Constitutional Tribunal of 24 November 2010, K 32/09.

Judgment of the Constitutional Tribunal of 16 November 2011, SK 45/09.

Judgment of the Constitutional Tribunal of 7 October 2021, K 3/21.

European Court of Human Rights

Judgment of the European Court of Human Rights of 21 February 1975, Application No. 4451/70.

Judgment of the European Court of Human Rights of 1 October 1982, Application No. 8692/79.

Judgment of the European Court of Human Rights of 26 October 1984, Application No. 9186/80.

Judgment of the European Court of Human Rights of 23 February 1994, Application No. 16757/90.

Judgment of the European Court of Human Rights of 22 February 1996, Application No. 17358/90.

Judgment of the European Court of Human Rights of 18 February 1997 Application No. 18990/91.

Decision of the European Court of Human Rights of 25 January 2000, Application No. 51501/99.

Judgment of the European Court of Human Rights of 15 February 2000, Application No. 38695/97.

Judgment of the European Court of Human Rights (Grand Chamber) of 5 October 2000, Application No. 39652/98.

Judgment of the European Court of Human Rights (Grand Chamber) of 5 October 2000, Application No. 33804/96.

Judgment of the European Court of Human Rights (Grand Chamber) of 11 July 2002, Application No. 36590/97.

Judgment of the European Court of Human Rights of 12 November 2002, Application No. 46129/99.

Judgment of the European Court of Human Rights of 15 February 2005, Application No. 68416/01.

Judgment of the European Court of Human Rights (Grand Chamber) of 30 June 2005, Application No. 45036/98.

Judgment of the European Court of Human Rights of 21 September 2006, Application No. 12643/02.

Judgment of the European Court of Human Rights of 10 October 2006, Application No. 69129/01.

Judgment of the European Court of Human Rights of 19 October 2006, Application No. 1855/02.

Judgment of the European Court of Human Rights of 23 November 2006, Application No. 73053/01.

Judgment of the European Court of Human Rights of 28 November 2006, Application No. 40765/02.

Judgment of the European Court of Human Rights of 17 January 2008, Application No. 14810/02.

Judgment of the European Court of Human Rights of 20 January 2009, Application No. 32971/03.

Judgment of the European Court of Human Rights of 19 May 2009, Application No. 18353/03.

Judgment of the European Court of Human Rights of 7 July 2009, Application No. 58447/00.

Judgment of the European Court of Human Rights of 27 April 2010, Application No. 23083/05.

Judgment of the European Court of Human Rights of 3 May 2011, Application No. 30024/02.

Judgment of the European Court of Human Rights of z 26 July 2011, Application No. 58222/09.

Judgment of the European Court of Human Rights of 12 June 2012, Application No. 31098/08.

Judgment of the European Court of Human Rights of 7 July 2015, Applications Nos 72287/10, 13927/11, 46187/11.

Judgment of the European Court of Human Rights of 25 April 2017, Application No. 31371/12.

Judgment of the European Court of Human Rights of 2 October 2018, Application No. 66580/12.

Judgment of the European Court of Human Rights (Grand Chamber) of 6 November 2018, Applications Nos 55391/13, 57728/13, 74041/13.

Judgment of the European Court of Human Rights of 9 April 2019, Application No. 11236/09.

Judgment of the European Court of Human Rights (Grand Chamber) of 1 December 2020, Application No. 26374/18.

Judgment of the European Court of Human Rights of 7 May 2021, Application No. 4907/18.

Judgment of the European Court of Human Rights of 2 December 2021, Application No. 36516/19.

Judgment of the European Court of Human Rights of 21 July 2022, Application No. 48762/19.

Court of Justice of the European Union

Judgment of the Court of Justice of 15 July 1964, C-6/64, ECLI:EU:C:1964:66.

Judgment of the Court of Justice of 17 December 1970, C-11/70, ECLI:EU:C:1970:114.

Judgment of the Court of Justice of 16 December 1976, 33/76, ECLI:EU:C:1976:188.

Judgment of the Court of Justice of 16 December 1976, 45/76, ECLI:EU:C:1976:191.

Judgment of the Court of Justice of 15 May 1986, 222/84, ECLI:EU:C:1986:206.

Judgment of the Court of Justice of 22 October 1987, C-314/85, ECLI:EU:C:1987:452.

Judgment of the Court of Justice of 13 July 1989, C-5/88, ECLI:EU:C:1989:321.

Judgment of the Court of Justice of 19 June 1990, C-213/89, ECLI:EU:C:1990:257.

Judgment of the Court of Justice of 8 June 2000, C-258/98, ECLI:EU:C:2000:301.

Judgment of the Court of Justice of 30 May 2002, C-516/99, ECLI:EU:C:2002:313.

Judgment of the Court of Justice of 15 June 2006, C-28/05, ECLI:EU:C:2006:408.

Judgment of the Court of Justice of 27 June 2006, C-540/03, ECLI: ECLI:EU:C:2006:429.

Judgment of the Court of Justice of 19 September 2006, C-506/04, ECLI:EU:C:2006:587.

Judgment of the Court of Justice of 25 January 2007, C-403/04 P, ECLI:EU:C:2007:52.

Judgment of the Court of Justice of 13 March 2007, C-432/05, ECLI:EU:C:2007:163.

Judgment of the Court of Justice of 15 April 2008, C-268/06, ECLI:EU:C:2008:223.

Order of the Court of Justice of 14 May 2008, C-109/07, ECLI:EU:C:2008:274.

Judgment of the Court of Justice of 3 September 2008, C-402/05, ECLI:EU:C:2008:461.

Judgment of the Court of Justice of 2 April 2009, C-394/07, ECLI:EU:C:2009:219.

Judgment of the Court of Justice of 21 September 2010, C-514/07, ECLI:EU:C:2010:541.

Judgment of the Court of Justice of 22 December 2010, C-279/09, ECLI:EU:C:2010:811.

Judgment of the Court of Justice of 28 July 2011, C-69/10, ECLI:EU:C:2011:524.

Judgment of the Court of Justice of 15 November 2011, C-256/11, ECLI:EU:C:2011:734.

Judgment of the Court of Justice of 17 November 2011, C-327/10, ECLI:EU:C:2011:745.

Judgment of the Court of Justice of 21 December 2011, C-411/10, ECLI:EU:C:2011:865.

Judgment of the Court of Justice of 6 November 2012, C-199/11, ECLI:EU:C:2012:684.

Judgment of the Court of Justice of 8 November 2012, C-40/11, ECLI:EU:C:2012:691.

Judgment of the Court of Justice of 19 December 2012, C-325/11, ECLI:EU:C:2012:824.

Judgment of the Court of Justice of 26 February 2013, C-617/10, ECLI:EU:C:2013:105.

Judgment of the Court of Justice of 26 February 2013, C-399/11, ECLI:EU:C:2013:107.

Judgment of the Court of Justice of 18 April 2013, C-463/11, ECLI:EU:C:2013:247

Judgment of the Court of Justice of 11 December 2014, C-249/13, ECLI:EU:C:2014:2431.

Judgment of the Court of Justice of 16 June 2015, C-62/14, ECLI:EU:C:2015:400.

Judgment of the Court of Justice of 6 October 2015, C-61/14, ECLI:EU:C:2015:655.

Judgment of the Court of Justice of 30 June 2016, C-205/15, ECLI:EU:C:2016:499.

Judgment of the Court of Justice of 26 July 2017, C-348/16, ECLI:EU:C:2017:591.

Judgment of the Court of Justice of 27 February 2018, C-64/16, ECLI:EU:C:2018:117.

Judgment of the Court of Justice of 17 April 2018, C-414/16, ECLI:EU:C:2018:257.

Judgment of the Court of Justice of 25 July 2018, C-216/18, ECLI:EU:C:2018:586.

Judgment of the Court of Justice of 23 January 2020, C-578/18, ECLI:EU:C:2020:35.

Judgment of the Court of Justice of 6 October 2020, C-245/19 and C-246/19, ECLI:EU:C:2020:795.

Judgment of the Court of Justice of 16 November 2021, C-748/19 to C-754/19, ECLI:EU:C:2021:931.

Judgment of the Court of Justice of 29 March 2022, C-132/20, ECLI:EU:C:2022:235.

Order of the Court of Justice of 8 September 2022, C-188/22, ECLI:EU:C:2022:678.

Supreme Court of the Republic of Poland

Resolution of the Supreme Court of 18 December 1968, III CZP 119/68, LEX nr 4655.

Resolution of the Supreme Court of 27 September 1980, U 1/80, LEX nr 19661.

Judgment of the Supreme Court of 12 July 2000, III RN 207/99, LEX nr 45255.

Judgment of the Supreme Court of 20 August 2001, I PKN 571/00, LEX nr 78998.

Judgment of the Supreme Court of 12 September 2001 rku, V CKN 1827/00, LEX nr 52401.

Judgment of the Supreme Court of 13 November 2003, I CK 229/02, LEX nr 106587.

Resolution of the Supreme Court of 2 December 2003, III CZP 90/03, LEX nr 82113.

Order of the Supreme Court of 27 January 2006, III CK 369/05, LEX nr 178249.

Resolution of the Supreme Court of 22 February 2007, III CZP 160/06, LEX nr 224581.

Judgment of the Supreme Court of 5 December 2007, I CSK 295/07, LEX nr 382064.

Judgment of the Supreme Court of 25 April 2008, II CSK 613/07, LEX nr 420867.

Resolution of the Supreme Court of 26 January 2012, III CZP 83/11, LEX nr 1102775.

Resolution of the Supreme Court of 18 December 2014, III SZP 3/14, LEX nr 1554560.

Resolution of the Supreme Court of 17 February 2016, III CZP 108/15, LEX nr 1977618.

Resolution of the Supreme Court of 23 March 2016, III CZP 102/15, LEX nr 200576.

Resolution of the Supreme Court of 5 December 2019, III UZP 10/19, LEX nr 2746933.

Judgment of the Supreme Court of 23 June 2020, IV CSK 520/18, LEX nr 3039810.

Order of the Supreme Court of 19 February 2021, I USK 89/21, LEX nr 3122707.

Resolution of the Supreme Court of 26 October 2021, III CZP 55/20, LEX nr 3246819.

Order of the Supreme Court of 11 January 2022, II USK 596/21, LEX nr 3342281.

Order of the Supreme Court of 25 January 2022, III CZ 58/22, LEX nr 3303514.

Order of the Supreme Court of 27 January 2022, III CZ 70/22, LEX nr 3329661.

Order of the Supreme Court of 23 February 2022, III CZ 31/22, LEX nr 3403021.

Order of the Supreme Court of 29 April 2022, III CZP 77/22, LEX nr 3361825.

Resolution of the Supreme Court of 26 May 2022, III CZP 86/22, LEX nr 3347779.

Resolution of the Supreme Court of 26 April 2023, III PZP 6/22, LEX nr 3523123.

Resolution of the Supreme Court of 9 April 2024, III CZP 59/23, LEX 3704216.

Resolution of the Supreme Court of 12 April 2024, III CZP 55/23, LEX nr 3715355.

Resolution of the Supreme Court of 30 April 2024, III CZP 60/23, LEX nr 37010114.

Common Courts

Order of the Court of Appeal in Kraków of 24 June 2013, I Acz 1051/13, LEX nr 1454488.

Judgment of the Court of Appeal in Białystok of 29 October 2020, III AUa 506/20, LEX nr 3089291.

Judgment of the Court of Appeal in Kraków of 2 July 2021, I ACa 174/21, LEX nr 322772.

Judgment of the Court of Appeal in Warsaw of 27 July 2021, VII AGa 658/20, LEX nr 3318281.

Judgment of the Court of Appeal in Szczecin of 20 September 2016, II Ca 278/16, LEX nr 2370345.

Order of the Regional Court in Katowice of 21 October 2021, IV Ca 311/21, LEX nr 3247618.

Judgment of the Regional Court in Katowice of 9 June 2022, IV Ca 167/22, not published.

Order of the Regional Court in Kraków of 27 July 2022, II Cz 353/22, not published.

Order of the District Court fo Poznań – Nowe Miasto i Wilda in Poznań of 22 December 2021, II Cz 120/21, LEX nr 3339644.

Order of the District Court for Katowice-Zachód in Katowice of 5 June 2022 roku, III Pz 5/22, not published.

Judgments of foreign courts

Judgment of the Federal Constitutional Court of 29 May 1974 (Germany), (https://www.servat.unibe.ch/dfr/bv037271.html).

Judgment of the Federal Constitutional Court of 22 October 1986 (Germany), (https://www.servat.unibe.ch/dfr/bv073339.html).

Judgment of the Federal Constitutional Court of 15 December 2015 (Germany), (https://www.bundesverfassungsgericht.de/SharedDocs/Entscheidungen/DE/2015/12/rs20151215_2bvr273514.html).

Index

Ius, Lex et Res Publica
Studies in Law, Philosophy and Political Cultures

Edited by
Barbara Janusz-Pohl
Anna Jaron

Vol. 20 Francisco J. Campos Zamora: Das Problem der Begründung richterlicher Entscheidungen. Eine Analyse auf der Grundlage der Theorie der juristischen Argumentation. 2021.

Vol. 21 Aneta Skorupa-Wulczyńska: Language Rights of the Citizen of the European Union. 2022.

Vol. 22 Mateusz Osiecki: International Legal Aspects of Aerial Terrorism. Methods of Law Enforcement in Aviation. 2022.

Vol. 23 Vladimír Sharp / Gabriela Blahoudková / Jakub Handrlica (eds.): Law, Pandemics and Ownership Restrictions. 2022.

Vol. 24 Piotr Kasprzyk / Anna Konert: Drones – Future of Aviation Law? Interference of Public Law in Private Law. 2023.

Vol. 25 Szymon Pawelec (ed.): Consensual Procedures in Criminal Law – Comparative Perspective. 2023.

Vol. 26 Dorota Pudzianowska: The Statelessness in Public Law. 2023.

Vol. 27 Bogusław Przywora / Aleksander Wróbel: Formalised Access to Pre-jurisdictional Free Legal Aid. Analysis based on Example of Ukraine, Poland, Great Britain and Sweden. 2023.

Vol. 28 Ewa Dawidziuk / Patricia Panero / Anna Tarwacka (eds.): Family, Law, and Society: from Roman Law to the Present Day. 2023.

Vol. 29 Marian Grzybowski / Bogusław Przywora / Aleksandra Syryt (eds.): Free Legal Aid, Theory, Legal Basis and Practice. European Standards. 2023.

Vol. 30 Karolina Gmerek: Trial as a Social Communication Occurrence. Interactions Between Professional and Non-professional Participants of a Trial. 2023.

Vol. 31 Paweł Wiliński (ed.): Effective Legal Remedies in Criminal Justice System. European Perspective. 2024.

Vol. 32 Olga Sitarz / Anna Jaworska-Wieloch / Jakub Hanc : On the (Non)existence of the Right to Religious Freedom of Persons Deprived of Liberty. A Reconstruction of the Normative Standard Based on Polish and German Regulations in Comparison With Empirical Studies. 2024.

Vol. 33 Marian Grzybowski / Bogusław Przywora / Aleksandra Syryt (eds.) : Free Legal Aid – A Comparative Approach. Volume 2. 2024.

Vol. 34 Dominik J. Gajewski (ed.) : Functioning of Administrative Judiciary in the Context of Economic Changes. 2024.

Vol. 35 Barbara Mikołajczyk : Older Migrants – Vulnerable and Excluded. Searching for Visibility in Universal and European Laws. 2024.

Vol. 36 Maciej Świder: The Exercise of the Right to a Fair Trial in the Era of the COVID-19 Pandemic. 2024.

www.peterlang.com

www.ingramcontent.com/pod-product-compliance
Ingram Content Group UK Ltd.
Pitfield, Milton Keynes, MK11 3LW, UK
UKHW021831100926
8556IPUK00004B/273